# EDITH WHARTON

## AN EXTRAORDINARY LIFE

# EDITH WHARTON

## AN EXTRAORDINARY LIFE

By

# ELEANOR DWIGHT

Harry N. Abrams, Inc., Publishers

For George, enthusiastic editor and traveling companion,
and for my children, Daphne Trotter, Willard Gardiner, and Sarge Gardiner

Project Director: Margaret L. Kaplan
Senior Editor: Harriet Whelchel
Designers: Carol Robson with Gilda Hannah

Library of Congress Cataloging-in-Publication Data

Dwight, Eleanor.
    Edith Wharton: an extraordinary life / Eleanor Dwight.
       p.    cm.
    Includes bibliographical references (p. 290) and index.
    ISBN 0–8109–2795–0 (pbk.)
    1. Wharton, Edith, 1862–1937—Biography.   2. Authors,
American—20th century—Biography.   I. Title.
    PS3545.H16Z643   1994
8138.52—dc20
[B]                            93–29751

Printed and bound in Hong Kong

Harry N. Abrams, Inc.
100 Fifth Avenue
New York, N.Y. 10011
www.abramsbooks.com

*Front cover:* Edith Wharton during World War I (courtesy Lilly Library,
Indiana University, Bloomington)

*Back cover, clockwise from top left:* Wharton, mid-1880s (Lilly Library);
c. 1884 (courtesy Beinecke Library, Yale University, New Haven); with
Bernard Berenson (Beinecke Library); with Catharine Gross at Hyères
(Lilly Library); writing at the Mount (Beinecke Library)

*Page 2:* Edith Wharton, c. 1885–86

# Contents

# PREFACE: EDITH WHARTON'S WORLD

O n March 22, 1905, Edith Wharton wrote in her diary: "Finished 'The House of Mirth.'" She had been working on her New York novel off and on for two years, and the first installment had appeared in the January 1905 issue of *Scribner's Magazine* even before she finished it. It came out in book form in October 1905 and sold extremely well—by the end of 1905 she had earned more than $20,000 (about $200,000 today). The book became a best-seller in 1906.

Although she had already published short stories, a book on decorating, a historical novel, and poems and essays about Italy, Wharton previously had reached a limited audience. Now, with *The House of Mirth*, she touched an important nerve, and readers rushed out to buy *Scribner's Magazine* to find out what would happen next to her heroine Lily Bart.

Wharton's friend Winthrop Chanler wrote to his wife, Daisy, that he was reading *The House of Mirth*: "It is a very remarkable book; New York society as it really is, as one really knows it, has never been written about before. The satire is so light, so deep, and so true to life. One knows all the people without being able to name one of them. Save I think Walter Berry in the hero, a little, and of course a sketch of the Mills."

The amassing of fortunes after the Civil War in America had enabled a fantastic life-style for the new rich. A lavish standard of living that included enormous mansions, landscaped estates, squadrons of liveried servants, stables full of horses and carriages, wardrobes of the latest Paris designs, jewels in profusion, sumptuous art collections and interiors—not to mention the rise and fall of those maneuvering for social position—all made for very interesting reading.

Wharton exposed the shallow values of this affluent "society" and their effect on a creative person growing up in that world—namely Lily Bart, an appealing character who was born into "society" yet existed on its fringes because she had no money. In the novel, Wharton explored the greed, extravagance, and pettiness of moneyed American families and the few possibilities available for human development in such a world. She showed marriage as the pivotal experience for a young woman—and how difficult it was to remain single and survive.

Like Lily Bart, Wharton had been born into the old New York society and she knew of the millionaires who were now breaking into it. She wrote to a friend in 1905: "I must protest, & emphatically, against the suggestion that I have 'stripped' New York society. New York society is still amply clad, & the little corner of its garment that I lifted was meant to show only that little atro-

Edith Wharton in 1905, just after having written *The House of Mirth*. When Wharton created Lily Bart and showed her social downfall and sad death, she had recently moved to the Mount, her new house in Lenox, Massachusetts. She wrote easily in the stillness of the country, and, with profits from her novel, she could now add stone walls to her sunken garden. Her group of regulars (including her new friend Henry James) came for motoring, enjoying the views, and hilarious conversation and fun in the evenings.

She was enjoying the success of her novel. She wrote to her publisher Charles Scribner: "It is a very beautiful thought that 80,000 people should want to read 'The House of Mirth,' and if the number should ascend to 100,000 I fear my pleasure would exceed the bounds of decency." She thanked him for sending her "these 'returns'—And by the way, I hope you got that photograph I sent you about ten days ago, with my eyes down, *trying to look modest*?!"

phied organ—the group of idle & dull people—that exists in any big & wealthy social body." To another letter she responded, "Social conditions as they are just now in our new world, where the sudden possession of money has come without inherited obligations, or any traditional sense of solidarity between the classes, is a vast & absorbing field for the novelist."

Wharton was forty-three years old before she made New York the subject of a novel. At the time, she was working through difficult personal conflicts while going forward in an increasingly productive career. Now she was ready to weave observations of the society about her and the strands of her own past into the fabric of her fiction. She claimed that earlier she had felt fashionable New York was too shallow to be interesting but finally decided that "a frivolous society can acquire dramatic significance only through what its frivolity destroys. Its tragic implication lies in its power of debasing people and ideals. The answer, in short, was my heroine, Lily Bart."

In *The House of Mirth,* Edith Wharton used her wonderful sensitivity to places and her descriptive powers to create a background of landmarks she knew in New York and its fashionable environs. She had an extraordinary ability to perceive and to remember whatever she saw: "I always saw the visible world as a series of pictures more or less harmoniously composed." She could remember indefinitely in all their detail, "rooms and houses, even those seen briefly, or at long intervals." She also felt strong reactions to nature—a "secret sensitiveness to landscape—something in me quite incommunicable to others, that was trembling and inarticulately awake to every detail of wind-warped fern and wide-eyed briar rose." She was alive to "a unifying magic beneath the diversities of the visible scene—a power with which I was in deep and solitary communion whenever I was alone with nature."

The novel is alive with city and country tableaux described in wonderful detail. It opens in Grand Central Station, a setting suggesting both the transient quality of Lily's existence and the power of the Vanderbilts, who owned the New York Central Railroad. Life in the American country house is depicted at a house party on the Hudson, at Bellomont (modeled after the country estate of the Odgen Mills family, friends of the Whartons').

The houses on Fifth Avenue and its side streets become the settings for Lily's adventures. These houses were not refuges for civilized living but a testament to social climbing. The two principles in the philosophy of Lily Bart's mother, who is determined that Lily find her place in this line of architectural extravaganzas, are that one must be decently dressed and, "whatever it cost, one must have a good cook." Simon Rosedale's new house is the first step in ascending the ladder, because it "attracts attention, and awes the Western sightseer." The Wellington Brys' house is the next stage, for it implies that "one has been to Europe, and has a standard. I'm sure Mrs. Bry thinks her house a copy of the

Illustrations from *The House of Mirth:*

*Above left:* "She lingered on the stairway, looking down into the hall below." On the first evening at Bellomont, Lily Bart experienced one of those moments in which "the sense of contrast was uppermost." In the opulent atmosphere, she savored the "external finish of life" and regretted "the meagreness of her own opportunities."

*Above right:* Gus Trenor, who feels that he can bully Lily and ask her for sexual favors because he has given her money, declares, "I mean to make you hear me out."

*Trianon;* in America every marble house with gilt furniture is thought to be a copy of the *Trianon.*"

Wharton drew on the social events she had witnessed as a young woman. According to Louis Auchincloss: "The supreme social rite of the [late 1800s] was not, as it would become in the 1920s and 1930s, the debutante party; it was the wedding. This was the ultimate example of Thorstein Veblen's theory of conspicuous consumption." The wedding presents, sometimes worth as much as a million dollars, "were displayed in a special chamber for the admiring guests; the newspapers speculated on the fortunes and the settlements on the couple about to be joined; the church and the bride's home were converted into greenhouses of floral profusion." In the mid-1890s, four young Vanderbilts—great-grandchildren of the commodore—were married, mostly to children of other millionaires: Gertrude Vanderbilt to Harry Payne Whitney, Consuelo Vanderbilt to the ninth Duke of Marlborough, Florence Adele Sloane to James Burden at Lenox, and Cornelius Vanderbilt III to Grace Wilson. Other American heiresses were marrying European nobility in very visible matches, such as that of the French Count Boni de Castellane and Anna Gould, daughter of

the millionaire Jay Gould. Wharton knew of these weddings and the great attention they brought, and she captures their spirit in her novel, so that when Percy Gryce becomes engaged to Evie Van Osburgh, it is clear he wants to merge another fortune with his own instead of marrying the impoverished Lily Bart.

Edith Wharton could depict this world with such energy, vitality, humor, and rage, and with such success, because she had known it too and felt its restricting and dehumanizing qualities. Since childhood she had struggled to be creative, imaginative, and productive in a world alien to her talents.

In the novel, Lily is valued only for her beauty and what is left of her social position. As critics have noted, the dazzling image she creates as the subject of Joshua Reynolds's painting *Mrs. Lloyd* in the performance of *tableaux vivants* suggests that she and others see herself as an art object, a prize for the connoisseur's collection. Photographs of Wharton in the 1870s and 1880s show her

When Florence Adele Sloane married James Abercrombie Burden in June 1895 *(shown at left)*, the *New York Times* reported that the wedding was "one of the most elaborate and costly affairs of the kind ever given in this country. The bride's trousseau cost $40,000. The bride's parents, Mr. and Mrs. William Douglas Sloane [she was Emily Vanderbilt and a social power in Lenox], hired the Curtis Hotel, one of the largest hotels in Lenox, for the use of the wedding guests." One hundred eighty broughams were brought from New Haven on fifty freight cars at the cost of forty dollars each to supplement the fifty found in Lenox to transport the guests.

Wharton humorously described a similar event in *The House of Mirth*: "The Van Osburgh marriage was celebrated in the village church near the paternal estate on the Hudson. It was the 'simple country wedding' to which guests are conveyed in special trains, and from which the hordes of the uninvited have to be fended off by the intervention of the police. While these sylvan rites were taking place, in a church packed with fashion and festooned with orchids, the representatives of the press were threading their way, notebook in hand, through the labyrinth of wedding presents, and the agent of a cinematograph syndicate was setting up his apparatus at the church door. It was the kind of scene in which Lily had often pictured herself as taking the principal part, and on this occasion the fact that she was once more merely a casual spectator, instead of the mystically veiled figure occupying the centre of attention, strengthened her resolve to assume the latter part before the year was over."

squeezed into perfectly fitted dresses, trying desperately to look beautiful but instead appearing rather timid and ill at ease. She too had thought that her looks and gowns from the Parisian couture houses Worth and Doucet would be her ticket to success (yet when she first met Henry James, the great writer did not even notice the wonderful hat and dress she had bought to impress him). At the beginning of the new century, when she had gained success as a writer, her new confidence shows in her regal and assured manner in photographs as she peers out from the fur-trimmed coats she wore in her Paris years.

Wharton herself said that growing old was "the most interesting thing that ever happened to her," Mary Berenson recalled. "She said she wasted her youth trying to be beautiful, but now that she has given up all hope she feels freer." Although Wharton had great respect for beautiful clothes, she cautioned women against paying too large a price for keeping up appearances. Lawrence Selden notices the struggles of Lily Bart: "As he watched her hand, polished as a bit of old ivory, with its slender pink nails, and the sapphire bracelet slipping over her wrist," he was aware of her need for luxurious surroundings and the amenities of wealth. She was "so evidently the victim of the civilization which had produced her, that the links of her bracelet seemed like manacles chaining her to her fate."

Lily Bart's unsuccessful quest for self-realization set off a correspondence in the *New York Times Saturday Review of Books* between readers in Newport and Lenox, where Wharton had lived. In reply, a writer purporting to be from Ocean Grove, Brooklyn, wrote, tongue-in-cheek:

These here letters signed Lenox and Newport give me a pain; any one would think from the fuss made over 'em that the writers was real swells. Ain't it plain that their poso de nyms was taken to convey that impression? The one feels better because what Mrs. Wharton says is only too true, while the other pretends to be real mad at having his set misrepresented. I'll wager neigher of 'em has ever sat in a par tear box at the opra. As one who sits in one of 'em odd Fridays and has the honor to be well acquainted with the Trenors, the George Dorsets, and even the Brys and Rosedale, who ain't quite first class even yet, let me say—though I hate to give away my friends—that Mrs. Wharton is quite correct. Her book ain't in the same class with Thackaray's or George Eliot's, but she has the up to date society novelists beaten to a frazzle. The only criticism I can make is that she would have been fairer to the smart set if she had run in a few pure, high-minded, cultured representatives like me, who are doing our best to discourage bridge and make the ladies stop smoking cigarettes.

# AN EXILE IN NEW YORK

Edith Wharton's past had many strands. Like her character Lily Bart, she had grown up in New York City. Her mother's ancestors, the Rhinelanders and Stevenses, and her father's clan, the Joneses, were all part of the polite society that had lived in New York City since the seventeenth century and traced their ancestry back to England and Holland. They were "old money," as opposed to Jay Gould and Andrew Carnegie, who had recently made fortunes in steel and railroads. The "old money" owned real estate that climbed inexorably in value as the boomtown of New York City spread up Manhattan Island. Many prudently invested their gains in banks. Wharton saw this patrician group as anti-intellectual and passive: none caught the "gold fever" of America's nineteenth-century entrepreneurs.

From the beginning, she was a maverick, so much more intelligent than anyone in her family. Looking back on her ancestors while she was writing her memoirs, she could find no eagles or fanatics and only one she would have wanted to be like—Ebenezer Stevens, her great-grandfather, who took part in the Boston Tea Party, rose to be a general of artillery in the Revolution, and afterward became an East India merchant.

Edith Newbold Jones's first known likeness, c. 1865

Another who stood out in the family was her maternal grandfather, Frederick William Rhinelander, because he loved to read. When he died in 1836 at the age of forty, however, his fortune was well depleted, and Edith's mother, Lucretia, and her brother and sisters grew up in a kind of genteel poverty at the family place near Hell Gate on the East River. When Lucretia married George Frederic Jones, her fortunes improved: he was the youngest of three surviving children of Edward Renshaw and Elizabeth Schermerhorn Jones, members of the prosperous Jones family. He graduated from Columbia University but never felt the need to work. His daughter, Edith, suggested later, however, that her mother's extravagance and her father's fixed income led to difficult periods.

The Joneses' neighborhood was bordered by Washington Square at Eighth Street, Gramercy Park in the East Twenties, and Madison Square Park at Twenty-third Street and Fifth Avenue. When Edith was born in 1862 in the house at 14 West Twenty-third Street, her brother Freddy was sixteen and Harry was eleven. During her childhood, they were often away at school; she was raised as an only child of elderly parents, with a large, socially prominent collection of cousins and aunts and uncles.

Just after the Civil War ended, the Jones family went to Europe. For six years they lived in Paris, Rome, and Florence and traveled in Germany and Spain. As Wharton explained, "The depreciation of American currency at the

The cosmopolitan Edith was not impressed when, at fifteen, she saw the figure of her great-grandfather Ebenezer Stevens in a painting at the Capitol: "It was a weary and bored little girl who trailed after her parents through the echoing emptiness of the Capitol, and at last into the famous Rotunda with its Revolutionary victories. [John] Trumbull was little thought of as a painter in those days . . . and when one panel after another was pointed out to me, and I was led up first to the 'Surrender of Burgoyne' [at Saratoga, New York, October 17, 1777, *right*] and then to the 'Surrender of Cornwallis', and told: 'There's your great-grandfather,' the tall thin young man in the sober uniform of a general of artillery, leaning against a cannon in the foreground . . . impressed me much less than the beautiful youths to whom I had just said goodbye at Annapolis. If anything, I was vaguely sorry to have any one belonging to me represented in those stiff old-fashioned pictures, so visibly inferior to the battle-scenes of Horace Vernet and Detaille."

close of the Civil War had so much reduced my father's income that, in common with many of his friends and relations, he had gone to Europe to economize," renting his townhouse in New York and country place in Newport.

It was a natural move for anyone in the Jones family. Like other well-off New Yorkers, they had often gone to Europe for a vacation or to improve their health on the "supposedly mild shores of Arno and Tiber." Edith's Aunt Margaret and Uncle Joshua Jones would be buried in the Protestant cemetery in Rome, and her father would die in Cannes in 1882. In 1866, however, he was in good health and an experienced traveler who had inherited the wanderlust from his own father.

Labeled "View from my Grandmother Rhinelander's country place at Hell Gate (about 1835)," this scene was painted by one of the tutors who taught the Rhinelander children at their country house way uptown, where George Jones would sail in his rowboat with its bed-quilt sail to court Lucretia Rhinelander.

George Frederic Jones lived through his eyes, as his daughter would later. He loved to visit art galleries, walk in gardens, and tour palaces and classical ruins. We know from his diary of an 1848 trip that he thought Pompeii the most interesting place in Europe, and, like many tourists of his time, he visited the Colosseum in the moonlight and traveled with the words of Lord Byron's *Childe Harold* in his mind. He loved the things his daughter would later care for. He was fussy over where he stayed and was sensitive to the charm and atmosphere of places. Staying near the Rhine River in August 1848, he wrote: "Spent the rest of the evening on the balcony enjoying the quiet and beauty of the place." He was aware of the architectural layouts of towns. He found Karlsruhe "a pretty city, well laid out & very regular, all the streets radiating from the palace like a fan." He had a wonderful visual memory. At the Ducal Palace in Florence, he was "astonished to find how perfectly I remembered the pictures and their respective positions," although he had not seen them in years. His diary is a collection of images, from "magnificent Gobelin tapestries in Paris" to the "beautiful gardens of the Luxembourg Palace." Like his daughter, he loved spectacles—events in which many elements worked together to produce an impression pleasing to the eye—a procession on the Champs Elysées, a fête in Rome.

The Jones family spent their first winter in Rome. The Risorgimento was sweeping the country; within four years the Papal States would surrender to the army of Garibaldi and Italy would be unified. The Risorgimento was to provide themes and settings for Wharton's stories, and one can imagine her recalling how she had lived as a child in Rome during the twilight of papal rule, as unconcerned Romans continued to enjoy the customary ecclesiastical spectacles. Then four years old, Edith beheld cardinals resplendent in red-and-gold robes within heavy coaches rumbling through narrow streets at twilight. She went to Saint Peter's, where "in the million tapered blaze the Pope [Pius IX, 'Pio Nono'] floated ethereally above a long train of ecclesiastics seen through an incense haze so golden that it seemed to pour from the blinding luminary behind the high altar." She remembered shrieking with ecstasy as she watched "the flowery bombardment of the Carnival procession from a balcony on the Corso."

From the Pincio Gardens above the Piazza del Popolo she and her friends could see Rome stretched out before them. The gardens were divided by wide walks and drives, shaded by trees and bordered by smooth lawns. Busts of artists and statesmen and fountains lined the avenues. Pio Nono would walk there, attended by chamberlains and *guardie nobili*, and the children would run up to receive his blessing. The band played under the palm trees on Thursday and Sunday afternoons, and crowds of people from every rank of Roman life gathered until the Ave Maria bell rang from the churches: "There we played,

Edith Jones's brothers, Frederic Rhinelander Jones *(top)* and Henry Edward Jones *(above)*

Edith's father, George Frederic Jones, attended the Episcopal church, sat on various boards, involved himself in philanthropy, and loved to travel. With the income from his inheritance, he could afford to live a life of "leisure and amiable hospitality." Edith later wondered "what stifled cravings once germinated in him."

Edith Jones as a child of eight, taken in 1870 during the Jones family's six years in Europe

dodging in and out among old stone benches, racing, rolling hoops, whirling through skipping ropes, or pausing out of breath to watch the toy procession of stately barouches and glossy saddle-horses which, on every fine afternoon of winter, carried the flower of Roman beauty and nobility round and round and round the restricted meanderings of the hill-top."

The Renaissance villas and gardens and the palaces of the Caesars on the Palatine were also her playgrounds. Edith and her mother wandered through the daisy-strewn lawns of the Villa Doria-Pamphili, among the statues and stone pines of the Villa Borghese and the fountains in the villas at Frascati. In later life she recalled: "I still meet . . . in the 'boschi' of the Pincio & the Boboli gardens, the ghosts of the romping children—the Harrys & Willies and Georgies—with a view to whose subjugation I practiced the arts of the ball & the skipping-rope, and shook out my red hair so that it caught the sun!"

In the 1860s the ruins of the Forum and the Palatine had not yet been restored. The cattle of the eighteenth century no longer grazed there, but the broken and ghostly remnants of the empire lay vulnerable to anyone who wanted to carry off pieces of marble, fragments of imperial vases and statues. Edith hunted for stones, blue and pink and green, which "cropped up through the turf as violets and anemones did in other places," precious bits of porphyry, lapis lazuli, and verd antique that once adorned the Palace of the Caesars.

Vivid memories of these Roman scenes remained with her, and the essence of "the lost Rome of my infancy" became the strong sensuous impressions of "the warm scent of the box hedges on the Pincian, and the texture of weather-worn sun-gilt stone," part of her idealized impressions of Europe.

George and Lucretia Jones knew some of the American writers and artists who since the 1840s had been congregating in Rome along with fashionable Bostonians and New Yorkers. They saw a great deal of Luther Terry and his wife, Louisa. Louisa Ward Terry was the sister of Julia Ward Howe and a leader of the expatriate American colony. Beautiful and adored, and generous to the poor, she gave away clothes, books, jellies, and "pumpkin pies for homesick American travellers." She had first come to Rome to marry the temperamental and gifted Thomas Crawford, considered the preeminent American sculptor of his time, with whom she had four children, including Marion, later the author of many historical romances set in Italy. In 1857 Thomas Crawford died of brain cancer, and in 1861 his widow married Luther Terry, less dynamic than her first husband but wonderfully kind, an artist who painted romantic landscapes.

Their daughter, Daisy, was Edith's age, and the little girls played together. Daisy had learned Italian, French, and German without effort, as Edith would also. Their favorite pastime was to gaze from the windows of the Palazzo Odescalchi, in the Piazza Santissimi Apostoli near the Corso, where the Ter-

The gardens of Il Pincio in Rome, where Daisy Terry and Edith Jones rolled hoops and played games in the shady avenues overlooking the dome of Saint Peter's

rys lived. As Daisy described it later, there was much to see, leisurely happenings on the streets, as well as splendid state weddings and funerals with all the participants dressed magnificently and partaking in fascinating ceremonies. The funeral of the Grand Duke of Tuscany, Francis VI, last of the Hapsburgs, involved "endless processions of monks, Knights of Malta, and diplomatic representatives. The Roman Senate sent three glass coaches with outriders and footmen." Another activity, devised by their nurses, was watching the archangel on the Castel Sant' Angelo flap his wings at noontime. But when the noon cannon fired from the Mausoleum of Hadrian, it always distracted their gaze, so they "never saw them flap and always looked in vain." Although Edith felt at home, to young Daisy Terry she was still an outsider. "Pussy" (a nickname coined by her mother) Jones, with her smart little sealskin coat and her long red-gold hair, was a *forestiera* who "would not have understood these things that we Romans knew about."

The Jones family went to Spain, as Edith's father had been reading William Prescott and Washington Irving's *The Alhambra*. The little girl now caught his enthusiasm for the road: "I recall only the incessant jingle of *diligence* bells, the cracking of whips, the yells of gaunt muleteers hurling stones at their gaunter mules to urge them up interminable and almost unscaleable hills." No inconvenience could dampen her excitement: "It is all a jumble of excited impressions: breaking down on wind-swept sierras; arriving late and hungry at squalid *posadas*; flea-hunting, chocolate drinking . . . being pursued everywhere we went by touts, guides, deformed beggars, and all sorts of jabbering and confusing people; and through the chaos and fatigue, a fantastic vision of the columns of Cordova, the tower of the Giralda, the pools and fountains of the Alhambra, the orange groves of Seville, the awful icy penumbra of the Escorial, and everywhere shadowy aisles undulating with incense and impressions."

Daisy and Arthur Terry, Edith's childhood friends in Rome in the 1860s, painted by their father

A Roman picnic: Luther Terry is at the far right in the back row. Daisy's half-sisters, Annie and Mimoli Crawford, are third and seventh in the first row.

After wintering in Rome, the Joneses moved to Paris. Although Edith had imagined stories before, it was in Paris that the elements of "making up" became a ritual. Even though she could not read, all she needed was a book with closely printed pages, heavy black type, and narrow margins. Novels with dense print were good, and the family's copy of *The Alhambra* even better. Summoned with the help of this device, the muse called "regularly and imperiously," and fantasies overwhelmed her. "I had only to walk the floor, turning the pages as I walked, to be swept off full sail on the sea of dreams."

In Paris she saw the Empress Eugénie driving down the Champs Elysées in an open carriage, "a little boy in uniform beside her on a pony, and a glittering escort of officers." Later she realized that this spectacle was a last vestige of the Second Empire, which would collapse the next summer. She and her procession "vanished in a crimson hurricane; and the whole setting of swaying carriages and outstretched ladies, of young men caracoling on thorough-breds past stately houses glimpsed through clustering horse-chestnut foliage, has long since been rolled up in the lumber-room of discarded pageants."

When the Franco-Prussian War broke out in 1870, the family escaped Paris for Bad Wildbad, a resort in Germany's Black Forest. There Edith caught typhoid and almost died. This illness marked the beginning of the severe fears that formed the dividing line between what she called her "little childhood" and the next stage: "Fear of *what*? I cannot say—& even at the time, I was never able to formulate my terror. It was like some dark undefinable menace, forever dogging my steps, lurking & threatening; I was conscious of it wherever I went by day, & at night it made sleep impossible, unless a light & a nursemaid were in the room." Her fears were associated with a particular place, in this case her own home. She was happy when out walking with her nurse and her dog; once she returned to where her family lived, she was seized by feelings of dread. Before being let into the house, she would stand on the threshold in panic, lest "It" catch her. She was thus haunted for the rest of her childhood.

In 1871 the family took a hotel suite in Florence. Edith learned Italian—she had already learned French and German—and walked in the Cascine gardens with the grown-ups and her dog Foxy. Now that she could read, the passion for "making up" had grown, and that winter in Florence "it became a frenzy." The little girl paced back and forth in the large, high-ceilinged, dreary suite overlooking the Arno. "The long vista of rooms, each communicating with the next through tall folding doors, was a matchless track for my sport." When the grown-ups were out and Doyley (Hannah Doyle, her childhood nurse) safe with her sewing, "I had the field to myself; and I still feel the rapture (greater than any I have ever known in writing) of pouring forth undisturbed the tireless torrent of my stories."

When writing her memoirs in the 1930s, Edith Wharton noted that, in her childhood, "the European background [was] everywhere preparing my eye and imagination to see beauty and feel the riches of a long historic culture. All unconsciously, I was absorbing it all." And she was not just any little American girl who had spent time as a child in Europe, for her abilities were extraordinary. She had an exaggerated way of seeing everything: she was hypersensitive to the details of a beautiful garden or gallery of paintings, yet at the same time haunted by fears and feelings of horror brought on by what she considered her own evil thoughts.

Her love of beauty was a tonic for an overbearing conscience that demanded she confess feelings of disgust or anger, confessions that then caused her to be punished. She had worked out in her mind "a rigid rule of absolute, unmitigated truth-telling, the least imperceptible deviation from which would inevitably be punished by the dark Power I knew as 'God.'" This conflict between her need to confess and the shame it produced caused her great uneasiness, what she called her "chronic moral malady."

It was in Europe that she had first begun to experience feelings of torture when she thought she was falling short of her high moral standards. One way to escape these feelings was through paying attention to pretty things—clothes, pictures, sights—or to read or to tell stories. The child craved to be pretty and in a beautiful place. She wrote to an aunt: "I wish you could have seen me in my white muslin at Elise's birthday party." This fantasy of being the center of attention and considered beautiful by others is one that recurs in her memoirs and in her fiction. To this visual precocity, which led her to experience life as if it were a series of tableaux, and her powerful response to beauty, was added another quality, a tendency to imagine herself as the principal actress in a beautiful and therefore pleasing scene, adored by all who beheld her. Such a scene is her earliest recollection, which begins both her memoirs, *A Backward Glance* and "Life and I." Edith, a small child dressed in her warmest coat and a pretty new bonnet, is walking up Fifth Avenue with her father. In her old age,

Hannah Doyle, or "Doyley," Edith's childhood nurse, remained a presence all her life. It was Doyley, not her mother, whom she always remembered as giving her warmth and affection when she was small. On All Souls' Day, when she thought about "all my dear, dead friends," she particularly missed Doyley.

when she wrote her memoirs, she commented that this first recollection was "produced by the two deepest-seated instincts of my nature—the desire to love & to look pretty. I say 'to look pretty' instead of 'to be admired,' because I really believe it has always been an aesthetic desire, rather than a form of vanity." She saw the world as a series of pictures and "the wish to *make the picture prettier* was, as nearly as I can define it, the form my feminine instinct of pleasing took."

Even stronger than her love of beauty was her fear of ugliness, of both ugly people and of ugly places, which she believed developed before her sense of beauty. "The ugliness stamped itself more deeply on my brain," she wrote, "& I remember *hating* certain rooms in a London house of my aunt's, & feeling for ugly people an abhorrence, a kind of cold cruel hate, that I have never been able to overcome." In Paris she remembered being repelled by the "small shrivelled bearded" mother of her dancing teacher, "whom I could not look at without disgust." She confided to a little boy that Madame Michelet looked like "une vieille chêvre," and "I was seized with immediate horror at my guilt; for I had said something *about* Mlle. Michelet's mother which I would not have said *to her* & which it was consequently 'naughty' to say, or even to think." As a critic has noted, an unexpressed feeling of hatred for her own mother was transferred onto this old woman. In this way Edith projected onto ugly people and places the fears, guilt, anger, and anxiety she felt and tried to confide but was then scolded for. Places assumed an unreal importance: magical refuges, boundless landscapes, or beautiful palaces juxtaposed against other locations dense with feelings of horror and dread, dark rooms that entrapped her, empty houses of loneliness or abandonment. Her strong feelings of rage or joy gave places personalities far beyond reality. Edith's own personality thus evolved from an amalgam of unusual qualities—her moral tortures and her need to escape them, her extraordinary visual precocity, her emotional response to beauty and ugliness, her tendency to see the visible world as a series of pictures, her narcissistic needs, and her instinct to please by "making the picture prettier."

From childhood, therefore, Edith projected these strong feelings onto the places she saw. While traveling with her family, who practiced their American routine abroad by going to the American church in Italian towns and seeing their American friends, she beheld the great monuments, landscapes, and architecture and responded profoundly. She would have disagreed with Alice James, who in 1888 warned her brother William against dragging his children around Europe: "What enrichment of mind and memory can children have without continuity and if they are torn up by the roots every little while as we were! Of all things don't make the mistake which brought about our rootless and accidental childhood. Leave Europe for them until they are old eno' to

Twenty-third Street where Fifth Avenue meets Broadway at Madison Square Park, mid-1870s. In 1857 a monument had been erected to honor William J. Worth, hero of the Seminole and Mexican wars, and this scene appeared on the endpapers of Wharton's book *New Year's Day*. She recalled, "The New York from which I received my most vivid impressions was only that tiny fraction of a big city which came within the survey of a much governessed and guarded litle girl."

have *the* Grand Emotion, undiluted by vague memories." Yet Edith Jones's early expatriate years shaped her life.

Although the ten-year-old Edith could not understand how "people who had seen Rome and Seville, Paris and London" could come back and live contentedly between Washington Square and Central Park, the Jones family did so in 1872. They did not return to Europe until 1880, when Edith was eighteen. The disappointment produced by the first impressions of her native country was keenly felt. She saw New York as a city of narrow, dark brownstone houses, offensively decorated with "smug and suffocating upholstery." Compared to the beautifully designed European cities, New York of the 1870s and 1880s did not measure up: "I was only ten years old, but I had been fed on beauty since my babyhood, and my first thought was: *'How ugly it is!'* I have never since thought otherwise, or felt otherwise than as an exile in America; and that this is no retrospective delusion is proved by the fact that I used to dream at frequent intervals that we were going back to Europe, & to wake from this dream in a state of exhilaration which the reality turned to deep depression."

New York in the 1870s had few monuments to its past, and no long history that was visually apparent; it was designed as a grid. Even so, young Edith's picture was distorted. When the Jones family returned to New York in 1872, it was a city of explosive energy, the business and commercial center of the nation during a period of unprecedented growth after the Civil War. In the air was talk of westward expansion, women's suffrage, the labor movement, and politics. The most publicized events of 1876 were the Centennial Exhibition in Philadelphia, Custer's Last Stand, and the Hayes-Tilden election, but none of these events figured in her memories of childhood, which were colored by a combination of elements—a poor relationship with her mother, fears, loneliness, and, one can guess, boredom: for an exceptionally intelligent child there simply was not much to do.

Edith Jones's world was small, and she projected her feelings of discontent onto her native city. She was a solitary, only child, "much governessed and guarded." The highlights in her life were Sunday church services, occasional evenings with her parents at the theater, walks in the park, studying with her governess, educating herself by reading in her father's library, and observing the rituals of her parents' social life. She was happiest in the summers, when the family went to their big gabled house in Newport and she could play with her neighbors and enjoy the outdoors.

From this time on, Europe and its architectural wonders, its beautiful gardens and the centuries of history evoked by them was the place that she associated with well-being, with exploration and discovery, with excitement and with civilization itself. New York had little to offer in comparison. She began to polarize her reactions, building imaginatively on the places that she knew. As she wrote to Mary Berenson in 1932, asking for advice on the writing of her memoirs: "I'm hopelessly stuck, and feel how much easier it would have been if I'd lived in Florence with picturesque people instead of stodging in New York!"

The Jones family moved back to 14 West Twenty-third Street, just off Fifth Avenue and diagonally across from Madison Square Park. Their house

Fifth Avenue at Twenty-third Street and Broadway at the turn of the century. The Jones house, which received a cast-iron facade in the early 1890s when it became a retail store, was number 14 West Twenty-third Street, the third one in from the corner on the south side. Across the street is the Fifth Avenue Hotel.

was a four-and-a-half-story brownstone in the Italianate style. It had a low stoop of four steps that led up to double doors crowned by a massive pediment. Beyond the vestibule, which was probably "painted in Pompeian red, and frescoed with a frieze of stenciled lotus-leaves," were her father's library, the conservatory, and the billiard room.

Upstairs on the second floor were the dining room and the drawing room, "a full-blown specimen of Second Empire decoration, the creation of the fashionable French upholsterer, Marcotte." The floor-length arched windows were "hung with three layers of curtains: sash curtains through which no eye from the street could possibly penetrate and next to these draperies of lace or embroidered tulle, richly beruffled and looped back under the velvet or damask hangings which were drawn in the evening." In the drawing room were huge pieces of Dutch marquetry furniture and a table of "Louis Philippe buhl with ornate brass hands at the angles." The table held a Mary Magdelene "minutely reproduced on copper," and in the dining room a Domenichino "darkened the walls."

Edith's room was on an upper floor; there she could amuse herself by scribbling her stories and poems on the brown wrapping paper she had saved. She also stared out her window at the goings-on at the Fifth Avenue Hotel across the street.

During the years Edith lived in New York with her parents, from 1872 to 1880, this enormous hotel was the center of the city's social, business, and political life. Visiting dignitaries stayed there—the Prince of Wales in 1860, and, soon after, Dom Pedro, the last Emperor of Brazil, as well as the Crown Prince of Siam and Prince Napoleon. At the outbreak of the Civil War the new hotel had become the headquarters of the forces organized to preserve the Union. Republican politicians made it their unofficial headquarters. The "Amen Corner" of the lobby was where Platt, the Republican leader, would sit and give instructions to his minions. It was thronged with just the sort of people the Jones family loved to shun. Years later Wharton's short novel *New Year's Day* opens with a couple being discovered in their affair as they escape the Fifth Avenue Hotel when a fire starts there. They are observed by "proper" New Yorkers, who, gathered for a family New Year's party, watch the fire from the windows of a house on Twenty-third Street.

Intrigued by Lucretia Jones's "beautifully flounced dresses," "painted and carved fans in sandalwood boxes," "ermine scarves," and "perfumed yellowish laces pinned up in blue paper, and kept in a marquetry chiffonier," Edith would hang over the stair railing in the evening to watch her mother sweep down to her carriage "resplendent in train, aigrette, and opera cloak." One of the child's favorite occasions was watching the annual unpacking of the "trunk from Paris, and the enchantment of seeing one resplendent dress after anoth-

While George Jones was interested in art and history, Lucretia Rhinelander Jones seemed aware only of the demands on a socially prominent woman. She dressed and entertained well, and, like Lily Bart's mother, she cared very much about society and "appearances."

Fifth Avenue and Fifty-fourth Street, looking north, 1874. Mary Mason Jones's house is in the right background at Fifty-seventh Street. When Edith Jones and her family returned from Europe in the early 1870s, New York was pushing its way northward from the Battery. The streets of lower Manhatan were filled with horses and carriages, and the two rivers thronged with tall-masted ships. Open country stretched north of Fifty-ninth Street. The newly landscaped Central Park offered a man-made wilderness for driving and strolling. The land to the east was sparsely settled; west of the park, cattle grazed in open fields. Elegant mansions from Italian and French models were just beginning to line upper Fifth Avenue; the Metropolitan Museum of Art would begin its rise at its new location in Central Park by 1880.

In addition to creating ritual scenes with all the tribe assembled for *The Age of Innocence,* Wharton pictured the town houses along Fifth Avenue. Everyone knew where everyone else had gone for dinner because they could identify the carriages that stood in front of the houses in the evenings.

er taken out of its tissue paper." (New York matrons were just beginning to patronize the couture houses in Paris.) Her mother had a beautiful figure, and "her sloping shoulders and slim waist were becomingly set off" by her wonderful gowns.

Despite the daughter's admiration for her mother's beautiful clothes, their relationship caused Edith much suffering. Her memories of her mother are of constant competition and power struggles. Unable to share the child's "secret life of the imagination," Lucretia was the insensitive enemy of the reading and solitude that nourished it. Mother and daughter struggled over trying to make Edith "like other children." Lucretia would invite them over to play, only to have Edith disappear because she wanted to be alone to "make up" stories: "I used to struggle on as long as I could against my perilous obsession, and then, when the 'pull' became too strong, I would politely ask my unsuspecting companions to excuse me." Leaving her mother to cope with the "nice little girls," Edith would rush to shut herself up in her mother's bedroom, where she "poured out the accumulated floods of my pent-up eloquence. Oh, the exquisite relief of those moments of escape . . . the rapture of finding myself again in my own rich world of dreams!" One can imagine the scoldings she received for such bad manners.

According to Edith, a little girl with larger tastes and questions was an enigma to this cold and insensitive beauty who cared most about her appearance and who could not discuss what puzzled her daughter. Lucretia Jones disappointed her daughter for not helping her make sense of contradictions in religious beliefs, nor for sharing her reading interests, understanding her fears, or even giving her any sex education before she was married. All profound subjects were off bounds—ladies did not talk of such things—and Edith grew up estranged, mystified, and resentful that her mother could not understand her.

She later wrote that there was little communication between her parents and that she, Edith, was her father's soul mate. Her father was sensitive, but his development was stunted by her mother, who could not share his "rather rudimentary love of verse": "My mother's matter-of-factness must have shrivelled up any such buds of fancy; and in later years I remember his reading only Macauley, Prescott, Washington Irving and every book of travel he could find, and I have wondered since what . . . manner of man he was really meant to be. That he was a lonely one, haunted by something always unexpressed and unattained, I am sure." While her father sat on the board of the Blind Asylum and the Bloomingdale's Insane Asylum and other boards, her mother's daily schedule included card leaving and other social calls.

The little girl shared in the activities of her family— they spent their life engaged in what was gracious and genteel, diversions and amusements, walks and drives in Central Park, evenings at the theater and opera, and dinners with friends. These patrician New Yorkers had a long list of *dos* and *don'ts* that would provide the conflicts for the more imaginative of Wharton's later characters. No tradesman was accepted in society. Business or sexual scandals were not tolerated. Edith was often lonely in what she saw as the "impoverished emotional atmosphere of old New York," yet when she ventured beyond, into poorer parts of the city, she was horrified by its "shameless squalor."

Although there were schools for girls at that time, Edith Jones was tutored at home by Anna Bahlmann, who later became her secretary. Edith remembered her as "an admirable finishing governess, and thoroughly fitted to interest a girl in literature, German or English," but "she never struck a spark from me, she never threw a new light on any subject, or made me see the relation of things to each other. My childhood and youth were an intellectual desert."

Having little guidance from adults, she found mentors in books and contentment in reading and writing. Books became her passion, and she was left to herself in her father's library, a small room on the ground floor of the Twenty-third Street house: "The room was lined with low bookcases where, behind glass doors, languished the younger son's meagre portion of a fine old family library. The walls were hung with a handsome wallpaper imitating the green damask of the curtains, and as the Walter Scott tradition still lingered, and there was felt to be some obscure (perhaps Faustian) relation between the Middle Ages and culture, this sixteen-foot-square room in a New York house

Edith's older brother Freddy, and his wife, Mary Cadwalader Jones (Minnie, *above*), lived in a big brick house on Eleventh Street, just off Fifth Avenue not far from Washington Square. Minnie was an accomplished, vibrant woman with a great many brilliant friends. Daisy Chanler remembered her house as full of books and old engravings, an island of refuge for her brother Marion Crawford and for Henry James, who always stayed with her when he was in New York.

Although Freddy and Minnie Jones's daughter, Beatrix Jones, later Beatrix Farrand, the garden designer, was ten years younger than Edith, they became close friends.

was furnished with a huge oak mantel-piece sustained by vizored knights, who repeated themselves at the angles of the monumental writing table." Her mother was "wholly indifferent to literature" but "had a wholesome horror" of what she called "silly books" for children. She forbade her daughter to read contemporary novels without her permission, so that Edith was rarely allowed to read one. Except for these interdictions, the collection of volumes Mr. Jones had inherited were at her disposal.

She remembered squatting on the thick rug, pulling open one after another the glass doors of the low bookcases, and dragging out book after book in a secret ecstasy of communion: "I say 'secret,' for I cannot remember ever speaking to anyone of these enraptured sessions. The child knows instinctively when it will be understood, and from the first I kept my adventures with books to myself." She thus marked off for herself a space where she could read, and this became an inner world also: "There was in me a secret retreat where I wished no one to intrude, or at least no one whom I had yet encountered."

She read prodigiously—English and French literature (Swift, Sterne, Defoe, Shakespeare, and Milton, and works of Corneille, Racine, La Fontaine, and Victor Hugo were available to her), all of Goethe's plays and poems, books on history and philosophy. Her parents gave her editions of Keats and Shelley for her birthday.

The library kept her memories of Italy alive and taught her secondhand how to understand and evaluate art. Art history and criticism were represented by "La Croix's big volumes, so richly and exquisitely illustrated, on art, architecture, and costume in the Middle Ages," by Joseph Gwilt's *Encyclopedia of Architecture,* works of Franz Kugler and Anna Jameson, and, above all, by the writings of John Ruskin, by far the most influential art critic of the late nineteenth century, who became the authority for travelers of Wharton's generation: "And then I came upon Ruskin! His wonderful cloudy pages gave me back the image of the beautiful Europe I had lost, and woke in me the habit of precise visual observation."

Although the little girl Edith Wharton later described in her memoirs was lonely and misunderstood, and found her friends in books and longed for an adult who could make sense of the confusing world for her, she was also observant and aware of the social goings-on of her family's set. She watched, listened, and remembered, her writer's capital accruing. Wharton recalled that, when she began to write as a small child, probably in Paris, she started "a story in which Mrs. Smith calls on Mrs. Brown, who says: 'If I had known you were coming I should have tidied up the drawing room.' Rebuke from my mother: Drawing rooms are *always* tidy. Discouraged, I abandoned my literary career." But she did not stop—back in New York, she wrote "sentimental poems and mawkish stories, blank verse tragedies, sermons—I loved writing sermons and

I really think I should have been an ornament to the pulpit"—and short lyrics "poured out with a lamentable facility."

She even managed to get published. A New York newspaper published a poem she submitted "in a moment of unheard of audacity," and a few years later, when she was fifteen, the *Atlantic Monthly* brought out a group of her poems that had been recommended by Henry Wadsworth Longfellow after a friend of her brother's had shown them to him. Soon after Longfellow's endorsement, her parents paid a Newport printer to publish a collection of her poems. On rereading her "oeuvre de jeunesse," however, the mature author concluded that, except for one poem, nothing showed "the slightest spark of originality or talent."

At sixteen, Edith wrote *Fast and Loose*, a sentimental novel of manners that, as Viola Winner points out, imitates as well as mocks the romantic stories the child somehow read on the sly, such as *Goodbye Sweetheart* by Rhoda Broughton and *Lucille* by Robert Lytton. It depicts life in high society in a semi-satirical vein and experiments with the kind of novel Wharton later was to perfect, "what she herself called 'chronicle novels,' in which the point of view indiscriminately shifts or is omniscient, and the author comments overtly on character and on social, philosophical issues." It is full of the wonderful details of the world of fashion in London, plus descriptions of Italy—a Roman street, an artist's studio, and the Villa Doria-Pamphili.

After writing the novel, Edith proceeded to offer comical and revealing reviews of it. She had *The Saturday Review* complaining that "whatever character Mr. Olivieri [her pseudonym] hopefully attempts to portray, we lose before long all the boundaries of its individuality, & find ourselves towards the welcome last page involved in a chaos of names apparently all seeking their owners." Her review for the *Pall Mall Budget* comments on the "melancholy band of nonentities which form the dramatis personae of this dolorous tale." In *The Nation*, after first stating that "the English of it is that every character is a failure, the plot a vacuum, the style spiritless, the dialogue vague, the sentiments weak, & the whole thing a fiasco," she asks the question, "Is not Mr. Olivieri very, very like a sick-sentimental school-girl who has begun her work with a fierce & bloody resolve to make it as bad as 'Wilhem Meister,' 'Consuelo,' and 'Goodbye Sweetheart' together, & has ended with a blush, & a general erasure of all the naughty words which her modest vocabulary could furnish?" The truth behind Edith's humor was that she was critical of herself and felt perhaps that her writing would be frowned on by her mother.

Indeed, alarmed at Edith's growing shyness, her passion for study, and her indifference to young people her own age, her parents "decided that, contrary to all precedent, I should be taken into the world at seventeen." The intellectual teenager thus made her debut one year early. "The step decided on,

Drawing by Edith Jones, age fourteen. A very bookish teenager intoxicated by words, Edith loved going to the services at Calvary Church near Gramercy Park with her father and listening to the melodious voice of the Reverend Dr. Washburn. She developed a crush on the minister and even learned Anglo-Saxon in the hopes of impressing him.

Edith Jones in 1876, several years before she was brought out a season early because "my parents decided that I spent too much time in reading."

there followed a feverish period of dress-making; & at last one evening, with my shoulders bare, & my head coiffée, for the first time, I followed my father & mother to a ball at the house of Mrs. L. P. Morton. I had hardly crossed the threshold of the ball-room before three men asked me to dance; I refused the first two in an agony of shyness, but consented to dance the Cotillion with the third, because he was 'much older,' & I had always known him. That evening was a pink blur of emotion—but after it was over my mother had no fears for me! For the rest of the winter, I don't think I missed a ball; & wherever I went I had all the dancers I wanted."

She was now launched into a society that demanded that a young girl be pretty and entertaining. Her lifelong shyness plagued her, but it was ameliorated by her social success. Her brother rescued her from the fate of being unpopular. Harry Jones was one of the most popular men in New York society, and his handsome friends, some ten or twelve years older, all of whom were among the leading "valseurs" of fashionable New York, paid lavish attention to her. "I tasted all the sweets of popularity. Oh, how I loved it all—my pretty frocks, the flowers, the music, the sense that everybody 'liked' me, & wanted to talk to me & dance with me!" Not only was she asked to balls, she was invited constantly to dinners with "the older girls" and the young married women, who then ruled New York society, so that she had more fun than the average debutante.

Although she made her debut at the house of Mrs. Morton, Delmonico's at Twenty-sixth Street and Fifth Avenue in the Joneses' neighborhood was the place for the "Assemblies," the most important of the big balls of the season, because only a few families had a ballroom (she remembered that the Goelets, Astors, Belmonts, Schermerhorns, and Mason Joneses "possessed these frivolous appendages"): "There were, I think, three Assemblies in the winter, presided over by a committee of ladies who delegated three of their number to receive the guests at the ballroom door. The evening always opened with a quadrille, in which the ladies of the committee and others designated by them took part; and there followed other square dances, waltzes and polkas, which went on until the announcement of supper. A succulent repast of canvasback ducks, terrapin, foie-gras, and the best champagnes was served at small tables below stairs, in what was then New York's only fashionable restaurant; after which we re-ascended to the ballroom (in a shaky little lift) to begin the complicated maneuvers of the cotillion."

In 1880 George Jones became ill and, fearing he might not survive another New York winter, his doctors advised a change of climate. So the Jones family, with a governess for Edith, left their house on West Twenty-third Street once again and boarded a ship for England. Edith did not mind at all leaving her new social life, for now she could enjoy the art and architecture of Europe

Marble Block, Fifty-seventh and Fifty-eighth streets and Fifth Avenue, 1875. When George Jones's cousin Mary Mason Jones had built her mansion at Fifty-seventh Street on the east side of Fifth Avenue in the 1860s, it sat there lonely on its faraway block. It was "a bold move which surprised and scandalized society. Fifty-seventh Street was then a desert, and ball-goers anxiously wondered whether even the ubiquitous 'Brown coupés' destined to carry home belated dancers would risk themselves so far a-field."

again. While in London she visited the National Gallery and spent "rapturous hours" making the "memorable acquaintance" of a number of paintings, particularly Franciabigio's *Knight of Malta*. Even more important were the paintings in the Salon Carré of the Louvre in Paris, the family's next stop. Years later she remembered "the first rush of sensation before the Giorgione, the Titian, and the Mona Lisa. I felt as if all the great waves of the sea of beauty were breaking over me at once—and at the same time I remember being conscious of the notice of the people around me and wondering whether I should be 'thought pretty in Paris.' "

The Jones family spent the winter of 1880–81 at Cannes at a quiet hotel terraced with flowers. The countryside was full of roses and jasmine, and Edith took long walks with her governess and rides with new friends through the cork and pine woods. She had been welcomed into a circle of French families "made up of kindly and rather frivolous people, to whom my secret dreams would have been as unintelligible as to my friends at home."

In the fall of 1881, however, came the expedition to Italy Edith longed for. She was reading Ruskin's *Stones of Venice* and *Mornings in Florence*, presents from her father, who had even agreed to "my whim of following step by step Ruskin's arbitrary itineraries." Ruskin's little volumes gave a meaning to their tours of Florence and Venice, a "sense of organic relation, which no other books attainable by me at the time could possibly have conveyed." Although her father was ill and they could not take many walks together, Edith was grateful for a guide as lively and amusing as Ruskin. Through Ruskin Edith felt she had joined the elite, those who saw many things "the average Baedeker-led tourist of that day certainly missed." Following Ruskin's itineraries, Edith and her father would have visited Santa Croce to view Giotto's frescoes of the life of Saint Francis in the Bardi Chapel, as well as Santa Maria Novella to see the Ghirlandaios, and finally the Piazza del Duomo to look at the sculptures on Giotto's bell tower there.

Ruskin became Edith's companion and teacher. In *Modern Painters* (which she read in her father's library), he devoted chapters to principles of color, chiaroscuro, space, and tone. He taught her to see all elements of a picture—sky, clouds, earth, mountains, foreground, water, vegetation. For someone like Edith, who saw the world as a series of pictures, Ruskin was a good model for the use of the English language to re-create these rich, suggestive images.

Although they never met (he died in 1900), she referred to him often, sometimes in praise, other times rebelling against his thinking. In *The Decoration of Houses* (1897), she and Ogden Codman blame him for interfering with symmetry and balance in decorating, and in *Italian Backgrounds* (1905), she criticizes him for leading travelers away from beautiful art. In *False Dawn* (1923), however, he is the knowledgeable, inspired seer, and in *A Backward Glance* (1934), with Shelley and Byron, he is a true connoisseur of Italy. Wharton saw Ruskin as "the best possible preparation for the enjoyment of the authors who afterward led me away from him."

Edith disagreed with the view often expressed by Ruskin that one must scorn Italian art after the mid-quattrocento, Tintoretto excepted, because it fails as an expression of faith and national character and that, by the same reasoning, Gothic art and architecture is mankind's purest accomplishment. She went on to enjoy much of what the master had condemned, especially the worldly art of the High Renaissance and the Baroque.

Ruskin had spent years carefully studying Venice's palaces and churches. Now father and daughter saw Venice, also, through Ruskin's eyes. They observed the architecture and painting Ruskin had written about so passionately, which had "arisen out of . . . a state of pure national faith, and of domestic virtue," though later she would criticize Ruskin for training art lovers "to pass without even saluting any expression of structural art more recent than the first unfolding of the pointed style," and she would praise the luxurious and theatrical eighteenth-century Venetian architecture that he disliked. The Jones family also went to Lucca, Pisa, and Milan. At Milan she did not like Leonardo's *Last Supper*, but *Ilaria del Carretto* at Lucca brought a "thrill of delight."

That Italian trip was to remain an important memory because it was the

Edith Jones in her late teens, about the time she returned to Europe. She wondered if she would be thought "pretty in Paris."

Performance of *Faustus* by an Italian opera troupe, from *Leslie's Illustrated Weekly,* 1870s. In the mid-1870s, on Mondays and Fridays, everyone met at New York's Academy of Music for the opera, "Wednesday being, for some obscure tribal reason, the night on which boxes were sent to dull relations and visitors from out of town." *The Age of Innocence* opens with a wonderful scene set at the academy in which the character of Ellen Olenska is introduced.

last she made with her father. He died in Cannes in the early spring of 1882 after being stricken by paralysis. Years later, she wrote, "I am still haunted by the look in his dear blue eyes, which had followed me so tenderly for nineteen years, and now tried to convey the goodbye messages he could not speak." His not being able to say goodbye prompted her to write, "I doubt if life holds a subtler anguish." With her father's death, Edith lost the companion who had taught her to read, who had taken her to church, the theater, and had been with her in all the important places. She remembered all her life "the tall splendid

"The Flower Party," in aid of the Northeastern Dispensary, given at Delmonico's, which, in the 1870s, moved uptown from Fourteenth Street to Twenty-sixth and Fifth. In the late 1870s and early 1880s, the big balls of the season (from January to Lent) were held at Delmonico's. Edith used it for a setting in *The Buccaneers*, the novel she never finished.

father who was always so kind, and whose strong arms lifted one so high, and held one so safely."

The family returned to New York, where Edith resumed a life dominated by the tastes of her mother. They moved into a house on Twenty-fifth Street west of Fifth Avenue, and, for the next three years, Edith had a succession of beaux. Just before her father died, she had had a flirtation with a New Yorker in Germany—he was courting another girl but "I liked the admiration, & he liked my sense of fun, and I believe it amused us both to keep his poor fiancée on the rack for a few weeks." In 1882 she became engaged to Harry Stevens. They had met in Newport two years before and were together constantly, in Newport and elsewhere, until their engagement was announced in August 1882. Harry had even stayed with the Joneses in Europe during Mr. Jones's illness. He was a prominent figure in New York society, although he moved in slightly different circles. Harry's mother, Mrs. Paran Stevens, a wealthy widow who was actively (and successfully) forcing her way up the New York social ladder, often met with resistance and resentment by the more established families such as the Rhinelanders and the Joneses: Lucretia Jones regarded her as pushy.

Mrs. Stevens seems to have been instrumental in ending her son's involvement with Edith Jones; the engagement was broken in October 1882. Edith's cousin Ethel King wrote to her sister Alice on July 15, 1883: "I think that if Pussy and Harry S. really cared much for each other, their respective mothers should not have sacrificed the children's happiness because of their own disagreements. I believe that 'Aunty P' gave Aunt Lu a piece of her mind, using very strong language in all probability, just as they were about to leave London." It has been suggested that Mrs. Stevens's motive may not have been social revenge but the desire to maintain control of her son's sizable inheritance from his father—$1.25 million worth of land to be received at age twenty-five or upon his marriage. In any event, Edith expressed little outward emotion at the breakup, though it seems she was quite shaken by it. (Harry Stevens died at age twenty-six, six weeks after Edith's marriage to Teddy Wharton.)

In 1883 Edith fell in love with Walter Berry, a distant cousin whom she saw in Bar Harbor, Maine. Berry, a young lawyer, shared her love of reading. Though he never proposed, they became close friends for life. In her old age, she described him as the "one friend in the life of each of us who seems not a separate person, however dear and beloved, but an expansion, an interpretation, of one's self, the very meaning of one's soul."

The same summer she began seeing Edward (Teddy) Wharton, a friend of Harry's. Teddy was good-looking, kind, and had a nice sense of humor. He was from a socially acceptable Virginia family transplanted to Boston. He had graduated from Harvard in 1873 and later joined the Knickerbocker Club in

New York. He had no profession but lived on an allowance of $2,000 a year from his parents. He was a fine social escort, and he and Edith shared a love of dogs and horses and travel. They were married on April 29, 1885.

Marriage was "a dark mystery" to Edith (just before her wedding day she had to ask her mother "what being married was like"), and, as a critic has pointed out, she had repressed the normal questions about sexuality girls ask and find the answers to. The shy and somewhat neurotic young woman was hardly ready for marriage, and she married someone with whom intimacy would be difficult.

Although he was fitted to play a leading role in Edith Wharton's social life and give her some companionship, Teddy could not enter her intellectual or aesthetic realms. She had picked a husband who by his nature—he would prove to be childish and dependent—was barred from her "secret life of the imagination" and could not understand her wide reading, her writing, or share her fantasies. As Edith's friend Gaillard Lapsley would write about Teddy years later, "In a sense he secured her in the world which she professed to have renounced but in fact cherished and valued to the end of her life." That she soon came to regret her decision is suggested by the fact that, beginning in the late 1880s, she wrote many stories and novels that center on unhappy marriages and divorces.

Edith Jones became Edith Wharton with relatively little fanfare at a church on West Twenty-fifth Street near the Joneses' new house. In the years after their marriage, Edith and Teddy Wharton kept a small house in New York City, where they would stay for short periods. In the closing years of the century, the look of New York was improving. Wharton recorded in her memoirs: "With the coming of the new millionaires the building of big houses had begun, in New York and in the country, bringing with it . . . a keen interest in architecture, furniture and works of art in general. The Metropolitan Museum was waking from its long lethargy, and the leading picture dealers from London and Paris were seizing the opportunity of educating a new clientèle, opening branch houses in New York and getting up loan exhibitions."

The Whartons set up permanent housekeeping, however, in Newport— the summer haunt of the Jones family—punctuated by yearly trips to Europe. Edith Wharton, aspiring writer and social critic, long familiar with New York's marble mansions and big new public buildings, could now observe their Newport counterparts, the enormous summer "cottages" of this flourishing Rhode Island watering place, and the hedonistic social life that took place inside them.

Edith Jones in the early 1880s

Pencraig, the Joneses' family
house in Newport

As a child, Edith Jones had loved Newport and remembered it later as the place in the country where she could play outdoors freely. In 1872 the Jones family returned from their six years abroad to "summer" at their house on the harbor side of the island. Pencraig had big gables, a view of the harbor, a cove for swimming, a boat landing, and lots of rooms for family and house-guests. Off the rocky point, Freddy and Harry Jones moored their catboats. Clematis and honeysuckle grew on the verandah, and a lawn sloped to a meadow filled with daisies in early summer.

Summer visitors had come to Aquidneck Island since the early nineteenth century. They lived in roomy houses on the harbor side (where the Jones's house was), or at the upper end of Bellevue Avenue, or stayed at the big hotels like the Ocean House. During the Civil War, Newport became the temporary home to the Naval Academy, which had been evacuated from Annapolis, Maryland. After the war, many writers spent time there—including Bret Harte, Oliver Wendell Holmes, Henry Wadsworth Longfellow, and Julia Ward Howe.

At the same time, summering grew increasingly popular and almost overnight fashionable New Yorkers began to crave seaside residences in Newport. Astors and Vanderbilts competed with each other and the nouveau riche to buy up ocean views and farmland along the cliffs parallel to Bellevue Avenue. By the 1890s, replicas of English country houses, French châteaus, and Italian palaces, blown up way out of scale by American architects, began to push up along the shore overlooking the Atlantic. Driving down Bellevue Avenue, one passed a succession of stone walls and ornate wrought-iron gates,

The southernmost side of Aquidneck Island, called "The Rocks," where Edith Wharton roamed as a child with her neighbors the Rutherfurds

each enclosing sumptuous summer homes with big trees, formal gardens, and enormous lawns stretching to the cliff edge.

In the early 1870s, after six years of touring and living in Europe, "pent up in hotels and flats," and being constantly watched by a nurse, Edith could now wander freely during summers in Newport. "There was inexhaustible delight in the freedom of a staircase to run up and down, of lawns and trees, a meadow full of clover and daisies, a pony to ride, terriers to romp with, a sheltered cove to bathe in." At last other children were within reach, particularly the Rutherfurd boys, who lived next door and with whom she shared tutors—there was lots of coming and going through the private gate between the two properties.

The thrill of being amid nature was what she remembered later. Lewis Morris Rutherfurd, her neighbor and a professor of astronomy at Columbia University known for his photographs of the moon, would take children and friends on Sundays for "walks over what we called the Rocks—the rough moorland country, at that time without roads or houses, extending from the placid blue expanse of Narragansett Bay to the gray rollers of the Atlantic."

During their rambles, she was struck by the beauty of the place and remembered not so much the comradeship of the other children, or the friendly talk of Mr. Rutherfurd, but her strong feelings about nature—"my secret sensitiveness to the landscape—something in me quite incommunicable to others, that was tremblingly and inarticulately awake to every detail of wind-warped fern and wide-eyed briar rose, yet more profoundly alive to a unifying magic beneath the diversities of the visible scene—a power with which I was in deep and solitary communion whenever I was alone with nature."

Daisy Terry at age seventeen—about the time she saw Edith Jones again at Newport

Many of the photographs taken from Wharton's collection were labeled in her own hand and are indicated as hers by quotation marks, as below.

"Edith Wharton about 1884—Mouton and Sprite"

And Newport was naturally beautiful; it was rich with wildflowers and shrubs growing in abundance in a spectacular seaside setting. As Newport's historian, Mrs. Van Rensselaer described the view from the famous Ocean Drive: "On one side of the drive lies the ocean in one of its ever varying moods, on the other there are lovely lichen-covered rocks, between which, in the scanty soil, eglantine, whortle-berries, and other shrubs grow in wild profusion. Early in the spring saxifrage nestles in every nook, while tall irises nod their purple heads amid the flag-leaves and cat-tails of the adjoining marshes. When the wild roses are blooming the edges of the road are gay with their pink blossoms, that give place to the red berries that hang on the bushes through the most rigorous winter weather, and with the bronzed green of the few clinging leaves make touches of color even in the gray days of February."

Mr. Rutherfurd had also organized an archery club, and his daughters, Margaret and Louisa, both older than Edith, "were among the most brilliant performers" at the club meetings. The contests made a strong impression on their young neighbor: "And a pretty sight the meeting was, with parents and elders seated in a semicircle on the turf behind the lovely archeresses in floating silks or muslins, with their wide leghorn hats, and heavy veils flung back only at the moment of aiming." They all competed for the prize of a gold bracelet. Edith saw them as young goddesses—and prototypes for characters in her later novels.

The Jones family had many cousins who came from New York to spend the hot months by the water. Her great-aunt Mary Mason Jones, her grandfather's sister-in-law, lived at Halidon Hill in the summers and helped to make it fashionable, "when the tide seemed to have set in the opposite direction, for at one period the cliffs attracted all newcomers." Mary Jones was the model for *The Age of Innocence*'s Mrs. Manson Mingott, the family matriarch who was considered outrageous because she lived north of Fifty-seventh Street and had French windows that opened out instead of pulling up and down.

As a teenager, Daisy Terry spent a summer at Newport while Edith Jones was there. They both were enjoying themselves in the company of young men. For Daisy, "the most entirely charming boy I had ever seen" was Wintie Chanler, just back from Eton and going to Harvard in September—"but it never for a moment occurred to me" that someday they would marry. Daisy would write long afterward that she "never felt quite in step with the Newport world. . . . I was too much interested in things that in no way pertained to the cogent business of youth"—as was Edith. Daisy also saw herself as too foreign: "I spoke with a strong Italian accent."

The two young women became close friends for life, an intimacy developed during the winters the Whartons spent in Paris while the Chanler family was living there. In so many ways, Daisy was Edith's soul mate, one of the

good women friends within her intimate circle. Daisy shared Edith's intellectual curiosity. They both were fluent in French, Italian, and German; they read widely, were connoisseurs of art and architecture, and enjoyed good conversation. Like Edith, Daisy had talent. Music was her passion. She wanted a musical career, and her teachers encouraged her. But her father opposed it, in an era when fathers had the last word: "'No,' he said when I once had the courage to tell him of my plan. 'No, I like you to work at your music, I want you to be an accomplished young lady, but not a professional.'"

"Dull" was Daisy's judgment of the fashionable world of Newport, "wholly taken up as it was with the externals of life, fine clothes, well-appointed houses, and smart turnouts." Edith would eventually agree, but for a time she enjoyed fine clothes, smart turnouts, and the Newport social scene. The Newport summer when she was a debutante, there were lots of houseguests at Pencraig, and she and her friends played tennis on the lawn. They organized swimming and mackerel-fishing parties, catboat races, and "an occasional

Catboat races, Newport: "Off the rocky point lay my father's and brothers' 'cat-boats', the graceful wide-sailed craft that flecked the bay like sea-gulls."

Driving on Bellevue Avenue, 1890s. The women in Edith's family were competitive and obsessed with etiquette. Edith's great-grandmother Rhinelander, the former Mary Robart, was said to have insisted that her daughter-in-law's carriage follow hers on the road to New York, even though the younger woman's horses were faster and her errand more urgent. After her marriage, Edith would feel obliged to apologize because her coach had inadvertently passed her mother's on Ocean Drive in Newport and given her mother "the dust."

excursion up the bay, or out to sea when the weather was calm enough, on one of the pretty white steam-yachts which were beginning to be the favorite toys of the rich."

Later, Wharton discovered that life as a married matron in Newport was a different matter. It meant facing a prescribed list of social obligations—entertaining, dressing with great formality and style, running a large household for family, guests, and servants, and calling and visiting. Social duties absorbed all of a woman's time. She remembered her mother being embroiled in these rituals: "Calling was then a formidable affair, since many ladies had weekly 'days' from which there was no possible escape, and others cultivated an exasperating habit of being at home on the very afternoon when, according to every reasonable calculation, one might have expected them to be at Polo or at Mrs. Belmont's archery party, or abroad on their own sempiternal card-leaving."

The drive was the important afternoon diversion in her mother's time. "Every day all the elderly ladies, leaning back in victoria and barouche, or the new-fangled *vis-à-vis,* a four-seated carriage with a rumble for a footman, drove down the whole length of Bellevue Avenue, where the most fashionable villas then stood, and around the newly laid-out 'Ocean Drive,' which skirted for several miles the wild rocky region between Narragansett Bay and the Atlantic." For this occasion one dressed as elegantly as if attending the races at Ascot or Auteuil: "A brocaded or satin-striped dress, powerfully whale-boned, a small flower-trimmed bonnet tied with a large tulle bow under the chin, a dotted tulle veil and a fringed silk or velvet sunshade, sometimes with a jointed handle of elaborately carved ivory, composed what was thought a suitable toilet for this daily circuit between wilderness and waves."

After their wedding, Teddy and Edith Wharton set up house in Pencraig Cottage, part of the Jones's property across Harrison Avenue from the family

Edith Wharton, c. 1889

house, Pencraig. Their first home consisted of four or five boxy rooms on each of the first two floors and five or six maids' rooms on the third to house themselves and their staff of servants, which at the time included Catharine Gross, her lady's maid; Alfred White, Teddy's manservant; a cook; and several housemaids and gardeners. Edith made a small garden there, which her friend Gaillard Lapsley described as "done with amazing skill to conceal the irregular shape of the scrap of land and the roads that held it on three sides."

In the late 1880s, Newport was entering the social period that would become legendary. New York society had originally transplanted itself there

*Above left:* Pencraig Cottage, where the Whartons lived in Newport after their marriage

*Above right:* "Pencraig Cottage Drawing-room"

Hoyt Gould, Lucretia Jones, and Teddy Wharton (sitting), Miss Edgar, a cousin, and Edith Jones (standing) at Newport, c. 1884

*Above left:* The Whartons with Edith's brother Harry (second from left) and friends

*Above right:* Edith Wharton, her brother Freddy, and his wife, Mary Cadwalader Jones

for the summer so families could enjoy the clear blue skies, the ocean breezes, the pleasant summer resort life by the sea, and each other, but, by 1890, a whirlwind of events had preempted pastoral holidays and Newport was becoming the showiest resort in the country. Mrs. William Backhouse Astor was the legendary leader—she lived at Beechwood on Bellevue Avenue, a "cottage" with high-ceiled piazzas to which she added a ballroom. According to Cleveland Amory, she regularly adorned herself in a diamond tiara, a "three strand diamond necklace, a dazzling diamond stomacher and several chains of diamonds in lesser spots." Daisy Chanler remembered how "she always sat on the right of the host when she went to dinner parties; she wore a black wig and a great many jewels; she had pleasant cordial manners and unaffectedly enjoyed her undisputed position. She gave very grand dinners and the great Astor ball was the social event of the season."

Mrs. Ogden Mills—a younger social leader and a model for a difficult society hostess in Wharton's novel *The House of Mirth*—also entertained lavishly and, according to Cleveland Amory, boasted that she could give a dinner for a hundred without calling in extra help (Mrs. Astor supposedly could give one for two hundred). Greenhouses burst with exotic plants, and stables of the enormous mansions were filled with as many as twenty different types of carriage. The Vanderbilts' help wore maroon livery, the Astors' wore blue.

The couple continued to see old friends who had summered in Newport for years, such as the Van Alens, the Goelets, the Winthrops, the Chanlers, and the Cushings. Edith was related to the Astors through her grandmother Jones, and she was friendly with the Vanderbilts. She dressed and acted the part of the socially sophisticated young woman—giving dinners and picnics, watching tennis and boating, and entertaining houseguests. They were "in" Newport's social world, a point Teddy was said to have made much of. An outsider once saw Teddy hitching a ride up Bellevue Avenue in a butcher's cart. Upon meeting Teddy later, he said, "Wharton, I hear you rode up the Avenue in a butcher's cart. I wouldn't do that if I were you." Teddy replied coolly, "No, if I were you I wouldn't do that either."

Although the Whartons shared tastes on the surface of life—houses, gardens, entertainments, and travel—they were deeply mismatched and often unhappy in these early years. Critics have made a good case for the fact that Edith was emotionally unready for intimacy, and the short works written during this period depict many portraits of unhappy couples. The woman abandoned by her husband for long periods of time and then expected to be sexually available to him when he returns is drawn in "The Duchess at Prayer," "The Lady's Maid's Bell," and other stories. The young woman often finds a sympathetic companion who is intellectually compatible to cheer her up during her husband's absences.

"ERW about 1898 with Jules, Miza and Mimi"

Teddy, who loved fishing and hunting, horses and dogs, found the milieu in Newport familiar and easy, but Edith struggled to balance her social obligations with her own interests—seeing to her house and garden, trying to write stories, and spending time with new friends such as architect Ogden Codman, publisher Daniel Berkeley Updike, and Egerton Winthrop. They also escaped to Europe for a long period each year.

In 1888 Edith enjoyed a welcome respite from Newport. She told her friend James Van Alen, "I would give everything I own to make a cruise in the Mediterranean," to which he replied, "You needn't do that if you'll let me charter a yacht, and come with me." Edith was twenty-six; Van Alen was forty-two and a widower. Van Alen's wife, Emily Astor, the oldest daughter of William Astor, had died in 1881, six years after their wedding. He had just completed Wakehurst, copied from a Tudor-style house in Sussex he had summered in, with many rooms brought from Europe. He was a good athlete and enjoyed traveling. His grandson would remember, "Grandfather enjoyed the company of the fair sex as well as good food and good wine and as a widower he was often rumored to be about to marry."

It turned out that Van Alen wasn't joking about the cruise. Edith was captivated. The upshot would be that for reasons of propriety—and to allow Edith to make all the decisions with a clear conscience—the Whartons insisted on paying half the expense, an expense which was equal to their combined income for the year, from Edith's trust and Teddy's allowance from his father. Edith's older brothers, her mother, and Teddy's father delivered their opinion: Mediterranean cruises were a "fad for the wealthy" like James Van Alen, but Edith remembered long after that, ultimately, "My husband said, 'Do you really want to go?' and when I nodded, he rejoined, 'All right. Come along then.' And we went."

The necessary money was supplied miraculously by an elderly childless cousin, who died and left Edith with a share of his fortune, "more than enough to pay for our taste of heaven." She kept a chronicle of the cruise, from February 18 to May 7, 1888, in which the names of her two companions are never mentioned—Van Alen is "our fellow traveler." The book is most professional; it foreshadows her first travel writings about Italy, which she began to publish eight years later. It shows her observant eye, lively writing style, her enthusiasm, energy, and even courage for travel, as well as her immense knowledge of art and architecture, history, plants and flowers, her self-confidence as an art critic, her sense of humor, and how much she enjoyed being boss. And it reminds us how different she was from those women in Newport who spent all their time in social activities.

The cruise began in Algiers and ended in Ancona, Italy. They stopped at Malta, in Sicily at Syracuse, Messina, Taormina, Palermo, and Argenti, then to the Cyclades, Rhodes, Smyrna on the Asia Minor coast, Mount Athos, Athens, the Ionian Islands, and the Dalmatian Coast, Spalato (Split), Ragusa (Dubrovnik), and Cattaro (Kotor). It was an ambitious itinerary, designed to follow part of the voyage of Odysseus. Wharton's travel journal describes adventures on primitive islands—many unknown to Americans—observing local religious festivals, climbing steep and narrow paths to isolated monasteries, riding through towns on donkeys, all excursions she delighted in.

Such travels were the high points of Edith Wharton's early married life. But even at home in Newport, she was making changes. In 1889 she began to see some of her poems and, later, stories published in *Scribner's Magazine*, although her periods of creativity alternated with bouts of uncertainty and depression. And in 1892 the Whartons moved from Pencraig to Land's End, a larger house with a garden on Coggeshall Ledge, which Edith paid for from her new inheritance. Although not on the scale of what the Vanderbilts were building, Land's End was well appointed, and in much better taste, Edith maintained. It was located just off Ocean Drive, close to the most fashionable cliffs, and afforded an incomparable view.

Edith Wharton in the late 1880s. Wharton wrote to her godson, Bill Tyler, on May 16, 1937, after the death of her dog Linky: "Once they found a boy who *understood what the birds said*; & I have always been that way about dogs, ever since I was a baby. We really communicate with each other & no one had such nice things to say as Linky."

Land's End before Edith Wharton bought it

Land's End marked not only a move toward the more fashionable part of the island, but also a symbolic move away from the Newport of her childhood and into the adult part of her life where she arranged her own affairs. Wharton equated being housed in a place of one's own choice with being an adult, and her fiction is filled with characters—for example Lily Bart in *The House of Mirth*, Mattie Silver in *Ethan Frome*, Sophie Viner in *The Reef*, and Charity Royal in *Summer*, who are homeless and thus never make it into an adult and independent state. Land's End was Wharton's first real home of her own, acquired at a time when she was struggling to create a new self.

Although she felt comfortable with her old Newport set, the social activities bored her. Her intellectual qualities, her love of reading, history, and European culture, set her apart. She was a natural new friend for Paul Bourget, the French novelist who came to Newport in 1893 on assignment to write his impressions of American life for the *New York Herald,* which became his book *Outre-Mer.*

When Bourget visited Newport with his new wife, Minnie, he was already a literary lion in France, author of several novels and a collection of critical essays, *Essais de psychologie contemporaine* (1883). The Bourgets had a letter of introduction to Edith from an expatriate Wharton cousin in Paris, and they were invited to Land's End for lunch. Edith was prepared: she had read all his novels—she never would like them—and admired the essay collection.

She did not know whom to ask to meet this accomplished writer and was too timid to imagine that "perhaps he preferred to take a family meal rather than to be part of a formal dinner," so she somewhat reluctantly invited the

Paul Bourget by J. Coraboeuf, 1902. Edith would always admire Paul's lively conversation, his "fundamental generous nature," and his "magnificently professional integrity." The Bourgets would prove to be ideal traveling companions on later motor flights: "There were so many questions about which we held the same opinions, so many tastes which we shared together, so many subjects which we could discuss as far as the eye could see!"

The Bourgets at Isabella Stewart Gardner's summer house, Beech Hill, Prides Crossing, with N. E. Thiébaut and T. R. Sullivan in September 1893, just after meeting the Whartons in Newport. Edith, who always scrutinized a new face, described Paul's "beautiful head, with its grave and tormented characteristics, its gay smile, its look always on the alert" and Minnie's "little acquiline nose, her grave remote eyes and sensitive mouth, in the delicate oval of a small face crowned by heavy braids of brown hair." About Minnie, she wrote: "From our very first meeting a deep-down understanding established itself between us." She was a rare being, "full of delicate and secret vibrations."

Bourgets to lunch with six or seven guests. "At least, I thought, they can enjoy the incomparable view of the sea (for we lived on the top of a cliff overhanging the Atlantic) for want of engaging in interesting conversations."

Years later, Wharton, who tended to picture herself as inept as a young woman despite others' impressions to the contrary, remembered their meeting: "What a thrill for a young woman passionately interested in literature, but who never dreamed of making herself part of the illustrious fraternity of writers! ... At the time of our meeting I knew almost no man of letters. I had always led a purely social life, and the idea of entertaining in my house a great French writer frightened me at least as much as it flattered me. Not sharing my husband's taste for the frivolous and monotonous life of Newport, I didn't realize how the kind of life which appeared to me so desperately banal could have a documentary attraction for a foreigner as curious for novelty as Bourget was."

It turned out that Bourget was enormously interested in Wharton's house and guests and also in the fact that a house in "this ultra-frivolous milieu" was filled with books; he returned often, "enchanted by the contrast between the quiet library of Land's End, with its great bay windows opening up on the immensity of the Atlantic, and the life of the Casino and of sports, yachting, bridge—sumptuous dinners and elegant dances which make up Newport's season."

Wharton credited the success of the meeting to her library and her Venetian consoles; however, Bourget found Wharton very interesting, perhaps too interesting. He found her so well informed that most likely it was she who became his model for the intellectual tomboy in *Outre-Mer*, "the girl who is up to the times, who has read everything, understood everything, not superficially, but really, with an energy of culture that could put to shame the whole Parisian fraternity of letters. The trouble is that nine times out of ten this mind, which is capable of assimilating everything, is incapable of tasting anything. It is an iron stomach . . . with no palate. Though like all the others she gets her gowns from the best houses of the Rue de la Paix, there is not a book of Darwin, Huxley, Spencer, Renan, Taine, which she has not studied, not a painter or sculptor of whose works she could not compile a catalogue, not a school of poetry or romance of which she does not know the principles." Bourget felt the intellectual tomboy was "the most striking illustration of the misdirected effort from which this civilization suffers, and the proof that effort can replace nature only to a certain point."

Bourget also drew the portrait of the socially active young lady—the double of the intellectual tomboy. This young beauty "is in the saddle before 9 in the morning." After trotting and galloping for two hours in the salt air, she returns at eleven in time to change her gown and go to the Casino, the fashionable place of meeting in Newport, where there is a tennis tournament. At half-past twelve "the beautiful horse woman of this morning . . . has left the Casino for a yacht, where she will take luncheon. I see her get into her carriage,

a very high *duc,* take up the reins, and go off at the full speed of a horse, guiding him with her supple and firm little hands, bravely, deftly, in her elegant costume and her jewels. . . . Half an hour later I find her in the electric launch which plies between her yacht and the wharf." After lunch, when "the inevitable dry champagne has flowed without stint," her party will disperse to the polo match. "This long day of comings and goings will close, like all the others, by a dinner party followed by a ball at the Casino or elsewhere." If you joined the two—the intellectual tomboy and the social young woman—you would have the complex personality of Edith Wharton at that moment, half socially accomplished postdebutante, half serious writer.

During his stay in the Rhode Island resort, Paul Bourget noted many illustrations of America's "misdirected efforts" and ravenous appetite for excess in

everything. "On the floors of halls that are too high there are too many precious Persian and Oriental rugs. There are too many tapestries, too many paintings. . . . The guest-chambers have too many *bibelots*, too much rare furniture, and on the lunch or dinner table there are too many flowers, too many plants, too much crystal, too much silver."

Bourget looked with amazement at the new palaces—first Wakehurst, a copy of a fifteenth-century house in Sussex, begun in 1884 by James Van Alen; then Ochre Court, the Ogden Goelet house, built between 1882 and 1892; and Marble House, with its white marble facade designed by Richard Morris Hunt for William K. Vanderbilt.

What went on inside these mansions was as amazing as the buildings themselves, because, "For the last thirty or forty years, thanks to their full purses, [Americans] have laid hands upon the finest pictures, tapestries, carvings, medals, not only of France, England, Holland, Italy, but also of Greece, Egypt, India, Japan. Hence they have in their town and country houses a wealth of masterpieces worthy of a museum."

That fall of 1893, the Whartons saw the Bourgets at Mr. and Mrs. Jack Gardner's country place in Brookline, Massachussetts, and again soon after in Paris. When the Whartons started spending more time in Paris, Paul Bourget introduced her to his literary and aristocratic friends. They both enjoyed social climbing, what Daisy Chanler called "the great game of eagle-or-swan-hunting." An unkind French critic wrote of Bourget, "He comes from that climbing and envious class, the lesser bourgeoisie, and is delighted to hobnob with authentic counts and barons of the old Faubourg Saint-Germain." Wharton shared this delight. The same critic goes on to expatiate on Bourget's wide knowledge of trivia, which must have intrigued Wharton: "He described dresses, coiffures, jewelry. . . . He is an expert upholsterer, an authority on bric-

In 1894 *Scribner's Magazine* ran a series of articles on American summer resorts. "Newport" was illustrated by W. S. Vanderbilt Allen.

*Above left:* "Yachting"

*Above right:* "The Ballroom of the Casino"

à-brac, a connoisseur in perfumes, a gourmet, a faultless dresser and a grand master of etiquette."

All her life, Edith Wharton longed for a soul mate. She was later to write in *The Writing of Fiction* that "the creative artist" works in "mysterious correspondence" with an ideal other. She continually looked for people with whom to share her impressions and ideas, friends who could understand her, see into her heart and her world of the mind and the eye, someone to fulfill her fantasy of that ideal other. Daisy Chanler would be one, as would Paul Bourget. Another important friend of this time was Egerton Winthrop. A descendant of Peter Stuyvesant of New York and John Winthrop, governor of Massachussetts, Egerton Winthrop worked in finance and sat on boards. He became a mentor for Edith Wharton, who credited him with explaining to her the social behavior of the New York of her young married years.

She made him the model for Benedetto Alfieri, uncle of the Italian playwright Vittorio Alfieri in her first novel, *The Valley of Decision.* Count Benedetto instructs the hero, Odo Valsecca, in the appreciation of fine art, especially in the classical taste, an aesthetic approach inspired by recent archaeological discoveries.

Knowing Winthrop, Wharton wrote, helped her to pass for the first time "from the somewhat cramping companionship of the kindly set I had grown up in, and the cool solitude of my studies, into the warm glow of a cultivated intelligence.... Besides being an ardent bibliophile, he was a discriminating collector of works of art, especially of the eighteenth century, and his house was the first in New York in which an educated taste had replaced stuffy upholstery and rubbishy 'ornaments' with objects of real beauty in a simple designed setting."

Egerton Winthrop painted by John Singer Sargent

He became one of those whom Wharton had wished for in her childhood to show her the relation of things to each other. He was "a lover of books and pictures," an "accomplished linguist and eager reader, whose ever-youthful curiosities first taught my mind to analyze and my eyes to see. It was too late for me to acquire the mental discipline I had missed in the schoolroom, but my new friend directed and systematized my reading, and filled some of the worst gaps in my education." He encouraged her to read French novelists and historians and literary critics of the day, and introduced her to "the wonder-world of nineteenth century science. He it was who gave me Wallace's 'Darwin and Darwinism,' and 'The Origin of the Species,' and made known to me Huxley, Herbert Spencer, Romanes, Haeckel, Westermarck, and the various popular exponents of the great evolutionary movement. But it is idle to prolong the list, and hopeless to convey to a younger generation the first overwhelming sense of cosmic vastnesses which such 'magic casements' let into our little geocentric universe."

Wharton felt, however, that he had not solved the problem of mixing society with his other interests, the same problem now puzzling her. She thought he "took far more trouble about the finish and perfection of his dinners than about the choice of his guests." He was "an intensely social being, and to such the New York of the day offered few intellectual resources. As in most provincial societies, the scholars, artists and men of letters shut themselves obstinately away from the people they despised as 'fashionable,' and the latter did not know how to make the necessary advances to those who lived outside of their little conventions."

Unlike Winthrop, Wharton after her marriage had not set herself up in New York society to entertain madly; her house was small and her interests wide. She felt that, although she "had always lived among the worldly," she "had never been much impressed by them." Winthrop would plead with her to fill the part he thought she ought to play in New York society: "But I suspect that he was secretly envious of an indifference to the world of fashion which he was never able to acquire."

Another potential soul mate was the architect Ogden Codman. From an old Boston family, Codman was about Wharton's age and had lived abroad as a child, for reasons of economy as she had. He was talented, fastidious, attached to his mother, and he loved gracious living.

While his parents lived in France, Codman had been encouraged by his uncle, John Hubbard Sturgis, an architect who designed the Museum of Fine Arts in Boston, to study architecture at MIT. He soon left to educate himself through looking and working as an apprentice. By 1893 he had offices in Newport, where he had summered since 1883, and New York City.

Wharton and Codman shared a way of looking at life, as well as a taste for eighteenth-century French and Italian palaces, and Codman saw Wharton's friends as potential clients. They immediately became pals and conspired to redo Land's End together and to promote Codman's career.

In the 1890s, she often wrote to him from Europe about the status of the remodeling, giving him general advice as well as her impressions of travel in France and Italy. She wrote from Milan on April 23, 1895: "I do hope you will be an angel & have the room ready & the paint dry when we arrive. You ought to for I am bringing you a lot of photographs of Mantua which will make you fall down & worship, & then tear your hair out to think you didn't go there. Imagine two or three hundred Villa Madamas & Papa Giulio's rolled into one, & you will have a faint, but only a *very faint idea,* of the Palazzo del Te & the Ducal Palace—I never dreamed such splendour was left."

Land's End was an ugly, overdecorated wooden house with large mansard roofs when Edith and Teddy Wharton bought it. With Codman's help they transformed it into a home with bright and airy rooms. The walls were

In his career, Ogden Codman designed twenty-one houses, remodeled a number of others, and decorated well over one hundred more in Newport, Lenox, Long Island, Boston, Philadelphia, New York, and France.

painted in a light color and filled with the Italian furniture the Whartons had brought back from abroad.

Wharton was, of course, involved in every detail. She wrote to Codman on April 7, 1897: "I want to talk to you when you come next week. The library is a real pleasure to us both & we consider it a *perfect success*. The morning room is in a state of suspense, as Sharp refuses to answer our numerous appeals for the chintz."

Outside they designed a small formal garden on the ocean side, in front of trellises that climbed the walls, at right angles to the house. Paths, hedges, and an obelisk created an enclosed garden between the house and the sea. In front of the house was a central forecourt. Wharton wrote on April 30, 1897: "The formal garden is booming. The paths are partly cut, the stone steps are being put in, & on Monday I am going to put out the standard privets. With regard to the pergola, I am perfectly willing to order the four columns if you think anything would be gained by doing so at once; but I think the matter needs study, owing to the fact that the verandah is slightly raised above the grade of the terrace & it will perhaps be rather a nice question how to 'marry' the pergola with the hedge on the one side & the verandah columns on the other. I want to talk it over with you when you come next week." And in May 1897: "The place is so absorbingly interesting that I can't stay indoors. The flower-garden is all laid out, the terrace nearly finished, the stone steps being set, & we are now going to campaign among the gravestone-makers around the cemetery in search of columns & urns."

In addition to hiring him herself, Wharton also helped Codman get a

At the Breakers, Codman created a subdued and elegant atmosphere, as can be seen in his drawing for Cornelius Vanderbilt's bedroom curtain wall. The spacious and airy rooms had simple paneled walls with exquisitely carved details and perfect proportions. As Pauline Metcalf points out, their relative simplicity of decoration contrasts with the overwhelming opulence of the downstairs rooms created by the well-known French firm of decorators J. Allard et fils, who preferred the flamboyant, gilded style of the Second Empire.

Land's End, designed in 1864 by Ogden Codman's uncle, John Hubbard Sturgis, for Samuel G. Ward

Although she used wallpaper in her drawing room at Land's End, Wharton later claimed that "it was well for the future of house-decoration when medical science declared itself against the use of wall-papers. These hangings have, in fact, little to recommend them."

One of the nicest rooms at Land's End was the glass verandah lined with panels the Whartons brought back from Italy. Caned furniture with graceful legs was grouped in front of the glass, through which one could see the garden with its appealing statue and, over the hedge and grass, the sea.

The garden at
Land's End

commission to design interiors at the Breakers, the mansion of Cornelius Vanderbilt II. He designed some thirteen dignified rooms on the two upper floors of this enormous house whose windows looked out over the sea. He wrote his mother on December 13, 1893: "Who do you suppose I have for a client? Teddy Wharton told me today that Mr. *Cornelius Vanderbilt* wants to see me at his offices at 11:30 tomorrow to talk about his Newport house and he wants me to do part!

"Just think what a client!! The richest and nicest of them all. I can scarcely believe it is true. . . . I am going to thank Mrs. Wharton who brought this about." The rooms were built in 1894 and 1895, and Codman thus became part of the mad building spree in which people competed with one another for the most sumptuous surroundings.

Codman's attitude toward his clients was complex. He was glad, even overjoyed to have the patronage of families like the Vanderbilts, and he enjoyed social events at their houses (telling his mother in letters how pretty Gertrude Vanderbilt was and how he took her into dinner). But then he pretended to be superior, too: "He continually made fun, in private if not in public, of the *arriviste* taste of the big-money families." The Codman attitude was to approve loftily only of "what took place in 'my rooms' on the second floor of the Vanderbilt palace, meaning the bedrooms and boudoirs he had decorated for the family's less spectacular moments."

For her part, Wharton wrote Codman continually, talking of what she saw and approved of and what she didn't. On May 1, 1897, for example: "Teddy hasn't yet rallied from the effects of the Whitney house. It must indeed be a Ghoul's lair. I wish the Vanderbilts didn't retard culture so very thoroughly. They are entrenched in a sort of Thermopylae of bad taste, from which apparently no force on earth can dislodge them."

The Whartons and Codman met in Versailles in the summer of 1896. Codman reported to his mother that Edith Wharton was not very strong, and she had sprained her ankle falling off her bicycle. He even did more sight-seeing than Edith, who "gets tired easily which shortens the pleasant visits to the museums but I go alone." He commented on the Whartons' fussiness to his mother: "The hotel is really very good. The W's seem to complain a shade less—they remind me of the Princess and the Pea." While Edith was laid up, he and Teddy took their bikes on the train to the Arc de Triomphe and bicycled part of the way back to Versailles.

Codman shared Edith's love for Europe's wonderful palaces and churches, whereas Teddy preferred spending more time in America. After the Whartons left for Italy, Codman wrote to his mother that Teddy Wharton "is always regretting Newport for which he is so well fitted. He is always sure a man ought to live in his own country and does not see that if a man really amounts

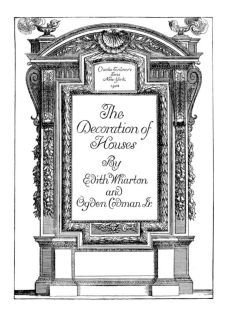

In *The Decoration of Houses*, at times the authors state seemingly rigid rules; for example, on how to hang pictures: "Pictures or prints should be fastened to the wall, not hung by a cord or wire, nor allowed to tilt forward at an angle." The following illustrations *(pages 53–55)* from the book highlight additional principles set forth by Wharton and Codman.

Sala della Maddalena, Royal Palace, Genoa, eighteenth century: "In the seventeenth century the introduction of the two-storied Italian saloon produced a state apartment called a *salon*; and this, towards the beginning of the eighteenth century, was divided into two smaller rooms: one, the *salon de compagnie*, remaining a part of the gala suite used exclusively for entertaining, while the other—the *salon de famille*—became a family apartment like the English drawing-room."

to anything he will make himself whatever he is. I never can see what he could amount to if he lived 100 years in America. I suppose he thinks some people there might look up to him and no one ever will here."

Wharton and Codman felt so much the same about rooms and houses that they wrote a book together, *The Decoration of Houses*, a statement on how to house oneself in elegance, beauty, simplicity, and practicality, a subject that absorbed Wharton all her life. Although she had avoided taking a large part in New York society, she liked to entertain small groups constantly, to be in the presence of beauty, to have large formal gardens, and this book was her manifesto on how to live with taste.

Years later Edith Wharton said she wrote the book to counteract the current decorating practices, for the architects of that day saw house decoration "as a branch of dress-making, and left the field to the upholsterers, who crammed every room with curtains, lambrequins, jardinières of artificial plants, wobbly velvet-covered tables littered with silver gewgaws, and festoons of lace on mantelpieces and dressing-tables." This meant throwing out the clutter, removing

Library of Louis XVI, Palace of Versailles: "It has already been pointed out that the plan of building bookshelves into the walls is the most decorative and the most practical. . . . When not set in recesses, the shelves [should form] a sort of continuous lining around the walls, as in the library of Louis XVI at the palace at Versailles."

Andrea Mantegna's ceiling of 1474 at the Sala Degli Sposi, Ducal Palace, Mantua: "There is no reason why a painter should not simulate loggia and sky on a flat plaster ceiling, since no one will try to use this sham opening as a means of exit; but the carpet-designer who puts picture-frames and human faces under foot, though he does not actually deceive, produces on the eye a momentary startling sense of obstruction. Any *trompe-l'oeil* is permissible in decorative art if it gives an impression of pleasure; but the inherent sense of fitness is shocked by the act of walking upon upturned faces."

the dark wood walls and furniture, letting in light, and focusing on what was really beautiful.

Both authors had an excellent eye and a natural sense of form. They saw that simplicity and harmony were the key to elegant rooms, and they understood that what was practical could also be beautiful—the well-crafted bookcase, the elegant hairbrush, the perfectly hung drapery, the handsomely carved mirror. In the past, "few purely ornamental objects were to be seen, save in the cabinets of collectors; but when Botticelli decorated the panels of linen chests, and Cellini chiseled book-clasps and drinking-cups, there could be no thought of the vicious distinction between the useful and the beautiful. One of the first obligations of art is to make all useful things beautiful: were this neglected principle applied to the manufacture of household accessories, the modern room would have no need of knick-knacks."

Although they admired the Italians and their splendid villas and palaces, the authors deemed Italian architecture more appropriate for court functions and suggested the reader look to eighteenth-century France and England for models for the private house.

Every room must have a purpose that reflects historical precedents and considers contemporary behavior. For example, "Pains have been taken to trace as clearly as possible the mixed ancestry of the modern drawing-room, in order to show that it is the result of two distinct influences—that of the gala apartment and that of the family sitting-room." Such "mixed ancestry" leads to confusion in the present, and the modern house owner should decide on the

Bathroom, Pitti Palace, Florence: "The chief fault of the American bath-room is that, however splendid the materials used, the treatment is seldom architectural. A glance at the beautiful bathroom in the Pitti Palace at Florence will show how much effect may be produced in a small space by carefully studied composition. A mere closet is here transformed into a stately room, by that regard for harmony of parts which distinguishes interior architecture from mere decoration."

function of his drawing room—will it be a *salon de compagnie* or a *salon de famille*? The first is out of place in the average house and is needed only where the dinners are so large that a gala apartment is needed—it should be gay and uncluttered with furniture. The *salon de famille,* on the other hand, is a room where people should be comfortable and should include a well-appointed writing table and chairs conveniently grouped about tables with lamps. Such identity quests for each room are necessary to properly design and furnish it.

After giving chapters on the historical tradition and general function, Wharton and Codman go on to analyze elements of each room—walls, doors, windows, fireplaces, ceilings, and floors—and then the rooms themselves,

In her chapters on doors, halls, and vestibules, Wharton emphasized the importance of spaces to human behavior and the house dwellers' need for security and privacy: "It should be borne in mind of entrances in general that, while the main purpose of a door is to admit, its secondary purpose is to exclude." The hall is "the centre upon which every part of the house directly or indirectly opens. This publicity is increased by the fact that the hall must be crossed by the servant who opens the front door, and by any one admitted to the house." The hall, therefore, "is like a public square in relation to the private houses around it," and its decoration should be formal and impersonal. She carried her ideas through in her hall at Land's End (*left*).

examining the historical raison d'être and suggesting how each should be decorated. The authors are adamant that one should stick to one purpose per room: "A room should have a distinct function," for "the tendency to combine functions is more likely to multiply dissatisfaction than to satisfy several needs at once."

Children's rooms are very important: "The room where the child's lessons are studied is, in more senses than one, that in which he receives his education," as well as where he develops his sense of beauty. Wharton is doubtless talking of herself when she says, "The aesthetic sensibilities wake early in some children, and these, if able to analyze their emotions, could testify to what suffer-

"Pencraig (Hall). My 2 portraits at 8 and 18 (by Edward May)"

ing they have been subjected by the habit of sending to school-room and nurseries whatever furniture is too ugly or threadbare to be used in any other part of the house." A child should be taught to distinguish between a good and bad painting, "a well or an ill-modelled statue," and should only read certain books, such as Geoffrey Chaucer's *Knight's Tale* and Sir Thomas Mallory's *Morte d'Arthur*.

From the beginning, the child should see art and life as intertwined. "The habit of regarding 'art' as a thing apart from life is fatal to the development of taste. Parents may conscientiously send their children to galleries and museums, but unless the child can find some point of contact between its own surroundings and the contents of the galleries, the interest excited by the pictures and statues will be short lived and ineffectual. . . . The child's mind must be prepared by daily lessons in beauty to understand the masterpieces of art."

It is the poor little rich children who suffer most, "since the presents received by those whose parents and relations are not 'well off' have the saving merit of usefulness. It is the superfluous gimcrack—the 'ornament'—which is most objectionable, and the more expensive such articles are the more likely are they to do harm. Rich children suffer from the quantity as well as the quality of the presents they receive. Appetite is surfeited, curiosity blunted, by the mass of offerings poured in with every anniversary."

"A good print may often be bought for the same price as a poor one, and the money spent on a china 'ornament,' in the shape of a yellow Leghorn hat with a kitten climbing out of it, would probably purchase a good reproduction of one of the Tanagra statuettes, a plaster cast of some French or Italian bust or one of Cantagalli's copies of the Robbia bas-reliefs." These suggestions aroused caustic remarks from readers, as Wharton and Codman were both childless.

Wharton and Codman knew that "good objects of art give to a room its crowning touch of distinction," but they also knew that collecting required "cultivation and judgment, combined with that feeling for beauty that no amount of study can give, but that study alone can quicken and render profitable." Taste was a quality they felt was currently in short supply in Newport and belonged to a bygone time when rich men were patrons of "the arts of elegance." Wharton was probably thinking of Egerton Winthrop, a collector whom she admired, in contrast to other owners of Newport mansions.

The authors end by presenting house decoration as an art with definite rules derived from seeing the house as a whole made up of parts. "In the composition of a whole there is no negligible quantity: if the decoration of a room is planned on certain definite principles, whatever contributes line and color becomes a factor in the composition. The relation of proportion to decoration is like that of anatomy to sculpture: underneath are the everlasting laws."

Yet individual tastes and needs should come first and not allow irrelevant past customs to dictate unless they provide necessary form and beauty. "One is unconsciously tyrannized over by the wants of others, the wants of the dead and one's predecessors who have an inconvenient way of thrusting their different habits and tastes across the current of later existences." This statement brings to mind the tortured relationships in Wharton's fiction and suggests that in writing the book she was dealing with problems of her own emerging identity and trying to make up for a time when her own needs were not considered.

Wharton's ideas on form in decorating are consistent with her ideas on form in fiction. According to Wharton, a work of art should be composed of parts assembled in harmonious balance, no part distracting the viewer from the impression of the whole. She despised details that do not reinforce the primary design. Her novels have balanced, architectural structures, and she used that sense of form to evaluate everything she saw, from clothing to interiors to gardens.

Although one might suppose in view of their other careers that Wharton's contribution was limited to the writing, she supplied many of the ideas as well. So Codman reported to his mother in January 1897: "We have now written about 100 pages. Mrs. Wharton is a great help, and is very much interested. She takes my notes and puts them into literary form, and adds a good deal out of her own head." Wharton assumed the leadership for the project, as she was the more industrious and determined to get things done. She contacted publishers, evaluated the success of each chapter, and also handled translating and indexing. Her friend Walter Berry helped with problems of organization. "This does not allow for any loafing," she wrote, after a deadline was postponed. She con-

In the library at Land's End, the decorating couple broke their own rules by including an overstuffed, comfortable sofa and chairs.

stantly prodded, admonished, and scolded, revealing her dominating personality, and her perfectionism. Before a meeting with an editor she wrote, "A good deal depends on the impression produced during this visit, as Mr. Brett sails next week, and I want him to have a clear report of the book and its appearance."

Codman's rendering of the fireplace wall in the library at Land's End

When other publishers rejected the book on decorating, it was natural for Wharton to show it to Scribner's Publishers, since *Scribner's Magazine* had published her poems and stories as they appeared. Once the book was accepted in July 1897, Wharton became obsessed with every detail.

Between July and November of 1897, Wharton wrote twenty-nine letters to Scribner's discussing the cover of the book, the wording, printing, and placement of its title, as well as the binding, paper, illustrations, introduction, and conclusion. Finally, on December 4, 1897, she wrote to William Brownell (Scribner's senior literary consultant and Wharton's second editor there): "I received three copies of *The Decoration of Houses*, and I must tell you at once how gratified I am by the appearance of the book. Paper, type of binding seem to me admirable, and Mr. Codman who is here with us, desires to join me in thanks to the Messrs. Scribner for the handsome and dignified dress in which they have clothed us."

*The Decoration of Houses* was an instant success. Even though Scribner's only published a small first edition "produced with great typographical care, probably thinking that the book was more likely to succeed as a gift book among my personal friends than as a practical manual," this was sold out at once and went through edition after edition because "people of taste were only too eager to follow any guidance that would not only free them from the suffocating upholsterer, but tell them how to replace him." It initiated a new style of decoration, drawing on classical models that combined simplicity, harmony, and beauty, which was carried on by others, such as Elsie de Wolfe, in rebellion against the earlier Victorian clutter.

By this time Wharton had taken over Codman's career. Since she knew many possible clients, they would plot on how to get their business, and then she would advise him on how to handle them. When the Whartons had returned from Europe in the autumn of 1896, Edith had been told by Codman's clients, "either directly or through a third person," that his charge of 25 percent was considered excessive. She advised him: "Human nature, take it all and all, is pretty much the same all over, & though when you make a general reputation you will find suckers who will pay any price because you are 'the Fashion,' you would not have found such in the beginning, and the people who *did* go to you, & whom you complain of as not being remunerative, went simply because they had more discernment than the average. You must count that in their favour. If you had continued to charge 25% the report would have spread and it would have done you harm. When I came home you had no clients, and those you had had were all talking loudly about your high prices."

On the Whartons' advice, Codman reduced his charges. Wharton could now claim that she had been right. "What was the result? You had fresh orders, *from the friends of former clients*." She thought he should put up with demand-

Interior of Egerton Winthrop's house,
Quatrel, designed by Codman

Interior of Egerton Winthrop's house,
Quatrel, designed by Codman

ing clients who might not want large jobs, for, "if they are pleased they will speak to others, & now & then an ideal client like C.V. & Mr. Bowdoin, will compensate for the others.

"I am not taking the client's view, I assure you; I am putting myself in your place, & I still say, be content to make very little money now in order to make a great deal more later. I cannot say anything else, for I do not honestly think it, & Teddy agrees with me."

When Codman was redoing her friend Egerton Winthrop's house, Quatrel, Wharton took an active interest; she wrote on May 1: "I can see no signs of Egerton's mantelpieces being put up. Do stir up the mantel man. I don't want you to get into the way of shirking small jobs for big ones. If you only *would* believe me when I tell you it's bad policy! The people who give you small jobs are always the ones who are on the lookout for being shirked, & require to be ménagés much more carefully than the millionaires—witness the Millers & Lispenard Stewart. It's no use to say—oh, but such poor clients aren't worth while. People who are not worth while directly may be so *indirectly*, & you can never tell, till afterwards, what a small job may bring you in the way of big jobs, nor, on the other hand, what incalculable harm the dictum may do you behind your back. I shall always preach this at you, as long as we're on speaking terms; for I *know* that success lies in this direction.

"I am very glad that Mr. Winthrop is to have the trellis. The boiseries are nearly up & *very* pretty, but I think the ceiling ornament too small to be in

Drawing room at 884 Park Avenue, New York. In 1896, Wharton asked Codman to help her with her little house in New York on Park Avenue near Seventy-ninth Street, her pied-à-terre for a couple of months each winter. Although it was very far uptown, "on account of the bicycling, I would rather be up there in a 'bicoque' [shack] than down town." On January 5, 1897, Codman wrote to his mother: "[Mrs. Wharton's] New York house will be a great success. . . . The things are so pretty. Just what I have always wanted to do myself. I never saw any one learn so quickly as she has, she gets very different things from what she did when I first knew her—I think we have both learned much and each has taught the other."

scale with the panel ornaments. Let us hope that he will like it, because he chose it. What are you going to do with his hall? It looks like the ragged edge of despair."

On June 17, from Newport, she wrote again to Codman in New York, informing him of possible trouble brewing with a client: "Just a line to say that Miss Kneeland, who has just come from Mrs. S. V. R. Thayer's at Tiverton, says the latter is much disappointed because you have done nothing about her boudoir."

In counseling Codman, Wharton showed excellent business sense, an awareness of appearances, and a devotion to detail. She was doubtless giving her friend the sort of advice and support she could use herself, and taking the interest in his career she would have liked someone to take in hers.

One friend with whom she could discuss her work was Daniel Berkeley Updike, a bachelor who was the head of the Merrymount Press in Boston and had met the Whartons when they were still living at Pencraig Cottage. Updike was responsible for the title page and binding of *The Decoration of Houses*, and he shared Edith's enthusiasm for perfection in printing and attention to detail. Updike's press printed Wharton's first collection of short stories and five of her other books. He often enjoyed the Whartons' hospitality at Land's End and, later, the Mount. They "were past masters in the art of entertaining; and in this there was between them a complete unanimity of taste."

When the Whartons and Codman later fought over Codman's bills,

Ogden Codman (right) and
Daniel Berkeley Updike (left)
with an unknown friend

Updike tried to "grease the wheels" and calm Codman down, reminding him that "we all of us are subject to lapses of temper, and lapses of judgment. I am. You are. Teddy Wharton is. But that does not mean that we are not sane people, but only we are not at all times well regulated people." At another time he wrote, "What you never will realize is that the 'W's really like you and are interested in you and hope that you are a little interested in them."

After periods of frantic activity, Wharton often would collapse and then withdraw from life for a time, sickened and exhausted, and try to recharge herself. After the publication of *The Decoration of Houses*, in the summer and fall of 1898, she was treated for depression by S. Weir Mitchell, a well-known physician and expert on neurasthenia. Her great love of houses and architecture sustained her during these times. She seldom lost interest in exploring new places, and she came to believe that a change of scenery was a good cure.

She was also sustained by her friendship with Sally Norton, one of six children of Charles Eliot Norton and Susan Sedgwick. Sally had lived in Europe as a child, was interested in art, a great reader, very religious, and had been brought up in a house filled with brilliant thinkers. A spinster, she took care of her aging father. Edith had met the Nortons through Teddy's family, and she began corresponding with Sally in the late 1890s. It was to Sally that she could tell things she could tell no one else—especially her feelings about her health. In the early 1900s, she wrote to Norton that she was hoping to see Mrs. Jack Gardner's new house, Fenway Court. The story that Berkeley Updike told years later was that she happened to be stopping in Boston just at the moment when Mrs. Gardner was arranging the interior of Fenway Court. Mrs. Gardner loved to veil her proceedings with an air of mystery, and she permitted people to have a peep at her house, admitted by a "postern" (which was merely a side door) at some precise and generally rather inconvenient moment. If this appointment was not exactly met, the "postern" was closed and the unfortunate late-comer left without. I think Mrs. Gardner rather enjoyed these early morning appointments, and perhaps also the failure of tardy guests to enjoy her hospitality. Knowing that Mrs. Wharton was in town, she sent word to her that if she wished to see the house and would arrive promptly at twelve minutes past eight in the morning, Mrs. Gardner would consent to show it to her. Mrs. Wharton replied that she was never up at that hour, and the invitation was declined.

On May 29, 1901, Wharton reported to Codman that they had been in Boston for ten days and enjoyed it immensely: "I saw the Sprague house and garden, The Public Library, all Mrs. Jack's new pictures, the outside of her palace (?) in the fens—"

Although her letters to Codman show a confident command of her life (and his), other feelings were lingering just below the surface. In preceding years, she had had trouble finishing her stories, experiencing spurts of creativity followed by periods of languishing. She had written her fiction editor at *Scribner's Magazine,* Edward Burlingame, in 1894, after he criticized her story "Something Exquisite," that she had "fallen into a period of groping.... Pray don't regard this as the wail of the rejected authoress—it is only a cry for help and counsel."

Miniature of Edith Wharton by Fernand Paillet, 1890

She struggled to write fiction, and she felt she would not truly be herself until she succeeded: "I continued to live my old life, for my husband was as fond of society as ever, and I knew of no other existence, except our annual escapes to Italy. I had as yet no real personality of my own, and was not to acquire one till my first volume of short stories was published." She wrote sporadically and the results were greeted by success, but they appeared slowly. It was a great triumph when her first volume of short stories, *The Greater Inclination,* appeared in 1899. She said later that its publication "broke the chains which had held me so long in a kind of torpor." She had finally shown that she could do what she wanted, which was to write.

To others at Newport she appeared fashionable and unapproachable and much too well turned out to be bookish. She showed them only one side of her complicated self. Years later her contemporary Maud Howe Elliot remembered: "Among the belles of my youth was Pussy Jones, who lived at Pencraig

Cottage. Our acquaintance was slight; she belonged to the ultra-fashionable crowd, and I in quite another group. Though the intellectuals and the fashionables sometimes met, they never quite fused. She was slender, graceful, and icy cold, with an exceedingly aristocratic bearing. We were all amazed when Pussy Jones brought out a book of verses in her early twenties. She soon forsook the world of fashion, which always claims her as its own, and, as Edith Wharton, took a leading place in the world of letters."

While she often put on this rather stiff and formal facade to those around her, Wharton let down her guard in her fiction and addressed openly whatever interested or troubled her at the time. Obsessed with the idea of suitably housing herself and creating order and beauty out of disorder, in the 1890s she wrote a number of stories where houses figure prominently as a framework for exploring the lives of many troubled characters; metaphors incorporating houses, furniture, and landscape views occur frequently in her work.

In her first published story, "Mrs. Manstey's View" (1891), a poor widow's good spirits depend on enjoying the view from the window of her boarding-house room. "The view surrounded and shaped her life as the sea does a lonely island." Mrs. Manstey possesses "the visualizing gift" that was so important to Edith Wharton, and she could infuse her images with fantasy. "She loved, at twilight, when the distant brownstone spire seemed melting in the fluid yellow of the west, to lose herself in vague memories of a trip to Europe, made years ago, and now reduced in her mind's eye to a pale phantasmagoria of indistinct steeples and dreamy skies. Perhaps at heart Mrs. Manstey was an artist; at all events she was sensible of many changes of color unnoticed by the average eye and, dear to her as the green of early spring, was the black lattice of branches against a cold sulphur sky at the close of a snowy day."

When a neighbor plans to build an extension that will block her view, Mrs. Manstey tries to prevent it and fails. She loses her only sustaining passion—her joy in seeing—and she cannot survive without it.

In Wharton's second story, "The Fullness of Life" (1893), the heroine sees her emotional life as a house full of rooms: "There is the hall, through which everyone passes in going in and out; the drawing room, where one received formal visits; the sitting room, where the members of the family come and go as they list; but beyond that, far beyond, are others rooms, the handles of whose doors perhaps are never turned; no one knows the way to them, no one knows whither they lead, and in the innermost room, the holy of holies, the soul sits alone and waits for a footstep that never comes." This wonderful metaphor suggests profound loneliness and sexual longing.

In 1898, Wharton described these early stories to her editor Edward Burlingame as being written "at the top of my voice." They were "the excesses of my youth," and "'The Fullness of Life' was one long shriek."

Wharton's settings and spatial metaphors reflect her aesthetic interest in houses and gardens and at the same time remind us that she was feeling trapped and unhappy in her marriage. These feelings were translated into images of obstructed views and empty rooms where women sit alone. To be suitably housed, along the lines set down in *The Decoration of Houses,* was one thing. To feel imprisoned was another. The illusion of freedom was important to her, and her spatial metaphors reflect this. Windows are associated with new understanding, "opening magic casements," and travel suggests escape from the limitations of life and exploration of new possibilities.

"Copy" (1901) concerns Mrs. Dale, a successful writer in her forties, "the novelist of the age," who is bored by the evidence of her new success—many letters about royalties, translations, and her new serials. When she is visited by an old friend, Paul Ventnor, she confesses to him that she feels it was years ago that they were "real people. . . . I died years ago. What you see before you is a figment of the reporter's brain—a monster manufactured out of newspaper paragraphs, with ink in its veins. A keen sense of copyright is my nearest approach to an emotion."

Surfeited with public attention, Mrs. Dale again wants a private life: "Don't talk to me about living in the hearts of my readers! We both know what kind of a domicile that is. Why, before long I shall become a classic! Bound in sets and kept on a top bookshelf—brr, doesn't that sound freezing? I foresee the day when I shall be as lonely as an Etruscan museum!"

In "The Muse's Tragedy," it turns out that Mrs. Anerton—supposedly the inspiration for the great poet Vincent Rendle—was never really loved by him. In "The Journey," a young husband dies and his wife finds herself hiding his body behind the sleeping-car curtains in a railway carriage full of curious strangers. Around the same time, Wharton also wrote two stories, "The Twilight of the God" and "The Line of Least Resistance," making fun of the opulence and greed of Newport.

Cynthia Wolff has noted that many of Wharton's early stories are autobiography barely disguised as fiction and do not stand on their own as polished tales. She calls these fictions "Landscapes of Desolation" and suggests that their often unhappy characters tell the real story of Wharton's life at the time. As Candace Waid points out, these early stories also voice Wharton's feelings of conflict between art and life and reveal her "anxiety at devoting herself to art."

During this time, Wharton often turned to her old friend Walter Berry, who became her mentor and adviser for many of her writings. He helped her to organize her ideas for *The Decoration of Houses,* and when she was blocked while working on her first novel, he said, "Don't worry about how you're to go on. Just write down everything you feel like telling." He wrote her affectionate, joking letters. He was understanding of her health problems and believed

The Casino on Bellevue Avenue in the 1890s

in her talent. In November 1899 he encouraged her to leave Newport, which had come to depress her, particularly in the winter: "The Dr. (Dr. W.B.) positively forbids your going back to sea air—will not answer for the consequences. *Do, please*, Edith think what it means to have a relapse: your winter ruined, littry biz null, general awfulness; on the other hand: in the fairy ring, and $500. Stories just falling off the end of the pen without effort."

By the end of the decade, Wharton had begun to make regular visits to the Berkshire town of Lenox, Massachusetts, staying either with her mother-in-law and sister-in-law or at the Curtis Hotel while she contemplated her next move. She was drawn to the countryside there. She found the views in the Berkshires more "picturesque" than in Newport, and she could assemble the foreground of fields, middle ground of woods and lakes, and background of blue hills and mountains into pleasing images. The relative calm of Lenox felt perfect. She wrote Ogden Codman in August 1900: "Dear Coddy, I should be proud to keep up my side of our correspondence, were it not that you have so impressed on my mind the fact that you hate Lenox and all that therein is. . . . The truth is that I am in love with the place—climate, scenery, life, & all—& when I have built a villa on one of the estates I have picked out, & have planted my gardens & laid out paths through my bosco, I doubt if I ever leave here—expect [*sic*] to go to Italy."

Also at the end of the decade, Lucretia Jones lay dying in Paris. Bedridden for more than a year, she died just after Wharton purchased her new property in Lenox, in late June 1901. Wharton would not remember her mother fondly. She continued to feel that her mother had misunderstood her and not properly cared for her, and, although she would have liked to be free of her

Tennis week at Newport at the turn of the century. Winthrop Chanler is the second seated figure on the left.

mother's influence, her bitterness toward her mother remained strong for the rest of Wharton's life.

Even after she moved to Lenox and built her large house on the hill, Wharton came back to Newport from time to time. Her letters to Sally Norton suggest that, by the fall of 1902, she was beginning to see the resort as a place whose pastimes and culture could be analyzed objectively. Newport was more than ever the place for gala balls, sports events, and competitive spending sprees, but "this life of lazy ladies and gentlemen" would no longer irritate or entrap: "I had a very pleasant week at Newport. Dry, brilliant weather (not a fog), magnificent tennis (I am a devout spectator of that game). . . . If you care for tennis I wish you had seen the final match between Larned and Doherty. It gave me a sense of being at a Greek game—the brilliancy of the scene, the festal dresses, the grace & ease of the two players, & the strange intensity of silence to which that chattering crowd was subdued. It seems to me such a beautiful game—without violence, noise, brutality—quick, graceful, rhythmic, with a setting of turf & sky."

Wharton often found inspiration for her writing during her Italian travels. Parma (whose cathedral is shown *above*), along with Mantua, became the model for her fictional duchy, Pianura, in *The Valley of Decision*.

In the early years of the Whartons' marriage, they crossed the Atlantic by steamer almost every spring, and Italy was their favorite destination. They would stop in Paris to see Edith's mother and then make their way to Switzerland and across the Alps, traveling by train and carriage. Edith was fascinated by the country, and she began to write about it continually. Readers of the period loved travel accounts. Travel sketches by William Dean Howells and Henry James had appeared beginning in the 1860s, and Wharton's friend Paul Bourget had just written *Sensations d'Italie* (1890). Amateurs also kept travel journals that sometimes made their way into print, and travel accounts were traditionally a socially acceptable form of writing for a lady. Edith joined the throng and, after almost every trip, wrote an essay for publication in *Scribner's Magazine*.

Writing about Italy was an important step in developing Wharton's confidence, as she enjoyed assessing art independently of earlier critics and finding new roads to old destinations—defying the guidebooks. She studied palaces and villas inside and outside for *The Decoration of Houses* and as settings for her fiction. The art and landscape moved her deeply. As she wrote Ogden Codman from Milan in 1895: "The older I grow the more I feel that I would rather live in Italy than anywhere—the very air is full of architecture—'la ligne' is everywhere. Everything else seems so coarse or banal beside it. I never weary of driving through the streets and looking at the doorways & windows and courtyards & walls & all the glimpses one gets. What an unerring sentiment for form! And if I could only get you to see that on this side of the Alps the Roman tradition continued unbroken, & that through what you call the barbaric period one may trace the same exquisite refinement & fitness of line & ornament—oh, there is nothing like it in the world, and it breaks my heart every time I have to leave it."

In her travels Wharton amassed an enormous store of images and impressions—fields of wildflowers, frescoes in a dark church, paintings in a gallery—which she translated beautifully into words, in both travel essays and short stories. In "The Fullness of Life," a woman (a barely disguised stand-in for Wharton herself) has died and is talking to the "Spirit of Life." She recounts how she and her husband could never appreciate the same things—his riding boots creaked in an irritating way. He did not share her love of art and travel, poetry and architecture. A pivotal episode occurred in the church of Orsanmichele in Florence, when she experienced a wonderful vision and felt herself being "borne onward along a mighty current." Life wove around her like a rhythmic dance in all its "varied manifestations of beauty and strangeness," and "wherever the spirit of man had passed I knew that my foot had once been familiar."

As she gazed at Orcagna's tabernacle, she saw it change into images from different periods of history. She was swept on

> past the alien faces of antique civilizations and the familiar wonders of Greece, till I swam upon the fiercely rushing tide of the Middle Ages, with its swirling eddies of passion, its heaven-reflecting pools of poetry and art. . . . The rhythmic blow of the craftsmen's hammers in the gold-smiths' workshops and on the walls of churches, the party cries of armed factions in the narrow streets, the organ roll of Dante's verse, the crackle of the fagots around Arnold of Brescia, the twitter of the swallows to which St. Francis preached, the laughter of the ladies listening on the hillside to the quips of the Decameron, while plague-struck Florence howled beneath them—all this and much more I heard, joined in strange unison with voices earlier and more remote, fierce, passionate, or tender, yet subdued to such awful harmony that I thought of the song that the morning stars sang together and felt as though it were sounding in my ears.
>
> My heart beat to suffocation; the tears burned my lids; the joy, the mystery of it seemed too intolerable to be borne. I could not understand even the words of the song; but I knew that if there had been someone at my side who could have heard it with me, we might have found the key to it together.

The unhappy woman, who desires a soul mate to share her interests, is much like Edith Wharton (who admitted this story was autobiographical): sensitive to beautiful art, imaginative and articulate, but more open to art than intimacy. When the Spirit of Life offers her someone with whom to share a dream house with a portico and beautiful columns, and to talk about Dante and art, she turns him down to tend to her husband's needs. Critics have commented on how the story parallels Wharton's own unhappy marriage; art, history, and travel gripped Edith's imagination in ways that Teddy simply could not share.

Nevertheless, traveling was at least a way they could enjoy being together. Since friends could also share her enthusiasm, and experience moments of enlightenment, she often brought them with her (as well as her housekeeper and personal maid, who made up her entourage). Egerton Winthrop was "responsive to beauty" and "patient over disappointments and discomforts." The Bourgets also measured up to her standard as travelers, particularly Minnie, who of the two was "more sensitive to the minor magic of scenes and

Wharton described her find: "The chapels of the Passion [at San Vivaldo] are about twenty in number, and as many more are said to have perished. They are scattered irregularly through the wood adjoining the monastery."

### A Tuscan Shrine.

*By Edith Wharton*

ONE of the rarest and most delicate pleasures of the continental tour- . . . his statements; and the only refu[ge] left from his oppressive omniscien[ce] . . .

places, the little unnoticed exquisitivenesses that waylaid one at every turn of the paths we followed." They developed a comfortable routine: "We generally settled ourselves say in Milan, Turin or Venice; then we would hire a large carriage to make excursions in the neighborhood. My husband, on a bicycle, went ahead of us to look around, procure rooms at the inn, and order meals, while we followed, in the slow trot of our tired horses, across the ravishing Bergamesque landscapes or the alpine valleys of Piedmont."

Off they would go, the women in their long skirts and hats and veils, the men in their knickers, climbing into carriages that lurched over bumpy roads and spending nights in hotels that were sometimes luxurious, sometimes primitive. Bicycling was also part of the fun—she wrote from Parma in 1896: "The roads in this part of Italy are capital, you can't fancy what fun it is to jump on one's bicycle at the railway station and fly about one of these queer little towns!"

In early March of 1894, Wharton was in Cannes, France; later in the month, she went down to Florence. She had heard about a religious shrine in the hills somewhere near San Gimignano, and she wanted to investigate it. At the monastery of San Vivaldo, she found a series of terra-cotta figures in the little chapels there and decided they had been misattributed to "an obscure artist of the seventeenth century," when she perceived they were obviously earlier. She was so fully persuaded of the importance of the terra-cottas that she had them photographed by Alinari Brothers in Florence, at her own expense, on the chance that *Scribner's* or one of the other magazines would like to publish an illustrated account of them.

This, her first travel essay, tells the story of her discovery. In a voice that is a bit shrill, she states that "Even Mr. Murray [John Murray, English publisher of travel guidebooks] does not know much of San Vivaldo," and "such information as he gives on the subject was refreshingly inaccurate"; yet she was surprised that he knew of it at all, since when Wharton inquired about San Vivaldo in Florence, she found that its name was unfamiliar "even among amateurs of Tuscan art."

Wharton was all for the fresh experience. She and her group deliberately approach San Vivaldo by way of San Gimignano because the guidebook said you could only get there from the other side: "One of the rarest and most delicate pleasures of the continental tourist is to circumvent the compiler of his guide book," who "has already been over the ground, has tested the inns, measured the kilometres, and distilled from the massive tomes of Kugler, Burckhardt and Morelli a portable estimate of the local art and architecture." When they dash out under the gateway of the medieval town, the Whartons feel "the thrill of explorers sighting a new continent."

At first, they are alone in the Tuscan landscape with its "slopes trellised with vine and mulberry . . . stretches of ash-coloured olive orchard; and here and there a farm house . . . guarded by its inevitable group of cypresses," but later they see workers in the fields and shepherdesses with flocks and oxen. Behind them the towers of San Gimignano pierce the sky. After an arduous climb, they finally arrive at the monastery, with its chapels containing terra-cotta dioramas of scenes from the Passion spread out in a lovely glade.

A monk greets them without surprise, "as though San Vivaldo were daily invaded by hordes of sight-seers." He repeats the traditional belief that the terra-cotta groups are the work of Giovanni Gonnelli, Il Cieco di Gambassi (the Blind Man of Gambassi), yet Wharton notes that the groups are uneven in quality and feels sure they were done by different artists. The figures in *The Descent of the Holy Ghost upon the Disciples* have an air of simplicity that suggests they are of "an earlier and less worldly period of art," while those of "*Lo Spasimo*, the swoon of the Virgin at the sight of Christ bearing the Cross," evi-

Wharton was keen to document her discovery: "My first care was to seek expert confirmation of my theory; and as a step in this direction I made arrangements to have the groups of San Vivaldo photographed by Signor Alinari of Florence [whose photographs are shown here]. . . . In the group of the Ascension [*above*] the upper part has been grotesquely restored; but the figures of the Virgin and disciples, who kneel below, are apparently untouched, and on their faces is seen that look of wondering ecstasy, that reflection of the beatific vision, which the artist excelled in representing."

*Lo Spasimo,* the swooning of the Virgin at the sight of Christ bearing the cross, "is the smallest of the groups, being less than life-size, and comprising only the figure of the Virgin supported by the Marys and by two kneeling angels. There is a trace of primitive stiffness in the attempt to render the prostration of the Virgin, but her face expresses an extremity of speechless anguish which is subtly contrasted with the awed but temperate grief of the woman who bends above her; while the lovely countenances of the attendant angels convey another shade of tender participation."

dence the "refined and careful modelling, reticence of emotion, and that 'gift of tears' which is the last attribute one would seek in the resonant but superficial art of the seventeenth century." Three groups—*Christ before Pilate, The Ascension,* and *La Maddalena ai Piedi* (The Magdalen Bathing the Feet of Christ)—she feels must have been executed by the same artist. In addition, "the careful modelling of the hands, the quiet grouping . . . the simple draperies, the devotional expression of the faces" all establish the figures as belonging to the fifteenth century. These stylistic similarities, reinforced by her recollection of a Presepio in the Bargello in Florence, led Wharton to associate the figures with the Della Robbias.

She went back to Florence to see the Presepio, which showed greater delicacy of treatment. The details of hair and drapery and the types of faces were, however, identical. It had come from San Vivaldo and was attributed to Giovanni della Robbia or his school. Professor Enrico Ridolfi (the director of the royal museums at Florence, who had told her there was every reason to accept the attribution to Giovanni Gonnelli) agreed that they were the work of an artist living at the close of the fifteenth or beginning of the sixteenth century, an artist of the school of the Della Robbias.

Wharton was pleased to experience "the rare sensation of an artistic discovery . . . in the heart of the most carefully explored artistic hunting ground in Europe," when she had been expecting an inferior imitation of the seventeenth-century groups at the more famous Sacro Monte at Varallo, which she had previously inspected. How could work of such artistic merit have gone unrecognized and be so long unknown? She attributed it to the seclusion of the monastery and that "the perception of differences in style is a recently developed faculty."

The aspiring art critic Bernard Berenson (whom Wharton had not yet met) did not agree with Wharton's assessment, however. After reading the

The Berensons' Villa I Tatti, in Settignano, c. 1908

travel piece in *Scribner's,* he and his companion Mary Costelloe had gone out to see the figures and returned home "scoffing at Mrs. Wharton's preposterous suggestion that any of them could have been by one of the Della Robbias." Mary Costelloe gleefully reported their conclusions to Isabella Gardner: "But, of course, the terra cottas have no more to do with any of the Della Robbias than they have to do with St. Gaudens." Wharton had the last laugh, however, and her opinion has been confirmed by modern scholars.

With the help of Mary Costelloe, Bernard Berenson would become the best known connoisseur, scholar, and authenticator of art of his era. (The first of his studies of Italian art, *Venetian Painters of the Renaissance,* was published in 1894, and it was in the same year he encouraged Isabella Stewart Gardner to buy Botticelli's *Tragedy of Lucretia,* initiating their long and fruitful collaboration.) At the time, however, he was still working to establish his own reputation.

Bernard Berenson in Venice, 1897

Wharton and Berenson (BB) eventually discovered many common interests (for example, BB and Mary, like Wharton, were enthusiasts of the works of Walter Pater and followed in his footsteps throughout Italy). They remained friends for almost thirty years, and perhaps no one came to know her better than he did, yet their first encounter was a disaster; years later they would laugh together when BB reminded her about it. As Mary Berenson noted in her diary for March 19, 1903: "Logan and I drove to La Doccia to meet the great Edith Wharton. We found BB there already, it was clear loathing her. We also disliked her intensely." (Logan was Mary's brother, Logan Pearsall Smith, who also would become Wharton's good friend.)

It was not until 1909 that Berenson and Wharton met again, by chance, at the writer Henry Adams's apartment in Paris—Berenson didn't recognize her. A week later, Adams gave a small dinner party at a restaurant, where Berenson and Wharton were among the guests. This time they charmed each other: she was "affable to the last degree," was BB's report to Mary, and he called on Wharton the next day. She confided somewhat boastfully to Sally Norton: "I saw a great deal of Berenson when he was in Paris a week or two ago, and we talked about you. I had never met him before, beyond an introduction once in Florence, years ago." By the next spring, she wrote him, "Why are the few, the very few nice people in the world always at the antipodes—each, that is, at a different one?" They would correspond continually until Wharton died.

During the 1890s, BB and Mary were in the process of moving to Florence; eventually they settled at the Villa I Tatti. They regularly saw other Anglo-Americans, such as Leo and Gertrude Stein, who spent time in that picturesque spot. Only a short walk away, at Settignano, was the Villa Palmerino, home of Vernon Lee (the pen name of Violet Paget). From an aristocratic English family, Lee was tall and masculine, a tremendous talker, outspoken and

Bernard Berenson around 1910, when he and Edith Wharton first became friends

Vernon Lee by John Singer Sargent. Lee wrote her "genius loci" sketches while visiting villas and Italian towns, carrying a notebook and recording her impressions; in the 1890s Wharton began to follow her example.

witty. She was a lesbian, and her constant companion at this time was Clementina "Kit" Anstruther-Thomson.

Berenson and Lee had a falling out when Berenson accused the two women of stealing his ideas on Florentine painting. Lee had already offended Henry James by dedicating her first novel, *Miss Brown,* a satirical portrait of society, to him. (She had intended to flatter him, but he found the novel offensive, though he never said anything directly to her about it.)

When Wharton first met Lee through Paul Bourget, she had already read and admired Lee's *Studies of the Eighteenth Century in Italy*, as well as *Belcaro* and *Euphorion*. "Vernon Lee," Wharton wrote later, "was the first highly cultivated and brilliant woman I had ever known." Lee had lived all over Europe—in England, France, Germany, and Italy—while she was growing up, like Edith Jones but more so.

When she was in Florence in 1894, Wharton visited Lee at Il Palmerino, where she also met Lee's half-brother, Eugene Lee-Hamilton. Formerly a secretary in the British Embassy in Paris during the Franco-Prussian War, he had suffered a nervous collapse and lay in a paralyzed state. He spent his days laid out on a stretcher in a dark room, but he wanted to meet the American writer, because he had read a sonnet of hers in *Scribner's Magazine*. Edith admired his poetry and later praised it in an article. After being paralyzed for years, Lee-Hamilton miraculously recovered and later visited the Whartons at Land's End, "rejoicing in his restored vigour, and keeping us and our guests in shouts of laughter by his high spirits and inimitable stories."

John Singer Sargent and Ralph Curtis were also old expatriate friends of Vernon Lee's who became friends of Edith Wharton's. Sargent and Lee had made friends as children while their families spent the winter of 1868–69 in Rome. Sargent and Curtis had been art students together in Paris. Curtis had been friendly with the Jack Gardners since he had shown them the sights of Venice when they visited in 1884; they often rented his parents' Venetian home, the magnificent Palazzo Barbaro, for a month or more at a time. It was Ralph

Vernon Lee by John Singer Sargent

Curtis and her old friend Henry James who led Isabella Gardner to Sargent, and they in turn became friends for life.

Curtis had aspired to be a painter, but after he married he became less a painter and more a bon vivant, an observer of the social scene, and a witty and regular correspondent with, among others, Bernard Berenson, for whom he created Hiram Slocum, an imaginary Bostonian and Harvard classmate who embodied all the characteristics of that "proper" milieu, which Curtis and Berenson enjoyed making fun of.

The Curtises eventually settled in France at the Villa Sylvia at Cap Ferrat, there to welcome many friends as houseguests. Ralph's wife was rich, which helped them maintain their life-style. Wharton's short story "The Verdict" (1908) concerned an artist whose talent was dissipated through a similar

Eugene Lee-Hamilton on his stretcher

marriage. Lise Curtis and others were indignant, but not Ralph. He wrote
Berenson that the story was banal and Edith could not have had them in mind.

Although Florence was not Wharton's favorite Italian town, in the 1890s
and the early years of the new century, she often visited her new friends there.
She also began what would be a lifelong practice—at Salsomaggiore, a health
spa in a nondescript town—of taking "the cure": inhalations for chronic nose
and throat problems.

In addition, she traveled through northern Italian towns, carefully studying their palaces. She loved Baroque art with its flamboyant movement, its
energy and wonderful details. She was also having fun buying Italian furniture
for Land's End, and she reported her successes and her impressions of Italy to
Ogden Codman. She wrote in 1896: "We left Paris about eight days ago, and
came to Italy by way of Milan—From there we went to Parma, Modena, then
to Bologna and Ferrara and yesterday we came here—tomorrow we are going
on to Rimini, Urbino, Ancona and Loreto, and by the end of the month we
expect to be in Venice." In June 1896, she wrote that they had just come from
Turin, where they had gone out to see the hunting lodge at Stupinigi built by
Juvara, "during every moment of which I simply *groaned* for you." She then
rapturously described the hunting lodge, dwelling happily on every dazzling
detail:

You can picture nothing more gay, pimpant & charming than the
whole suite of rooms—Versailles, though of course much grander
does not compare with it, to my mind, in charm & suggestiveness—

There is one very curious thing about the palace—no "stucchi" are used anywhere. The ceilings are all painted, & the walls either frescoed or hung with silk. There are no tapestries, either, & no boiseries, & even the doors and shutters are almost without mouldings, & depend entirely for their effect on the exquisitely varied paintings which adorn them.

We found it rather hot in Italy, & like an idiot I persuaded Teddy to come here [Aix les Bains], & we arrived yesterday. I had always heard it was a most beautiful place, & fancied it was like Baden or Hamburg, but it is the most ghastly hole I ever got into, & I think we shall soon decamp. I don't know where to. The fact is that Italy spoils me for everything else. I only wish it wasn't quite so hot there. It is really awfully poky in Europe in summer, for the nice, interesting places are all hot and fetid, & the cool places too dull for words—& one does get so weary of living objectlessly in hotels, for more than three months!

The malaise Wharton described became the starting point for one of her best tales, "Soul's Belated," which she finished in the early summer of 1898. The story opens with an American couple, who are not married, traveling together on an Italian train headed north from Bologna. They are trying to avoid discussing a disagreeable subject—a "thing" that arrived in the mail that morning—the notice of Lydia's divorce from her husband, Tillotson. Her life with her husband had been disappointing—"a series of purely automatic acts in the commodious Tillotson mansion on Fifth Avenue." Although unhappy, she had not considered leaving her husband until she met her present traveling companion, Gannett. "It was her love for Gannett that had made life with Tillotson so poor and incomplete a business." She and Gannett had gone off together

Beginning in the 1890s, Edith went regularly to the Salsomaggiore Terme near Parma to "take the cure" for her asthma and throat problems. Teddy and friends would often accompany her. Teddy's role during the Whartons' trips was to be the good-natured diplomat who smoothed ruffled feathers and took care of practical matters. Sybil Cutting—a younger British friend who had married a favorite friend of Wharton's, Bayard Cutting, and who would eventually marry two more of Wharton's friends, Geoffrey Scott and Percy Lubbock—recalled an evening together at Salsomaggiore. In the dining room, after Edith had sent many dishes back to the kitchen, "her husband would pass a hand rather wearily through his hair as he leant back after the conflict." He also had to apologize when she snubbed two middle-aged American ladies in the hall after dinner. "Oh, Pussy, don't you see the duchess?" he cried. Edith gave a stiff bow in the direction of the group, and then led her foursome straight to the lift. Sybil remembered: "Mr. Wharton was all confused apology—that was easily seen. 'While she is taking the cure my wife,' he said, 'has to rest a great deal—she feels cold too.' 'Yes,' said the duchess serenely, 'I noticed the chill in the air.'"

Cutting also described a shopping trip in Florence in 1903. Edith brightly examined the wares, "chests of drawers, writing-tables, cabinets filled with china and glass, walls covered with every variety of mirror," and then "pounced" on an attractive object and began to bargain. Once the bargaining was over, "Mr. Wharton took in hand the rest of the business."

and had traveled "like the flight of outlaws" through Italy, Dalmatia, and Transylvania, "persisting in the tacit avoidance of their kind."

They had enjoyed being alone, but now that Lydia learns that she is officially divorced, she feels worse; she finds herself in the position of not being free, as if Gannett "owed her something." Everyone would now think he must marry her to "'stand the damage.' . . . She knew not whether she most shrank from his insisting too much or too little . . . whichever way she turned, an ironical implication confonted her: she had the exasperated sense of having walked into the trap of some stupid practical joke."

Seeking a respite in their wanderings—"we can't travel forever can we?" asks Gannett—they end up at a fashionable Anglo-American hotel on one of the Italian lakes and lose themselves in the crowd. Gannett, a writer, remarks, "Queer little microcosms, these hotels! Most of these people live here all summer and then migrate to Italy or the Riviera. The English are the only people who can lead that kind of life with dignity—those soft-voiced old ladies in Shetland shawls somehow carry the British Empire under their caps. *Civis Romanus Sum*. It's a curious study—there might be some good things to work up here."

It turns out that this hoped-for refuge has a social hierarchy that is hauntingly familiar. The hotel is given its "certain tone" by the annual visit of Lady Susan Conduit (an earl's daughter), who, with the help of Miss Pinsett, rates everyone's social acceptability. Lydia soon realizes the importance of the respectability she thought she didn't care about. The story is one of the first of many Wharton would write on the conflicts produced by characters seeking freedom but ultimately unable to break free from social constraints, and it reflects obvious aspects of Wharton's life at the time. It is one of her many stories about divorce.

In 1899 and 1900 the Whartons again traveled in northern Italy—this time with the Bourgets—where they sought out more religious shrines of the kind she had discovered at San Vivaldo. The group would approach the shrines through the Italian landscape, and Wharton would assemble her impressions in a series of pictures: peasants working the fields, villages "where every window displays its pot of lavender or carnations." After arriving at the shrines, Wharton watched the Italian peasants being moved by religious art and came away with "a renewed sense of the way in which, in Italy, nature, art and religion combine to enrich the humblest lives." She too was moved by the tableaux within the curious chapels and was able to lose herself in another world, "somewhere between art and life."

In making these trips Wharton felt she was seeing the real Italy—the Italy of the people—not what other tourists saw. She relished all the elements that combined to produce the magical effects of a church service: the music, the murmurs of the prayers, the incense, the votive offerings on the walls, the hushed darkness, the flickering candles. She witnessed how the religious pilgrimage was central to the Italians' daily lives. In the evenings, back at the inn, she and her friends would talk over the days' adventures: "After a joyous day of healthy fatigue, what did we talk about, settled in front of spaghetti and chianti? About everything, it seemed to me, the spirit of Bourget was intensely open, his culture vast, his memory completely filled with recollections of his literary and social beginnings."

Her essays about the trips to the shrines were original and fresh because of the unusual nature of these trips, and because of her insights and enthusiasm. Similarly, in her pieces on Parma and Milan, she caught her reader's attention by hyping the ordinary and avoiding the celebrated tourist attractions, such as the cathedral and Leonardo's *Last Supper*, which she leaves out entirely. In "Sub Umbra Lilliorum" and "Picturesque Milan," she praises instead the Italian creative spirit as in flower boxes in windows of old palaces, carved wooden doors, churches built over the ages and—one of her favorite places—the gracefully arcaded Ospedale Maggiore.

Wharton's Milanese highlights are dark arches brightened by fruit stalls, churches festooned with garlands and nosegays. She finds the city streets "full of charming detail—*quattro cento* marble portals set with medallions of bushy-headed Sforzas in round caps and plaited tunics; windows framed in terracotta wreaths of fruit and flowers; iron balconies etching their elaborate arabesques against the stucco house fronts; mighty doorways flanked by Atlantides, like that of Pompeo Leoni's house . . . and of the Jesuit seminary; or yellow-brown rococo churches with pyramids, broken pediments, flying angels, and vases filled with wrought-iron palm-branches"; in short, the way the Italians exuberantly expressed their creativity and genius everywhere.

During these trips to Italy, Wharton began to envision a novel set in the past. This novel, to be called *The Valley of Decision,* would take place in the eighteenth century and include the impressions of her travels, her fascination with palaces and churches, and the history they suggested, in short, all the culture of this period. She felt that the eighteenth century in Italy had been upstaged in everyone's minds by the Renaissance, and she wanted to bring it to life in a novel. After all, George Eliot had written a novel about Italy, *Romola,* set in Florence during the Renaissance. Why couldn't she? And besides, Wharton felt she had the "visualizing gift" and George Eliot did not.

She had read reports of eighteenth-century writers about what it was like there just before the French Revolution: in Venice, a wild hedonistic life, all-girl orchestras, trysts in convents, masked Venetians able to lead double lives, the impromptu Italian theater, the commedia dell'arte, the new performances of opera, the strange custom of *cicisbeism,* whereby an Italian husband permit-

*Sacri monti* shrines crown many mountaintops in northern Italy. Although they were listed in Baedeker's guidebook, they were too inaccessible for the typical grand tour of the nineteenth-century tourist; rather, they served as summer refuges for Italian farm families, who might walk thirty or forty miles to reach the holy place. The *cappelle,* or chapels, are small buildings spaced throughout the pine woods around the main church so that families can stroll from one to another in the pleasant shade. The finest groups of figures are in the chapels at Varallo (seen here in the distance), where Wharton went with the Bourgets in the spring of 1900. Each contained a tableau of life-size terra-cotta figures brightly painted and posed dramatically before a frescoed background, creating a diorama illustrating the major events of Christ's life. These scenes were central to the religious education of peasants who could not read. At the center of the constellation of small chapels was a massive rococo church.

ted his wife to be escorted by another man, the mad gaiety at Carnival time; visitors described the new excavations at Pompeii and Herculaneum. And, as Wharton wrote her publisher, William Brownell, "As far as I know no novel has ever dealt with this particular period of Italian life." If Wharton worked with the primary sources, she would have all this fresh material to fashion in her own way.

The period appealed to her because it was a time of conflict, when the small principalities were breaking up, and yet, "All the old forms and traditions of court life were still preserved, but the immense intellectual and moral movement of the new regime was at work beneath the surface of things." She tried "to reflect the traditional influences and customs of the day, together with the new ideas, in the mind of a cadet of one of the reigning houses, who is suddenly called to succeed to the dukedom of Pianura, and tries to apply the ideas of the French encyclopedists to his small principality. Incidently, I have given sketches of Venetian life, and glimpses of Sir William Hamilton's circle at Naples, and of the clerical milieu at Rome. . . . The close of the story pictures the falling to pieces of the whole business at the approach of Napoleon." She had chosen an enormous subject—a panorama of Italy in the past and a plot in which young people try to right all the wrongs of an ancient society.

Her central character was a nobleman, Odo Valsecca, a distant cousin of the Duke of Pianura, her fictional duchy modeled on Parma and Mantua. A serious intellectual who also had a gift for living life, he embodied a dualism that was at this point fascinating and even troubling Wharton: he was a sociable being and also an intellectual. He had read the French *philosophes*, frequented the underground meetings of unbelievers in Turin, and yet he loved to enjoy himself, too.

His mistress, Fulvia, is also an intellectual, one of the few bluestocking heroines in Wharton's fiction. An idealist, she revises Pianura's constitution. The people hate her, however, for being too liberal, for demanding too many reforms too quickly, and for her influence over Odo; ultimately, she is assassinated. Odo, too, falls prey to political intrigue and ends in exile and disillusionment. The dreams of these two idealistic young people are extinguished by complicated realities they come to understand too late.

By contrast, Odo's wife, whom he married for political reasons, is a rather shallow and conventional woman. She and Fulvia together become one of the first of many double heroines in Wharton's fiction. Here, Maria Clementina represents the social side of her creator, Fulvia, the intellectual and idealistic.

Writing *The Valley* gave Wharton a chance to use all her impressions of Italy. The architecture she had recently seen becomes the background for the rituals of the public life, the rooms of the palaces the settings for the private lives of these troubled characters. The scenes she creates resemble the many paint-

Gaudenzio Ferrari's *Crucifixion* at Varallo "is fitly the culminating point of the series."

At Oropa, over the mountain pass from Varallo, is the Sanctuary of the Black Virgin. Coming upon it after a three-hour carriage ride six miles up into the mountains above the town of Biella gratifies any traveler's demand for the "momentary escapes from the expected," one of Wharton's travel requirements. As the winding road rises higher through woods and along ridges, the settled area is left behind. Although an occasional shrine marks the route, nothing prepares one for the last turn when the huge Baroque buildings suddenly loom through the mist.

ings of pageants and crowds assembled in the great squares, such as those by Gentile Bellini and Vittore Carpaccio, which she had seen many times. She also used descriptions and episodes from the books of eighteenth-century travelers—particularly Goethe, whose descriptions of journeys on the Brenta and the goings-on at Sir William Hamilton's villa in Naples went right into her book. She reproduced every detail of the time—the clothes, the perfumes, the masks, the games, the appearance of the life of all classes.

This was the first time Wharton had used architecture symbolically to give authenticity to her scenes. When Odo makes his triumphal entry into Pianura on the day of his coronation, he observes all the symbols of the city's power and past: "The crenellations of Bracciaforte's keep, and just beyond, the ornate cupola of the royal chapel, symboliz[e] in their proximity the successive ambitions of the ducal race; while the round-arched campanile of the Cathedral and the square tower of the medieval town-hall sprang up side by side, marking the center of the free city which the Valseccas had subjugated." As the people pour forth to shout their welcome, the noise of cannon, bells, and voices are merged. Odo passes the houses of the important persons of Pianura, who will play a part in his downfall. Later, Odo and his courtiers enter the cathedral; the great doors shut behind him, separating him from his subjects.

In her later novels, Wharton created similar scenes in which an important character is the center of attention, often partaking in a ritual, while surrounded by others and placed in front of an architectural background. These scenes, rich in details that the reader can interpret symbolically, show her protagonists in relation to their world. In her fiction about New York society, Grace Church, Fifth Avenue, Grand Central Station, and the old Academy of Music will have their own meanings.

*The Valley of Decision* is Wharton's *Bildungsroman,* the first of many of her

"The Farnese theatre [in Parma] is one of those brilliant improvisations in wood and plaster to which Italian artists were trained by centuries of hurriedly-organized *trionfi*, state processions, religious festivals, returns from war, all demanding the collaboration of sculptor, architect and painter in the rapid creation of triumphal arches, architectural perspectives, statuary, chariots, flights of angels, and galleons tossing on simulated seas: evanescent visions of some *pays bleu* of Boiardo or Ariosto, destined to crumble the next day like the palace of an evil enchanter."

novels about the struggle of young people to grow up. Although it takes place in Italy, it incorporates subjects she personally was concerned with at the time—a trivial, hedonistic society that left little room for the gifted idealist, corrupt, inefficient authoritarian institutions like the government and the church, and censorship of intellectual exploration. Perhaps she set her first effort at long fiction in the Italian past because many of its subjects were too close to the bone to treat in a New York setting just yet.

Wharton sent regular installments of *The Valley* to Walter Berry. In October 1899 he wrote to her, "The Valley is altogether delightful, and I don't wonder at the fun you get out of it. . . . If *moeurs* à la Casanova are to be introduced your fortune is ready made." He advised her on episodes, figures of speech, and style. During the three years she worked on the novel, he encouraged her when she was depressed and sympathized when she was sick. He applauded her going to Europe, "because doing what one wants is the best medicine," and "being bored is a great part of your obscure and interesting case."

In the end, reviewers of *The Valley of Decision* felt Wharton was more successful creating the background—the social panorama of Italian life—than creating lively characters. She explained that her characters were "just little bits of broken glass," designed to reflect "fragments of the great panorama," and that "Italy is my hero . . . or heroine, if you prefer."

This illustration for *The Valley of Decision* (not used) provides details about eighteenth-century Venetian dress, architecture, and pastimes.

Wharton did extensive research for her novel and read many travel accounts of eighteenth-century visitors to Italy, including the *Italian Journey* of Goethe, whose description of a voyage on the Brenta on a *burchiello* (in September 1876) was embellished for Odo's trip (pictured here) in the novel.

In *The Valley of Decision*, Wharton got the chance to work out what she believed about religion, politics, and philosophy, and, within the world of eighteenth-century Italy, dealt with conflicts that fascinated her. She played with the question of reform in a society that for years had been corrupt and decadent, and she emerged with a realistic answer. People must compromise and live within the world as it is. Although they talk a great deal about freedom, her characters only experience it figuratively through the release of travel.

After she finished *The Valley*, Wharton considered a sequel. Richard Watson Gilder, editor of *Century Magazine* and a friend in Lenox, said he would welcome one. She even began one, entitled *The New Day*, set in Italy in the 1830s. Book 1 was to be "The Land of the Dead," Book 2 "The Eleventh Hour," with a Book 3 not yet named. Ten characters are listed, along with the dates of Odo's death and the births and deaths of the other characters.

Her notes suggest *The New Day* was to be another panorama of a period of Italian history, the Risorgimento, contrasting liberal and conservative forces. The pivotal point was most likely to be a choice the hero must make between the security offered by expedient loyalty to the Austrian rulers of Pianura and the danger inherent in supporting Italian unification and rebellion against foreign occupation. The novel would again render settings, customs, dress, and philosophical and political issues in impeccable detail.

Wharton was still considering this sequel during the spring of 1902 but Berry discouraged her. He said that he hated "'continuations,' fundamentally. I never wanted to know what the son of Marius would have done. If you want to play with a Risorgimento (some day) start it fresh. Of course a bastard always has a peculiar charm, especially to religious people (Quere: Is it because J.C. was a bastard?),—a fact which might benefit the sale of the 'sequel,'—but please *don't*. That N.Y. novel ought to come next anyhow. Do that off the reel, and then you can think of a brand new hero afterwards. That's my advice!" Apparently, she took it, because, after one version of the opening scene and several fragmentary versions of the next two scenes, the narrative breaks off.

In 1903 she urged Edward Burlingame at Scribner's to take the six travel essays she had written since 1894 and put them together into a book. She added several others, including one called "Italian Backgrounds," to unify the volume: "This essay will be the longest in the volume, and its thesis fits the whole book: namely that the most interesting Italy is the one in the background behind the official guide-book to Italy." On September 4 she wrote, "Italian Backgrounds is making a jolly essay—it is a subject I have long had in mind, and it is such fun to do it."

In Rome in February, she wrote to William Brownell: "I see lots to say about the Rome that no one cares to write about—seventeenth-century Rome. Twentieth-century Rome is very pleasant, by the way, though they have pulled down lots of nice things and built up lots of horrors since I was here nearly eight years ago. The new quarters are encroaching daily, and are as ugly as anything in New York—but oh, such sunshine, such heavenly air, such violets in the grass of the Villa Borghese, while you poor things are probably being whirled off your feet by a blizzard at the Flat Iron corner."

*Italian Backgrounds,* published in 1905, sums up what Italy meant to Wharton. Her concept of traveling becomes an art form, one that forces the voyager to comprehend and respond to this evocative country. In a 1909 review of the book *Italian Cities* by Evangeline and Edwin Blashfield, she expressed this idea: "The only possible plea on which the average writer can speak of Italy is that of having lit on some unnoticed place, some unrecorded phase of art, some detail insignificant enough to have dropped out of the ever-growing catalogue of her treasures." If he treats "the great landmarks" and boldly heads his chapters with immortal names—[he] must expect to be measured by another standard. He who has anything to say about Rome, Florence or Siena must justify himself by saying it extraordinarily well."

This is just what Wharton did. In the essay "Italian Backgrounds," she chose the devotional pictures of the early Renaissance, with their conventional foregrounds showing the holy family in predicitable dress, and their revealing backgrounds—showing the landscape of the painter's home region, the mountains and plains he knew so well—as the metaphor for her understanding of Italy. Most travelers see only Italy's foreground—the famous monuments, paintings, and sculptures. Only a few explore the background—the region claimed by the true lover whose intimacy with Italy has been earned through study and devotion. As critics have pointed out, however, Wharton knew the foreground thoroughly before she approached the background.

When discussing Rome, therefore, Wharton challenged the nineteenth-century attitude toward the Baroque, which was "acknowledged only in passing by art historians and travellers as a decadent, far too prolonged and regrettable phase of the late Renaissance." Wharton admired Rome as "the most undisturbed Baroque city of Italy" and presents the wonderful Baroque monuments as hidden treasures to be discovered.

For Wharton, the "exuberances of the seventeenth century," with its great number of successful Baroque buildings, "the grandeur of their scale, and the happy incidents of their grouping," illustrated better than in any other place "the collective efforts of which the style is capable." She praised the architect and sculptor Giovanni Lorenzo Bernini for giving expression to artistic forms required by the new tempo of life. Bernini's remodeling of Rome appealed to Wharton, for she had always advocated the well-planned city, the sculpturing of space. She argued not just for the well-designed building but for a well-designed group of buildings creating a pleasing complex.

Fascinated since childhood by spectacles, processions, and the public life of the aristocracy, she saw these Baroque buildings as representing "essentially a style *de parade*, the setting of the spectacular and external life," in contrast to the "more secluded civilization of the Renaissance." It was "the pomp of a revived ecclesiasticism" that blended with the elaborate etiquette of Spain and growing taste for country life to create this "sumptuous *bravura* period" of Baroque art.

Wharton's travels in Italy and her love of the country inspired her and allowed her to disagree with Ruskin and Goethe, those Italophiles she had loved in her youth. Writing the essays enabled her to renew her childhood passion for this country whose history and ideas were written in its architecture and evocative places. She articulated all the dimensions of her response to travel—her reactions to "that sophisticated landscape where the face of nature seems moulded by the passions and imaginings of man."

# LENOX: HOUSES AND GARDENS

By the turn of the century, Wharton divided her time between Europe and Lenox. She wrote Sally Norton from Lenox on May 10, 1901, "The country is beautiful and the apple blossoms are just showing themselves"; and in June 1902: "Lenox has had its usual tonic effect on me, and I feel like a new edition, revised and corrected, in Berkeley's best type. It is great fun at our place now too—everything is pushing up shoots—not only cabbages and strawberries, but electric lights and plumbing."

Although Lenox was now a resort like Newport—a watering place for the rich—it had a different history and a different landscape. Originally the home of Mohican Indians, Lenox and nearby Stockbridge were settled by whites in the middle of the eighteenth century. The town of Lenox, named for Charles Lenox, Duke of Richmond, flourished—it had an iron foundry, marble quarry, hearthstone mill, and glass factory. In 1782 its citizens petitioned to have Lenox declared the shiretown, and by 1816 the County Courthouse was completed. Until 1868, the courthouse was the center of Berkshire life, drawing lawyers, judges, litigants, and spectators as new businesses cropped up.

The area became the home of the intelligent and cultivated, like the Sedgwick family, who moved to Stockbridge in 1821. Catherine Sedgwick was a successful author of fiction, and her home was a gathering place for the literati of the day. English author Anna Jameson, Charles Sumner, and Harriet Beecher Stowe, among others, visited Sedgwick and fell in love with the scenic country of mountains and lakes. Oliver Wendell Holmes made his summer home in Pittsfield and wrote about a friend's house in Lenox as "one of the most beautiful spots I ever saw anywhere; perfect almost to a miracle." Lenox developed

Main Street, Lenox, before 1909

By July 1902, Wharton was enjoying her new territory near Lenox: "The rides are beautiful . . . and the trees and meadows look really English in their luxuriance," she told Sally Norton. "I haven't done any reading either. I usually spend my mornings at the place, working over the house and garden, and my afternoons in long rides from which I come home stupid with fresh air."

a reputation as a refuge for the intelligentsia: Nathaniel Hawthorne, Herman Melville, actress Fanny Kemble, Longfellow, and other artists and writers came to be associated with it. As early as 1846 the town had begun to change into a resort where the world of fashion spent summers and autumns while waiting for the opening of the winter season back in the cities.

Newcomers bought up the land that had been previously farmed and on their new acres built magnificent estates—neighbors competed to own the more beautiful dwelling and the best views. As one writer described it at the turn of the century: "The town was . . . an inland Newport where blue mountains were the equivalent of sand and rolling surf. . . . Topographically Lenox is a sort of 'saddleback,' with the villa of Charles E. Lanier, Esq., 'Allen Winden,' high in the pommel and her Congregational church at the other end high in the rear, or *vice versa,* whichever you chose to call it, the land sloping off to the east and west from these eminences. From either side of 'Allen Winden,' whose name suggests its elevation, the land descends, to the west to two little lakes": the Stockbridge Bowl and Laurel Lake.

By the turn of the century, some seventy-five enormous estates—owned by rich New Yorkers like the William Sloanes, the Anson Phelps Stokes, and the Giraud Fosters—surrounded by extensive, parklike grounds, overlooked the landscapes at different angles of vision. All varieties of architecture were

The Curtis Hotel in Lenox

Giraud Foster, Edith Wharton's Lenox
neighbor, at his house, Bellefontaine

represented: the Swiss chalet, the Tudor castle, the colonial mansion, the
French château, and the Italian villa.

On June 29, 1901, the Whartons bought 113 acres of land for their new
home from the Sargent family. Originally called Laurel Lake Farm, it consisted of farmland, wetland, and forests containing red maple, black and white
birch, hickory, and oak trees. White pines were the most common evergreen.

Edith Wharton had kept a close watch on the building that had occupied
rich Americans in the 1880s and 1890s. Now it was her turn. With the profits
from the sale of Land's End, she set about to create a place that expressed her

Shadowbrook, the "cottage" of Anson
Phelps Stokes, which, before the com-
pletion of George Vanderbilt's Biltmore
in Asheville, North Carolina, was the
largest house in the country

ideas laid out in *The Decoration of Houses* and drew on her memories of European villas and palaces.

It was logical that she would use Ogden Codman for her architect. He could easily do the sort of house Wharton would like, and they could have fun working together. Soon after they began planning the house, however, trouble began. Codman and Teddy disagreed on Codman's new commission of 25 percent, and he refused to change his terms. Codman collected his grievances, which he reported to his mother. He hated the long trips to Lenox and answering to the Whartons' constant bossy demands, and he was longing for his first European vacation in five years.

By the early spring of 1901, he wrote to his mother that the tiff, which had become the concern of all their friends, was about over and "I think myself that Teddy was the whole trouble and not Pussy. Meantime [Francis L. V.] Hoppin is *doing the house* which lets me out of a very disagreeable business as Teddy and I would have come to blows over the bills." Still, Codman hoped to get out of the situation with his reputation intact: "If Hoppin is troublesome and unsatisfactory as he no doubt will be, the more she will be sorry she did not come to me."

Edith wrote to him on March 25, 1901, urging that they remain friends:

I was very glad to get your letter, for it is always a pleasure to know that a friendship on which one has set great store has been worth something to the other "contracting party." In fact, it is of much more importance to me that we should maintain our old relation as good friends than risk it by entering in the new and precarious one of architect and client. We are in such close sympathy in things architectural that it would have been a pleasure for me to work with you, but perhaps after all we know

Edith, Teddy, and dogs exploring their land at "the Mount when we first bought it" each other too well, & are disqualified by that very fact for professional collaboration. At any rate having avoided that peril, I feel that our escape ought to unite us more closely, and now that you need not be on your guard against me as a client, perhaps I shall be all the more useful as a friend. I shall certainly try to be, for it has always been a great interest to me to follow your work and try to make people understand what it represents; and I hope you will not be too busy to be interested in *my* undertaking, and to come and talk over our plans some day when you have the time to spare.

Although Codman wished to salvage his friendship with Edith, he would have liked her to have been as emotionally involved in their disagreements as he was: "Altho I did not want much to do the house I cannot help feeling that I would have been better pleased if they had been *more upset* about it. The fact is to our mutual surprise we seem perfectly able to get *on without* each other. I fancy it *jars* both—"

Codman learned through the grapevine that "[Hoppin] is having an awful time with the house, . . . She telegraphs for him every day or two and fusses terribly over every detail. He told me himself that he hated the journey to Lenox and the house is not started yet. He has been cut down in every way, the house is to be of wood stuccoed not brick, and he has had to make three sets of plans. It has not been begun yet!! I consider myself well out of it."

Despite the annoyances, however, his protestations suggest he felt real regret, as Pauline Metcalf points out, that he was not doing the house of such a unique client. To rationalize his decision, Codman continually compared the Whartons to other clients who had treated him better, and he reminded himself of Edith's idiosyncracies: "I always knew that she has always rather gone out of her way to be rude and people don't seem to be willing to put up with it. However I shall continue to stand up for her as she was kind and helpful to me long ago and as long as I am not working for her I have nothing against her. The more unreasonable she is with Hoppin and the more he complains of it the better will people understand why I did not want to build the house."

Although Hoppin remained the official architect and Edith Wharton was the prime mover for the project, Codman was rehired later to design some of the interiors. This episode caused yet another rupture in the fabric of their friendship and they fought again later about bills.

*Lenox Life* reported on Saturday, August 17, 1901, "The foundations for the new residence of Mr. and Mrs. Edward Wharton are being completed, and lumber and brick are arriving for the superstructure. Nelson Martin, of Lee, has the contract for 160,000 bricks for the house. Barnes & Jenks, of Pittsfield, have the grading contract." By the time the Whartons had moved into the

This photograph of the approach to the house was taken soon after it was finished. The service road branches off from the main drive; the island in between had recently been planted.

house a year later, they had also completed the kitchen garden, driveway, the three terraces down the hill, and a lime walk (a row of fragrant linden trees) laid out on the lowest terrace to connect two formal gardens.

During construction Edith Wharton was involved in every detail. She wrote to Codman in 1901 about the tapestries in the library:

> The change of tapestries you suggest would not do as the two tapestries of which you have sketches are alike in colouring and composition, whereas the one I intend to put in the library is absolutely different. I don't care to have the chimney in the drawing room moved, but surely, as the tapestries match so perfectly in the essentials—i.e. colour and composition—the fact that one is narrower than the other need not matter, since you can put an extra narrow parcel on each side of the smaller tapestry. I am dreadfully sorry that the bust can't be recessed over the drawing room chimney. Could it be done by making a small chimney-breast? Of course they did have them in Louis XIV houses—I hope you have sent Hoppin the gallery plan. Please do it today, if you haven't already, for I know that there will be pretexts for delay at that point if we don't give them the alternative promptly.

Teddy also got into the act. He wrote to Codman on May 11, 1902: "You are at times a demon and have lots of really bad qualities, but I forgave all your baseness of character when I saw the work (wood-work) in Puss's boudoir, which is more than half up. It is perfectly delightful to look at and does your taste credit."

The Mount was a step up from Land's End. Sited on a hill, the house gave off a feeling of power and authority, and the long drive (in this case through sugar maples) brought visitors past beautifully tended woods and fields, stables, and into the forecourt in front of the house. On the east was the terrace

The gallery at the Mount, which acted as a hall linking the principal rooms. "When the floor of the hall is of marble or mosaic,—as, if possible, it should be,—the design, like that of the walls should be clear and decided in outline," Wharton proclaimed in *The Decoration of Houses.*

These two views of the library at the
Mount illustrate the principle in *The
Decoration of Houses* that "the general
decoration of the library should be of
such character as to form a background
or setting to the books, rather than to
distract attention from them. . . .

"Nowhere is the modern litter of
knick-knacks and photographs more
inappropriate than in the library. The
tables should be large, substantial, and
clear of everything but lamps, books
and papers—one table at least being
given over to the filing of books and
newspapers. The library writing-table is
seldom large enough, or sufficiently free
from odds and ends in the shape of pho-
tograph-frames, silver boxes, and
flower-vases, to give free play to the
elbows."

In September 1904, *Berkshire Resort
Topics* reported approvingly: "Mrs.
Wharton's literary tastes naturally lead
to the conclusion that her library must
be one of the most interesting rooms in
the house. . . . The coved ceiling is
white, and the oak floor is covered with
rugs. Comfort seems to have been
sought in the furnishings; and tapestries, paintings and statuary relieve any
appearance of staidness which may be
intimated by the long rows of books."

surrounded by balustrades that overlooked the gardens. The Mount signaled
prestige yet enabled Wharton to enjoy an intimacy with the land.

Compared to the other Lenox cottages, the Mount was smaller and organized around certain principles that made it perfect for its owner. Its thirty-
five rooms were spacious and airy, of pleasing proportions, with subtle details,
and each had a definite purpose. Edith Wharton's bedroom was on the second
floor, next to a boudoir, bathroom, and a dressing room, which made a little
apartment that could be shut off from the rest of the house. In the mornings,
she could write there, looking out of the window at her garden on the north
side, where she had planted a profusion of flowers. Downstairs was the pan-

eled library for her many volumes, the drawing room, dining room, a den for Teddy, and a gallery on the west side. The house had eight servants' rooms on the top floor, three guest rooms on the bedroom floor, a bedroom and dressing room for Teddy, and Edith's suite. On the ground floor were dark winding halls and rooms of the servants' world—a kitchen, scullery, servants' dining room, and the laundry.

The house is a mixture of styles. As Richard Guy Wilson writes, "The completed house, gardens, and grounds show Edith's architectural enthusiasms and are a perfect example of the American Renaissance impulse."

While the exterior configuration was copied from a Colin Campbell plate of Belton House (which was then attributed to Christopher Wren), the interior, a typical Codman "H" layout, was not as grand as its English inspiration. The gardens also reflect different styles and might serve as a symbol of Wharton's divided cultural loyalties—her love of both the garden styles of Europe and the American countryside. The profusion of flowers in her flower gardens and the wild and woodland gardens can be called English, yet David Bennett notes that "parts of the American landscape are allowed to intervene between house and garden, enveloping, overshadowing, being preserved as reminders—native trees, especially elms were retained; rock outcrops were highlighted and exposed (especially the one on the front lawn); an extensive system of paths for walks and rides extended into the woodland, and linked the Mount's grounds to adjacent estates, too."

Edith Wharton's niece Beatrix Jones (later Beatrix Farrand) was involved from the beginning in the layout of the grounds. She had studied horticulture with Charles Sprague Sargent, the first director of the Arnold Arboretum near Boston, then being created by Frederick Law Olmsted and Sargent, who became her mentor. Soon after 1895 she had begun to practice what she called "landscape gardening," receiving commissions from well-to-do patrons in Tuxedo, New York, and Newport. In 1899 she became one of the founders of the American Society of Landscape Architects, along with Samuel Parsons, John C. Olmsted, and others.

In the first decade of the new century, Edith Wharton and Beatrix Jones were coming of age professionally at the same time. Edith helped Beatrix get commissions in Lenox and Newport. In Lenox, in addition to helping the Whartons, Jones drew plans for gardens for Giraud Foster at Bellefontaine, William Douglas Sloane at Elm Court, and Harris Fahnestock at Eastover. Jones's style in garden design combined a wonderful sense of the French and Italian classical layouts with a profusion of planting, using her superb knowledge of flowers and shrubs. She had an excellent eye and an instinctive sense of how to work a garden into the landscape, which worked well with her aunt's own grasp of spatial relations.

The bill for the panels like the one above the fireplace in what Wharton called "my sitting room" set off the twenty-year war between Wharton and Codman. Walter Berry's photograph is on the mantel at left.

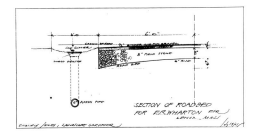

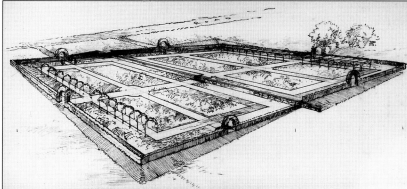

*Above left:* Drawing by Beatrix Farrand of the drainage system for the driveway at the Mount, 1901

*Above right:* Drawing by Beatrix Farrand for the large kitchen garden, which was next to the driveway before one reached the stables

The stables and driveway in the snow. The driveway was designed to bring the visitor in through the trees to the house, sited on a hill looking southeast out over lawns and terraces and fields to Laurel Lake and the Berkshire hills beyond.

Jones oversaw the two-thousand-foot driveway, which traversed a graceful right angle from Cross Road (now Plunkett Street) to the entrance of the house. It was made up of three parts—the eight-hundred-foot straight section of sugar maple allée, which ran from the road past the stable, then a curving section that turned downhill to the right into the woods, and another curve to the left into the forecourt in front of the house. On the right were the woods, on the left the gatehouse, greenhouse, and stables. A stream crossed the driveway, ran under the formal garden, and then reappeared in the meadow.

When Wharton and Codman first envisioned the house, they had thought the ground floor would extend from the forecourt side on the west all the way through to the terrace side on the east, creating a kind of grotto effect as at the Villa Cetinale near Siena. Blasting through the rock, however, turned out to be too expensive. The ground floor thus consisted of a gallery or hall—behind that was a service area with a furnace room—from which one mounted stairs to the right and onto the piano nobile, where the drawing room, dining room, and library were lined up enfilade in the French fashion on the terrace side of the house. Moving from the forecourt, through the entryway, then up the stairs and out onto the terrace, the visitor experienced a powerful progression of spaces, culminating in a dramatic view out over the countryside.

In designing her house Wharton had wedded herself to the land and could be clearly aware of the landscape and the weather. She wrote to Sally Norton in April 14, 1902: "The country wore its grimmest New England look. Yesterday it snowed, hailed & rained in pleasing alternation—today it blew an icy gale, that seemed to tell the green buds they needn't think of showing themselves for weeks. Quel pays!" Several years later, she returned to the Mount from Paris to find "winter weather. . . . Here we have the furnace lit and fires burning, and an autumnal wind howls in the chimneys. But the much needed rain has come, and when the weather changes the country will be radiant." The countryside became a friend who was alternately forbidding and threatening in bad weather and nourishing and loving in good. Wharton's way of strengthening her tie to the land was to garden, to tame the wilderness by sculpting the land and growing flowers and vegetables.

Wharton wrote to Sally Norton on September 30, 1902: "We have been in the new house ten days and enjoyed every minute of it. The views are exquisite and it is all so still and sylvan—I have never seen the Michaelmas daisies as beautiful as this year—the lanes are purple."

From the start the Mount was a great success. At Lenox she could partake in both her social and creative worlds without constant conflicts. She frequented some of the parties of other cottagers and she also knew hard-working creative people like the sculptor Daniel Chester French and his wife, Mary, who liked to write; Joseph Choate, the well-known lawyer; and the editors of *Century Magazine,* Richard Watson Gilder and Robert Underwood Johnson.

Teddy and Edith took part in many of the local goings-on. Teddy's sister Nannie Wharton was on the town planning board. Edith Wharton brought flowers to the flower show and acted as a judge. They belonged to the Lenox Club, went to meetings of the Village Improvement Society, and supported the library. Teddy played golf and they both rode horses. They were part of the cottagers' world but could resist being swamped by social obligations. They also imported their own friends for frequent house parties.

Edith's sister-in-law Minnie Jones and her niece Beatrix Jones came often, as did old friends from Newport like Daniel Berkeley Updike, Ogden Codman, Wintie and Daisy Chanler, James Van Alen, Eliot Gregory, Minnie and Paul Bourget, and Egerton Winthrop. Friends from New York included the Walter Maynards, Robert Minturn, Gaillard Lapsley; from Boston, Bay and Bessy Lodge, Sally Norton, Ralph Curtis. New friends like Henry James, John Hugh Smith, Robert Norton, Howard Sturgis; business friends like Clyde Fitch as well as George Dorr, Brooks Adams and his wife, William Buckler,

The site of the Mount in the snow

The Mount in the snow

her cousin Herman Edgar, Florence LaFarge, William King Richardson, the Jusserands from Washington, and Mr. and Mrs. Cass Canfield would also visit the Mount in summer and fall.

Two of Edith's closest friends at the time were Henrietta Haven and her sister Ethel Cram. Ethel was a beautiful, auburn-haired woman with very white skin and green eyes. She played the piano beautifully and did social work. Daniel Berkeley Updike wrote of her: "Ethel Cram was perhaps the person who had most influence with [Edith] of any woman at that period, for she had intellectual capacities that Edith respected, and clear and unswerving views which gave her certainty on matters about which Edith was not so sure. . . . To Ethel Cram, who was a woman of the world without being a worldly woman, Edith listened."

In many ways, however, the Whartons were different from the other owners of the large country houses and gardens. Although Edith Wharton shared certain activities with the other socially prominent people at Lenox, her role as novelist made her spectator to the social life as well as participant. She wrote to Sally Norton after returning from Newport: "The Vanderbilt entertainment was just what you say—but for a novelist gathering documents for an American novel, it was all the more valuable, alas!"

Her mounting reputation as an important writer set her apart from her neighbors. In January of 1902, *The Valley of Decision* came out to good reviews.

"The Mount—Bay and Bessy Lodge"—and Teddy. George Cabot Lodge (called "Bay") was the son of Senator Henry Cabot Lodge and a close friend of the Whartons', whose houseparties often brought together friends of unusual talent. Ethel Cram's niece remembered later that Edith found many people in Lenox dull and that she gathered around herself "intellectual and self-satisfied groups" of guests whom Ethel Cram and Henrietta Cram Haven could also enjoy.

In addition to her help with laying out the driveway and the kitchen garden, Beatrix Jones Farrand must have also given Wharton advice on the siting of the house and the planting of the two enclosed gardens at the Mount. Farrand was familiar with all the concepts in her aunt's book—such as the role flowers play in a garden, the importance of enclosure, the ways of contrasting light and shade, the subtle use of stone and garden ornaments. She paid attention to practical problems, however, and was less gifted in describing a garden's "magic."

By 1907 Wharton had gained confidence from the success of her books and had become friends with a number of writers. As she wrote later: "In the company of people who shared my tastes, and treated me as their equal, I ceased to suffer from the agonizing shyness which used to rob such encounters of all pleasure."

After her divorce from Freddy, Minnie Jones supported herself with the help of Edith, who was always generous to her. She acted as Edith's U.S. agent when Wharton was in France. In an article in *Harper's Weekly* in 1903 (from which this reproduction was taken), Jones defended society women and noted their generosity and social work.

Elizabeth (Mrs. James
Donald) Cameron by
Fernand Paillet, 1889

Henrietta Cram Haven by
Katherine Arthur Behenna,
c. 1900

Ethel Latimer Cram by
Katherine Arthur Behenna, c. 1895

Bessy (Mrs. George Cabot) Lodge
by Carl Weidner, 1895–1900

Emily (Mrs. William Douglas) Sloane
by Fernand Paillet, 1891

She already had two volumes of short stories in print, as well as *The Decoration of Houses*, and, while she was living in Lenox, she wrote two more novels, *The House of Mirth* and *The Fruit of the Tree*, a travel book on France, a book on Italian villas and gardens, and many travel essays, poems, and short stories drawing on the social activities and settings.

Daniel Berkeley Updike reported that many people were intimidated by Edith Wharton. One day the two of them went to "see an old lady with several unmarried daughters at a moment when one of Mrs. Wharton's earlier books had been published. One of the younger ladies thought it sad, another morbid, a third unpleasant. Mrs. Wharton replied, cleverly but with some impatience, to these charges, and the mother, seeing her elderly brood routed by these rejoinders, said in a majestic tone, 'In short, Mrs. Wharton, as a family we demand cheer!' I don't know why I was dragged along to pay this visit on a hot summer's day, but as we left the house Edith whispered, 'I think they thought it was a visit of Isabella d'Este and Aldus Manutius.'"

Wharton's sense of humor about foolish people did not make her popular. All her life, people would read her fiction and discover themselves or their friends in it. Before she had even moved into the Mount, she offended the William Sloanes, owners of the enormous shingle-style palace Elm Court in Lenox, by her short story "The Line of Least Resistance," published in *Lippincott's* in October 1900, depicting a rich man bullied by servants and children and a spendthrift, bossy wife. In 1899 Henry T. Sloane (William's brother) had separated from his wife, Jessie, who ultimately ran away with Perry Belmont. In

Edith Wharton at Lenox, photographed by Katherine Haven

"ERW and Jules at the Mount"

this story Edith Wharton described all the details of their marital struggles in a way that no one could mistake.

Ogden Codman reported the incident to his mother: "Her story about the Sloanes finished her with all the Sloane Vanderbilt hangers on who are now barking at her like a lot of yellow dogs. You can see Mrs. Willy Sloane did not like the story in Lippincott's and the Whartons *wrote and apologized* for it. Mrs. Sloane is the local queen of Lenox so everybody in the place sided with her. . . . People in glass houses ought not to throw stones."

Despite their indignation, however, Henry's brother and sister-in-law, William Douglas Sloane and his wife, the former Emily Vanderbilt, who had great power in Lenox, went to lunch at the Mount in September 1902 to celebrate the new house's being finished.

Edith Wharton's passions while at Lenox were gardening, reading, and writing. There she could work without the interruptions that plagued her in New York. In 1905 her excuse to Daisy Chanler for not reading Henry Adams's "Mont-Saint-Michel and Chartres" right away was that "it is too obviously meant to be read with recueillement, on our shady terrace, with all the books I want within reach, & great stretches of time in which to turn the matter over as one reads." She handed the as-yet-unpublished book on to Mr. Sedgwick after a "passing dip into it," which refreshed her and "started all manner of long turns and thought."

At the Mount, Wharton settled into a productive writing routine. According to Berkeley Updike: "Her writing was done early in the day, though very little allusion was made to it, and none at all to the infinite pains that she put into her work or her inexhaustible patience in searching for the material necessary to perfect it. By eleven o'clock she was ready for friends and engagements, for walking or garden-work."

"Mitou, Moza, and Nicette"

Even though she was working on her American novel and was happy about her new house, Wharton's personal life was complicated. Although her marriage had settled into a routine, Teddy Wharton experienced bouts of neurasthenia and their relationship grew more difficult. While she was coming into her own as a writer, making new literary friends, he was cut out of this part of her life. He enjoyed his sports, managed the big property, which he adored, and continued to oversee her trust funds, but he became more and more unhappy and developed manic-depressive symptoms—one moment he was in high spirits, the next in deep depression.

Thus, in January 1903, soon after moving into the Mount, the Whartons went to Italy for a long visit on the recommendation of Teddy's doctor. The success of *The Valley of Decision* had established Edith as an authority on seventeenth- and eighteenth-century Italian architecture, and Richard Watson

Gilder asked her to write a series of articles for *Century Magazine* on Italian villas and gardens, to be illustrated by Maxfield Parrish. She could think of many
reasons not to accept Gilder's offer—"I can't actually write the text for another year or more, though of course I could take notes on the spot"—but she
found the idea of working with Maxfield Parrish, who had previously done
illustrations for her story in *Scribner's*, "The Duchess at Prayer," irresistible.

Edith Wharton's assignment was a timely one. Having just begun her
own garden at Lenox, she was now off to study the great Italian gardens she
had known since childhood. Yet her extensive research, energetic visiting of the
villas, and serious attitude toward her subject reflected Wharton's view of herself as a disciplined scholar and critic, not a dilettante. She read books in German, French, and Italian in preparation for the project, including Montaigne's
descriptions of the Medici Villa Castello near Florence, and the English gardener John Evelyn's account of his visit to Roman villas in 1644. She studied
old plans and engravings from the seventeenth century and those of Percier
and Fontaine from the beginning of the nineteenth on Roman villas, as well as
Peter Paul Rubens's drawings of Genoese villas, and prints of Giuseppe Zocchi
and Giovanni-Francesco Costa's etchings of villas on the Brenta.

Between January and June 1903, the Whartons visited more than seventy villas and gardens. Six articles were published, about one every other month, starting with the November 1903 issue and ending with the issue of October 1904. *Century* brought out the articles as a book later in 1904, adding an index and bibliography. Wharton organized the book by region, dealing with the villas of Florence, Siena, Rome and its environs, Genoa, Lombardy, and the Veneto. She was more interested in the gardens than the villas, and she added photographs of her own and drawings to Parrish's illustrations.

The Whartons landed first in Genoa, where villas were built either "against masses of luxuriant foliage and above a far-spreading landscape" or "on narrow ledges of waterless rock," with "an outlook over the serried roofs and crowded shipping of a commercial city." Genoa, so wonderfully located, was then becoming the ugly industrial port it is today. Many villas had disappeared and "the other beautiful country houses which formerly crowned the heights above Genoa, from Pegli to Nervi, have now been buried in the growth of manufacturing suburbs, so that only the diligent seeker after villa-architecture will be likely to come upon their ruined gardens and peeling stucco facades."

From Genoa they went to Rome to see the villas on the hills of the great city and in the surrounding campagna. She wrote from there to her old Roman playmate Daisy Chanler: "I have thought of you very often in scenes which are so associated with you. We have been here a month, & we leave, alas, the day after tomorrow, with a sense at once of regret & repleteness. I think sometimes that it is almost a pity to enjoy Italy as much as I do, because the acuteness of my sensations makes them rather exhausting."

On this trip, Wharton was less charmed by the natives' response to their surroundings, and she experienced the old feeling that she was alone in her rapturous reactions to the beauty around her: "When I see the stupid Italians I have met here, completely insensitive to their surroundings, & ignorant of the treasures of art & history among which they have grown up, I begin to think it is better to be an American, & bring to it all a mind & eye unblunted by custom." Only Daisy's friend the Countess Pasolini seemed to know anything of art and architecture, and she was "like a cultivated English or American woman in her sense of beauty & her knowledge of the past. She has done everything imaginable to add to our enjoyment here, & her house is like a London salon, where people lunch & dine when they want to meet, instead of going thro' the everlasting Roman tea-drinking which consumes so many precious hours."

Edith took one of the first motor trips of her life from Rome north to visit the enormous cinquecento fortress-villa and gardens designed by Vignola for Alessandro Farnese at Caprarola. The United States ambassador George Meyer provided the car, "probably the most luxurious, and certainly one of the

Valmarana by Maxfield Parrish. Wharton admired Parrish's illustrations (here and on page 105) but considered them a bit too whimsical for her text: "[They] should have been used to illustrate some fanciful tale of Lamotte-Fouqué, or Andersen's *Improvisatore*."

In *Italian Villas and Their Gardens* (from which the illustrations on pages 103–5 are taken), Wharton begins with the early Tuscan gardens. Although they were no longer within the castle walls, they continued the earlier pattern of the medieval designs, and were for the most part two-dimensional series of garden rooms. They were far less innovative for their time, the late quattrocento, than those soon to be built in Rome.

The cinquecento villas near Rome, with their exciting terraces descending the hillside, their water stairs, their many statues, were Wharton's favorites—particularly Caprarola, "a garden to look out from," and Lante, one "to look into." For her there was nothing in all Italy like Caprarola *(below)*: "The audacity of placing that row of fantastic terminal divinities against reaches of illimitable air girdled in mountains gives an indescribable touch of poetry to the upper garden of Caprarola. There is a quality of inevitableness about it—one feels of it, as of certain great verse, that it could not have been otherwise, that in Vasari's happy phrase, it was *born*, not *built*."

It is this idea of "inevitableness" that becomes her criterion for judging the success of the gardens. As for Lante *(above and opposite, above left)*: "so far does it surpass, in beauty, in preservation, and in the quality of garden-magic, all the other great pleasure-houses of Italy, that the student of garden-craft may always find fresh inspiration in its study."

Wharton only once mentions the influence of ancient Roman architecture on the architects of the Renaissance, when describing the grotto bath of the Villa di Papa Giulio on the Pincio, a slight reference to such a large ingredient in Italian villa architecture, the

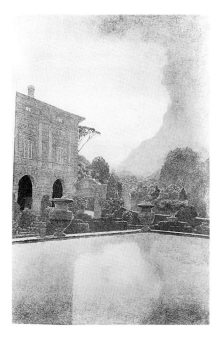

influence of the classical Roman retreats. Later studies have shown how extensively the Renaissance architects imitated them.

The appearance of the enormous villa parks of Rome in the seventeenth century again changes the direction of Italian garden architecture. Representing a new attitude toward nature, the garden is landscaped near the house with formal parterres, statues, and fountains that give way to groves of trees and other natural effects such as fields and lakes. Wharton found these gardens inferior, lacking "the architectural restraint and purity of detail which mark the generation of Vignola and Sangallo."

Isola Bella (completed in 1671), the unusual island garden shaped like a pleasure craft with ten terraces, which seemed to float like a boat in the beautiful Lake Maggiore *(above right)*, was for some critics "too complete a negation of nature." But in that romantic environment, "the almost forced gaiety of" the enchanting lake surrounded by towering mountains, Wharton thought the gardens worked.

By the eighteenth century, Italian gardens came to be considered artificial by tourists who sighed for "glades planted 'after Poussin,' and for all the laboured naturalism of Repton and Capability Brown." Now, "the enthusiasm for the English garden swept over Lombardy like a tidal wave, obliterating terraces and grottoes, substituting winding paths for pleached alleys, and transforming level box-parterres into rolling lawns which turn as brown as door-mats under the scorching Lombard sun." Wharton felt that this new English style pretended to be natural, but was no more so than its predecessor: "Both these manners *are* manners, the one as artificial as the other, each to be judged, not by any ethical standard of 'sincerity' but on its own aesthetic merits."

Wharton was also critical of the huge French gardens like Vaux-le-Vicomte and Versailles: "One is conscious, under all the beauty, of the immense effort expended, of the vast upheavals of earth, the forced creating of effects," and that entire villages were leveled to produce these great effects. The Italian garden art, on the other hand, "concealed itself," because the Italian gardener recognized "the natural advantages of his incomparable landscape" and fit them together into his plan, as at the Villa Scaasi in Genoa *(below)*.

fastest, then procurable." Even so, it was "only a sort of high-perched phaeton without hood or screen, or any protection from the wind." She sat on a high seat like a coachman's box. "In a thin spring dress, a sailor hat balanced on my chignon, and a two-inch tulle veil over my nose, I climbed proudly to my perch and off we tore across the Campagna, over humps and bumps, through ditches and across gutters, windswept, dust enveloped, I clinging to my sailor hat." She thought it the most beautiful excursion she had ever made in Italy. "The view on the ridge between Ronciglione and Caprarola, looking down on one side on the Lago di Vico, and on the other on the wide plain with Soracte springing up from it in 'magnificent isolation' was like one of Turner's Italian visions." (Not long afterward, Edith bought the first of the succession of motorcars that were to serve her during a lifetime of European touring in style.)

From Rome they traveled north by carriage with William Buckler, an old friend from Newport, and his wife, stopping at "Viterbo, Montefiascone, Orvieto and the delicious villas near Siena." Edith took photographs, made notes, and searched for useful books on locations and original plans of gardens. To Buckler, she was modest, affectionate, and humorous. She did not "lay down the law. . . . As to facts she might express confident certainty, and if she did, was apt to be right. But in no circumstances would she insist that a mon-

The magnificent grounds of the Boboli Gardens in Florence, Wharton wrote, were "laid out by il Tribolo, continued by Buontalenti, and completed by Bartolommeo Ammanati. . . . A horse shoe-shaped amphitheatre has been cut out of the hillside, surrounded by tiers of stone seats adorned with statues in niches and backed by clipped laurel hedges, behind which rise the ilex-clad slopes of the upper gardens. This amphitheatre is one of the triumphs of Italian garden-architecture."

ument or a picture could properly be seen and appreciated only in her way. For her the appreciation of 'a sight' was cooperative."

From Siena, they went on to Florence, where Vernon Lee helped to locate the less well known places. From Florence, Wharton wrote to Sally Norton: "I felt like a new being when I got up to Siena. Here also I feel splendidly, but I am doing far too much, as I know a few people living in the villas outside Florence, & the temptation to go & take tea on a terrace at Fiesole or at San Miniato interferes with my real work, which is hunting up & photographing villas."

Visiting the villas in those days was hard work: "We seemed to be always either rushing through the villas in order not to miss our train, or else, the villas exhaustively inspected, kicking our heels for hours in some musty railway-station." Often the Italians themselves were unaware of the old gardens, and Wharton found it difficult to get information even from "those living on the spot." To them, a "garden" meant "a humpy lawn with oval beds of cannas encircling a banana plant, and I wasted a good deal of time before learning that I must ask for *'giardini tagliati,'* " or formal gardens.

By the time they got to Florence and had seen twenty-six villas, "many unknown or almost inaccessible," she decided she should be paid more for her hard work. As the Whartons and their party worked their way north through Lombardy to the Veneto, Edith wrote to Richard Watson Gilder:

> You know, of course, that I do not 'live by my pen' & did not expect
> these articles to pay the expenses of our Italian trip; but neither did
> I realize how much they would increase our expenses!—In Rome, when

The garden at Bellefontaine. Poking fun at pretensions and imitations, Wharton wrote in *Italian Villas and Their Gardens* that "a marble sarcophagus and a dozen twisted columns will not make an Italian garden; but a piece of ground laid out and planted on the principles of the old garden-craft will be, not indeed an Italian garden in the literal sense, but, what is far better, *a garden as well adapted to its surroundings as were the models which inspired it.*"

I was continually on the hunt, I had to make long carriage excursions three or four times a week, & at Viterbo & Siena all the villas were from five to ten miles distant, & meant a carriage for the afternoon or for the day. Here I find I must not only take long drives into the country, but go & stay at several small places in the neighborhood, & drive from there to villas otherwise inaccessible. In addition, I have taken innumerable photographs, wh. I have developed on the spot in order to classify them, & I have had to buy old books on gardens & villas in order to make sure that I am not missing any important villas still existing. All this has increased our expenses considerably—especially, of course, I mean, the trips to out of the way towns & the long drives—& though you may think such investigations are unneccesary for the magazine articles, you will appreciate, I am sure, how much they will add to the value & importance of the book, & to its selling capacity.

The Whartons returned from Italy in the spring, and once Edith had finished writing the articles, the *Century* editors Richard Watson Gilder and Robert Underwood Johnson found fault with their seriousness. She wrote them a strong letter in reply: "As to changing the character of the articles, that seems to me almost impossible. If I had understood that you wished the 'chatty' article on Italian gardens, of which so many have been written, & forgotten, in England & America, I should have told you at once that I was not prepared to undertake the work." She couldn't imagine combining "a study of the architectural values of Italian villas & gardens with anecdotes & small talk."

*Italian Villas and Their Gardens* shows Wharton's wonderful understanding of how spaces relate to one another. Her sensitivity to place and her ability to describe "garden magic" enlivens the book. She explains how this magic was created and how charm and enchantment "can be produced by anything so dull and monotonous as a mere combination of clipped green and stone-work." She advised the reader to study the garden in relation to the house, and both in relation to the landscape. The villa was usually built on a hillside above a series of terraces and gardens that descended the slope below. The focal point below the terraces was a fanciful fountain or a circular pool. The visitor's eye was drawn to a variety of sights—statues, fountains, and ironwork, formal parterres, greenery, and pools—forming a dramatic vista unfolding in perspective.

We know what it is like to be inside a pleached allée, "an ancient tunnel of gnarled and interlocked trees, where a green twilight reigns in the hottest summer afternoon." With a tone of authority, she tells us that "the plan of the garden at Castello is admirable, but in detail it has been modernized at the cost of all its charm." Her eye picks up stylistic differences, as when she writes about the amphitheater of the Boboli gardens in Florence: "It belongs to the pure

Pastoral statues and obelisks on the Mount's terrace balustrade framed views to the distant lake and the Berkshire hills beyond. Petunias and other flowers bloomed in wooden boxes before the balustrade.

Renaissance, without trace of the heavy and fantastic *barocchismo*," which later "began to disfigure such compositions in the villas near Rome."

She explains what an Italian garden is and is not. It has no flowers and little lawn, as the summers are too hot in that southern country. The total success of this kind of landscape depends on the more permanent effects of marble, water, and evergreen trees and shrubs, which, skillfully blended, achieved "a charm independent of the seasons." She intended her readers to apply the principles in their own gardens, and, since flowers were terribly fashionable in America and England, and the "modern" garden lover craved "successive pictures of flower loveliness," this was a radical idea.

Wharton highlights the great contribution of the Italian Renaissance garden architect: "His garden must be adapted to the architectural lines of the house it adjoined," and it also must fit naturally into the surrounding landscape, so that the garden helps the house blend into the landscape.

Gardens should combine beauty with utility—one of Wharton's favorite principles. The garden must fulfill the needs of the "inmates" of the house, providing them with walks in the shade, bowling greens drenched by the sun, accessible parterres and orchards. Wharton was very sensitive to the personal qualities of gardens. They must provide privacy, intimacy with nature, as well as mystery. The correct imaginative grouping of their parts—"in the converging lines of its long ilex-walks, the alternation of sunny open spaces with cool woodland shade, the proportion between terrace and bowling-green, or between the height of a wall and the width of a path"—to make up the whole was important, as was distribution of shade and sunlight and the contrast of straight lines of masonry and rippled lines of foliage

The Villa Gamberaia in Settignano is "probably the most perfect example of the art of producing a great effect on a small scale" because it combines almost all the excellences of the old Italian garden: free circulation of sunlight

and air, "abundance of water; easy access to dense shade; sheltered walks with different points of view; variety of effect produced by the skilful use of different levels; and, finally, breadth and simplicity of composition."

Wharton did not expect everyone to duplicate the gardens at Caprarola or the Villa d'Este at Tivoli (although some rich Americans like Pierre du Pont at his Longwood gardens in Pennsylvania tried). She wanted the reader to learn from observing Italian gardens and copy them not "in the letter but in the spirit," and transfer something "of the old garden magic to his own patch of

Wharton's landscaping at the Mount reflected her interest in vistas with foregrounds and backgrounds, as in this view of the pond with Laurel Lake beyond. The Whartons' working farm was visible from the house on a hill between the pond and lake.

On the south side of the house, Wharton eventually built her "sunk garden" (after receiving money for *The House of Mirth*), erecting walls on three sides. The garden was organized with flower beds around a circular basin with a fountain.

ground at home." The secret, Wharton maintained, was that a garden must be "well adapted to its surroundings."

Returning from Italy in the late spring of 1903, Wharton picked up work on her grounds at Lenox. After six months of visiting the old retreats on olive tree–covered slopes all over northern Italy, she returned to the Berkshire countryside to find it parched and dry. Her initial reaction to America was violent. She felt "more acutely than ever the contrast between the old & the new, between the staid beauty and tradition & amenity over there, and the crassness here." She told Sally Norton:

> My first few weeks in America are always miserable, because the tastes I am cursed with are all of a kind that cannot be gratified here, & I am not enough in sympathy with our "gros public" to make up for the lack on the aesthetic side. One's friends are delightful; but *we* are are none of us Americans, we don't think or feel as the Americans do, we are the wretched exotics produced in a European glass-house, the most déplacé & useless class on earth! All of which outburst is due to my first sight of American streets, my first hearing of American voices, & the wild, dishevelled backwoods look of everything when one first comes home! You see in my heart of hearts, a heart never unbosomed, I feel in America as you say you do in England—out of sympathy with everything.

She went on to describe her disappointment over the new garden: "It is very pleasant to be taking one's ease in one's own house, but out-of-doors the scene is depressing. There has been an appalling drought of nine weeks or more, & never has this fresh country looked so unlike itself. The dust is indescribable, the grass parched & brown, flowers & vegetables stunted, & still no promise of rain! You may fancy how our poor place looks, still in the rough, with all its bald patches emphasized."

The Whartons' head gardener had failed them, "whether from drink or some other demoralization," and there was little to show for all the money they had spent on the place while they were in Italy. "I try to console myself by writing about Italian gardens instead of looking at my own." That summer and the next she worked on the flower garden below her bedroom window, planting rectangular beds and, eventually, white petunias around the tank of water.

After 1905, when *The House of Mirth* was the best-selling book in New York and she had extra money, Wharton built two stone walls to enclose the other formal garden on the southeast side of her house (a retaining wall had been built earlier). She was probably advised again by Hoppin, who made three visits that October. The east wall was pierced with openings to view the lake

e of Wharton, Lenox, Mass.

and landscape. A grape arbor connected the stone piers, and in the center of
this enclosed cruciform-shaped space was a round pool and fountain and statues in the niches of the wall. The effect was that of a *giardino segreto*.

Although she incorporated non-Italian elements—by massing the beds
with wonderful flowers, using extensive stretches of lawn, and highlighting the
New England countryside with its woods, fields, and view of the lake—Wharton's love for Italian gardens shows clearly in her design of the grounds at the
Mount. Like Italian villas of the sixteenth century, the house is sited with terraces descending down the hill, and the house and gardens have a strong axial
quality. (Codman's early sketches for the house are reminiscent of the Villa Pra-
tolino, a Medici villa near Florence with a strong axial layout, which Wharton
mentioned in her book.) She could look out from her terrace and see how the
garden and the enclosing landscape "formed part of the same composition."

A visitor at that time described the effect of Wharton's gardens, noting
the magnificent view "of the nearer and farther hills for miles, with half a
dozen lakes flashing to the sun. . . . On one side there is a rock garden of great
beauty, and the shrubbery, curving like an approaching wave, edges the lawns
nobly. But it is the double sunken gardens, set down into the hill, that are the
distinction of the place. Each has its central fountain, surrounded by geometrically shaped beds separated by narrow gravel paths and planted with brilliant
flowers of contrasted hues. At their lower edge stand marble walls in the Italian style, with openings that permit exquisite glimpses of the view, and, at the
same time, form a lovely background for a few of the taller flowers and some
choice rose-trees." The visitor found that when you looked down upon the two
gardens from the broad veranda, "the glory of their coloring actually vibrates

On the slope below the terrace, grass steps led to Wharton's rock garden.

in the sunlight: Yet, framed as they are in spacious green, they do not clash with the distant prospect."

Edith Wharton was a regular exhibitor at the flower shows in Lenox. On August 5, 1904, at the annual exhibition at the Lenox Horticultural Society, she took third prize in the six perennials class, first in the twenty-five annuals class, second prize for her sweet peas, and second for her Shirley poppies, as well as second for her double poppies, second for her dianthus, first for her penstemons, third for her lilies, first for her hollyhocks, and first for her carnations. Most of these were doubtless raised in her new greenhouse.

Daniel Chester French, who designed gardens himself, and his wife, Mary, who lived nearby in Glendale, occasionally visited the Mount. Mary French described how everything Edith Wharton did "was perfectly and artistically done. When she sent flowers to the flower show, I remember how perfectly each little cluster was tied up and labelled neatly in her own handwriting, and when we went to her place, she and Mr. French would wander about the

Aerial drawing of the Mount showing the driveway, flanked by sugar maples, coming in from the road at top right—beside it is the large kitchen garden with the stables just below—and continuing on to the house with its terraces and formal gardens sited on the hill (bottom left), surrounded by meadows and woods.

grounds, exchanging ideas, she courteous enough to ask his advice, but artistic enough to need little from any one." She felt the Mount and its grounds were "an example of what can be done in landscape gardening by developing every little natural beauty, instead of going in with preconceived ideas and trying to make it like some other beautiful place to which the lay of the land bears no resemblance whatever."

In *The House of Mirth,* which Wharton wrote at Lenox when the garden was in its first stages, several scenes describe the landscape at the Mount and show her attitude toward nature. When Lily Bart is at Bellomont contemplating her strategy of impressing Percy Gryce, a potential rich husband, she pauses on the mansion's terrace: "The terrace at Bellomont on a September afternoon was a spot propitious to sentimental musings, and as Miss Bart stood leaning against the balustrade above the sunken garden, at a little distance from the animated group about the tea-table, she might have been lost in the mazes of an inarticulate happiness." By Sunday, however, when Lawrence Selden arrives, Lily decides to forsake her pursuit of dull Percy Gryce and talk to her more appealing friend. As in later novels, the natural surroundings become a

The flower garden combined walks; panels of lawn; arborvitae topiary; and beds of flowers, including stocks, hollyhocks, phlox, physostegia, annual dianthus—predominantly in shades of pink, white, and red, but with some blue and purple—*Delphinium grandiflorum,* and platycodons, all surrounded by a hemlock hedge. The setting of the geometrically shaped flower garden, with paths and grass panels, into the more natural landscape is typical of Beatrix Farrand's later work.

The central pool in the flower garden, with its dolphin fountain, was surrounded by a hedge of white petunias. Rock outcroppings and the roof of the spring house appear in the meadow beyond.

As Daniel Berkeley Updike remembered years later: "Edith was conscious of my half-hearted interest in horticulture, and on one particularly dull autumn afternoon when she was directing some planting, I asked her if there was not something I could do—hoping that there wasn't! With a malicious glint in her eye she replied, 'Yes you can pick off the withered petunias that border the fountain.' If you have ever tried that particular task you will realise the punishment inflicted."

background for a frank and moving exchange: "Lily had no real intimacy with nature, but she had a passion for the appropriate and could be keenly sensitive to a scene which was the fitting background of her own sensations. The landscape outspread below her seemed an enlargement of her present mood, and she found something of herself in its calmness, its breadth, its long free reaches. . . . She could not herself have explained the sense of buoyancy which seemed to lift and swing her above the sun-suffused world at her feet. Was it love, she wondered, or a mere fortuitous combination of happy thoughts and sensations? How much of it was owing to the spell of the perfect afternoon, the scent of the fading woods, the thought of the dullness she had fled from?"

As Mark Alan Hewitt writes, "Wharton used the country as Shakespeare did in *Midsummer Night's Dream,* as a liberating setting for romance and the discovery of emotional truths." Wharton herself felt liberated and enjoyed a sense of play while busying herself with her gardens. In June 1905, she told Sally Norton that rain prevented her from going to Williamstown to see President Roosevelt accept an honorary degree: "But the flowers come *easily* first. I am really growing besotted about gardening!" That summer her flower garden was looking beautiful and she pleaded to Sally to come see it: "It is really what I thought it never could be—a 'mass of bloom.' Ten varieties of phlox, some very gorgeous, are flowering together, & then the snapdragons, lilac & crimson stocks, penstemons, annual pinks in every shade of rose, salmon, cherry & crimson— Hunnemannia, the lovely white physostegia, the white petunias, which now form a perfect hedge about the tank—The intense blue *Delphinium chi-*

The Mount seen from the flower garden. The shutters are closed against the heat of the day and the awning shades the terrace.

*nense,* the purple & white platycodons, &c—really, with the background of hollyhocks of every shade from pale rose to dark red it looks, for a fleeting moment, like a garden in some civilized climate." In August she announced that she had thirty-two varieties of phlox.

When creating her places, Edith Wharton enjoyed getting advice from others, including her friend George B. Dorr, an energetic and interesting Boston bachelor who was beginning his effort to create Acadia National Park on Mount Desert Island in Maine. On September 3, 1904, she wrote to Dorr, thanking him for his help with landscape design problems: "Your path is finished, & the task of planting its borders now confronts me; & we are just about to attack the laying out of the path from the flower-garden to the little valley which is to be my future wild garden." That November she wrote him again, reporting that in October they had planted white pines in the rough ground between the house and stables. Two years later, she invited Dorr to see the changes she planned for the garden: "We are going to begin the new barn & farm house as soon as we get back & this, & other thrilling incidents of the same kind, will make the Mount one of the most interesting places in the world in 1907." They also exchanged notes on flowers: "What you say of the phloxes makes my mouth water, for I have tried to get as many good varieties as possible, & am especially keen for new colours. If there is any really good novelty, wd. you not ask your manager to send me the name & colour? And won't you, by the way, come to us some time next month or in Sept., & see the George Dorr path, the new pond, & other improvements?"

By then, however, the prospect of keeping the Mount was uncertain. Wharton had begun a new life in France, including an affair with W. Morton Fullerton, a writer and friend of Henry James's whom she had met in Paris in the spring of 1907. That fall he had visited her at the Mount. She saw him again in Paris in January and February 1908, and, soon after, they became lovers.

The garden continued to mature despite Wharton's frequent absence, and, when she began spending more time in Paris and even stayed in Europe for the summers of 1909 and 1910, it improved wonderfully. By July 3, 1911, she could rave: "The heat is bad, and so is the drought; but in spite of both the place is really beautiful, and so much leafier & more 'fondu' than two years ago that I was amazed at the success of my [efforts]. Decidedly, I'm a better landscape gardener than novelist, and this place, every line of which is my own work, far surpasses the House of Mirth." From Lenox that same year, she wrote:

> The most wonderful incident of my return was the finding here of my devoted and admirable head gardener [Thomas Reynolds] who had, as you know, given me "warning" months ago & had finally said, as a great favour, that he wd stay till July 1st! Now it turns out that, when it came to the point, he *could not go*: he loved too much the work of our hands, and in the first two minutes of our talk, without a definite word, it was understood between us that he stays as long as I do. I never saw a more mouvant example of devotion to one's calling. He *couldn't* miss the first long walk with me yesterday afternoon, the going over every detail, the instant noting, on my part, of all he had done in my absence, the visit to every individual tree, shrub, creeper, fern, "flower in the crannied wall"—every tiniest little bulb and root that we had planted together! It is the sort of emotion a good gardener very rarely gets in this country where so few people with places care about them intelligently, and really work on them; and he sacrificed for it the prospect of a secure future and unlimited sway over some millionaire's orchids!

Wharton spent the entire summer of 1911 at the Mount, yet she knew its days were numbered. Although her affair with Fullerton had ended by 1911, Teddy's sickness was making life unbearable. In 1910 she had learned that he had squandered some of her money buying real estate in Boston and had kept a mistress in an apartment there. She hated the idea of divorce—it was socially unacceptable, but more than that, it suggested a kind of chaos, promiscuity, and casualness in human affairs that she detested. She tried to forgive him and be loyal to Teddy, but it was difficult. He would go off fishing or for a cure, improve, then enter a manic state and collapse into deep depression again, becoming a cringing child. As Ogden Codman reported to his mother: "Teddy has just sail'd in the Provence to join [Edith] having been terribly strange here and nearly driven the poor Willy Whartons mad too. He is so restless, and cannot stay anywhere long nor does he know what he is doing much of the time.

"His chief delusion is that he has lost all her money and nothing is left. He sits in the corner of the room and weeps with his face to the wall. This is his usual state, but he has intermissions of thinking he has made a vast fortune, and going about with a *wad* of bank notes giving them away right and left.

"Is it not awful!!!"

Very shortly after the gardener Thomas Reynolds had agreed to stay on at the Mount in 1911, he left anyway. The Whartons' relationship had declined irretrievably, and Edith made the difficult decision of separating from Teddy. The Mount was becoming too expensive to keep, and, after a great deal of equivocation, Edith concluded that it would have to be sold. They received a good offer in August. Edith chose to turn this and all other legal matters over to Teddy, and she sailed for Europe that September, returning only briefly to cosign the papers for the sale.

The loss of the Mount was a great disappointment to Wharton. When writing Daisy Chanler in 1929, she recalled her Lenox days fondly: "Your delightful letter full of green gallops & sunny garden-loiterings filled me with the longing for such country joys. I used to have them at Lenox and gave them up with real regret." Her friend Gaillard Lapsley also remembered how happy she had been there: "I can see her again this time in less detail on a radiant summer day at Lenox. We had driven to the post-office where I got down to send a telegram for her and as I returned I saw her in the trim, two-seated open carriage with a light fringed cover like an old fashioned pony phaeton, her coachman in front and a pair of smart cobs. The fashions in those days were often obliterating and the big garlanded hat and spotted lace veil, the tight corset, the ruffles and flounces of the summer frock would have absorbed most women's identity, but Edith's eyes and intelligence and the disciplined animation of her face mastered them all."

# "THE MOTOR-CAR HAS RESTORED
# THE ROMANCE OF TRAVEL"

With the Mount, Edith Wharton had created a wonderful place for entertaining friends, a setting that afforded her the privacy to write and acres of land where she could indulge her love of nature and plant her gardens. She could also take up her other passion, traveling, in a fresh way. In their new automobile, the Whartons made excursions over the winding and hilly roads with the same intensity and curiosity they had shown on voyages in Italy and Greece. The motorcar enlarged Edith's world and changed her way of seeing it.

After 1904, she no longer went to Italy each spring (except to Salsomaggiore to take the cure)—France became the new European destination of her heart. Thus, the New York / Europe dichotomy she had fixed in her mind since childhood now shifted to contrast the New England countryside with the sophisticated landscape and cities of France. She would often stay at the Mount late into the fall to enjoy the colors of autumn and the still whiteness of the snowy landscape; then she would move to 884 Park Avenue for part of the winter before going off to Europe in the spring.

Her motor excursions—both in America and France—provided scenes that turned up in her writing. In her memoirs, she would describe how the settings of the novellas *Ethan Frome* (1911) and *Summer* (1917) were the result of explorations "among villages still bedrowsed in a decaying rural existence, and sad slow-speaking people living in conditions hardly changed since their forebears held those villages against the Indians." She collected her observations about France in a series of travel articles, eventually published in book form as *A Motor-Flight Through France* (1908), which opens with the sentence, "The motor-car has restored the romance of travel."

The motorcar did restore romance—in many ways—to Edith Wharton and her friends. For Wharton, the zealous traveler, the discovery of motoring—a much nicer way of getting around than taking a train or riding in a carriage with horses to worry about—allowed her to travel all the time, even when she was at home, and traveling always healed her. Thanks to this new technological invention, the car, she could enjoy more intensely the countryside and her experience of the past, which she associated with it.

Her motoring life seems to have begun in 1902. On June 7 she wrote her friend Sally Norton of "chartering" an automobile in Pittsfield, and in 1903 she got another taste of the new sport when she rode in the automobile of the American ambassador to see the gardens of the villas Caprarola and Lante for her articles on Italian villas and gardens. On January 24, 1904 (her forty-second

Teddy Wharton (seated) and Paul Bourget at Les Plantiers, "a little peach-coloured villa above the peach-orchards of Costebelle," near Hyères

birthday), she wrote to Sally Norton about the Whartons' new car, which was "of moderate speed and capacious dimensions." Teddy had brought it down from Paris to Costebelle to be with the Bourgets, who had a villa there. While there they made a number of delightful excursions. Then they journeyed in the motor to Grasse, from where they planned to wander gradually down to Rome and perhaps Naples, although they would have to wait for better weather, as warmth and sunshine were so necessary for Teddy.

Wharton was happy, and she enjoyed the Riviera as never before, for, as she wrote, "our long flights across the hills & along the shore take us into the heart of the country, & steep us in warm bright air." They were enchanted with their motor, "with the escape from the railways, the charm of exploring new roads, of being able to flit from point to point as the fancy takes us. The rest and refreshment of spending so many hours daily in the open air are incalculable, & when I think how housebound you poor dears must have been through this iron winter I wish I could have you here and carry you with us through olive groves and rose fields & along the shores of a radiant blue sea."

She raved about this new way of seeing the landscape and towns: "We don't want to give up the trip to go ignominiously by train, missing all the beauties of the road between here & Pisa." They went to Cannes from Grasse, were storm-bound for ten days, then had a brilliant day and went on to Monte Carlo over the old Corniche road across the mountains. "There was a fresh fall of snow on the mountains & everything was indescribably clear-cut and radiant. The next day we meant to 'proceed,' as the English papers say of the travels of royalties, but there was a raging tearing mistral, which everyone said would put an end to the bad weather. So we stayed over, & behold today the clouds are banking up & we shall have rain again!" Wharton felt that the whole quality of touring was different, "for there is no end to the exploring one can do, in a carriage of which the horses are never tired. We hope to start Rome-ward the day after tomorrow, spending the first night at Alassio, the second at Nervi, the third at Spezia or Pisa." She apologized for the monotony of her letter, "which is all weather and motor, but really they are my only topics, for one sees no one who is interesting in these places, & as for new books, I can find none."

The invention of the gasoline engine in the second half of the nineteenth century made the automobile possible. At first it had been generally considered only for sport, but by the 1890s the number of car manufacturers had increased, and by the early 1900s cars began to appear on the road, replacing horse-drawn vehicles as a means of transportation.

Being out in the open air had a tonic effect on Wharton. In her motor she enjoyed a quick but direct look at the passing landscape, leaving her with constantly shifting vistas and scenes to observe—a fantastically efficient way to collect mental pictures. She was now free of the tyranny of the train schedule, and

Minnie Bourget in the back of the Whartons' car, with chauffeur Charles Cook looking on

of the waiting in stations, and could be in complete control of the itinerary. Although she was sick in the early spring of 1904, by May 5 she was able to report: "Soon as I was on my legs again we started on an enchanting motor-trip across France to Pau & down to the borders of Spain, & then up through Périgueux, Limoges, Bourges & Blois to Paris. Every step of the way was a delight, for we had perfect weather & saw unforgettable things, but the long days in the open air, & the rush of new impressions, had a stupifying effect, & I could not keep my eyes open at night when we reached our destination."

Paul Bourget (driving), with Teddy Wharton and Minnie Bourget in the back seat of the Wharton's car and Cook looking on

Her new intimacy with the landscape brought to her mind frequent comparisons between the charms of Europe and America. She motored to Cambridge, England, "& saw the exquisite 'Backs' in their glory—limes & beeches in fresh radiant leaf, the turf sown with daisies, the gardens glowing with spring flowers, the old mellow walls bathed in pale sunshine." Then she sounded the old cry: "How much we miss in not having such accumulated beauties to feed on now & then at home! I enjoy them so keenly that the contrast makes me miserable, & I think it almost a pity for an American who loves the country ever to come to England."

The Whartons' joy over their first "dear motor" was short-lived; they sold it to avoid paying duty when they went back to America in June 1904. Soon after their return, however, they bought another car and continued their new pastime at the Mount. This event merited newspaper coverage: "Mr. Edward R. Wharton has joined the ranks of the automobilists, having purchased this week, through the agency of Thomas S. Morse, a very handsome Pope-Hartford light touring car of ten horse-power, with removable tonneau and brass trimmings. Mr. Morse received the order on the morning of the Fourth. At eight o'clock the following morning the car was bought at the factory, and on Thursday morning Mr. Wharton and Mr. Morse went to Hartford and returned in the afternoon with the machine."

Local motor tours were planned with the care and excitement of a European vacation. Edith Wharton wrote repeatedly to Sally Norton at Ashfield about routes: "I merely wanted to know which villages to pass through . . . [in our] little sputtering, shrieking American motor, in which we hope to see something of the country." On July 18, 1904: "Teddy brought it from Hartford (70 miles) in 5 hours on its first run, climbing Becket mountain on the way."

In her old age she recalled the fun: "The other day, in going over some old letters written to Bay Lodge by Walter Berry, I came on one dated from the Mount. 'Great fun here,' the writer exulted; 'we motor every day, and yesterday *we did sixty-five miles'* (in triumphant italics)." She remembered how "one set out on a ten-mile run with more apprehension than would now attend a journey across Africa." The blue hills seemed to tantalize the imagination and promise mysteries as the adventurers delighted in "penetrating to the remoter parts of Massachusetts and New Hampshire, discovering derelict villages with Georgian churches and balustraded house-fronts, exploring slumbrous mountain valleys, and coming back, weary but laden with a new harvest of beauty, after sticking fast in ruts, having to push the car up hill, to rout out the village blacksmith for repairs, and suffer the jeers of horse-drawn travellers trotting gaily past us."

The Whartons ventured ever farther afield. The *Berkshire Resort Topics* informed its readers on August 13: "Mr. and Mrs. Edward R. Wharton start-

Walter Berry (left), Alice Warder, Ellen Warder, Teddy Wharton, and Elizabeth Warder at Beverly Farms, Massachusetts

ed out Tuesday for their first long tour in their new Pope-Hartford car and will spend a week or ten days in the eastern part of the state. On Tuesday they toured to Worcester, going Wednesday to Groton, and on Thursday to Beverly [Farms]. They are accompanied by Mr. W. V. R. Berry, of Washington, who has been their guest for some time at 'the Mount.' "

In August 1905, Edith and Teddy motored to Cornish, New Hampshire, lunched with Maxfield Parrish, "& saw that divine view of Mount Ascutney, the most beautiful I have ever seen in America." In August 1906 they had a typical adventure—as Edith told Sally Norton:

> !!!!!!!Seven minutes from your door we were in a ditch, & hiring a local "team" to pull us out!!!!! As Cook remarked: "It never rains but it pours over this way!"
>
> Still, it was not very bad, though I could not resist this sensational beginning. About a mile from Ashfield we met a nervous man & woman in a buggy. Their horse was as calm as a mill-pond, but as soon as they saw us they turned him up the bank, thus projecting the buggy at right angles across the narrow road. We tried to squeeze by in the space they left, but the whole edge of the road gave way under us, & we sank seven fathom deep in mud! I wish you could have seen Cook look at his over-turned car!—Well, the neighbourhood soon assembled, the "team" pulled us out undamaged, the village philosopher remarked: "Thar's a spring under the ro'd just thar," & 35 minutes later we were

skimming along as well as ever, & I was saying: "Thank goodness Sally didn't come!"

I said it louder still when, near Pittsfield, a wild rain-storm descended on us, & we raced home the rest of the way with the fire balls crashing behind.

It was *not* a good day for a beginner at motoring, but we took no harm, & finished off the evening by reading the *Symposium.*


Although Wharton's memories of the automobile were of exploration and excitement, the motorcar could be a dangerous presence on the road, and romance and adventure could turn quickly to catastrophe. At the end of July 1905, her great friend Ethel Cram was fatally injured in an accident that occurred when her horse was frightened by the appearance of a motorcar on the road.

The Whartons and the Cram family, which included Ethel; her sister, Henrietta Cram Haven; and their mother, Katherine Sargent Cram, who lived at Highwood (now the site of Tanglewood), saw each other constantly. Their servants were even related—Catharine Gross, Edith's housekeeper, was the Crams' butler's sister-in-law. Mrs. Cram felt that Edith treated Teddy—as well as Teddy's mother and sister, whom she avoided—terribly. The Crams thought Teddy was dull, too, although he did take the children to the Whartons' stable to see the carriages on display.

Ethel Cram and Edith Wharton were devoted supporters of the Lenox library, and, on the day of the accident, Ethel had taken two of her nieces, Charlotte Winthrop and Katherine Haven, up there from Highwood to sort books. On the way home in their horse-drawn cart, they met a friend, Carlos de Heredia, pushing his motor, one of the first in the area, up a hill. Their frightened horse shied, got the reins caught under her tail, and ran away. As Ethel tried to free the rein, her skirt caught the wheel, and she was dragged forward, kicked in the head by the horse, and pulled out of the cart. The two girls escaped unhurt when the horse finally made a sharp turn and broke free from the cart.

Ethel was brought home with a fractured skull; she was operated on and lived two months without regaining consciousness. Edith Wharton anxiously followed the condition of her friend. She wrote to Sally Norton on July 23: "You will have seen in the papers that since yesterday there is some slight hope of Ethel's recovery. The *Drs.* are amazed—but she continues to 'function' normally, & take nourishment, & each day seems to add a little to her strength. As to the awful question—*what* will she come back to? That must remain unanswered; but cases have been known where the mental power was recovered completely after a fracture of the skull. There is no sign yet of returning consciousness."

Henry James, Edith and Teddy Wharton, and Charles Cook in the car at the Mount. James had been "won over to motoring, for which the region is, in spite of bad roads, delightful—the mountain-and-valley, lake-and-river beauty extends so far, and goes so on and on and on that even the longest spins do not take one out of it." He described enjoying "the Whartons' big strong commodious new motor, which has fairly converted me to the sense of all the thing may do for one and one may get from it. The potent way it deals with a country large enough for it not to *rudoyer*, but to rope in, in big free hauls, a huge netful of impressions at once— this came to me beautifully, convincing me that if I were rich I shouldn't hesitate to take up with it. A great transformer of life and of the future!"

By August 23 she had heard that "alas there has been no change, & the only change we can hope for is long in coming," and on September 15: "Ethel died this morning. One can only give thanks, for the bitterness of death is long past. Even now, I shudder to think of the effect that this two months' agony have had on Henrietta & the future of her child. How often I have thought of that article of Dr. Baldwin's during these terrible weeks! I am sure I should have the 'triste courage,' in such a case, to let life ebb out quietly—should not you?" Wharton believed in euthanasia and wrote many times in her life that a swift death was better than lingering and suffering, but with Ethel Cram's death she lost a great friend.

Ethel's niece Katherine Haven was too young to go to the funeral, but she well remembered "sitting at the window, watching the long line of carriages move off in the pouring rain and my Nanny telling me the rain was the angels in heaven weeping over the death of such a lovely person. . . . When my Aunt Ethel died Pussy [Edith Wharton] arrived with a poem she had written in memory of her, and Marnie [Mrs. Cram] refused to do anything about it, and said it was cheeky of her to want to publish [it]. Mummy wept and there was a terrible scene."

Motoring was central to the house-party activities at the Mount, and Edith's new friend Henry James was one of her happiest passengers. The new motor played a big part in the fun. James took to readily, as it magnified his appreciation of the countryside.

Wharton had first met Henry James one spring in the late 1880s at a dinner party in Paris given by the Edward Boits. Several years later, in Venice,

Edith Wharton, Henry James, and Howard Sturgis at the Mount. James reached the Mount in the middle of October 1904 and wrote to Howard Sturgis on the 17th: "The social life, not unnaturally, is the note of this elegant, this wonderful abode. . . . It is an exquisite and marvellous place, a delicate French chateau mirrored in a Massachusetts pond (repeat not this formula)." It was "a monument to the almost too impeccable taste of its so accomplished mistress. Every comfort prevails, and you needn't bring supplementary apples or candies in your dressing-bag. The Whartons are kindness and hospitality incarnate, the weather is glorious-golden, the scenery of a high class. . . ."

their Boston friend Ralph Curtis invited the Whartons to the Palazzo Barbaro to see the great writer. On both occasions Edith longed for the great man to notice her: "It would never have occurred to me that I had anything but my youth, and my pretty frock, to commend me to the man whose shoe-strings I thought myself unworthy to unloose." During their second meeting, Edith was bursting with compliments for *Daisy Miller* and *The Portrait of a Lady,* but James noticed neither the hat she had chosen to get his attention "nor its wearer—and the second of our meetings fell as flat as the first."

It was her writing that finally captured the master's attention. Minnie Jones, one of James's great friends, sent him Wharton's first volume of short stories. James was immediately interested in an American who, like himself, was fascinated by Europe and whose first novel took place in Italy, as his *Roderick Hudson* had. Although they came from somewhat different backgrounds—the Jameses, a very intellectual family, were descended from Irish settlers who had made money in upstate New York, while the Joneses had been socially prominent but less accomplished New York City dwellers since the eighteenth century—Wharton and James had been in many of the same places. As children (James was eighteen years older), both had experienced constant European travel (James's first memory was an image of the column in the Place Vendôme), and both had lived in Newport (although at different times—his Newport was pre–Civil War) and knew the cultivated, upper-crust Yankees who lived along the Eastern Seaboard—in Washington, Philadelphia, New York, and Boston—in the second half of the nineteenth century.

After reading Wharton's story "The Line of Least Resistance" in *Lippincott's Magazine* and tactfully commenting, "It only suffers a little, I think, from one's not having a *direct* glimpse of the husband's provoking causes—literally provoking ones," James went on to "applaud, I mean I value, I egg you on in, your study of the American life that surrounds you. Let yourself go in it & *at* it." After the publication of *The Valley of Decision,* he wrote her: "Profit, be warned, by my awful example of exile & ignorance.... All the same DO NEW YORK!"

Because she was drawn to life abroad as a subject for her fiction and as a place to live, James warned Wharton to avoid a kind of international schizophrenia that he felt he had fallen subject to. He saw her as a younger version of himself, whom he could counsel. Like Wharton, James had spent years searching for the right place to live and had finally chosen London. It was there

Friends on the terrace at the Mount

that they met again in 1904—they had lunch together—and again just before she sailed for home in May. This time they hit it off right away. She wrote later that the reason was that, in the interval, "I had found myself." They had a "common sense of fun," and she found that "the real marriage of true minds is for any two people to possess a sense of humor or irony pitched in exactly the same key, so that their joint glances at any subject cross like interarching search-lights." She was "no longer afraid to talk to Henry James of the things we both cared about; while he, always so helpful and hospitable to young writers, at once used his magic faculty of drawing out his interlocutor's inmost self."

Over the next twelve years, their friendship went through many stages—from master and pupil to guest and hostess, traveling companions, perhaps to surrogate brother and sister (James's only sister, Alice, had died in 1892), coconspirators, and doubles. Wharton was always being told, to her annoyance, that her work was imitative of James's. For his part, James would sometimes find her overenergized and intrusive, the Angel of Devastation who swooped down in her large motor and carried him off. Later he would be the voyeur in her affair with Morton Fullerton; when he was sick, she was nurse, he patient; and when, after a brief illness, he died, she, still hardy and productive, survived to mourn and remember him.

Although James was America's great novelist, Wharton always made more money. Her luxurious life-style often puzzled him and made him feel awkward. As the story goes, when Wharton told James she was buying an expensive motorcar with her proceeds from *The Valley of Decision*, he replied, "With the proceeds of *my* last novel [*The Wings of the Dove*], I purchased a small go-cart or hand-barrow on which my guests' luggage is wheeled from the station to my house. It needs a coat of paint. With the proceeds of my next I shall have it painted." She, the perfect housekeeper and successful moneymaker, had little patience with his "anxious frugality." In *A Backward Glance*, written almost twenty years after James's death, Wharton remembered how, during visits to Rye, they would be served a "dreary pudding or pie" for dinner and consume a quarter or a half of it. The pie would then reappear at a later meal, "with its ravages unrepaired."

In late summer 1904, James, who had lived in Paris and London and not crossed the Atlantic since 1884, returned to America to tour the country and give lectures. From New Hampshire in September, he wrote to Wharton, who had begged him to come to the Mount: "I don't know that anything has yet (since last Tuesday [August 30, when he had docked in New York]) so contributed to persuade me that this first phase of repatriation isn't a mere lurid dream." Then he described the atmosphere in New Hampshire, where he was staying with his brother William: "The conditions are very pleasant & interesting to me—the Domestic Circle blooming, for the poor celibate exile, with

Wharton was able to share her enthusiasm for reading and make literary jokes with Walter Berry, shown here on the balustrade of the Mount terrace. They talked about "society" in a way that suggests Lily Bart's conversations with Lawrence Selden in *The House of Mirth*. They were both "inside" society but could analyze it, too, as Berry wrote: "I suppose you are keeping up the society end and dining out with Egerton, Bayard, & Co." In another letter to Edith in Lenox, he wrote that he had heard Teddy was at Newport: "He just had to see the nobs, I suppose. What *would* he think of this land where no one dresses for dinner."

Wharton wrote Berry from the Mount in the summer of 1906: "Caro mio, you must have been frizzling like the gente in the cammino acceso (you see I put you in Purgatory, because you have the hope of coming back to Lenox) for here we have been up to our chins in the Lake of Humidity ever since you left." She had been "'lying round' & reading Dant', & I *did* pine for you when I came to that divine 27th, & the 'divina foresta' at the opening of 28, & the most superlative 30th. It is too bad that we should have struggled together through the desert to part on the verge of the divina foresta."

Walter Berry with one of the Whartons' dogs in the flower garden niche at the Mount, which Ogden Codman had designed for the garden at Land's End

the rich flowers of a new generation; & all the New England beauty of forest, mountain, lake & general Arcadian ease making its own appeal to the pulses of old—very old—association, of remembered youth—when everything that is now behind was before. I am finding again my old (young) eyes & imagination, & it is rather exquisite."

Later, as he toured America, traveling first in the East, then to the South, and out to California, he was dismayed by what he saw. He witnessed "the gouging out of fortunes without the creation of a true civilization." What he missed was "a sense of place . . . of attachment, stability and unity." There was no "cult of permanence, no tranquility." When he visited old haunts, he saw in the buildings themselves symbols of the swiftly changing American culture. In New York City, his childhood church had vanished and his boyhood home was a factory. The skyscrapers he considered "usurpers of the past," the hotels offered "an immense promiscuity." The South was a "ghost of itself."

His voyage was punctuated, however, by the generous hospitality of friends who welcomed him for visits, including his new American friend Edith Wharton, who invited him often to the Mount. At the beginning of October 1904, James was enjoying the beauty of the American autumn in Salisbury: "I am here I believe on the very fringe of your country. . . . It is a ravishing land, & we see your blue hills, & if I 'owned,' as they say, a motor I would come over to pay you an anticipatory call." He had just visited Hill-stead, the house of the American art collector Alfred Pope: "What weather (yesterday at the really exquisite Farmington, for instance!) and what invraisemblable beauty of country."

Wharton planned a house party for the middle of October 1904, which would include James, Walter Berry, and Howard Sturgis. Berry was then practicing law in Washington. Occupied with business trips and briefs, he was not always able to appear at 884 Park Avenue or the Mount exactly when he or Wharton would have wanted, but they were together often. In December 1902 he wrote to her: "Speaking of weather, I had such a good dream of summer, last night. You were sitting under a tree somewhere (it must have been in one of your boscos), and I was stretched out on the grass with my head in your lap, and you were reading aloud."

Howard Sturgis was another transplanted exotic. The son of a Bostonian, Russell Sturgis, who was a banker in London, he was born in England and educated at Eton and Cambridge. Edith had seen him in Newport in the 1890s. He had just written a novel, *Belchamber*, about love affairs among the British aristocracy. His house in Windsor near London, Queen's Acre (or Qu'acre), would be a happy gathering place in the future years for James, Wharton, Gaillard Lapsley, and others.

They were all reading the first volumes of Madame Karénine's life of

Richard Watson Gilder and Maria Landsdale in the garden at Four Brooks Farm, 1907. Gilder, Wharton's friend and editor at *Century* magazine, lived on the Tyringham Road, southeast of Lenox. He and Wharton often traded talk on houses and gardens, and he followed the progress of construction of the Mount, including "the slimy swampy process" of laying the hall "in terrazzo." Gilder's garden, also based on ideas collected abroad, was enclosed by a stone wall to give it an Italian feeling and to keep the chickens out.

George Sand, and they named the "large showy car which always started off brilliantly and then broke down at the first hill" Alfred de Musset. The next one, a "small but indefatigable motor which subsequently replaced 'Alfred' was naturally named 'George.'" In those days, "motor-guides still contained carefully drawn gradient-maps like fever-charts, and even 'George' sometimes balked at the state of the country roads about Lenox."

The group's itinerary included visits to Mary and Daniel Chester French as well as Charles Eliot Norton and his daughter Sally. Edith described the journey back from the Nortons' home at Ashfield: "It almost makes a lyric poet

Mark Twain, F. H. Scott, Richard Watson Gilder, and an unidentified friend at Four Brooks Farm

Daniel Chester French and his nieces with the plaster cast of *America* (now in front of the New York Custom House) at Chesterwood, August 1905. French, his wife, Mary, and their daughter lived near Stockbridge. A garden designer as well as a sculptor, French had laid out several places for friends that were subtle celebrations of the Berkshire landscape, for he made the most of what was already there, the orchards, woods, and old walls.

French set his own garden between the woods and his studio, where trolleys on a railroad track (shown at *right*) transported his sculptures outdoors so he could see how the light fell on them.

Full-size plaster cast of Daniel Chester French's statue of George Washington (now at Place d'Iéna, Paris) at Chesterwood in the summer of 1899

out of me! We had no rain but a sky of flying gleams & leaden cloud—the most beautiful, perhaps, for our austere New England landscape. The road by Plainfield Savoy is far more beautiful than the one we came by, & from Savoy to Cheshire we crossed a desert region of lakes & rolling field & forest, enclosed in sombre hills, & all so remote, uninhabited & tragic under the dark sky, that one might have heard Milton's airy tongues that syllable men's names whispering through their solitudes."

For Edith Wharton, the Nortons were wonderful friends who belonged to an intellectual New England group she was glad to penetrate. She and Sally corresponded constantly about books, and they shared the belief that travel was the best means of dealing with the spells of depression they both suffered from time to time. In December 1905, Wharton wrote that "changing the scene"— making trips abroad or to Washington, Boston, or North Carolina—was the

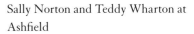

best tonic: "I am so sorry that you have had this breakdown.—No one knows better than I do (at least few know better) the unalterable weariness of pulling out of the tide of life into a dry dock for repairs—the first time one does it there comes a certain refreshment; after that, though no doubt the physical effect is good, the mental and moral results are less exhilarating. But I can't agree with the Dr. that a complete change, like Rome, would be bad—I am trying to speak disinterestedly & I believe I do! I am sure that a new environment, a change of mental activity, is more refreshing in such cases as yours & mine than withdrawal into a back-water of existence where one singly watches life sliding by at a distance."

Charles Eliot Norton was one of New England's great intellectuals—a friend of Thomas Carlyle, Matthew Arnold, Charles Dickens, and John Ruskin. He had met Ruskin while traveling in Europe and came to share his ideas on art. He had written books on his travels to Europe, and articles on art for the *Atlantic Monthly* and *North American Review,* where he was coeditor with James Russell Lowell. He was a poet and founder of the Archeological Institute of America. In 1862 (the year of his marriage and Wharton's birth), he joined the Saturday Club, which included Hawthorne, Longfellow, Lowell, Ralph Waldo Emerson, Louis Agassiz, and Samuel Ward. They all dined once a month at the Parker House in Boston. Norton had been Harvard's first professor of art history, beginning in 1875. When Wharton was working on *The Valley of Decision*, Norton lent her books and took an interest in her novel.

Charles Eliot Norton loved Ashfield for its unspoiled rural quality, which he idealized. His feelings about the American landscape ran parallel to Whar-

Charles Eliot Norton

ton's. In a letter to John Ruskin in 1873, he drew a European / American comparison that anticipates Wharton's later comments on the subject: "The surface of Italy has been moulded by the hands of men, like clay on the potter's wheel. England has been shaped by the English of two or three thousand years into a curious image of themselves. But here the soil has not been worked long enough to show many marks of old labour, and nature at once reasserts her full rights over the fields that man deserts after but a partial conquest of them. . . . Nature certainly did not show half so much poetic imagination in the construction of America as she did in Europe. She finished you off with exquisite elegance, and she left us very much in the rough."

On February 8, 1905, Henry James wrote Wharton from George Vanderbilt's Biltmore (the largest private house in the country) in Asheville, North Carolina: "The whole land here is bound in snow & ice; we are 2,500 feet in the air; the cold, the climate, is well nigh all the 'company' in the strange, colossal heart-breaking house; & the desolation & discomfort of the whole thing— whole scene—are, in spite of the mitigating millions everywhere expressed,

Sally Norton with her niece and father in the garden at Ashfield

THE MOUNT.

Aug. 7th /06.

No sooner safely at the Mount again! Behold me hastening with prolific Pen, To say (an act which you can hardly blame) That I should greatly like some more o' the same.

Edith Wharton to Charles Eliot Norton, August 7, 1906:
"No sooner safely at the Mount again,
Behold me hastening with prolific pen,
To say (an act which you can hardly
  blame)
That I should greatly like some
  more o' the same."

indescribable." It was a strange experience, "but I can't go into it—it's too much of a 'subject': I mean one's sense of the extraordinary impenitent madness (of millions) which led to the erection in this vast niggery wilderness, of so gigantic & elaborate a monument to all that *isn't* socially possible there. It's, *in effect,* like a gorgeous practical joke—but at one's own expense, after all, if one has to live in solitude in these league-long marble halls, & sit in alternate Gothic and Palladian cathedrals, as it were—where now only the temperature stalks about—with the 'regrets,' sighing along the wind, of those who have declined."

Wharton herself visited Biltmore later that year. She wrote Sally Norton on December 26, 1905, describing the "big Xmas fete for the 350 people on the estate—a tree 30 ft high, Punch & Judy, conjuror, presents & 'refreshments.' It would have interested you, it was done so well & sympathetically, each person's wants being thought of, from mother to last baby." The weather was great and the walks through the park a joy to see—"great sheets of fruited ivy pouring over terrace walls, yellow stars still shining on the bare branches of the nudiflora, jasmine, & masses of juniper, heath, honeysuckle, rhododendron & laurel making an evergreen covert so different from our denuded New England lanes." Wharton, who was used to enjoying the settings of the very rich, was not as oppressed as James by Biltmore. She loved staying at the enormous place and found it easy to write there.

She spent the winter of 1904–5 in New York City at 884 Park Avenue. James came to visit, and she did not go abroad until April. She was in Salsomaggiore in May and by June back at the Mount. James came again that spring, and they again took frequent motor trips. Anticipating his visit, he wrote her on June 7 that "it will be delightful to have your traveller's tale, & I feel as if those days wd. be a really deep draught—of the Pagellino vintage." The

Whartons' current motorcar was named Pagellino, after yet another of George Sand's lovers, Dr. Pietro Pagello, who replaced Alfred de Musset briefly after having been the composer's doctor in Venice in 1834. As Lyall Powers has explained, their naming the cars for George Sand's lovers came to have erotic associations for Wharton and James.

Back in England in November, James wrote on the 8th that he admired *The House of Mirth,* which he had just finished in the November edition of *Scribner's,* "& especially the last three numbers of it; finding it carried off with a high, strong hand & an admirable touch, finding it altogether a superior thing . . . I wish we could talk of it in a motor-car: I have been in motor-cars again, a little, since our wonderful return from Ashfield; but with no such talk as that."

Again he returned to his memories of the flights; his thoughts, he said, "wing their way back to Pagello & his precious freight (have you read the luridly interesting little vol. *George Sand & sa Fille,* by the way?) & hover about him as he so greatly adventures & so powerfully climbs . . . to his flights & his swoops, & even more to his majestic roll in the deep valleys, with a wistfulness in which every one of those past hours lives again. . . . Won't you come out with Pagello, & a luncheon-basket, & feign at least an intention of purchase—taking me with you to do the lying? I will show you all those the Abbeys haven't yet bought."

The Whartons did visit James in England: they made a short motor flight in April 1906. On April 26, they sent a postcard to Charles Eliot Norton from Canterbury. Teddy and Edith then spent the last two weeks of May touring France from the Channel coast into Clermont-Ferrand—and visited George Sand's house at Nohant. James was unbearably jealous: "A few days after you had sloped away to France I said to myself suddenly: 'They're on their way to Nohant, d--n them! They're going there—they *are* there!' It came to me as a jealous, yet so tenderly sympathetic, conviction—out of the blue. You hadn't spoken of it. So you owe me the *récit.* There has been, you know, no *récit* (of the impression of the place) of any sort of authority or value but George's own. How you must have *smelt* them all!"

The impressions Wharton collected on this trip in France became an article in the *Atlantic Monthly* in December and the first part of her book *A Motor-Flight Through France,* published in 1908. While the essays in *Italian Backgrounds,* written between 1894 and 1903, were the work of a writer who saw herself as an ingenue, the French pieces were written more quickly and are the work of a professional. Wharton was intent on making instant pictures of what she saw, savoring the original, fresh experience free of past impressions.

Traveling in her auto, she hurried from place to place, receiving images quickly and organizing her experience according to what she was seeing that day in that place, not (as in the case of the Italian essays) around a single excur-

sion, taken slowly by carriage and highlighted, or an impression of a city made over time. The result is a constant barrage of pleasing scenes: the flowers in well-tended village gardens, the great cathedrals, and the large and sweeping views available to the auto rider, such as the sky overarching the wide rolling landscape or the sudden approach to a town appearing over a hill. Her romantic, hyberbolic praise of France signals that France was replacing Italy as the imaginary receptacle for her fantasies and her longings. In France, she found the art of life exemplified at every level of society:

> Never more vividly than in this Seine country does one feel the amenity
> of French manners, the long process of social adaption which has pro-

duced so profound and general an intelligence of life. Every one we passed on our way, from the canal-boatman to the white-capped baker's lad, from the *marchande des quatre saisons* to the white dog curled philosophically under her cart, from the pastry cook putting a fresh plate of *brioches* in his appetising window to the curé's *bonne* who had just come out to drain the lettuce on the curé's doorstep—all these persons (under which designation I specifically include the dog) took their ease or pursued their business with that cheerful activity which proceeds from an intelligent acceptance of given conditions. They each had their established niche in life, the frankly avowed interests and preoccupations of their order, their pride in the smartness of the canal-boat, the seductions of the show-window, the glaze of the *brioches*, the crispness of the lettuce. And this admirable *fitting into the pattern*, which seems almost as if it were a moral outcome of the universal French sense of form, has led the race to the happy, the momentous discovery that good manners are a short cut to one's goal, that they lubricate the wheels of life instead of obstructing them.

French castles, cathedrals, and the French village as a geographical and social unit fascinated her. The castles and the churches evoked a sense of history as well as religious inspiration. The spell of the cathedral at Bourges derived from "the mixing of the ingredients so that there rises from them, as one stands in one of the lofty inner aisles, with one's face toward the choir, that breath of mystical devotion which issues from the very heart of medieval Christianity." In Normandy: "A deep delicious thatch overhangs the plastered walls of cottages espaliered with pear-trees, and ducks splash in ponds fringed with hawthorne and laburnum."

In the south, the ruins tell their story. Provence is "thick with history, and in the ancient principality of Orange the layers are piled so deep that one wonders to see so few traces of successive dominations in the outward aspect of its capital." Of the Mediterranean spring, she wrote: "One's first feeling is that nothing else matches it—that no work of man, no accumulated appeal of history, can contend a moment against this joy of the eye so prodigally poured out. The stretch of coast from Toulon to Saint Tropez . . . has a peculiar nobility, a Virgilian breadth of composition. . . . After packed weeks of historic and archaeological sensation this surrender to the spell of the landscape tempts one to indefinite idling."

In June 1906, the Whartons were back in America, and the summer was spent at the Mount. In November James wrote to suggest another Nohant visit: "Perhaps if you have the proper Vehicle of Passion—as I make no doubt—you will be going there once more—in which case *do* take me!"

Carte Postale handwritten text:

CARTE POSTALE

A utiliser seulement dans le service intérieur
(France — Algérie — Tunisie)

*March 23d 1907.*

Partie réservée à la correspondance — Adresse du destinataire

*Near this wonderful little old church in Poitou we affectionately think & talk of you & wish you were here to tell us more about it. Henry James. Edith W. Teddy*

*M Charles Eliot Norton, Esq. Shady Hill Cambridge, Mass. États Unis.*

Collection C. Siaud, phot., Chauvigny

16 — CHAUVIGNY (Vienne) - Chapiteau de l'église Saint-Pierre

Edith, Teddy, and Henry James sent a postcard to Charles Eliot Norton when they were touring from Nohant to Poitiers in the early spring of 1907: "Near this wonderful little old church in Poitou we affectionately think & talk of you, & wish you were here to tell us more about it. Henry James, Edith W., Teddy."

In May 1907, they did make another motor flight—James and Teddy and Edith. On May 15, Edith wrote to Charles Eliot Norton from Pau: "Our whole journey through the Poitou was full of wonder for me, & as for the return by the Morvan, when I saw for the first time Avallon, Vézelay, & Auxerre, there was a sense of suffocation from the excess of suggestions received. This France is so rich, so varied, so packed with old 'états d'âme' & their visible expressions! . . . Mr. James has left us last week, after giving us two months of a companionship unfailingly delightful, wise & kind." Years later, Edith described the Nohant visit with James: "I had been there before and knew how to ingratiate myself with the tall impressive guardian of the shrine, a handsome *Berrichonne* who could remember, as a very little girl, helping 'Madame' to dress Maurice's marionettes, which still dangled wistfully from their hooks in the little theatre below stairs."

James had known personally a number of the illustrious pilgrims to George Sand's house, such as Flaubert, Maupassant, Alexandre Dumas fils, and other writers, who would visit Nohant "in the serene old age of its tumultuous châtelaine." Fascinated by every detail of the scene, he was deeply moved "by the inscriptions on the family grave-stones under the wall of the tiny ancient church—especially in the tragic Solange's: *La Mère de Jeanne*—and absorbed in the study of family portraits, from the Elector of Saxony and the Mlles Verrier to Maurice and his children. He lingered delightedly over the puppet theatre with Maurice's grimacing dolls, and the gay costumes stitched by his mother; then we wandered out into the garden, and looking up at the plain old house, tried to guess behind which windows the various famous visitors slept. James stood there a long time, gazing and brooding beneath the row of closed shutters. 'And in which of those rooms, I wonder, did George herself

After James left the Whartons in the spring of 1907, he went to Italy for what would be his last visit to the country that had stirred his emotions in the 1860s, when he had seen it as "that beautiful disheveled nymph." He spent time in Rome and four days near Florence at Edward Boit's, where this photograph of him with the Boits and Howard Sturgis was taken—at the "really quite divine—'eyrie' of Cernitoio, over against Vallombrosa, a dream of Tuscan loveliness & a really adorable séjour."

sleep?' I heard him suddenly mutter, 'Though in which, indeed'—with a twinkle—'in which indeed, my dear, did she *not?*'"

James wrote to a friend that he was "immersed in a wondrous motor-tour through the centre and the wide and entire south of this wonderful and most interesting country, . . . France seen in this intimate and penetrating way (for that's how we *are* seeing it) is of a captivating charm (to the intelligent mind), and my companions—[the] Edward Whartons—are full of kindness, sympathy, curiosity and all the right elements of amenity and convenience—to say nothing of travelling arrangements (with servants sent on ahead by train everywhere to have our rooms ready and our 'things out'), which makes the whole thing an expensive fairy-tale."

After finishing *The House of Mirth* in 1905, Wharton started a new novel, which she finished in the winter of 1907 in Paris. *The Fruit of the Tree* records the death of two marriages and the sadness that occurs when husband and wife are not bound by common passions—one is a social butterfly, the other has serious dreams and hard work to do. In the novel, Wharton dealt with the social conditions of workers in New England mill towns in a way that recalls her similar preoccupations in *The Valley of Decision*. She also incorporated a subject that was ever fascinating to her—the building of houses and creating of order in people's lives, in this case those of the workers.

The setting for the book came to Wharton during her trips around the Berkshire countryside. She was interested in the other side of life there, not just the lives of rich socialites but also those of the people who lived in the villages and worked in the mills. John Amherst, like Odo, has fantasies about improving things for the poor workers; unlike Odo, his reforms are successful although his personal life remains sad.

The idealistic hero appealed to Wharton, and she would return to him again in her war fiction. Perhaps creating these do-gooders was her reaction against the many men she had known growing up in New York. Like her brothers, they were, as Gaillard Lapsley wrote, "men living on allowances or private means, who had often studied law and may even have had an office, but no practice, idle persons without responsibility or much conscience." Also like *The Valley* and many later novels, *The Fruit of the Tree* has a double heroine: one woman, Justine Brent, is hard working, serious, and idealistic; the other, Bessy Westmore, is a conventional socialite, pleasure-loving and athletic.

The novel deals with the issue of euthanasia—a subject that had preoccupied Wharton since the sad accident of her friend Ethel Cram. She hoped this controversial subject would attract readers. She reported the reaction of one reader: "I have had a *furious* letter from a lady of Winona, Minn., who says she has 'struck Justine Brent off her visiting list' because that unhappy person, 'preferring happiness to life or honor,' gave her blackmailer her husband's wedding gift as a bribe! If the book excited such violent emotions in its readers, it ought to be a success."

The novel is also filled with longing for a new relationship—one in which things of the mind are shared with a loved one. In the spring of 1907, having just finished *The Fruit of the Tree*, Edith Wharton met Morton Fullerton. She wrote Sally Norton from Paris: "Your friend Fullerton, whom we see frequently, is writing a series of charming articles on the Rhône valley in the Revue de Paris. Do you ever see it? He is very intelligent, but slightly mysterious, I think."

The winter of 1906–7 marked the beginning of Edith Wharton's life as an expatriate. America was her *patrie,* the country of her birth and allegiance, and Lenox the place in America where she had used her wealth and ideas to create her ideal dwelling and garden. Europe up to this time had been her dream world, a place to explore endlessly, always renewing the magic of her childhood experiences and studies. Now she began to rearrange this relationship. No longer merely a visitor from the New World, she gradually relegated her life in New York and Newport, even Lenox and the Mount, to the background and created a new life for herself in France.

That winter she rented the apartment of the George Vanderbilts in the Rue de Varenne, a setting worthy of any French aristocrat. Her narrow old street connected the Boulevard des Invalides to the Boulevard Raspail. Each house turned its stony facade to the passersby, but, once inside, the guest or "inmate" could enter the past and imagine what life had been like there in the eighteenth century.

These monumental *hôtels* had enormous wooden entrance portals and wonderfully carved facades. Beyond the entrance, the visitor entered a courtyard to find a house that was part of what once had been a complex of related service buildings surrounding the cobblestoned interior court—stable, carriage house, and servants' quarters—set off by gardens of shrubs and parterres. On the ground floor was a large hall. Then a curving staircase swept up toward the *piano nobile,* where the ceilings were high and the rooms decorated in the style of Louis XV or Louis XVI, reflecting the ambience of the per-

Between 1885 and 1914, Wharton crossed the Atlantic almost yearly. During her lifetime, she probably made between sixty and seventy crossings altogether. Henry James called her the "pendulum woman." When she embarked on her last voyage from New York to France in 1923 (after receiving an honorary degree at Yale), she wrote in her diary: "Same old Atlantic." In this 1907 postcard to Sally Norton, she rhapsodized, "Splendid voyage in splendid ship—Rested at last!"

Rue de Varenne from the Boulevard des Invalides, 1908. Wharton lived at 58 Rue de Varenne for two winters and then at number 53 until 1920 (both are near the horizon here). Magnificent houses lined the street: Number 78–80 was the Hôtel de Villeroy, built in 1724; at number 73 the Hôtel de Broglie, 1735; number 72, the Hôtel de Castries, 1700. Number 56 was the Hôtel de Gouffier de Thoix and number 47 the Hôtel de Boisgelin. At number 57, the Hôtel Matignon, built in 1721, has been since 1958 the official Paris residence of the prime minister of France.

fectly arranged rooms Wharton and Codman had enthusiastically described in *The Decoration of Houses* ten years before.

Wharton had often visited the city—her mother had lived there alone after her father died. Her brother Harry now had a flat in the Place des États-Unis, which she had used sometimes when he was away. The old neighborhoods of the Faubourg Saint-Germain breathed history. The avenues were laid out in a handsome and thrilling way; the public gardens were charming—the Luxembourg was not far away—and the walks beckoned. In Paris she was discovering the literary world of the salons, a phenomenon with no American counterpart. She was fascinated by French aristocrats. As R. W. B. Lewis has noted, she had a "fondness for lineage and continuity. . . . Her snobbery was an

Rue Vaneau, which adjoins the Rue de Varenne, 1906

The Auberge du Bourdon at 64 Rue de Varenne. In February of 1907, Teddy wrote Sally Norton from the Rue de Varenne describing the good effects of their move on Edith: "I never knew her better in ten years. Our experiment of taking six servants, two dogs, our motor & chauffeur, Cook, has worked perfectly. . . . I have had [the old motor] all done over as new for Paris, with electric light inside, & every known accessorie for comfort. You know I am no good on Puss's high plane of thought, but you will agree that no lady of talent is as well turned out as she is." He ended: "We are most comfortable, & as all the servants are taking French lessons, I feel the cause of education is being advanced."

integral part of her historical imagination." Wharton wrote later about her years in the Rue de Varenne: "All those years rise up to meet me whenever I turn the corner of the street."

Wharton described her new place to Sally Norton in January 1907: "Well—we are peacefully established in this very beautiful apartment, with charming old furniture, old Chinese porcelains & fine bronzes, against an harmonious background of *real* old boiseries (the hôtel was built in 1750), in the heart of the most delightful part of Paris, & just two steps from my dear 'Minnie-Pauls.'" (Minnie and Paul Bourget lived down the street and around the corner on the Rue Barbet de Jouy.) Entrenched in these surroundings, she set out to fit the pieces of her life into a pleasing pattern of dinners, teas, luncheons, theater, guests—including French intellectuals and aristocrats—motor excursions to nearby towns, and writing.

Henry James came to visit in March 1907. After motoring with the Whartons in their "chariot of fire. . . . It's the old travelling-carriage way glorified and raised to the 100th power" into central and southern France for ten days, they all returned to Paris to spend most of the month of April in their "beautiful old house in the heart of the Rive Gauche, amid old private *hôtels* and hidden gardens. . . . I tasted socially and associatively, so to speak, of a new Paris altogether and got a belly full of fresh and nutritive impressions."

Returning to Paris just before Christmas 1907 after another summer at the Mount, Wharton began to immerse herself in the culture of France, seeking to gain acceptance from Faubourg society and to expand her circle of good friends to include more Frenchmen and women. As always, she sought out people who shared her tastes, rare people who had the "ineradicable passion for good talk." She also hoped to discover for the first time total human communion with a man, Morton Fullerton, the attractive expatriate American living in Paris whom she had met there the previous spring.

Fullerton had visited the Mount in October 1907 and had encouraged her hopes in a subtle way. They had gone for a drive over the snow-dusted roads and had had to stop while the chains were put on the wheels of the car. While waiting, they had sat together on the ground and smoked, and they had noticed witch hazel blooming on a wet bank. The night he left, Wharton began writing in a long-discarded diary because at last she felt she had found "someone to talk to." She would not have opened her "long-abandoned book," she wrote, "if you had not enclosed that sprig of wych-hazel in your [thank-you] note . . . the note in itself might have meant nothing—would have meant nothing to me—beyond the inference that you had a more 'personal' accent than weekend visitors usually put into their leave takings." The witch hazel told her "that you knew what was in my mind when I found it blooming on that wet bank in the woods."

During the winter and spring of 1908, she kept two diaries—one a record of her social schedule, with mentions of the times she saw Fullerton and her intimate feelings briefly noted in German, and the other, taken up again at the Mount the previous October, in which she wrote frankly and openly, as if to her lover.

In mid-March 1908, she reported to Sally Norton: "I enjoy Paris more & more, as I get hold of more agreeable & interesting people." And she had grown closer to Fullerton. She had begun with "Dear Mr. Fullerton" and ended with "Sincerely Yrs" in a mid-January letter, but by February things started to change. They traveled to Herblay. That night she described their excursion and noted, in German, "We were together." On February 26 he came into her box at the theater: "Ach, gott—gott—" she wrote later. She began to see him constantly. Witch hazel, "the old woman's flower that blooms in the autumn," had kept its promise.

Wharton's eagerness to be with Fullerton merged with her love of France, and their affair became indelibly linked in her memory with Paris, Herblay, and the other beautiful medieval towns around Paris that the lovers would savor together as sightseers. She wrote to Sally Norton: "I am sunk in the demoralizing happiness which this atmosphere produces in me. Dieu que c'est beau after six months of eye-starving! The tranquil majesty of the architectural lines, the wonderful blurred winter lights, the long lines of lamps garlanding the avenues & the quays—je l'ai dans mon sang [it is in my blood]!"

It was the excursions to the country and riding together in the motor that Edith Wharton described in her diary as the happiest times with Fullerton:

W. Morton Fullerton

And we had another dear half-hour, coming back from St. C[loud] last Sunday in the motor. It was snowing—the first snow of the winter!—& the flakes froze on the windows, shutting us in, shutting everything else out.... I felt your *dearest* side then, the side that is simple & sensitive & true ... & I felt that all that must have been, at first, so unintelligible before to you in me & in my life, was clear at last, & that our hearts & our minds met....

I should like to be to you, friend of my heart, like a touch of wings brushing by you in the darkness, or like the scent of an invisible garden, that one passes on an unknown road at night.

Later, she recalled the places they enjoyed together: "Herblay ... Montfort l'Amaury . . . Provins . . . Beauvais . . . Montmorency . . . Senlis . . . Meudon. . . . What dear, sweet, crowding memories!" While visiting the old town of Senlis with its gray stone buildings, the church at Beauvais with its soaring choir, Wharton shared with Fullerton what she loved.

They could see each other more easily that early spring in Paris because Teddy's mental and physical illness took him away. He went to stay with the Curtises in the south of France from February 12 to 21 and sailed to America on March 21. Sometime in February or March 1908, Edith Wharton and Morton Fullerton became lovers.

Their closeness of thought was coupled with strong sexual feelings, yet beneath her joy Wharton constantly feared that she would not please her lover for long. The alternation of joy and despair was continual: "Sometimes I feel

that I can't go on like this: from moments of such nearness, when the last shadow of separateness melts, back into a complete néant of silence, of not hearing, not knowing—being left to feel that I have been like a 'course' served and cleared away!"

She had long been fascinated with the love story of Paolo and Francesca, and, quite unself-consciously, she used the scene from Dante's *Inferno* depicting their first passion. In *The Inferno* Francesca describes how she and Paolo came to the same moment:

*La bocca mi baciò tutto tremante:*
*Galeotto fu il libro, e chi lo scrisse;*
*Quel giorno piu non vi leggemmo avante.*

He kissed my mouth all trembling:
A Galleotto was the book, and he who wrote it;
That day we read no further.

She wrote in her diary on February 17, "Quel giorno piu"; on March 27, "galeotto fu il libro"; and on April 7, "non vi leggemmo avante."

On May 3 they went to Beauvais with Henry James, who had come over to Paris from Rye to spend two weeks with Edith and sit for his portrait by Wharton's friend Jacques-Emile Blanche. Wharton and Fullerton's trip to Herblay in February had been to find the house of the writer Hortense Allart, whose name became the new name of the Wharton motorcar. They traveled with James in the spacious Hortense, but the situation was changed, for now Wharton and Fullerton were lovers and James did not yet know it.

Fullerton had not wanted to go to Beauvais, "objecting that with H. J. it would not be like our excursions à deux," but he wrote her the next day telling her "how delicious it all was." She confided in her diary: "I think you really found it so. . . . Alone with you I am often shy & awkward, tormented by the fear that I may not please you—but with our dear H. J. I felt at my ease, & full of the 'motor-heureuse' that always seizes me after one of these long flights through the air." She rapturously described the trip: "History & romance & natural loveliness every mile of the way—across the windings of Seine & Oise, through the grey old towns piled up above their rivers, through the melting Spring landscape, all tender green & snowy fruit-blossoms, against black slopes of fir—till, a last climb brought us out above the shimmering plain, with Beauvais choir rising 'like a white Albi' on its ledge."

The trio had lunch together, a "lazy, happy luncheon in the warm courtyard of the Hôtel d'Aupleléne, with dogs & children playing, canaries singing, flowers blooming about the little fountain—the coffee & cigarettes in the sunshine, & the slow stroll through the narrow streets first to St. Etienne, then through the bright variegated fair which filled the Grande Place—till, guided by you, we reached the little lane behind the cathedral, I saw, far up against the blue, the soaring, wheeling choir—'saw it turn,' as you put it, cosmically spin through space. . . . Then, inside, the sense of glad upward rush of all these converging lives—'gladness,' as H. J. said, is the dominant note within the church —the mystic impression of something swung aloft, suspended, 'qui plane' in supernatural levitation."

While James made the tour of the ambulatory, they sat outside on the steps in the sunshine. Fullerton asked her, *"Dear, are you happy?"* For Wharton, "that made it all yours & mine, that drew the great miracle down into the compass of our two hearts—our one heart . . . . . . ."

On May 19, four days before she was to leave for Lenox, she wrote, "I am always glad to go with you to some new place, so that in the empty future years I may say, going there alone: 'We were here together once.' It will make the world less empty." They had walked in the Tuileries gardens and found a seat under the trees on the terrace above the Seine. She felt that, in the two months of April and May,

> I have drunk of the wine of life at last, I have known the thing best worth knowing, I have been warmed through & through, never to grow quite cold again till the end. . . .
>
> Oh, Life, Life how I give thanks to you for this! How right I was to trust you, to know that my day would come, & to be too proud, & too confident of my fate, to take for a moment any lesser gift, any smaller happiness than this that fate had in store for me.
>
> How often I used to say to myself: 'No one can love life as I do, love the beauty & the splendour & the ardour, & find words for them as I can, without having a share in them some day:—I mean that dear intimate share that one guessed at, always, beyond & behind their universal thrill!—And the day came—*the day has been*—and I have poured into it all my stored-up joy of living, all my sense of the beauty & mystery of the world, every impression of joy & loveliness, in sight or sound, or touch, that I once figured to myself in all the lonely days when I used to weave such sensations into a veil of color to hide, the great blank behind. . . . .

As she packed to leave on May 22, Wharton brought out her gowns, and, like Lily Bart in her shabby room at the end of *The House of Mirth*, she remembered the story that each one told: "On the bed, the sofa, easy chair, the dresses, cloaks, hats, tea-gowns, I have worn these last six months. . . . There is the black dress I had on the first time we went to the Sorbonne, to hear B.—lecture last December. I remember thinking: 'Will he like me in it?' And of how many of the others, afterward, I had the same thought, and when he noticed one of my dresses, or praised it, *quelle joie!* I used to say to myself: 'It must be becoming, or he never would have thought it pretty.'

"There is the tea-gown I wore the first night you dined with me alone. . . . You liked it, you said. . . . And here is the dress I wore the day we went to Herblay, when, in the church, for a moment, the Veiled Happiness stole up to me."

She sailed for America on May 23, and, at sea on May 25, she wrote:

When I am gone, recall my hair,
Not for the light it used to hold,
But that your touch, enmeshèd there,
has turned it to a younger gold.

Recall my hands, that were not soft,
Or white or fine beyond expressing,
Till they had slept so long & oft,
So warm & close in your possession.

Recall my eyes that used to lie
Blind pools with summer's wreckage strewn.
You cleared the drift, but in their sky
You hung no image but your own.

Recall my mouth, that knew not how
A kiss is cradled and takes wing
Yet fluttered like a nest-hung bough
When you had touched it like the Spring.

Back in America at the end of May, she was desperate. "Arrived yester-day. At sea I could bear it. Ici j'étouffe." Her heart was torn by "death pangs of separation." Back at the Mount in the summer of 1908, she tried valiantly to overcome her loneliness, but she longed to be in Paris and imagined the scenes she had known with Fullerton there. She would work steadily at her novel in the mornings, steep herself in books, and take long walks, "& all seems going well, till suddenly I stop & say:—'Tomorrow is *Saturday*'—or: 'The last time I wore this dress it was at Meudon . . .' & there's all the work to do over again, the stone to roll up hill once more!—"

In the early part of 1909, Wharton returned to Paris, where they continued the affair. They even spent a month together traveling in England that summer.

Many have asked how W. Morton Fullerton, an intelligent but not very nice man, was the one who succeeded in gaining entry into Wharton's heart. Was it because he came with the right letters of introduction, he was literary, an expatriate American from New England? His father was a minister, his mother a very intelligent woman who channeled her own creative desires into the upbringing of her family and the encouragement of her children, particularly her older son. He had grown up in Waltham, Massachusetts, near Boston,

W. Morton Fullerton in his rooms

and had gone to Phillips Andover Academy; he had been a brilliant student at Harvard.

After graduating magna cum laude, in 1890 he had taken a job at the *Times* in London, where he became friendly with Oscar Wilde and Henry James. James had responded to Fullerton's irresistible sensual quality. He wrote to Fullerton in September 1900, "I want in fact more of you. . . . You are dazzling, my dear Fullerton; you are beautiful; you are more than tactful, you are tenderly, magically *tactile*. But you're not kind. There it is. You *are* not Kind."

Fullerton continued to work for the *Times* in Paris, where he had covered the Dreyfus trial. He had written articles on French politics and a book, *Terres Françaises*, which, as Wharton wrote, "was crowned by the French Academy, & which I have frequently heard men of letters here speak of as the best 'appreciation' of French scenery & history ever written by a foreigner." Fluent in French, as she was, he could join her at the gatherings of both Americans and French.

Like Wharton, Fullerton had left America looking for a more cosmopolitan life, and he was well equipped to appreciate Paris on the same level as she. He had the mind to share her interests—the quick responses, the deep understanding. He was charismatic, and he put their love on a high, idealistic plane, as she did.

In the second year of their affair, however, matters of a different kind began to mar the picture. Wharton had always suspected Fullerton would tire of her, but she was not prepared to discover the extent of his varied and colorful sexual history. He had been married to a French actress, had had affairs with men and many women, including Margaret Brooke, the Ranee of

Sarawak, and that year he became engaged to his cousin, Katherine Fullerton. As Gloria Erlich writes about his many lovers, "To each he gave the sensation of a unique, transcendent love for a brief period, then moved on to the next."

Wharton had given herself to this man who had not much, in the conventional sense, to give her in return. Somewhat of a con man, he pretended to have a larger post at the *Times* than he really did, and he in no way planned a long union. Yet he had an unusual magnetism, an immediacy, a capacity for romantic sexuality that she could not resist, and she surrendered herself completely to her feelings. But he was soon difficult: he would not write her for long periods; he would be affectionate and familiar and then play with her feelings by cruelly distancing himself.

In addition to her disillusionment with Fullerton, Wharton also faced the ever increasing concern of her husband's health, which was becoming worse and worse. Teddy had experienced bouts of nervous sickness ever since they had settled in Paris for the winters. He did not speak French well and was unhappy in the company of Edith's French intellectual friends. During this confusing and distressing period, Wharton made James her confidant. To the news of her problems with Teddy and her affair with Fullerton, he wrote affectionately to her and advised her to "only sit tight yourself & *go through the movements of life*. That keeps up our connection with life—I mean of the immediate & apparent life; behind which, all the while, the deeper & darker and the unapparent, in which things *really* happen to us, learns, under that hygiene, to stay in its place. Let it get out of its place & it swamps the scene; besides which its place, God knows, is enough for it! Live it all through, every inch of it—out of it something valuable will come—but live it ever so quietly; &—je maintiens mon dire—waitingly!"

Wharton and Fullerton traveled for a month in England together in that summer of 1909. Wharton, however, had to busy herself and James with a plan to get money for Fullerton because he was being blackmailed by a former mistress. As James wrote her in July: "I hope the sum he has to pay to the accursed woman isn't really a very considerable one, or on which the interest for him to pay will be anything like *as* burdensome as what he has been doing."

By late summer of 1909, Wharton was insisting on a change in her relationship with Fullerton. "It is impossible, in the nature of things, that our lives should run parallel much longer. . . . I know how unequal the exchange is between us, how little I have to give that a man like you can care for, & how ready I am, when the transition comes, to be again the good comrade you once found me." The affair with Fullerton worked its way from rapture to disappointment—it ended in the summer of 1910—and then to another state. She continued to see him as a friend, playing the role of adviser and mentor and taking over his career—she urged him to leave the *Times* and critiqued his writing.

Despite her complicated personal life, Wharton could take heart that her liaison with Paris was continuing. Her diary entries during 1908 reveal her efforts to become part of the Parisian social scene. Though she was shy and a bit stiff, she was not timid, and she could be a charming, cultured conversationalist. In addition, she came to the Paris season of 1908 armed with a new celebrity stature. As she explained in *A Backward Glance*: "When we finally settled in the rue de Varenne, 'The House of Mirth,' then appearing in the *Revue de Paris,* was attracting attention in its French dress, partly because few modern English and American novels had as yet been translated, but chiefly because it depicted a society utterly unknown to French readers." The book's success was so great that translations of her short stories (*The Valley of Decision* was her only other novel at the time) "were in great demand in the principal French reviews."

The Rue de Varenne apartment was an attractive place for entertaining. She and her household staff were skilled in managing lunches, teas, and dinners; they had been doing it at the Mount for years. She committed herself to lessons to improve her spoken French and Italian, one session of each per week (even though she had read, written, and spoken both languages since childhood, she was teased about her archaic forms of speech derived from the books she had read).

Her enthusiasm for the new friendships she was making grew. She reported to Charles Eliot Norton in March: "We see very interesting people here, & I like the life more & more. I like especially André Chevrillon, Taine's nephew, whose admirable books on India & the East you probably know, & who is a man of the finest *quality* all through. M. Victor Bérard, the author of the big book 'Homère et les Pheniciens,' is another of the same kind." To top it off, "in [Parisian] society the average of intelligence is certainly higher than elsewhere, & one is less likely to spend a dull evening."

In addition to cultivating new friends among French aristocrats, intellectuals, writers, and artists, Wharton renewed friendships with Americans she had known as a girl when the Jones family lived in Cannes. Henry White, now American ambassador, and his wife, Margaret, acquaintances from Newport and Lenox, entertained her often. Other Americans living in Paris included Wharton's brother Harry, her cousin Le Roy King, Professor Baker from the Sorbonne and his wife, the Ralph Curtises, and Daisy Chanler.

The senior American expatriates were the Walter Gays, who kept an apartment in Paris and a château in the country near Fountainebleau, where they entertained Teddy Wharton in December 1908 for several days of shooting—Gay was reputed to be the best shot in France—and took him with them to a gala dinner party at historic Vaux-le-Vicomte.

Like William Wetmore Story in Rome a generation before him, Walter Gay had come from Boston to Paris at the age of twenty and stayed there. He

Walter Gay's reaction to life in the present was typical of many in his American group. As Daisy Chanler described it, he wanted to preserve "a bygone world, a setting of a human life more sensitive, more finished, than the life we are able to lead among noisy machines and machine-made objects; an age when things were made by skillful workmen with tools fitted to their hands, not turned out by factories where men are the servants of powerful automata." Walter Gay's paintings capture that ambience of an earlier time.

had established his reputation as a painter of fashionable French interiors and was awarded the Legion of Honor in 1906. Gay was married to Matilda Travers, a New Yorker and an old friend of Edith Wharton's. Daisy Chanler was another close mutual friend, who said of Walter Gay, "He knew how to give a room an intimate sense of life, to make you feel that charming people had just left it, and that rooms and furniture had belonged to other charming people long ago."

Yet another old friend from America was Henry Adams who, like Wharton, was often in Paris. In 1891 they had shared impressions and Adams had been impressed by how much she knew about art and French history. Brilliant and restless, the super-traveler, historian, and scholar had enjoyed a kind of salon in his own Washington home where his wife, Clover, had been the center until her death in December 1885. At seventy years old in 1908, he took part in Parisian salon life with Edith Wharton and reported on their activities in his letters. After sitting down with Wharton and the Bourgets at tea, he wrote:

Henry Adams with Elizabeth (Lizzie) Cameron (third from left) and friends in Clarens, Switzerland, in 1902. The beautiful much younger wife of senator James Donald Cameron of Pennsylvania had been close to both Henry and Clover Adams in the Washington days, and, after Clover's death, Lizzie became for Henry many things—companion, the recipient of regular letters, his ideal woman—in short, he adored her. Although since 1885 he had lived what he called a "posthumous existence," with Lizzie he kept his promise to act as a "tame cat." They were intimate in many ways but were probably never lovers.

"Mrs. Wharton really does make a social effort, and I approve it"; as for the Bourgets: "The Bourgets are Bourgeoises,—very!"

Wharton gave Adams a big rush of invitations between the time he arrived in Paris on May 3, 1908, and she left on May 23 to go back to the Mount. Often included were Morton Fullerton, with whom she was spending as much time as she could, and her houseguest Henry James, whose social life she also managed during his Paris stay. On May 5 she invited Adams to tea, on May 8 to an informal lunch at the embassy with James, William Dean Howells, and his daughter. On May 10 she asked him for tea with another group. An embassy dinner followed on May 13, and tea elsewhere on May 14. On May 17 he was her guest at a small dinner party with mutual friends the Ralph Curtises and William Richardson. On May 19 she took him to Jacques-Emile Blanche's studio to see his "rather brutal Sargenty" portrait of Henry James. On May 20 Adams and Wharton dined alone, with Robert Grant, an old mutual friend, coming by afterward. On May 21, they had dinner again, with Daisy Chanler and her daughter Laura, who had charmed Adams on their trans-Atlantic boat trip together in early May. Finally they had tea on May 22. At her three teas for Adams, only one other person was a guest twice. Her salon was taking shape, with Adams as a regular *de fondation*.

Adams reported to a friend, Mrs. La Farge: "Down here at this end of the town I have been playing more or less with Mrs. Wharton who keeps a saloon now-a-days, and knows people. Her tastes are eclectic enough—not quite so extensive as Miss Marbury's, but quite general." And, recounting to his friend Elizabeth Cameron the vigorous social life of an "aged Pierrot," he wrote: "Luckily Pussy Wharton—as a few irreverent contemporaries still call her—sailed yesterday, after spoiling me by planting me in her *salon*. I told her what fate waited her, and how she was floating into the fauteuil of Mme Récamier before the fire, with Chateaubriand on one side and Barante on the other, both drivelling; only Chateaubriand would be Henry James and Barante would be Henry Adams. She has her little suite, but they are not passionate. The Bourgets and so on; Blanche, the young painter. . . ; Fullerton, the young Times correspondent; in short, a whole train of us small literary harlequins who are not even funny."

He concluded, "And she goes to plays and things, and reads," which from Adams passed for another compliment. By 1910 Adams would admit that his expatriate American group in Paris was "more closely intimate, and more agreeably intelligent, than any now left me in America" and "Edith Wharton is almost the centre of it."

Adams characterized himself in amusing roles: "My only complaint is that I am oldest, and have to do the sage. Damn that!" Again, "I've nothing to complain of. Nobody seems to care to read by my light, but by whose light does anybody read?" Although his spoken French was good enough for ordinary conversation, he could not keep up in a salon conversation of intellectuals making witty and insightful remarks, something he enjoyed doing and did with brilliance in English. As Viola Winner has noted: "There was also perhaps an element here of personal and family pride and disappointed hopes: Edith Wharton was a 'literary luminary'; he would be introduced as an eminent historian but he was hardly well known as such, not even in his own country. As the grandson and great-grandson of American presidents and ministers to France, he was theoretically the equivalent of princes, but experience had taught him that his equality would not be recognized."

For Adams, who was keenly aware of contemporary politics and cultural issues, the Belle Epoque was a decadent era; he saw Faubourg society as isolated from the intellectual mainstream—"a totally disintegrated crowd." Yet while he tended to denigrate Faubourg society, Wharton idealized it. Through her Faubourg contacts she met French writers, artists, and university people who became lifelong friends.

Among her new French friends were Charles du Bos, a young critic and translator, and the painter Jacques-Emile Blanche, both of whom she had met through Paul Bourget. Bourget had arranged for Du Bos to translate *The*

Jacques-Emile Blanche painting a gathering that included Jean Cocteau and "The Six," a group of young musicians and composers whom Daisy Chanler came to know in Paris after the war. Darius Milhaud, Georges Auric, Arthur Honegger, Francis Poulenc, Germaine Taillefer, and Louis Durey (who soon retired) were, in Daisy's view, "the vanguard of bold modernity; some of their work seemed unnecessarily harsh and discordant." She liked Poulenc best. Once a week they would play two-handed piano together.

*House of Mirth,* and during this work together Du Bos and Wharton became friends. The most fashionable portrait painter in France at the time (it was to his studio that Wharton sent her houseguest Henry James to have his portrait painted), Blanche also painted still lifes, landscapes, and even interiors like Walter Gay. He acquired a reputation as a critic of art and literature, publishing many critical studies of art, as well as *Cahier d'un Artiste* (1915–19), a six-volume account of civilian life in Paris during World War I, and *Aymeris* (1919), a novel based on his own life.

In later years, Wharton would often spend a fortnight or so at Blanche's seventeenth-century family manor house in Offranville, "advising us on the flowers and trees for the garden." While she was there, Blanche recalled, "with her famous chauffeur, comfortable motor, her old German maid, our home assumed suddenly another air; there was something brighter in the atmosphere." She loved the beautiful Norman landscape with its endless green and gold fields, and she took "long motor runs to old châteaux, ruins, and parcs," delighting in meeting aristocrats living in their country seats. "She would endlessly ask us about their previous lives, their family connections. . . . She would sit for hours in my studio, when I painted flowers; soon the technique of the

*Above left:* Jean Cocteau and Jacques-Emile Blanche at Offranville, c. 1912

*Above right:* Jean Cocteau and Hilda Trevelyan painted by Jacques-Emile Blanche

novelist was discussed. At that time (1908–14) Jean Cocteau, a brilliant, astounding youth, would spend weeks at Offranville with us. We both wrote a play for Sacha Guitry's theatre. The Guitrys had a villa near Saint Wandrille on the banks of the Seine. Our rather incompetent, childish comedy, every evening [was] read aloud by Jean to Edith and my people, one scene or the other."

Wharton also visited the Blanches at their house in Auteuil: "Blanche, besides being an excellent linguist, and a writer of exceptional discernment on contemporary art, is also a cultivated musician; and in those happy days painters, composers, novelists, playwrights—Diaghilev, the creator of the Russian *ballet*, Henry Bernstein, whose plays were the sensation of the hour, George Moore, André Gide, my dear friend Mrs. Charles Hunter, the painters Walter Sickert and Ricketts, and countless other well-known people, mostly of the cosmopolitan type—met on Sundays in the delightful informality of his studio, or about a tea-table under the spreading trees of the garden."

Blanche missed out on Wharton's humor, finding her "too serious," never, according to Madame Blanche, having "a real, good raging laugh." As someone at home in two countries himself, he noticed that she was becoming out of sync with time and place: "She loved Europe, she loved and knew France, England, Italy better than any native—yet remained an American of the old fashion—alien, I suppose, to the present manners, customs of her compatriots."

Wharton managed to be invited to the most fashionable events of the 1908 Paris season: from new plays, good or bad, including dress rehearsals (at one, "All Paris there," she noted); opening night at the Opera; current exhibitions at the Louvre and the Petit Palais; the gallery opening of the new exhibition of Walter Gay's paintings ("lots of people, great success"); Salon concerts and lectures; the sale of an art collection at a Louis XV *hôtel* (again, "lots of people"); to the investiture of a popular new member of the Académie Française; a reception at the U.S. Embassy ("horrid crowd"); and an important debate in the Chambre des Deputies (Ambassador White gave her passes with Fullerton to seats reserved for the president of France; they listened for an hour along with Mrs. Roger Wolcott).

Her great ally in her Parisian social campaign was the Comtesse Rosa de Fitz-James, whose salon was the meeting place of some of the most distinguished people in Paris. The occasion for their meeting, which Wharton would always remember, was the kind of spectacle she loved, one of the "unchanged and distinctive events of Parisian life"—a ceremony for the induction of a new member of the Académie Française, held in its historic building. Paul Bourget, who was a member, had obtained two hard-to-get tickets. He invited Wharton and, because Minnie could not go, arranged for the Comtesse de Fitz-James "to take me under her wing." That she did, and, "before we had struggled to our places through the fashionable throng battling in the circuitous corridors of the Institute, she and I had become friends."

As Wharton remembered her, she was not beautiful—she was "a small thin woman, then perhaps forty-five years old [about Wharton's age], with a slight limp, which obliged her to lean on a stick" and to put a footrest under her lame leg while sitting down. Her hair had turned white, and her features were "sharp," but, with her "eager dark eyes" and "disarmingly guileless smile," she must have been charming. Henry James found her so and looked forward to seeing her when he visited. In 1908 he wrote Wharton: "Rosa, I trust, really plays up—not, I mean, in special deeds, but in *character*, candour & fidelity. I seem to *feel* she does." Henry Adams also fell under her spell when they met in 1909 at Wharton's apartment.

Austrian by birth, the comtesse spoke English "almost perfectly" and welcomed foreigners like Wharton to her salon. She was Jewish and, like Wharton, an ardent Dryfusard. Because of her "international promiscuities," a few among the "irreducibles" of Faubourg society would always shun her.

In the Faubourg society, Wharton found a "continuity of social relations

[that] particularly appealed to me." She had tried to create the equivalent at the Mount by inviting a steady flow of congenial houseguests to offset the often dull social routine of the Lenox summer colony. At Lenox, culture tended to be perceived as antisocial, Wharton felt, whereas in Paris, "where politics so sharply divide the different classes and coteries, artistic and literary interests unite them." Rosa de Fitz-James's salon was her ideal: "I have never known easier and more agreeable social relations than at Rosa de Fitz-James'." She enjoyed her role there—"I soon became an habitual guest at her weekly lunches and dinners"—where the men always outnumbered the women, and she described it later, perhaps again rationalizing her preference for France over America:

> In a French *salon* the women are expected to listen, and enjoy doing so, since they love good talk, and are prepared by a long social experience to seize every allusion, and when necessary to cap it by another. This power of absorbed and intelligent attention is one of the Frenchwoman's greatest gifts, and makes a perfect background for the talk of the men. And how good that talk is—or was, at any rate—only those can say who have frequented such a *salon* as that of Madame de Fitz-James. Almost all the guests knew each other well, all could drop into the conversation at any stage, without groping or blundering, and each had something worth saying, from Bourget's serious talk, all threaded with golden streaks of irony and humour, to the incessant fire-works of Tardieu, the quiet epigrams of Henri de Régnier, the anecdotes of Taigny and Gabriac, the whimsical and half-melancholy gaity of Abel Bonnard.

Rosa was an expert at blending compatible groups. In *A Backward Glance,* Wharton's word picture of her is endearing: "In and out among her guests Madame de Fitz-James weaving her quiet way, leaning on her stick, watching, prodding, interfering, re-shaping the groups, building and rebuilding her dam, yet somehow never in the way, because, in spite of her incomprehension of the talk, she always manages to bring the right people together and diffuses about her such an atmosphere of kindly hospitality that her very blunders add to the general ease and good humor."

Considered an accomplished hostess (Bernard Berenson called her "the best hostess I have ever known"), the comtesse was not a good guest. When she came to dine at Edith's, small parties always composed of her friends, the effort "seemed to embarrass and fatigue her." Wharton guessed it was from trying to restrain herself from playing the hostess: "She appeared to feel that she ought to be directing the conversation, signing to the butler to refill the wine-glasses, trying to reshape the groups into which the guests had drifted after dinner."

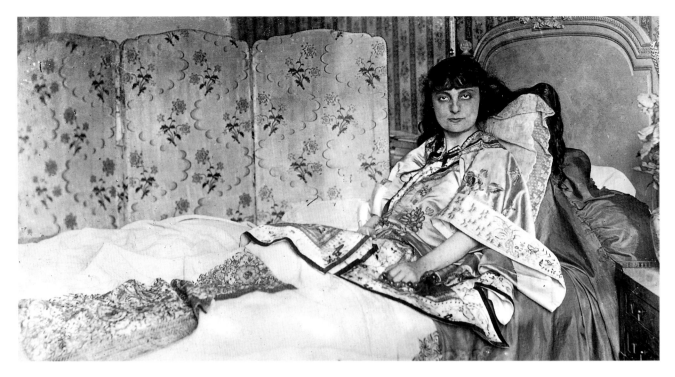

Repressing this impulse was so tiring "that she always fled early, with an apologetic murmur."

Despite Rosa's idiosyncrasies, she and Edith would remain friends, and they saw each other often. Wharton's diary for 1908 includes more than twenty occasions together—sometimes just the two of them but usually with other guests for dinner or the theater. Before the war, the two women even took a motor trip together in Spain with their friend Jean du Breuil de Saint Germain, but it was not a success. Spain was "all really so glorious & amazing & deep & dense, & cuts such long vistas in so many different directions," but, as Wharton complained to Daisy Chanler, her traveling companions weren't able to respond to her need to share her feelings evoked by childhood memories of the trip with her parents.

In 1908 Wharton also saw a lot of Comtesse Jane d'Oilliamson, whom she had made friends with as a child while in Cannes during her father's last illness. The comtesse translated Wharton's short stories for publication in a Paris literary magazine; she sometimes came over after dinner and they would work late into the night.

A new acquaintance was the Comtesse Anna de Noailles. They had first met in 1906 through Paul Bourget and were brought together again in 1908 at one of Rosa de Fitz-James's dinner parties. Anna de Noailles was also a celebrated writer, the irrepressible star of the Parisian literary world since the turn of the century. Beautiful and lively, brilliantly dressed, intellectual but emotional, outspoken, and self-centered, she charmed most everyone. Wharton

Anna de Noailles, one of the three women Wharton met who she felt had the real gift of conversation

was instantly attracted to Noailles and to her poetry, a personal communion with nature, romantic and pagan in spirit, which Wharton compared favorably to that of Walt Whitman, one of her favorite poets.

She and Wharton eventually drifted apart as their other interests pulled them in different directions. By the time Wharton wrote her memoirs, she remembered the poet as a great talker, whose conversation "resembled the most expensive fireworks." An exasperated Noailles in-law is said to have complained, "She starts quoting Plutarch the moment she comes into the room, and I can't allow that sort of thing in my house." Wharton may have shared this exasperation on occasion: "I do not remember ever seeing Madame de Noailles, the poetess, at Madame de Fitz-James," she wrote. "Poets are usually shy of salons, and so are monologuists like Madame de Noailles, whose dazzling talk was always intolerant of the slightest interruption."

Another new friend, to whom Wharton was drawn immediately, was l'Abbé Mugnier, a regular at the Fitz-James salon and a celebrity himself within Faubourg society. Dressed in sandals, worn soutane, and archaic tricorn hat, he was a welcome guest in every house and was often called on for confession, advice, and consolation. The Duchesse de Noailles, aware of his friendship with her daughter-in-law Anna, once consulted him. He was bemused by her concerns: "The old duchess is simply content to see Matthew [her son] and his wife under the same roof! 'One must keep up appearances,' she told her son. She cannot conceive of a divorce among the Noailles." Knowing Anna, he concluded, "Evidently this mother-in-law has no influence whatsoever over her daughter-in-law."

Writing later, Edith remembered l'Abbé Mugnier's profound kindness and keen intelligence, also "his quick sense of fun and irony," which was "so lined with tender human sympathy that the good priest is always visible behind the shrewd social observer." L'Abbé Mugnier's active social life and catholic intellectual attitudes vexed his superior, the archbishop of Paris, and he was eventually removed as vicar of his church, Sainte Clothilde. He continued, however, to find his way back to the houses of his friends in the Faubourg Saint-Germain. His guardian angels were the beautiful Comtesse de Castries (about whom the archbishop had complained when she was the widowed Mme. de Contades) and Princesse Marthe Bibesco, another of the lively French writers of the Belle Epoque. The Comtesse de Castries provided the exiled abbé a car and chauffeur to get him to and from the Faubourg and a secretary to help with his letter writing.

At Rosa's, Edith met her neighbors the Comte and Comtesse d'Haussonville (both were models for Proust, he for the Duc de Guermantes, she for the Marquise de Cambremer), and through Bourget she met Charlotte de Cossé-Brissac and her constant companion, Gustave Schlumberger, who were also good friends with the Berensons. Charlotte was witty and attractive, emancipated and adventurous. At Blanville, just south of Chartres, she entertained at the ancestral château of her late husband's family, where she had redone the formal gardens. Schlumberger was a distinguished archaeologist and a large man "who looked like a descendant of one of the Gauls on the arch of Titus," according to Wharton, who liked him.

In addition to those who lived there, many of Wharton's friends and acquaintances visited her in Paris. Between 1909 and 1911, Bernard Berenson was in and out of the city often, doing business for the Duveens and enjoying himself, and he became a regular among Wharton's new Paris set. Among those who also passed through were Egerton Winthrop, James Van Alen, Moncure Robinson, the Bayard Cuttings, William Richardson, Eliot Gregory, her publisher Charles Scribner, the Giraud Fosters, and, in April 1910, Theodore Roosevelt.

Roosevelt had left the White House in 1909, and, after eleven months traveling and hunting in Africa, he visited Austria-Hungary, England, France, Belgium, Holland, Italy, Germany, and Scandinavia giving speeches and meeting with kings, queens, and crowds of interested Europeans. He had written

Theodore Roosevelt at the American Embassy in Paris, April 1910

to Robert Bacon, the new American ambassador, to arrange a visit with Wharton in Paris. On April 25 she asked him to tea at 53 Rue de Varenne, along with Jules Jusserand, André Tardieu, Victor Bérard, André Chevrillon, the Comte d'Haussonville, Morton Fullerton, and others. Wharton wrote Fullerton that no women were invited: "He is as averse as you to social life." Teddy, who was not at all well, made the effort to appear "out of regard for Mr. R[oosevelt]."

The president was impressed with Fullerton and wrote later, "What an able fellow he is!" Roosevelt hoped he would come to the reception at the embassy the next day. Fullerton did not because he felt that, in the "Embassy crush," he would have "fumbled with my ideas, and undone the impression made at the Wharton tea." He wrote later that Edith was "disappointed, almost indignant, and thought me a fool."

Percy Lubbock recalled his visits to the Wharton apartment in the Rue de Varenne: "It seemed, with the passing days, a fortress of beauty and security to be lodged in, as the guest surrendered to the calm attention of the household, the soundless regularity of the ministrations to his ease."

The early morning hours, when Edith sequestered herself to write—"a gay little note thrown off as it were between chapters, would appear for the guest on his breakfast-tray, with a greeting and a plan for the day"—were for the guest a choice opportunity to do beautiful work of his own "in such a fostering atmosphere: in this exquisite little study, for example, overlooking the quiet cité, where the writing table is stocked . . . with everything imaginable to tempt a writer's hand—if that could fire his brain."

Percy Lubbock, 1906

Lubbock described the morning walk, which Wharton never liked to miss. Off they would go,

> briskly stepping out through the cool grey streets, away to the river, the bridge—to that other Paris which seems . . . to tick and click so neatly in the clockwork of its morning industry. No aimless loitering for anybody and certainly not for us; it is a precise round that we follow, with an errand to be accomplished in its place. The errand, I must say, was apt to prove, without warning, to be Edith's appointment with her tailor or her dentist, and you find yourself suddenly left in a doorway for an unspecified term; these people who live by the clock keep time for themselves, and when the companion drops out of the *horaire* he must hang in suspense till it includes him again. I think we most of us remember that we have waited for Edith in a good many doorways— till she reappears, without explanation or embarrassing apology, and we resume the time-table together and trip home to lunch.

Wharton was always changing her apparel; Lubbock remembered that "her things never seemed suitable for two consecutive occasions." And the food was perfect: "'I must warn you,' Henry James had said to me, in thoughtful reminiscence, on the eve of my first visit to the Rue de Varenne, 'against the constant succession, in our dear Edith's hospitality, of succulent and corrupting meals.' They were his words, and I couldn't improve them."

When she returned to Paris from Lenox in the summer of 1909, Wharton stayed at the Hotel Crillon on the Place de la Concorde, her refuge between apartments that year and at the start of the war. Each time she moved her

The Hotel Crillon (shown here in the left background) had opened in 1907, nine years after its arch rival, the Ritz. Wharton preferred the Crillon and made fun of the Ritz, calling it the "Nouveau Luxe" in her fiction.

The Hotel Crillon breathed history, elegance, and power. Housed in parts of two old palaces, masterpieces of eighteenth-century architecture designed by Jacques Gabriel, a celebrated architect, it was constructed on an order issued by Louis XV in 1758. The rooms were sumptuously and appropriately appointed, the walls hung with tapestries. The Place de la Concorde—one of the most famous squares in Paris—was the site of victory parades, funeral processions, and the arrival of sovereigns. It was one of Edith Wharton's favorite "places" imbued with history and meaning.

household in later years, she would set up temporary housekeeping at the Crillon. It was her home away from home.

In 1909 she wrote John Hugh Smith from the Crillon, "Here I am again, in a very nice apartment up in the sky, overlooking the whole of Paris." She had found a new apartment, "nearly opposite 58 rue de Varenne [at 53]"—looking "south over the Cité de Varenne & the Doudeauville Gardens." She took Henry Adams up to see the new quarters, not yet occupied, and he reported, "Of course it was in a state of total confusion, but I could see enough of it to make me vastly envious of that devotion to the Rue de Varennes which would sacrifice so much in order to live there." January 1910, when she moved into the new apartment, marked the beginning of her permanent transfer from America to France.

That same month, a natural disaster struck Paris: the Seine flooded for the first time since 1746. Unprecedented rains had been falling south of Paris since January 15. By the time the flood crested on January 28, a vast, malodorous lake covered half of Paris. The metro was flooded, the bridges submerged in a roaring torrent. The waters reached almost to the door of 53 Rue de Varenne. Wharton watched the Comtesse de Fitz-James's footman get to her front door in a rowboat. "Fifty thousand refugees sheltered in public buildings, while President Fallières tasted soup in improvised kitchens, congratulated the society ladies who cooked it, and talked sympathetically to cheering victims. . . . Sewers burst in the streets, or rose hideously in cellars, and rats fled through the boulevards. Plank bridges for pedestrians were built along the main thoroughfares, looters were ducked by infuriated crowds, and the police interrupted, in the nick of time, a lynching on the Pont d'Ivry."

Three times in February the river rose again. Edith wrote to Lizzie Cameron how she "managed to keep quite dry in the rue de Varenne, & to pre-

The Rue de Constantine, where Rosa de Fitz-James lived, during the flood of 1910

serve our electricity & telephone, so we have not had a moment's discomfort.—
Paris is sad to see, as you may imagine, & it will be months before the ravages
are repaired. If it could only have happened in Omaha!" She found her new
apartment "a Paradise! No earthly epithet would do justice to its merits. It is
as pretty as it is comfortable, & so flooded with sun that I have had to rush to
Audrain for awnings."

These crowded years in Paris were some of the most productive of Wharton's
life. In the early morning hours, while her houseguests entertained themselves,
she wrote religiously. All the feelings associated with her transplanting herself
to France and her complicated relationships fueled her fiction. After her affair
with Fullerton, she was able to describe strong, vital relationships and all the

feelings associated with love—possessiveness, jealousy, sadness, rejection, and bliss. Sexual passion became her subject for some time. As Judith Fryer writes: "By 1911 the affair was over, but this newly experienced passion would give an increased range and depth to her fiction, and her characters, from this point on, would have alternatives to entrapment, even if they did not use them or made bad use of them."

She made Paris the setting for a number of her fictional works—*Madame de Treymes, The Reef,* and *The Custom of the Country,* as well as several short stories in which she addressed her feelings of loyalty to America, her impressions of Americans in Paris, and her respect for French culture.

In her novella *Madame de Treymes* (1907), she makes obvious comparisons between French and American manners. It was written before she met her many new French friends, and it seems more about James's *The American* than about Faubourg society. John Durham looks out on the Tuileries Gardens to see the "vast and consummately ordered spectacle of Paris," which appears to have been planned "as a background for the enjoyment of life, instead of being forced into grudging concessions to the festive instincts, or barricading itself against them in unenlightened ugliness like his own lamentable New York." In this novella, the French aristocrats are sophisticated and devious. John Durham wants to marry Fanny Malrive, who has been separated from her French husband for years, but he cannot extricate her from a powerful and scheming family represented by clever Madame de Treymes, who does not play the game according to open, American rules.

In *The Custom of the Country,* the chronicle of the mad, energy-filled midwesterner Undine Spragg, Wharton took on French and American mores with new enthusiasm. She had begun the novel at the Mount in 1907, and she worked on it until 1913. The materialistic, immensely ambitious Undine (who might be a heroine of the 1980s) tears back and forth across the Atlantic looking for the good life but with none of the subtleties, the complexities, the nuances of meaning that Wharton and her group cherished. Although Undine is culturally antithetical to Edith Wharton, she has, as a critic has pointed out, the same energy and talent for conquering new worlds.

The novel is sharpened by Wharton's satirical treatment of the wealthy and pretentious, for example, Popple the portrait painter, whom everyone in the world of fashion wants to sit for because he paints pearls so well. At this time, when Wharton was transplanting herself to France, she was voicing anti-American sentiments to justify her move. She associated America with materialism, greed, fascination with business, and money-making and France with deeper, finer values.

Wharton managed to insert an expository essay on the differences between French and American marriages: "Why does the European woman

interest herself so much more in what the men are doing? Because she's so important to them that they make it worth her while! She's not a parenthesis, as she is here— she's in the very middle of the picture." In America, "all the romantic values are reversed. Where does the real life of most American men lie? In some woman's drawing-room or in their offices? The answer's obvious, isn't it? The emotional centre of gravity's not the same in the two hemispheres. In the effete societies it's love, in our new one it's business. In America the real *crime passionnel* is a 'big steal'— there's more excitement in wrecking railways than homes."

This American girl shows her worst qualities to the French when she tries to sell the priceless Boucher tapestries that have been in her French husband's family for generations. Her husband despairs that, like other rootless and homeless Americans, Undine "can never understand about the things that make life decent and honourable for us." Undine does manage to get the tapestries, as her soul mate and former husband, Elmer Moffatt, reappears to rescue her from her latest entrapment and appoints himself the next person to try to gratify her consuming appetites.

In *The Reef,* which she finished in August of 1912, Wharton worked and reworked her feelings about her affair with Morton Fullerton. Her central character is Anna Leath, an old New Yorker about Wharton's age who has had

*Above left:* Walter Gay's *Open Window* overlooks the courtyard of the Château du Bréau, Seine et Marne, France, where the Gays lived.

*Above right:The Long Gallery* at Château Courances by Walter Gay

a disappointing early marriage and now, in the middle of her life, hopes for a second chance at happiness with George Darrow, whom she knew as a girl. She had married her first husband because she was dazzled by his expatriate style and possessions: "In the atmosphere of West Fifty-fifth Street he seemed the embodiment of a storied past. . . . That she should be so regarded by a man living in an atmosphere of art and beauty, and esteeming them the vital elements of life, made her feel for the first time that she was understood." Yet she finds that she has been deceived by surfaces, that Fraser Leath, like James's Gilbert Osmond, is an effete collector, conventional and cold, and his beautiful French château, Givré, is a house of loneliness.

Ultimately Darrow betrays Anna and she cannot forgive him. In the scenes of doubt and hurt and forgiveness and trying to start over, Wharton wonderfully shows the reality of betrayal and the feelings it generates. Anna alternates between feelings of outrage and jealousy and of forgiveness. Near the end of the novel, she looks back at her own past "through the tears of disenchanted passion. . . . There it lay before her, her sole romance, in all its paltry poverty, the cheapest of cheap adventures, the most pitiful of sentimental blunders." She longs to be with Darrow and love him, but she cannot because he is inseparable from her sense of betrayal at his duplicity and the jealousy his past generates.

Wharton wrote *The Reef* around a large wonderful old house in Burgundy, the habitat of expatriates who were drawn to the ambience and elegance of the old place. It was perhaps modeled after the Château Courances—where she went to stay with her friend the Marquise de Ganay—or Blanville, the home of Charlotte de Cossé-Brissac's family, or the Château du Bréau, owned by the Walter Gays. Although Henry James criticized the French setting as inappropriate, the château, filled with its anxious inhabitants, allowed Wharton to evoke characters all caught up in a tangle together, who take constant walks down to the river, into the woods, around the property, as if to try to find ways to escape.

*The Reef*'s Givré is a wonderful example of how Wharton used architecture symbolically in her novels. In *The House of Mirth*, she had depicted Lily Bart's experience in architectural terms—starting her off at Bellomont and finishing her sad story in the boardinghouse room. Now Givré reflects Anna Leath's story. It sums up the different stages in Anna's experience, suggesting both a life of romantic possibilities and a life imprisoned and limited. When she became engaged, "the mere phrase 'a French château' had called up to her youthful fancy a throng of romantic associations, poetic, pictorial and emotional; and the serene face of the old house seated in its park among the poplar-bordered meadows of middle France, had seemed, on her first sight of it, to hold out to her a fate as noble and dignified as its own mien."

The château at first was a projection of her fantasies onto an outward symbol. Later, "the house had . . . become to her the very symbol of narrowness and monotony," reflecting her disappointment with her marriage to her rigid husband. "Then, with the passing of years, it had gradually acquired a less inimical character, had become, not again a castle of dreams, evoker of fair images and romantic legend, but the shell of a life slowly adjusted to its dwelling: the place one came back to, the place where one had one's duties, one's habits and one's books, the place one would naturally live in till one died: a dull house, an inconvenient house, of which one knew all the defects, the shabbiness, the discomforts, but to which one was so used that one could hardly, after so long a time, think of one's self away from it without suffering a certain loss of identity." Finally, the château and the inner life of the character seem to merge in a symbolic unity as Anna passes from the romanticism of youth through disillusionment and into an appreciation of reality. Louis Auchincloss writes that

> the role of Givré is justified simply by Mrs. Wharton's ability beautifully
> to delineate it. It is the best of all the wonderful houses in her fiction,
> shimmering in color yet clear of line, like an early impressionist canvas,
> or like a painting by Walter Gay, . . . As the story unfolds we see Givré
> in different lightings. We see [it] . . . first in the light of a mild October
> afternoon, the breadth of its grassy court "filled with the shadow and
> sound of limes." We see its garden at noon when the sunlight sheets
> with gold "the bronze flanks of the polygonal yews." We see it in the
> deep blue purity of a mistless night when the moon blanches "to unnat-
> ural whiteness the statues against their walls of shade."

Wharton also used the house to show how the past and the present intermingle. When George Darrow stands framed in the doorway of the farthest drawing room, and moves toward Anna "down the empty pale-panelled vista, crossing one after another the long reflections which a projecting cabinet or screen cast here and there upon the shining floors," he suddenly is displaced in her mind by the figure of her husband, now dead, "whom, from the same point, she had so often seen advancing down the same perspective. . . . Fraser Leath used to march toward her through the double file of furniture like a general reviewing a regiment drawn up for his inspection."

Written in Paris though not set there, *Ethan Frome* (1911), with its descriptions of love, rivalry, dependency, and disappointed hopes, reflects many of Wharton's emotional experiences, including the feeling of being controlled by other people's illnesses. During the time she was writing the novel, Henry James was deeply depressed, as was Teddy, and she felt she was taking care of both of them. Although she was still married to Teddy, she longed to be free to enjoy her love for Fullerton. For *Ethan Frome* she also went back to her memories of early rivalries and attachments in her family, when she saw herself as her father's little darling.

In this story, Wharton created a nightmarish triangle of characters. Ethan is sensitive, intelligent—a potential artist, or even a hero—yet he lacks the emotional strength to pull himself out of the little village of Starkfield and go to Florida to create the new life he dreams of. When he falls in love with Mattie, his wife's cousin, who has come to help on their poor farm, he gains new strength and happiness. His jealous wife, Zeena, insists that Mattie leave, and he becomes trapped between the woman who inspires him and the woman who drains him. A failed suicide attempt leaves both Ethan and Mattie maimed and in the hands of Zeena, who, now that she has a power over them, becomes capable and strong, swapping roles with Mattie, the new whiny invalid.

In returning to Massachusetts for her setting, Wharton had another ax to grind. As she said later in *A Backward Glance,* she had for a long time felt that the writing of the local colorists wasn't realistic. Her own vision of "life as it really was in the derelict mountain villages of New England . . . [was] utterly unlike that seen through the rose-coloured spectacles of my predecessors, Mary Wilkins and Sarah Orne Jewett." Jewett's tales—*The Country of the Pointed Firs* and others—and the fiction of Mary E. Wilkins Freeman describe strong, capable heroines, connected to the land as farmers and gardeners and interpreters of its beauty, who delight in family and community despite their loneliness. Wharton showed a grimmer side of rural life in *Ethan Frome*.

Her version of the New England countryside used as the setting is her beloved western Massachusetts landscape, but not as perceived by the wealthy estate owner who looked over carefully maintained flower beds at idyllic views of fields, woods, and hills during the summer months. It is the landscape of the "snow-bound villages of Western Massachusetts . . . grim places, morally and physically: insanity, incest and slow mental and moral starvation were hidden away behind the paintless wooden house-fronts of the long village street, or in the isolated farm-houses on the neighbouring hills." It is the same landscape that Charles Eliot Norton described to Ruskin in 1873—where life on the farms was too "lonely, too hard, too monotonous" for the bright young people.

Wharton had known of a sledding accident in Lenox involving five local teenagers in which one was killed and two badly hurt; she knew one of the victims, Kate Spencer, who had worked at the library. Perhaps she also remembered another image of a "smash up," which had come to her when she was missing Fullerton desperately. On June 5, 1908, she had written him from the Mount: "This is one of the days when it is more than I can bear . . . 'almost,' since I am here & the lake is là-bas—& I *am* bearing it. But just now, when I

heard that the motor, en route for Hâvre, had run into a tree & been smashed (bursting tire), I felt the wish that I had been in it, & smashed with it, & nothing left of all this disquiet but a 'coeur arrêté.' . . . So the total result seems to be that I, who always took life on its own terms, now want it only on mine!"

Disappointing sales of *Ethan Frome* contributed to the necessity of selling the Mount. The sale took place in June 1912. With the Mount gone, Edith's separation from Teddy became final (their divorce was granted on April 16, 1913), as did her estrangement from America.

She rationalized her move in letters to Sally Norton: "One is so consoled & nourished by all the quiet beauty of the old countries, & by the richness of reference that feeds one's imagination at every turn. The most earnest self-searching will *not* discover in me the least regret for having left America. I would go back there tomorrow to live if I thought it necessary, & get many things out of my life there; but I *shouldn't like it*, & I like everything—almost!—here."

She now began a series of mad travels that cut a wide swath across Europe. In October 1911, needing the support of old friends, she and Walter

*Pages 172–74:*
While traveling in Italy in October 1911, Edith Wharton and Walter Berry sent a series of postcards to Henry James.

*Above:* From Verona, October 9: "Parma, Sabbioneta, Mantua—and *this*! Just off to Vicenza now. I hope the Neo-Paddington surpasses the original as far as the new 50 h. p. Mercedes excels our plodding Hortense. Come & see!!!—E.W."

*Below:* From Petrarch's House, Arquà Petrarca, October 11 (in Berry's hand): "Without the Worm the Beaks are growing starker, / The more so in This Room; and if Petrarca / Could live again he'd sing: 'We want the aura / Of Henry more than all the lure of Laura!' / Arquà, Oct. 11 / W.B. / E.W."

RAVENNA - Chiesa dei SS. Giovanni e Paolo
*(Campanile del VI secolo)*

From Ravenna, October 13: "In such a place, in ties unholy, / How could he live with La Guicciole?— / Between the Exarchate & Guicciole / Compelled to make a choice, oh which shall he / Forsake forever?—No less grave / *Our* problems by this sad sea wave:— / Th' Italian accent's wilful truancy / Is *such* a check upon our fluency! / E.W. / W.B."

From Rimini, October 15: "A flashing word to mark the giro's gesta / Merceding through the land of Malatesta / Hoping the Trin will not forget the Gemini / But send a counter-thought from Rye to Rimini.     W.B.     E.W."

Berry had traveled to Italy. They urged James to join them, but he declined, so they sent him postcards regularly.

In the summer of 1912, escapes to friends' houses made things bearable for a time—she had been with the Bourgets and Berensons in Avignon and then gone to Genoa, Lerici, and Florence to stay with the Berensons—but she returned to Paris because she found it "impossible to hire a good typewriter but in big towns (& difficult there), so I thought I had better come back here to my own. As the weather is very cool and pleasant & I get out of here every afternoon in the motor there is no hardship in being here at present, & I have my books, & a few friends in or near Paris—the Du Bos at La Celle St. Cloud, the Huberts at Marly, etc." She traveled again the following summer—including a trip to Sicily with Berry—but wrote from Cologne: "By next year I hope I shall have a small place of my own somewhere, for I detest these midsummer roamings."

In August 1913, Wharton and Bernard Berenson toured Germany together. He had come into her life just when she was beginning to realize that Morton Fullerton must find his way out of it. The roller coaster of emotions she had been experiencing with Fullerton, as well as with Teddy's and Henry

RIMINI - Tempio Malatestiano.
S. Sigismondo in trono e Sigismondo Pandolfo Malatesta genuflesso.
(Piero della Francesca).

James's illnesses, was overwhelming. One can suspect that some of the longing and passion awakened by Fullerton was absorbed by Berenson, who was ready to be the comrade she then needed.

Although she thought Fullerton "wanted me to write what was in my heart," to Berenson she wrote what was in her mind or before her eyes. They had a great gift in common—the gift of "seeing"—and what distinguishes her letters to BB are the dazzling descriptions of where she had been and what she had seen. In a typical letter, written in 1912, she told him: "I almost cried when you describe your emotions at the descent from the Passo dell'Aprica to the Valtellina. It is the most beautiful scene in Italy to me—perhaps because I was so happy when I saw it." In 1913, on her return from Sicily, she wrote: "I'm coming back with my mental and visual trunks so full that the left-outs are not bothering me. I don't think I could have squeezed in much more!" And from Paris in 1917, " 'I need you every hour.' You're the one person who understands everything—*from the centre all round to the sea.*' "

Most women who were attracted to Berenson, however, were attracted to him physically, as he to them, and the result would likely range from a brief encounter to a prolonged love affair. Yet despite the intensity of their first meetings in Paris during the waning of her love affair with Morton Fullerton (to hear Berenson tell it years later), they were never lovers.

In fact, BB's wife, Mary Costelloe Berenson, also became an intimate. She had been sharing BB's life for fifteen years and would remain his devoted soul mate throughout all the bumps of their relationship. In 1912 Mary spent three days in Paris at Edith's apartment, without BB, and Wharton shared with her the manifestations of Teddy's mental illness. Mary wrote to her mother-in-law, "Mr. Wharton's mania leads him to buy houses and motors for music-hall actresses, to engage huge suites in hotels and get drunk and break all the furniture and to circulate horrible tales about his wife."

And Mary gave her own family a sympathetic report about the great Mrs.

From I Tatti, October 17: "Climbing cliffs & fording torrents / Here we are at last in Florence, / Or rather perching on the piano / Nobile, at Settignano. / Doing picture galleries? No, sir! / Motoring to Vallombrosa, / Pienza, Siena, tutte quante, / High above the Dome of Dante; / Then (compelled by the busy lawyer) / Back to France by a scorciatoia. / E.W.—W.B.—"

Edith Wharton wrote Berenson on August 10, 1912, from Pouges-les Eaux: "Falsefleeting Bernhard, From this very dim Naxos, Ariadne sends her pardon to her deceiver!—Only she rather wishes you wouldn't flaunt the guilty splendours of Carlsbad in the face of the lady you deserted to enjoy them. If you could see Naxos, you'd appreciate your cruelty.

"My news is brief & uninteresting. I spent three weeks in England with Howard S., Henry J. & the Cliveden-Astors. Then three days with les Blanches near Dieppe, ten in the rue de Varenne waiting for my book & the rain to finish (wh. only the former did); & then I came here."

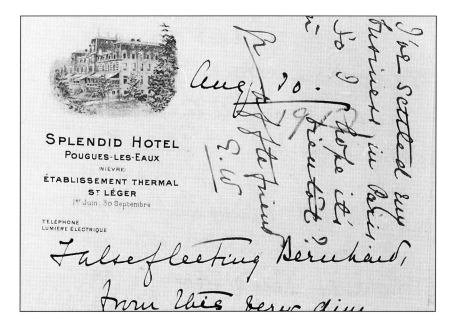

Wharton: "Mrs. Wharton is really very nice, so easy to get on with. Indeed she is more *our* sort than most people—more than any Latin person could *possibly* be. Our past is the same as hers, a tempered New Englandism, and she has never quite got over the Henry Jamesy sense of contrast. . . . She *is* heavy-handed, but when you like her it becomes rather endearing. I think she is a very good friend to her friends."

One could wonder what Mary had in mind writing her Quaker family about someone "more our sort than most people," when she had left her first husband and their small daughters to take up a most unconventional life with hardly "our sort" of man—a Jew born in Lithuania. But of course what Mary meant by "our sort" were the brainy expatriates who had grown up in or had known America after the Civil War and then had come to Europe searching for an atmosphere of the fine and beautiful that America's plunge into the modern world seemed to have discarded.

Like Wharton, Berenson depended on income earned as a professional and, with Mary's help, worked hard to earn it by handling an enormous volume of requests for art opinions—in one year, 137 from the Duveen firm alone—and by constantly adding to his precious store of knowledge the seminal lists he and Mary put together, aiming to catalogue all the Italian painters and their paintings by inspecting all candidates personally, wherever they could be found: hidden away in Italian churches, palaces, and villas, or in museums and private collections throughout Europe and America.

When Berenson and Wharton went to Germany together in 1913, Wharton had just finished *The Custom of the Country* and was corresponding with Scribner's about the proofs. She was exhausted yet delighted to be in Ger-

*Letter from Edith Wharton to Berenson from La Bourboule, September 11, 1912: "Ariadne Avenged is my name, but I'm really a poor forgiving Christian. . . . [I] have now come to this hideous village simply because it gives me a new motoring centre on the same level & I want to swallow all the high air I can—"*

many—after "the yearning of a life time" she had at last made it to "Goethe Country." She and Berenson were reading Werther. She told him, "What a voice and how new it must have sounded in 1774. Even now it is clarion like in its freshness."

Berenson found his traveling companion alternately infuriating and charming. She was accompanied by her customary entourage: Cook, the chauffeur; her agent, White; a maid; and her little dog, Nicette. Berenson felt that her cushioned way of life deprived her of many experiences: since she could not conceive of taking a glass of water anywhere but at a hotel, she could never wander around the streets and was distanced from all experience by her luxury. Although Berenson also enjoyed traveling first class, it was the first time he had come to Berlin as a "Ritzonian," and it reduced the city to "a place of museums, theatres, and drives" and therefore for him made it quite unreal.

Whenever they arrived at a hotel, Wharton would become disturbed by the arrangement of furniture in the rooms and the defects in the bathrooms. In Dresden, the fact that "in her room the bed was so placed that she would not

*Postcards from Wharton and Berry in France to Mary Berenson, April 1913: "For our first menu we venture to suggest: / Minestrone / Ravioloni / Polloni di Bressoni / Sparagoni / Articiocchoni / Formaggioni, / Ed altri generoni. Edith / W.B."*

*Above left:* Letter from Edith to BB while they were at Cologne in August 1913: "Dearest BB: Things are not brilliant this morning, & there is no doubt that I must lie up for a week anyhow.

"Come in & see me on your way out, & let us arrange whatever plan will least interfere with you. The motor will take you on your way, if you will first—this afternoon or tomorrow—drop me off somewhere in a greener & less malodorous spot. I waste no words over my despair—*you must know*—but I'm almost sure I can join you later on if it fits with your plans.          E.W."

*Above right:* Letter from Wharton and BB in Dresden to Mary Berenson, August 24, 1913: "Dearest Mary, We have had three such good days here that, in spite of the pictures & the music Berlin is holding out to us, I am sorry to be just jumping into the motor! Then the sun came out, & warmed our backbones for the first time, & it has been so delicious looking out from my windows at the Elbe, over the really Villa d'Esteau garden of this romantically situated hotel where only man & food are vile."

be able to read in the morning nearly drove her into hysterics. In fact she is often on the verge thereof."

Berenson witnessed the two sides of Wharton—that of the writer and of the perfectionist who always had to be "situated" in a particular way in relation to the world. Places were charged with significance. She could easily suffer from the old feelings of entrapment or enclosure which she projected onto a room or a house. She set herself up in bed each morning and wrote on a writing board. She also loved to spend long intervals in bed reading books. Where the sunlight came from, therefore, was an important element of a suitable hotel room.

Although she was a fatiguing companion because she was so fussy about hotels, food, and waiters, and "a misdirection in the car makes her fall back in all but a faint," Berenson found her "such good company most of the time. Her sense of significant little things of human motive is as acute as of the best French people, and far better than of any other English-speaking person known to me." Later he wrote to Mary: "Her company is delightful. She is ready to talk & to listen on so many topics & nothing is too small for her if it be characteristic or significant or a point of contrast."

At Cologne, however, Wharton wrote, "the whole year's wave of fatigue seemed to roll over me again & I went to pieces & had to admit I wasn't up to such a long flight." So they retreated to Oberhof, a "green place" where she could "patch myself up." She had written to Berenson to "ask d'avance if you would so far modify our itinerary as to give me three or four days in some green woody *walky* place where I can recover my nerves before we attack the big towns? You see I'm essentially a country person, and pine in towns in summer; and when I'm rather overdone, as I am at present, the feeling becomes a phobia."

Yet while Edith was keen for her "Waldeinsamkeit" (sylvan solitude),

Berenson longed to examine paintings in the city galleries. As he told Mary in a letter from Dresden: "Yesterday P.M. we walked thro' the North Italian pictures together. It is clear art is a sealed book for her. She sees only that in the subject wh. appeals to her literary sense or better still that wh. happens to illustrate an anecdote within her range of interests."

During their trip in Germany, Wharton often exasperated him—"a meal scarcely goes by without her returning every dish"—but then she could also be "a simply enchanting companion. We sat through nearly four hours at the opera listening ecstatic and spellbound to Strauss's 'Rosenkavalier' and I felt that she was enjoying it as much & in the ways that I was, although she is always very much more keen about the situation & anecdote than I am." A critic has pointed out that, since the sexual element was kept out of their relationship, they could enjoy being friends, and they both preferred friends of the opposite sex. Their friendship thus embraced the contradictions in both of them.

Unfortunately, the trip to Germany provided only a brief respite for Wharton. A letter written on January 12, 1914, betrayed her harried condition. She had gone to New York for Beatrix Jones's wedding, which had taken place after Christmas of 1913, and she was relieved to be back home in France: "Oh the long breath I drew when I tumbled out of the NY maelstrom into my berth in the France, & thence, after a smooth reposeful trip, into the profounder quietness of the rue de Varenne! I'm very glad I went 'over' for that little glimpse, but hotel life in one's native place especially after as long an absence as mine is a soul-destroying thing, & I'm only just begining to piece my inward self together again." Her little group was diminished—Charles and Zezette du Bos were on the Riviera, the Walter Gays in America—"& I'm less & less disposed to make new acquisitions, to throw out feelers. So I've crawled into a kind of Esquimau hut." On New Year's Eve, 1913, she had written to Daisy (whose husband was recovering from a serious operation): "I'm so glad to hear such good news of Winty—What you *have* been through, my poor Daisy. I hope 1914 will make up. I don't feel as if anything *cd* obliterate 1913 for *me*!"

# THE GREAT WAR, "A CALAMITY UNHEARD OF IN HUMAN ANNALS"

Ordre de Mobilization Générale on a Paris wall. In villages throughout France, the *tocsin,* the ringing of the church bells, alerted the men and frightened the women.

When Archduke Franz Ferdinand of Austria and his wife, Sophie, were assassinated at Sarajevo on June 28, 1914, Edith Wharton, like most Europeans, had already made summer vacation plans, "a quick dash to Barcelona and the Balearic Islands," for the most part by motorcar with Walter Berry in her usual style. She had also rented a house, Stocks, near Henry James in Rye, to carry out at last "my life-long dream of a summer in England." Her household staff had closed the apartment in Paris and was already at Stocks preparing for her arrival.

At the end of July, Wharton and Berry were returning from Spain to Paris by motorcar. She wrote Bernard Berenson from Burgos on July 26, reporting on the trip. Her letter ends, "I shall be at the Crillon on the 31st for a night only, probably—then on to England." She hoped to find him in Paris "ready to come to Stocks with me!"

Then, as an afterthought, "The international news in this morning's paper here is pretty black. I wonder?"

Although Wharton and Berry had been out of touch, as it turned out they were to be eyewitnesses to the transition from peace to war. On July 30, north of Poitiers, they picnicked by the roadside under apple trees at the edge of a field: "The serenity of the scene smiled away the war rumours which had hung on us since morning." The night before, patriotic crowds had kept them awake.

Thunderclouds had banked the sky all day long, but by the time they reached Chartres in the afternoon, the town was saturated with sunlight. Inside the cathedral: "At first all detail was imperceptible: we were in a hollow night. Then, as the shadows gradually thinned . . . there burst out of them great sheets and showers of colour." Writing in 1915, Wharton rhapsodized over the experience: "All that a great cathedral can be, all the meanings it can express, all the tranquilizing power it can breathe upon the soul, all the richness of detail it can fuse into a large utterance of strength and beauty, the cathedral of Chartres gave us in that perfect hour."

They arrived in Paris at sunset. As they drove to the Hotel Crillon: "Under the heights of St. Cloud and Suresnes the reaches of the Seine trembled with the blue-pink lustre of an early Monet. The Bois lay about us in the stillness of a holiday evening, and the lawns of Bagatelle were as fresh as June. Below the Arc de Triomphe, the Champs Elysées sloped downward in a sunpowdered haze to the mist of fountains and the ethereal obelisk; and the cur-rents of summer life ebbed and flowed with a normal beat under the trees of the radiating avenues. The great city, so made for peace and art and all humanest graces, seemed to lie by her river-side like a princess guarded by the watchful giant of the Eiffel Tower."

The next day, Friday, July 31, Paris was "thundery with rumours." Everyone speculated. "War? of course there couldn't be war! The Cabinets, like naughty children, were again dangling their feet over the edge." Austria-Hungary had declared war against Serbia on July 28. That Friday, Russia ordered general mobilization. The next day, Germany declared war against Russia, and mobilization of the French Army began. Germany's declaration of war against France came on August 3, and Great Britain's declaration of war against Germany on August 4, after the German Army invaded Belgium (compelled to do so, as a German diplomat explained to the remonstrating British ambassador, in order to get into France "by the quickest and easiest way").

Saturday, August 1, Wharton watched the happenings from the Hotel Crillon. Her descriptions of the scene revolved around the architectural backdrop of her beloved Place de la Concorde, the center of the action.

The afternoon began quietly. Around 4 P.M. a few passersby stopped to read "a little strip of white paper" posted on the wall of the Ministère de la Marine on the Rue Royale (next to the Crillon on a corner of the Place de la Concorde). "The group about the paper was small and quiet." They were reading the order for general mobilization. "Like a monstrous landslide," Wharton wrote, "it had fallen across the path of an orderly laborious nation, disrupting its routine, annihilating its industries, rending families apart, and burying under a heap of senseless ruin the patiently and painfully wrought machinery of civilization. . . ."

By evening, strange new crowds flooded past the restaurant window on

Horses being requisitioned for the army. Millions of horses died during the Great War.

Motor vehicles requisitioned for the army. Taxis were exempted at the beginning; General Gallieni later commandeered them to move the Paris garrison to the front to make a critical attack during the Battle of the Marne.

the Rue Royale where Wharton and Berry were dining. Everyone was walking because the military had comandeered all buses. Most of the crowds were reservists, accompanied by wives, family, and friends, "carrying all kinds of odd improvised bags and bundles" on their way to the railway stations. Wharton's impression of the reservists was of a "cheerful steadiness of spirit . . . serious but not sad." Caught among them were bewildered tourists trying to get out of France, "their luggage pushed before them on hand-carts."

Wharton had little sympathy for the tourists and their "wild rushes to the station, bribing of concierges, vain quests for invisible cabs, haggard hours of waiting in the queue at Cook's," only to return to their fashionable hotels, like the Crillon, with their "resounding emptiness of porterless halls, waiterless restaurants, motionless lifts." What chiefly troubled them was that "they could get no money, no seats in the trains, no assurance that the Swiss frontier would not be closed before they crossed the border."

A unit of foreign volunteers marching through the Place de la Concorde. "Italian, Romanian, South American, North American," Wharton wrote, "each headed by its national flag and hailed with cheering as it passed."

Inside the restaurant where Wharton dined that Saturday evening, service was slow, because so few waiters were left to serve, and was made even slower by a Hungarian band, "befrogged and red-coated," who poured out patriotic music, thus putting on the diners "the ever-recurring obligation to stand up for the Marseillaise, to stand up for God Save the King, to stand up for the Russian National Anthem, to stand up again for the Marseillaise." One can imagine Wharton laughing at her own growing annoyance, as she bobbed up and down, waiting for the next course—she was notorious for complaining about less than perfect food or service—when she heard someone growl from outside the window: "Et dire que ce sont des Hongrois qui jouent tout cela [And to think it's a bunch of Hungarians who are playing that game]!"

As the evening wore on, the thickening crowds outside the restaurant window began to join in the war songs the band was playing. "Down the rue Royale, toward the Madeleine, the bands of other restaurants were attracting other throngs, and martial refrains were strung along the Boulevard like its garlands of arc-lights." Looking back later, Wharton concluded, "It was a night of singing and acclamations, not boisterous, but gallant and determined." All during this night, another crowd, moving with the reservists, streamed to the Gard du Nord and the Gard de l'Est, the stations for trains to the frontiers.

It was the beginning of the Great War, as those who lived through it came to call it. Wharton spent most of the time working in Paris—the target for bombs from German airplanes and zeppelins and, beginning in March 1918, shells from "Big Bertha" (she called it "Mme Laonnois"). Wharton came back one evening to find that a shell had landed in the courtyard of her former apartment at 58, Rue de Varenne.

In retrospect, the Great War turned out to be the unique catastrophe of Western history. The evil forces it let loose produced horrors on a scale most observers could not imagine during the extraordinarily beautiful summer of 1914. Yet some did. On Friday, July 31, the Archbishop of Canterbury preached in Westminster Abbey, "The thing which is now astir in Europe is not the work of God, but of the Devil." That same day, André Gide wrote in his journal, "We are getting ready to enter a long tunnel full of blood and darkness." On August 5, the day after Great Britain entered the war, Henry James prophesied that "the plunge of civilization into this abyss of blood and darkness" would be "too tragic for any words." On August 29, Ralph Curtis wrote Bernard Berenson: "I fear it will be a long & terrific carnage."

And so it was. By May 1915, James in England would write Wharton in Paris: "*Everyone* is killed who belongs to anyone here, & one looks straight and dry-eyed, hard & arid, at those to whom they belonged." And in November 1915, Wharton wrote that the war had grown into "a calamity unheard of in human annals."

The courtyard at 53 Rue de Varenne. Readers of *Fighting France* must have been startled by Wharton's descriptions of the women with dogs watching the men go off to war in the first days of August 1914. A fanatic dog lover herself, Wharton was pleased to note "the small but significant fact that every one of them had remembered to bring her dog"—a doubtful statistic, surely—"snugly lodged in the bend of an elbow" (like Wharton's Pekinese), from which "scores and scores of small serious muzzles, blunt or sharp, smooth or wooly, brown or grey or white or black or brindled, looked out on the scene with the quiet awareness of the Paris dog." For Paris going to war, "It was certainly a good sign," she lamely concluded, "that they had not been forgotten that night."

Her friend Jacques-Emile Blanche wrote about Wharton after her death: "During the war, Mrs. Wharton behaved splendidly on all occasions. She worked marvels, the gallantest, pluckiest among hundreds of women heroes, always optimistic, in high spirits, energetic, undefatigable—yet sometimes she looked on the verge of collapsing—we would call her Our American Field Marshal (as Joffre, or was it Foch?) described her after the war." Those who worked for her gave her other nicknames, "La Révèrende Mère" or "Madame, l'Intendante Générale," wrote Blanche, "because one could picture her at the head of a convent, of a hospital, of a factory, or bank."

In the days that followed the outbreak of the war, Paris changed before Wharton's eyes: "When an armed nation mobilizes, everybody is busy, and busy in a definite and pressing way. It is not only the fighters that mobilize: those who stay behind must do the same. For each French household, for each individual man or woman in France, war means a complete reorganization of life."

Wharton also reorganized her life. After the first few days in Paris, she ceased to be a spectator. She moved back into her apartment on the Rue de Varenne and, perhaps caught up by the spirit of the French reservists she had watched go to war, she too went to war for France in the most effective way an American woman could in Paris. She committed all her energy to the French cause until final victory more than four years later.

In her wartime work, Wharton displayed enterprise, common sense, and enormous energy. She drew on those reforming impulses she had expressed in *The Valley of Decision* and *The Fruit of the Tree*. In the strange way that Wharton's fiction often foresaw her life, the heroes of these novels—Odo Valsecca and John Amherst—sought to improve conditions for their people. That each person have a home was one of Wharton's most profound concerns, and she had a deep impulse to create good working and pleasant living conditions in other lives. She had done it for herself and her guests; now she helped unemployed Parisian women, and soon, French and Belgian refugees.

As Paris had been emptied of men who had gone into the army, hotels, restaurants, shops, and workrooms had closed and women and children were left destitute. The women needed work, so, in early August 1914, Wharton helped set up a workroom in a big empty flat in the Faubourg Saint-Germain. As she explained to Berenson:

Finding that no one had thought of coming to the help of the unemployed work-girls, I have opened a work-room where I feed them & pay them 1 fc a day. My companions (mostly unknown to me) have come to my aid, & we have 20 women working already, & I long to enlarge it & take in many more. The silly idiot women who have turned their drawing-rooms into hospitals (at great expense), & are now making shirts for the wounded, are robbing the poor stranded ouvrières of their only means of living, & the Red Cross is beginning to be severely criticized by the Syndicat du Travail for its immense work-rooms where femmes du monde do the work the others ought to have—so my "ouvroir" has excited a good deal of interest, & I hope we may get help to carry it on. So far we have about 2,800 fcs, which enables us to keep 30 women for about 2 months, perhaps more—

"Mme. Wharton's Ouvroir" was expanded to employ about sixty women, constantly turning over. It included several skilled seamstresses, so that "we decided to try for orders for fashionable *lingerie,* instead of competing with the other ouvroirs by making hospital supplies." They were soon doing a thriving business in "unexpected lines, including men's shirts (in the low neck Byron style) for young American artists from Montparnasse!"

Edith's first efforts to help the cause were interrupted by a trip to England at the end of August 1914, for which, like a stranded tourist, she personally went through the ordeal of obtaining the necessary papers. She wrote Bernard Berenson on August 22 with all the enthusiasm of beginning a holiday: "I'm coming over next week, next Thursday probably. I shall count on you *much* and *long* at Stocks." Wharton and her entourage with motorcar reached Stocks on August 27 and were met at the boat by Henry James, with whom they dined at Rye that evening.

Having crossed the channel with a stream of refugees, Wharton must have experienced something of what befell Charles Durand, her unassuming hero of "The Refugees" (1930), who managed to escape at the same time: "At Boulogne he found himself caught in the central eddy of fugitives, tossed about among them like one of themselves, pitched on the boat with them, dealt with compassionately but firmly by the fagged officials at Folkestone, jammed into a cranny of the endless train, had chocolate and buns thrust on him by ministering angels with high heels and powdered noses, and shyly passed these refreshments on to the fifteen dazed fellow travellers packed into his compartment."

Upon reaching Stocks, she realized that leaving Paris had been a mistake. She sought to justify herself to Sally Norton: "I hardly know with what feelings I sit down & write to you in this still & lonely place where I had dreamed of being so happy with my friends, & of seeing you among them! I am all alone here, & without the heart to ask any one to join me. I feel as if this immense burden of horror could best be borne alone for the present." (Yet Wharton was not completely alone; James, Percy Lubbock, and Gaillard Lapsley came to visit.) She explained that she had decided to leave her *ouvroir*

in the very capable hands of the young woman who founded it with me, & come over here for a few weeks' rest. My servants & luggage were all here, & I had been picnicking in the rue de V. with a bonne à tout faire & a maid; & I thought it seemed foolish not to enjoy Stocks for a while. I left, therefore, on the 27th, & the very next day came the dreadful news of the German advance & the probable siege of Paris, & I felt like a deserter! It was a perfect thunderbolt. I was seeing every day people in touch with the different ministries, & everyone thought the war would

Throughout the war, Pauline-Eulalie-Eugénie d'Harcourt, Comtesse d'Haussonville, was president of the Women's Central Committee of the Aid Society for Military Wounded. She chose Wharton to open the first charitable *ouvroir* in the Faubourg Saint-Germain.

be fought out in Belgium & on the northern border. You can understand how I feel—as if my co-workers must think I had planned my flight when I said I was going off for three or four weeks.

She tried to get back to Paris through the French Embassy (Ambassador Cambon was a friend). Meanwhile, somewhat quixotically, she wrote her landlady in Stocks, Mrs. Humphrey Ward, for permission to turn part of her house into a convalescent home. Then she exchanged residences with Mrs. Ward, moving into her London house to be nearer news of Paris, "for this loneliness in which I sit inactive seems to make things worse if the worst can be made worse." Cook and her car arrived back from France, bringing all kinds of news: "Cook says Paris is perfectly calm, & *the Russians are in France*. An Indian contingent has also arrived. Kitchener was in Havre for a day while, he, Cook, was waiting for his boat & presumably went to the front."

Cook and Wharton weren't the only ones spreading this Russian rumor. As the German armies thundered toward Paris, anxious civilians fell victim to a mass delusion. James wrote Wharton in August 30 that he had heard of "the passing through England in guarded secrecy these last 48 hours of a big Russian contingent shipped from Archangel landed at Aberdeen & now being injected into France by (presumably) Ostend. It is *much* corroborated—& though I hate premature crowing risk a faith in its making a difference! If it be true, however, we shall know nothing whatever of it until every man has been landed." Wharton replied at once, expressing reservations, and he in turn responded, enclosing "a regular gem of evidence," a photograph clipped from the *Daily Mail*. He asked Wharton to examine "the dress, the caps and the boots of the so-called Belgians" shown disembarked at Ostend: "If they are not straight out of the historic, or even fictive, pages of Tolstoy, I will eat the biggest pair of moujik boots in the collection." Plus, a friend of his had heard from a man who had a letter from a brother (or friend) saying trainloads of Russians

A workroom of one of Wharon's charities, probably a sewing class for older girls and women at a Children of Flanders hostel

had been passing through Sheffield and "they *are* a rum-looking lot!" Such an enormous quantity of "this apparently corroborative testimony from *seen trains*, with their contents stared at and wondered at, have within two or three days kept coming in from various quarters."

By September 3, an official denial from the War Office led James to concede that "the 'Russian' legend doesn't very particularly hold water," though he still was not fully convinced: "The only thing is that there remains an extraordinary residuum of fact to be accounted for. It seems difficult that there should have been that amount of variously-scattered hallucination, misconception, fantastication or whatever—yet I chuck up the sponge!"

Wharton reported to Berenson that Walter Berry intended to stay in Paris and attach himself to the U.S. Embassy if the Germans came. Like Wharton, he was totally committed to the cause of France, which meant doing everything to bring the United States into the war as her ally (he served as president of the American Chamber of Commerce in Paris from 1917 through 1923). He often helped Wharton in her war work, when she needed him; it was he who looked after the *ouvroir* in her absence that September.

The fate of Paris would not be determined until around September 7, as the "Miracle of the Marne" unfolded with attacks by the British Army and French Sixth Army in front of Paris on the right flank of Von Kluck's retreating German Army. Wharton got back soon afterward and wrote Sally Norton on September 27 from the Rue de Varenne, "I regret very much not having been in Paris during the week of the panic." She reported to BB that "most of the fluffy fuzzy people have gone, & the ones left are working hard & seeing each other quietly.—Last night Fullerton, Victor Bérard & W dined here, & we laughed till 11:30."

The repulse of the German forces around Paris was followed by a race to the sea between the British and German armies, resulting in a bloody dead heat around Ypres. By the end of 1914, "the grey reality of the trenches" gripped the armies facing each other from the North Sea to Switzerland. The French Army had already suffered more than 900,000 casualties.

The mood in France had changed radically. Many Americans who had enjoyed the Parisian life before the war went home. On July 26, 1914, Henry Adams had written from his home near Paris: "War seems now actually upon us. We must go home I suppose, and wait till peace," and he did. His friends Elsie de Wolfe, Anne Morgan, and Elizabeth Marbury were stranded in Spain and in Brides-les-Bains in Savoie, near the Italian border, when the war started in early August: their French chauffeurs, called up by general mobilization, abandoned them and went off to join the army; because passenger trains were recruited for transporting troops and they were unable to drive their own large motors, these women—formerly so mobile—became faced with new chal-

A great grandson of William Backhouse Astor, Captain Winthrop Chanler, Daisy Chanler's husband, had never worked in peacetime. Daisy called him "a born soldier"—he had fought and been wounded in the Spanish-American War. War for him was the "Great Adventure," and he served with distinction in the U.S. Expeditionary Force— "our little foot-ball team of an army" —on the French and Italian fronts, beginning as an aide to General William Walker, an old friend, "sportsmen both and ardent fox hunters." He wrote Daisy: "We walked along a road with a high wall on our right; a lot of bersaglieri were lying along under the wall waiting. The shells and shrapnel flew over us and cracked about us. I confess I was scared for the first time of my life—I really had the sensation of fear. I do not know why for I have been shelled before and shot at often. Perhaps, and very probably, there was loss of sleep and too much tobacco. As we walked by the bersaglieri I could hear them say 'Americani, Americani!' So I had to keep a stiff upper lip and look encouraged and not 'duck' when the shells passed over."

He wrote her about going to a dressing station to watch "the wounded brought, dressed and shipped in motor ambulances to rear hospitals. Some were badly hurt. It is a very good schooling for a soldier's nerves to look at wounded before breakfast. I can stand pretty near anything now."

lenges. They finally got themselves to Le Havre in Normandy, where they had tickets to sail for America in September (they returned later to join the French war effort). Meanwhile, casinos and hotels, formerly the playgrounds of the rich, were transformed into hospitals.

Many Americans who had been in France pressed urgently for the French cause once they reached home. Many others failed at first or even later to share Wharton's enthusiasm, from President Wilson, whom she often derided, to mothers fearful of sending their sons to slaughter, to Henry Adams, who wrote soon after the war started: "I have stiffly held my tongue and listened while everyone chatters, but as yet I see no light. I see none in the triumph of either party. If we wipe Germany off the map, it is no better."

Bernard Berenson's first reaction was that "Germany, not France, is fighting for Europe and Western civilization." He was incautious enough to express this opinion to Ralph Curtis, adding, "I am unable to contemplate the triumph of France without horror." Curtis replied indignantly, "You and Enver [Enver Pasha, pro-German leader of Turkey] appear to be the only friends the Kaiser has left," and added a postscript, "Hy Adams writes me with a sadly shakey hand that the Kaiser is insane." Adams reported to Elizabeth Cameron in November, "Even those who first talked German have shut up," as Berenson soon did. As an anti-German gesture, he took the "h" out of his first name, and, by June 1915, he was writing Wharton, "The will of nine tenths of Americans individually is to crush Germany at all costs." Berenson also tried but failed to mollify Curtis, who charged "Herr BB" that "you don't really believe in anything or anybody, so I for one limit my confidence in you."

Did Wharton ever learn about all this? Maybe. In her novel *A Son at the Front* (1923), just before the war starts, the artist Campton asks himself about his new patron, "the big banker and promoter" Jorgenstein: "But, if there were a war, on what side would a cosmopolitan like Jorgenstein turn out to be?"

Berenson eventually returned to Curtis's good graces, however; in 1918 he stayed in the Curtises' Paris apartment. By the end of the war, he was working for the United States, in effect as a spy, reporting on what people were saying in Paris salons. Henry James once ventured his impression that "humanly speaking," Edith Wharton was "worth six of BB."

Soon after her return to Paris, Wharton contacted Elisina Tyler to set up a meeting with her in Paris to discuss war work. They were social acquaintances: Elisina and her second husband, Royall Tyler, had once been invited to tea at 53 Rue de Varenne; they were in awe of their famous hostess. On October 11, Wharton wrote Tyler that she had just received her lovely reply, a postcard of a château: "It seems all to belong to that old world we used to know, so long ago—more than two months now!" She explained her feelings of helplessness in England and how she had rushed back to Paris to "plunge up to the chin in the managing of a work-room, which keeps me busy from dawn to dinner every day. It is awful to be quiet a minute, & think of the crashing ruins all around one, & I'm so glad to be absorbed in the price of sweaters and the cut of flannel shirts."

After their October meeting, almost overnight Tyler evolved into Wharton's partner in all her charitable enterprises. The bond between them grew to include the Tylers' infant son and, eventually, Elisina's baby grandson. The Tylers provided Wharton the family she never had, and Elisina's constant attentions gave her a sense of security.

They both worked flat out, pushing themselves to the limit physically and emotionally. Both followed the day-to-day operations of the various facilities, and, when one was on vacation, the other was writing almost daily to consult. Wharton, fiercely energetic herself, recognized Tyler's management skills and made no important decision without first getting her approval. The only serious misunderstanding between them came about when Tyler, in an unguarded letter written while Wharton was on vacation, seemed to have consented, on behalf of the enterprise, to turn over its operations to the American Red Cross. Wharton was shocked but even then used extraordinary tact in explaining to Tyler that only she and Walter Berry had the official power to make that sort of decision.

Wharton's war work had many facets, but its common theme was that if someone was in distress, she would respond. When the flood of refugees from Belgium and northern France overwhelmed Paris in the fall of 1914, she was recruited to help "these other people, dazed and slowly moving—men and women with sordid bundles on their backs, shuffling along hesitatingly in their tattered shoes, children dragging at their hands and tired out babies pressed against their shoulders: the great army of the Refugees."

Wharton and her friends agreed that "the first need was for some kind of a decent shelter for the poor creatures on their arrival. After that there would be time to try to provide for their future.

"In response to our appeal, generous friends put at our disposal three large houses, and the American Hostels for Refugees were founded, in connection with the already existing French committee, which had taken the name of 'Le Foyer Franco-Belge.' We had between us $500 in cash and a collection of more or less infirm furniture. We begged right and left for beds and blankets, we hired linen and cutlery, and within a fortnight we had opened two houses with beds for a hundred, and a third with a restaurant for 550 and a free clinic and dispensary—the latter as necessary as the beds and food, for the poor creatures we sheltered were almost all ill from hunger, fatigue and the horrors they had undergone."

Elisina Tyler, Wharton's partner in her war work and her close friend in the last years. She wrote Daisy Chanler about Elisina in 1926: "And I knew you wd like her, & understand her, better after seeing her chez Elle. When one gets past that funny little 1875 mincing manner there is much to be enjoyed & appreciated—& her fundamental qualities are admirable."

One hostel had a restaurant, a clinic, and a workroom staffed by 50 women (the number eventually grew to 120), "turning out clothes for our depot and also taking orders for hospitals," all operated at an expense of about $150 a month. A central bureau was set up in large offices, given by the Comtesse de Béhague, in the Champs Elysées. Among those who helped register, and distribute tickets for food, clothing, and lodging, were Wharton's friends Charles du Bos, the composer Darius Milhaud, Jacques-Emile Blanche, and André Gide. Geoffrey Scott and Percy Lubbock joined later.

The project drew on Wharton's organizational talents. While their mothers were sewing, the children played in a day nursery, a big pleasant room opening on a courtyard. "Then there is a singing class, and a class in designing, and we hope to start a sewing class before long. Another useful addition to our work is the English class for grown-ups, which is given free of charge at one of our hostels by the British Young Women's Christian Association and attended by the many young men and women among our refugees to whom English will, after the war, be a valuable business asset."

After Wharton and her group had taken care of shelter, clothes, and food for the refugees, they began to think of their future. They started an employment agency, and, by the end of the first year, they had found work for 3,400 refugees: "It is a figure to be proud of, for many refugees were small shopkeepers who knew no trade, others were familiar only with trades which the war has temporarily suspended, and many spoke only Flemish and were, therefore, of little use in any line." By the end of the first year this charity was running efficiently and Wharton could cite impressive statistics:

| | |
|---|---:|
| Refugees assisted | 9,229 |
| Meals served | 235,000 |
| Garments distributed | 48,333 |
| Refugees cared for at free clinic and dispensary | 7,700 |
| Refugees for whom employment has been found | 3,400 |
| Refugees receiving permanent assistance | 3,000 |

Wharton was as level-headed as any modern social worker in anticipating the problems some refugees were beginning to cause: "Finally there are immense numbers whom we have helped out by financial assistance, small sums to tide them over an emergency, or a weekly allowance to eke out the 25 cents a day the Government allows them. In many cases such timely help has enabled a man to get a job, a mother to provide proper food for a sick child, a peddler to buy the stock-in-trade for his hand cart.

"But we are now entering on our second year, with a larger number to care for, and a more delicate task to perform. The longer the exile of these poor

School of Lace-Makers for the Children of Flanders Rescue Committee.

bottle of medicine fur an invalid at home, or a bundle of cigarettes for a soldier. Nothing makes our women as happy as to send a little present to one of the friendless men at the front. When we are working for the trenches or the ambulances their fingers fly twice as fast, and I know that often their savings go

to find food and shelter. The first attempts to accommodate them were not systematic or successful, and in October a few French friends who had been trying to lend a hand in straightening out the confusion came to me for advice.

They were horrified at the misery they had seen, and they felt that the first

were familiar only with trades which the war has temporarily suspended, and many spoke only Flemish and were, therefore, of little use in any line.

go and see the results of the doing, a

Wharton described her war charities in "My Work among the Women Workers of Paris," for the *New York Times Magazine,* November 28, 1915.

people lasts, the more carefully and discriminately must we deal with them. They are not all King Alberts and Queen Elizabeths, as some idealists expected them to be. Some are hard to help, others unappreciative for what is done for them. But many, many more are grateful, appreciative, and eager to help us to help them."

Wharton's third charitable effort was organized in early 1915 as the Children of Flanders Rescue Committee, "my prettiest and showiest and altogether most appealing charity." As she reported to the *New York Times:*

> Last April the Germans suddenly began to shell the few remaining towns of uninvaded Belgium. . . . There was no military advantage to be gained by shattering Ypres, Poperinghe, Furnas, and the other beautiful old towns of Western Flanders. There was just so much beauty to be destroyed, there were so many more thousands of harmless civilians to be ruined or slaughtered, and so Germany did it.
>
> Well out of those awful ruins . . . poured hundreds and hundreds of little children. Some were picked up in the cellars of wrecked houses, some were living on offal in the bomb-swept streets, others were gathered in from abandoned farms, from burning villages, from the very trenches, and trainload after trainload of them came streaming into Paris last Spring. When the first detachment started the Belgian Government asked me to receive sixty of them—little girls—with the good Flemish Sisters in whose care they came. I called on a few friends to help; we were given a vacant house near Paris, and forty-eight hours later the sixty pitiful little creatures had come.

The Rescue Committee opened five houses in or near Paris to care for nearly 900 people, including the nuns and about 200 infirm, "old men and

Belle Alliance, the château in Groslay near Paris that housed a convalescent home for tubercular women and children

Children walking with the nuns at Belle Alliance

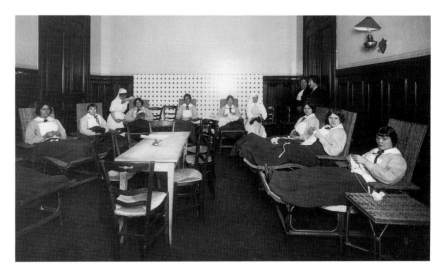

Recreation room for women at Belle Alliance

*Above left:* Refugee children from Flanders

*Above right:* Elderly refugees from Flanders at the hostel at Sèvres

women who are 'children' too, for the second time, and could not be left alone in the ruins." They started lace-making schools for the older girls, to give them a means of livelihood. They solicited funds for an industrial school for the boys. Wharton ended her *New York Times* article with the plea: "Help us! O all you happy peaceful people at home, if I could show you what we are seeing and hearing over here every day and every hour, I say again I should not have to beg of you: I should only have to tell you what I need!"

In addition to the three core charities, in the spring of 1916, Wharton was made vice-president of the committee in charge of Les Tuberculeux de la Guerre, which was devoted to helping cure French soldiers who had contracted tuberculosis in the trenches.

There is no question that Wharton enjoyed her war work. She was passionately committed to the French cause, and she also loved being part of the action, not being relegated to the passive role that women by custom were expected to play. She often visited the front, ostensibly to inspect hospitals and bring supplies, but also to report on the goings-on to American readers.

The military zone, that area behind the front line subject to martial law, was prohibited to civilians without a laissez-passer from the French High Command. (In 1914, while the German Army threatened, Paris itself was within the military zone.) General Joffre, commander-in-chief, exercised absolute control. His policy was to prohibit access to journalists and other civilians, even "highly placed French officials," as Wharton was pleased to note.

A few influential civilians were allowed in, however, even close to the front line. Wharton's friend Robert Grant had seen "the horrors of war under protection" in 1914, and, in the summer of 1915, Wharton and Berry became the first civilians to visit the reconquered part of Alsace. After they had climbed up to an artillery observation post on a hill overlooking the German positions,

Wharton and Berry with two French officers. Getting to and from the front-line trenches demanded stamina, particularly from a woman of fifty-three. The car had to be left well behind the line, from where they would hike a long way, except in the Vosges, where they began by taking a long ride on mules into the mountains, Wharton "an eager grotesque figure bestriding a mule in the long tight skirts of 1915." In Lorraine they climbed the Butte de Mousson, a steep hill, the highest in the area. In the Vosges they climbed through a forest to the crest of a hill, then into a walled and roofed tunnel that wound down the hill: sometimes the roof was so low they had to bend nearly double: "It is hard to guess the distance one covers in creeping through an unlit passage with different levels and countless turnings; but we must have descended the hillside at least a mile" before they reached a half-ruined farmhouse overlooking the valley floor. Then they plunged underground again and began to descend into another and darker tunnel: "We were in pitch blackness, and saved from breaking our necks only by the gleam of the pocket light which the young lieutenant who had led the party shed on our path," until they reached another half-ruined farmhouse on the valley floor, the French front-line outpost. And then they faced the climb back up the hillside under the same conditions.

she wrote James, "When [novelist Auguste-Maurice] Barrès was here about 10 days ago Recouly took him over the same ground, but they were unable to get to Pt. à Mousson, as it was being bombarded, so we were in luck yesterday." A friend of Wharton's, Raymond Recouly, was aide-de-camp to General Humbert, the army commander there. Wharton did not know the general, but she came armed with a letter of introduction and managed to lunch with him.

Wharton's visits to the military zone provoked mixed reactions: at times she found the sight of the armies "an invigorating spectacle," and there was an excitement in seeing so many people she could imagine passionately dedicated to her French cause. But she also felt the horror of it. She hated the spectacle of the French villages, for her the symbol of good living and ancient traditions, now grotesquely transformed. Many were empty and deserted; in others, the churches were filled with wounded and the houses destroyed. The beautiful landscape was scarred, and the old monuments—her contacts with the past—were battered.

Wharton made each excursion in her own car, with Berry and a picnic basket along, for "jolly picnic lunches around boards resting on trestles," not unlike her peacetime motor flights through Italy and France. Her new impressions mixed with old travel memories: Cassel, a walled town in the north, reminded her of San Gimignano: "As we took the windings that led up to it a sense of Italy began to penetrate the persistent impression of being somewhere near the English Channel." She still sought unusual adventures in hard-to-reach places—the trenches qualified as adventures that set her above the conventional traveler, just as Wharton set herself above other American women who did some charitable work and military zone sightseeing and then went home to regale friends with war stories.

In her short novel *The Marne* (1918), Wharton satirized these women in the character of Mrs. Belknap. Though she had not been strong enough to be a real nurse, before leaving Paris at the end of 1914, she had "donned a nurse's garb, poured tea once or twice at a fashionable hospital, and, on the strength of this effort, obtained permission to carry supplies (in her own motor) to the devastated regions." But Mrs. Belknap was constantly upstaged by other returned Americans "who had been nearer the front, or had raised more money, or had had an audience of the Queen of the Belgians, or an autograph letter from Lord Kitchener."

Wharton obviously took pride in the fact that she *did* carry supplies to the devastated regions in her own motorcar, "laden to the roof" with whatever medicines, bandages, cigarettes, and chocolates could be packed in, along with Berry and herself, Cook to drive, the escorting staff officer, and maybe a military guide. She did raise a lot of money for her charities, most successfully in the United States. She did have an audience of the Queen of the Belgians during one of her excursions, at La Panne on the Belgian coast. And, more than once, she did get as close to no-man's-land as any French soldier.

Between February and August 1915, soon after trench warfare had stabilized the front, Wharton and Berry made five or six excursions into the military zone, the region to the northeast of Paris in France and Belgium. Most lasted about a week. By the end of August, they had explored "the whole sleepless line" from Dunkerque on the English Channel to Belfort, the ancient citadel between the Jura and Vosges mountains. "Once within the military zone *every* moment is interesting," she wrote James.

As civilians of a neutral country, Wharton and Berry were afforded extraordinary privileges, but the military authorities took care not to have them exposed to unnecessary dangers. They were not allowed to visit any sector where serious fighting was anticipated, and granting the pass itself depended

Whenever Wharton turned up among a group of soldiers, she became the center of attention—and she enjoyed it. In the Vosges, "the soldiers gathered round us as the motor stopped—throngs of chasseaus-à-pied in faded, trench stained uniforms—for few visitors climb to this point, and their pleasure at the sight of new faces was presently expressed in a large Vive l'Amérique! scrawled on the door of the car. L'Amérique was glad and proud to be there." In Nieuport, they drove up while a regiment of Zouaves in their red fezzes were relaxing at a band concert. At the approach of their motor, "knots of cheerful Zouaves came swarming out of the ground like ants." Wharton and Berry joined the audience and then had their picture taken with the colonel, his officers, and some of their men.

Anna de Noailles at the front with Comte Étienne de Beaumont, who had organized an ambulance service for the French army

After the appearance of the May 22, 1915, issue of *Le Rire ROUGE*, a humor magazine, Wharton wrote to Alice Garrett: "Have you seen the last no. of the *Rire?*—We took Abel Faivre with us, & he's made such a good sketch of us at Gerbéviller! Walter's expression whenever I suggested visiting a hospital or doing anything good was caught to a line. We had such a wonderful trip, & I can talk John down any time he explodes shells at me *now*. A *très bientot, pas?*" The caption beneath Faivre's caricature, "Ce n'est que ca!", or "What's all the fuss about?", is rather mean, despite Wharton's enthusiasm about the drawing in her letter.

In ruined villages near the front, Wharton and Berry met several brave nuns who had stayed behind to protect civilians when "ces satanés Allemandes" occupied their villages. Here they may be in Clermont with Soeur Gabrielle Rosnet, "a small, round active woman with a shrewd and ruddy face," who could not address the German commander by his rank "because he was so tall that I couldn't see up to his shoulder-straps."

on what was going on in the area that day. They would be passed down the chain of command, required to stop at each headquarters for a further pass, which would be issued or not as the local commander saw fit. "One can't be sure of permits nowadays," she wrote James in March 1915. At least once, after a four-hour wait, permission was refused. On her first trip to the Vosges front, Wharton did not reach the front-line trenches; on the next trip, she did.

Wharton found or made friends among the staff escorts who passed her party along. Paul Boncour, Minister of Foreign Affairs after the war, escorted her into the trenches in Alsace. Raymond Recouly and Jean-Louis Vaudoyer were prewar friends who helped her out when called on; Henri de Jouvenal, Colette's second husband, recognized her and helped at Verdun. One pass was impossible because of a pending attack, until a staff captain who had read *The House of Mirth* persuaded his colonel to allow them through—but they must drive fast, the colonel said.

A typical excursion included a reception, often a lunch party, at the headquarters of the top commander for the area, for example, General Humbert or General Dubail, army commanders, or Admiral Ronarc'h, who commanded the French coastal troops. On August 14 at Reims, they lunched with General Humbert and his staff at headquarters, a stone and brick château set in a sleepy park with pampas grass, geraniums, rustic bridges, winding paths, the typical peacetime country place of Wharton's Parisian friends. But though the rooms still contained handsome tapestries and furniture, the tables were spread with military maps and aerial photographs. During a day trip to the reconquered part of Alsace on August 17, 1915, they were given the equivalent of a state reception in Dannemarie, the administrative center of the French occupation government. The heads of the military and civil administrations were their escorts. She noted with approval that the children and officials in this formerly German part of France spoke German and the local dialect, as well as French. Schoolgirls and -boys sang the "Marseillaise" and were observed studying under teachers who had them well in charge. "This exercise of tact and tolerance," Wharton reported, "seemed to proceed not from any pressure of expediency but from a sympathetic understanding of the point of view of this people of the border."

The military authorities trusted Wharton and Berry to travel unescorted entering and leaving the military zone, with someone in charge of them only after they picked up their staff officer guide at the first headquarters stop and before he was dropped off there when they headed home. With all road signs removed, they risked getting lost, but, as in Wharton's peacetime motor flights, the experience of blundering onto out-of-the-way scenes only added to the excitement.

Returning from Verdun, they took a haphazard turn onto a muddy byroad with long lines of 75s (the famous French light artillery) ranged along its banks "like grey ant-eaters in some monstrous menagerie." The motorcar then came upon a village "swarming with artillery and cavalry." Everyone was on the move as the car wheeled into the crowd: "Our arrival caused such surprise that no sentry remembered to challenge us, and obsequiously saluting *sous-officiers* [well below the ranks Wharton was used to dealing with] instantly cleared a way for the motor," as it sped through the crowd and out the other side on what must have appeared to be an important mission, the distinguished civilian with white moustache and his stately consort traveling alone. Wharton wrote, tongue in cheek, "It seems improbable that we were meant to be there. . . . So, by a happy accident we caught one more war-picture, all of vehe-

Ruins of the Gothic cathedral at Nieuport

The northern front (Nieuport) in 1915 merely previewed what was to come. Beginning February 16, 1916, for more than ten months the German and French armies attacked and counter-attacked each other furiously around Verdun. This battlefield finally account-ed for close to 1,250,000 casualties, of whom about 420,000 died. On July 1, 1916, a day still mourned in England, the British Army, outnumbering the Germans 7 to 1, attacked uphill along the Somme. Before nightfall 21,000 of the attackers had died with nothing to show for their sacrifice. The British would suffer more than 2 million casu-alties on the western front after July 1, 1916. What was left of the French Army's spirit was broken on the Chemin-des-Dames. As Alistair Horn wrote: "On April 16, 1917, the French infantry—exhilarated by all they had been promised—left their trenches with an élan unsurpassed in all their glorious history. . . . Angry, demoralized, bitterly disillusioned men flooded back from the scene of butchery. By the following day, there had been something like 120,000 casulties."

ment movement [including soldiers dodging Wharton's car] as we passed out of the zone of war."

It's a wonder that a vigilant military policeman, despite Wharton's "splen-did permesso," did not take them for spies (a spy hunt was underway there) as the motor continued on its lonely and erratic course on deserted roads within the military zone, stopping from time to time to ask soldiers the way: "One is in luck if one comes across a sentinel who knows the name of the village he is guarding." Heading home again from Saint Omer after an excursion to the northernmost part of the western front—from Ypres to Dunkerque—Whar-ton and Berry again left the main road and took an adventurous shortcut across rolling country. What happened next was another "happy accident," the grandest of military spectacles: "Over the crest of a hill, we saw surging toward us a mighty movement of British and Indian troops. A great bath of silver sun-light lay on the wheat-fields, the clumps of woodland and the hilly blue hori-zon, and in that slanting radiance the cavalry rode toward us, regiment after regiment of slim turbaned Indians, with delicate proud faces like the faces of Princes in Persian miniatures. . . . Then came a long train of artillery; splendid horses, chattering gun-carriages, clear-faced English youths galloping by all aglow in the sunset. The stream of them seemed never-ending."

A less glorious sight was that of the lines of soldiers the French called éclopés (literally, "the crippled"); the British, more charitably, called them "shell-shocked." Wharton described them as "the unwounded but battered, shattered, frost-bitten, deafened and half-paralyzed wreckage of the awful struggle. These poor wretches, in their thousands, are daily shipped back from the front to rest and be restored; and it is a grim sight to watch them limping by, and to meet the dazed stare of eyes that have seen what one dare not picture."

One can't but wonder how Wharton judged the performances of the *éclopés* in what she saw as the character-building experience of fighting in the Great War. The French Army sometimes treated them brutally. She visited "a colony" of them near Verdun, called "the African Village" by other soldiers: "The poor devils" sleeping on straw crammed together, "with nothing I could see to be thankful for but the fact that they were out of the mud, & in a sort of fetid stable-heat. It was *awful*—& the Directeur du Service de Santé was so complacent!... For a Horror-of-War picture, that one won't soon be superceded. At least I hope not!"

Wharton was often close to artillery fire. In the Vosges: "The big guns were all about us, crouched in these sylvan lairs like wild beasts waiting to spring; and near each gun hovered its attendant gunner, proud, possessive"— a metaphor mixed with enthusiasm—"important as a bridegroom with his bride."

On the northern front, the artillery fire was on a massive scale. The roar of the British bombardment "seemed to build a roof of iron over the glorious ruins of Ypres." At Nieuport, "the incessant crash of guns stretches a sounding board of steel." At Cassel, she recalled being waked by "a terrific clatter" from a Taube (German scout plane) overhead, "and all the guns in the place were cracking at it!" She was half-asleep: "By the time this mental process was complete, I had scrambled up and hurried downstairs and, unbolting the heavy doors, had rushed out into the square. It was about four in the morning, the heavenliest moment of a summer dawn, and in spite of the tumult Cassel apparently still slept."

A few soldiers who were standing around assured her the German plane had just disappeared into a cloud. She did not report how they reacted to her sudden rush into the square but admitted, "I had the sense of having overdone my excitement and not being exactly in tune; so after gazing a moment at the white cloud, I slunk back into the hotel, barred the door and mounted to my room." On her way up, she was startled by another crash, "and a drift of white smoke blew up from the fruit-trees just under the window." A gun hidden below "in one of those quiet provincial gardens" had fired a parting shot.

She went back to sleep, but, an hour or two later, "the hush was broken by a roar like the last trump." This time it was the German siege gun firing from Dixmude. Five times its shells landed while she was dressing, "a noise that may be compared—if the human imagination can stand the strain—to the

The mayor of Gerbéviller, in front of the ruins of his home. Wharton wrote to Charles Scribner at the end of June 1915: "I have been given such unexpected opportunities for seeing things at the front that you might perhaps care to collect the articles (I suppose there will be five) in a small volume to be published in the autumn. I am in hopes of being able to give you some interesting photographs for the Lorraine article. Those taken by the soldier who was with us are too small to be satisfactory, but I have sent for the films and think I can have them successfully enlarged. I am sorry there has been a delay about getting them, but I hope they will go to you, with the article, in about ten days. I shall have some good photos of the last trip also."

simultaneous closing of all the iron shop-shutters in the world." No one in the hotel seemed perturbed. When she left Cassel, she passed where the shells had landed. One had converted a cabbage field into a crater like Vesuvius. "There was a certain consolation," she concluded, "in the discrepancy between the noise and the damage done."

From the start, when the German Army stormed through Belgium, Wharton had developed a loathing beyond reason for the enemy. Near the front her imagination took over and transformed the invisible German enemy into a supernatural evil force, a menace heightened by the contrast with the beauties of nature along the quiet sector of the front, in Alsace and the Vosges, where she and Berry were permitted to travel. She became obsessed by the destruction of nature by the brutality of mankind.

German prisoners were "beasts," like those she saw in the Argonne, "much less famished and war-worn than one could have wished." Even Anna Bahlmann, her lifelong servant, was "too ineradicably 'Boche!'"

She accepted most reports of atrocities, although some were true and some were not. She had written Sally Norton on September 27, 1914: "As to the horrors & outrages, I'm afraid they are too often true. . . . Lady Gladstone, head of the Belgian refugee committee in London, told a friend of mine she had seen a Belgian woman with her ears cut off." She repeated stories told her by survivors. In one, German soldiers were destroying the village of Gerbéviller house-by-house and bayoneting the inhabitants. An old woman, "hearing her son's death-cry, rashly looked out of her door. A bullet instantly laid her low among her phloxes and lilies; and there, in her little garden, her dead body was dishonored." Wharton does not say how.

Wharton's car in a ruined town. She noted, "War is the greatest of paradoxes: the most senseless and disheartening of human retrogressions, and yet the stimulant of qualities of soul which, in every race, can seemingly find no other means of renewal." She was deeply ambivalent, at the same time sad, proud, and fascinated: "If one could think away the 'éclopés' in the streets and the wounded in the hospitals, Châlons would be an invigorating spectacle. When we drove up to the hotel even the grey motors and the sober uniforms seemed to sparkle under the cold sky." She remembered and agreed with Tolstoy: "'It was gay and terrible,' is the phrase forever recurring in War and Peace."

In the Argonne, in a village about four miles west of Les Eparges, "the trampling of cavalry and the hauling of guns had turned the land about it into a mud-flat." In May she wrote from Nancy while enjoying a bunch of pink peonies on her writing table, which "were not introduced to point the stale allegory of unconscious nature veiling man's havoc," but were "put on my first page as a symbol of conscious human energy coming back to replant and rebuild the wilderness."

Other terrible casualties were the "bits of the past that give meaning and continuity to the present." In the ruined village of Auve, she imagined "what it must have been as it looked out, in the blue September weather, above the ripening pears of its gardens to the crops in the valley and the large landscape beyond." She lamented the destruction of "the photographs on the walls, the twigs of withered box above the crucifixes, the old wedding-dresses in brass clamped trunks, the bundles of letters laboriously written and as painfully deciphered"—all the reminders of the past.

As she traveled across the war-devastated landscape, Wharton moved in and out of the consciousness of the present horror. In June of 1915, the empty houses at Ypres were still standing, and from afar the town presented "the distant semblance of a living city, while nearby it is seen to be a disembowelled corpse." As she approached, she saw that windows were smashed and facades torn away, "with the different stories exposed, as if for the stage-setting of a farce. In these exposed interiors the poor little household gods shiver and blink

Excerpt from the front page of the *New York Herald*, June 7, 1915. The *Lusitania* had been torpedoed by a German U-boat in May 1915. Neither the author of this poem, which Wharton translated, nor any details about its publication in Germany are mentioned. It begins:

"The swift sea sucks her death shriek under

As the great ship reels and leaps asunder;

Crammed taffrail-high with her murderous freight,

Like a straw on the tide she whirls to her fate.

A war ship she, though she lacked its coat,

And lustful for lives as none afloat."

like owls surprised in a hollow tree. A hundred signs of intimate and humble tastes of humdrum pursuits, of family association, cling to the unmasked walls . . . the poor frail web of things that had made up the lives of a vanished city-full, hung dangling before us in that deathly blast."

Once while picnicking in Alsace, Berry and Wharton were forced to move so as not to draw the Germans' attention: "We retreated hurriedly and unpacked our luncheon-basket on the more sheltered side of the ridge. As we sat there in the grass, swept by a great mountain breeze full of the scent of thyme and myrtle, while the flutter of birds, the hum of insects, the still and busy life of the hills went on all about us in the sunshine, the pressure of the encircling line of death grew more intolerably real. It is not in the mud and jokes and every-day activities of the trenches that one most feels the damnable insanity of war; it is where it lurks like a mythical monster in scenes to which the mind has always turned for rest."

Yet for Wharton the most thrilling part of her 1915 excursions were the visits into the frontline positions, the actual trenches, and coming to know the dangers lurking there. In Alsace, Wharton and Berry ended up "on the extreme verge of the defenses, on a slope just above the village over which we had heard the artillery roaring a few hours before. The spot where we stood was raked on all sides by the enemy's lines, and the nearest trenches were only a few yards away." In a forest in the Vosges, a sharpshooter fired at the sound of their voices; his bullet hit a tree "a few yards ahead." Wharton was allowed to peep around the corner of the trench: "I looked out and saw a strip of intensely green meadow just under me, and a wooded cliff rising abruptly on its other side. That was all. The wooded cliff swarmed with 'them,' and a few steps would have carried us across the interval; yet all about us was silence, and the peace of the forest." At Pt. à Mousson, in an observation post within a chapel on the hilltop: "In trying to show me something, Walter put his hand (not his arm, only *his hand*) through the window of the chapel, & instantly one of the artillery officers pulled him back & said, 'Prenez garde, Monsieur. On pourrait vous voir!'" She wrote to James, "You may imagine the sense it gave me of almost feeling their breath in our faces."

The unique VIP treatment Wharton and Berry received must have been based partly on the French High Command's calculation that Wharton would produce effective propaganda for the French cause, if given the opportunity. The pair were already identified in France as prominent and outspoken champions of America's entry into the war, with Wharton's reputation as a writer well established in the United States and Berry's reputation as an American business lawyer steadily growing in Paris. Given the opportunity, Wharton delivered. The reports she wrote, each one done immediately after the trip ended, became a series of articles in *Scribner's Magazine*. In late 1915, Scribner's published them together in book form as *Fighting France,* which became a best-seller in the U.S.A.

Wharton was constantly raising funds for her charities. In the United States, she put Minnie Jones in charge of writing to friends for donations, organizing events in Newport, Bar Harbor and New York, Philadelphia and Boston, and overseeing "Edith Wharton Committees" for donations. Wharton had photographs and movies taken of the refugee hostels and schools to send to contributors, and she wrote most of the thank-you notes herself.

A major fund-raising effort for which Wharton was the prime mover, *The Book of the Homeless (Le Livre des Sans-Foyer),* was published in early 1916 by Scribner's in New York and Macmillan in London. The concept of such a book was not new. Another fund-raising book for French refugee relief, *The Book of France,* had been published in England. Henry James had contributed, and he sent Wharton a copy when she wrote to ask his help for her own. As for England, James reported: "Very numerous are the publications of sorts on behalf of which such appeals have been made, and are being made here.... The little demon of an Elizabeth Asquith," the prime minister's daughter, had got something from him, "for a book of her own which up to now has never come out."

But Wharton wrote a persuasive proposal to Scribner's and was accepted. She handled all the business arrangements, something she had learned from promoting her own books. She also contacted most of the writers, artists, and musicians who contributed.

The cover of the book reads, "Edited by Edith Wharton," but most of her editing would have been done through her imaginative translations from the French (she translated all the contributions written in French, except for an Edmond Rostand poem translated by Walter Berry), which tended to highlight the anti-German sentiments many of her French contributors expressed. Because of time pressure, many of those writing in English sent their contributions directly to Scribner's.

Henry James, her chief assistant, worked with enthusiasm: "And in the glitter, the prospective of the book, I take the greatest interest—surely it *will* corruscate as no like constellation has ever done before." They worked together by exchanging letters. For him she became, "Dear Rédactress in-chief." She responded with, "Dear Rédacteur."

Although he wrote Joseph Conrad and Thomas Hardy, James warned Wharton not to expect much: "I haven't for instance much hope of Conrad, who produces by the sweat of his brow and tosses off, in considerable anguish at the rate of about a word a month." As for Hardy: "He is aged, newly married, without facility or current inspiration, I think; and it is many a year since

One hundred seventy-five copies of *The Book of the Homeless* were made up as deluxe editions, on special paper with an even larger format, fifty of them (at $75 each) with four facsimiles of manuscripts and a second set of illustrations in portfolio. These interested book collectors at the time. Now they are rare and valuable.

As the frontispiece states, the book was sold for the benefit of two of Wharton's charitable enterprises, the American Hostels for Refugees (with the Foyer Franco-Belge) and the Children of Flanders Rescue Committee. At the end of Wharton's preface, the reader is instructed where to address donations in the United States or France. Minnie Jones was Wharton's chief U.S. liaison.

Sketch of André Gide by Theo van Rysselbergher from *The Book of the Homeless*

Ambrose Vollard helped Wharton obtain Renoir's contribution, a charcoal drawing he had just made of this wounded soldier, his son.

I've seen anything from him anywhere at all of the occasional nature—if indeed I've ever seen it." But both men surprised James with a contribution.

Wharton rounded up contributors from her circle of friends, including Paul Bourget, Henri de Régnier, Anna de Noailles, Jacques-Emile Blanche, Jean Cocteau, Walter Gay, Edmund Gosse, Robert Grant, Barrett Wendell, and Mrs. Humphrey Ward, plus acquaintances like Max Beerbohm, Edmond Rostand, Leon Bakst, composer Vincent d'Indy, and General Humbert. James pulled in William Dean Howells and Rupert Brooks (posthumously through his literary executor: "Rupert B. should of course be cited as the late R.B.," James instructed—a detail that would somehow get overlooked).

The book begins with a two-sentence letter from General Joffre—still "le Commandant en Chef" in August 1915—then a two-page introduction by Theodore Roosevelt, followed by Wharton's preface. Joffre wrote in French. Wharton's translation on the facing page dents his style: "écrite avec un peu de sang français" became "partly written in French blood." She may have thought him flippant or not forceful enough.

Roosevelt's tone was admonitory. He noted that "the neutral nations of the civilized world should at last wake up to the performance of the duty they have so shamefully failed to perform." Specifically, "the part that America has played in this great tragedy is not an exalted part. . . . We owe to Mrs. Wharton all the assistance we can give."

Wharton's preface describes the work of her two charities for the Belgian refugees in straightforward specifics that leave the reader impressed with her compassion and common sense and the effective way the work was being carried on. It ends with an elaborate metaphor to describe the book: "You will see from the names of the builders what a gallant piece of architecture it is, what delightful pictures hang on its walls, and what noble music echoes through them. But what I should have liked to show is the readiness, the kindliness, the eagerness, with which all the collaborators, from first to last, have lent a hand to the building. Perhaps you will guess it for yourselves when you read their names and see the beauty and variety of what they have given. So I efface myself from the threshold and ask you to walk in."

As literature, however, most of the contributions are nondescript. Understandably, the prevailing theme is war. Writing in the summer of 1915, the first anniversary of the war's beginning, many pronounced loathing for the German enemy: A short poem by Howells ends with: "The little ones he hurled, Mocking that Pity in his pitiless might—The Anti-Christ of Schrecklickeit." James, who shared Wharton's visceral anti-German views, called it "fine and forcible and most feeling" and "really grim and strong and sincere"; when Howells had second thoughts and tried to withdraw it, James persuaded him not to.

For Robert Grant: "The world is beset by a monster." In his poem "The

Undergraduate Killed in Battle," George Santayana admonished: "Ah, demons of the whirlwind have a care, What, trumpeting your triumphs, ye undo!" Hardy's poem "Cry of the Homeless" is addressed to "Instigator of the ruin—Whichsoever thou mayst be / Of the mastering minds of Europe / That contrived our misery—"

In Wharton's own contribution, "The Tryst," the poet interrogates a refugee mother from "the North." The Germans have shot her husband and child and looted their village: "The streets are foul with the slime of the dead / And all the rivers run poison-red / With the bodies drifting by." Would the refugee like to escape to a safe haven? No, she replies, because when her men come home victorious, she wants to be there to "go in to my dead":

> Where my husband fell I will put a stone,
> And mother a child instead of my own,
> And stand and laugh on my bare hearth-stone,
> When the King [of the Belgians] rides by, she said.

James and Conrad contributed long and interesting essays based on their own war experiences: James, with British soldiers in the hospital he had organized and his memories of the first volunteers of the American Civil War; Conrad, in managing to escape through Germany with his family as the war was breaking over central Europe. General Humbert and Academicien Barrès retold sentimental war stories involving heroic French soldiers that could be expected to stir American readers.

Jean Cocteau's poem "La Mort des Jeunes Gens de la Divine Hellade" mourns for the dead young men of all armies: "Fearless they sought the land no sunsets see, / Whence our weak pride shrinks back, and would return, / Knowing a pinch of ashes in an urn / Henceforth our garden and our house shall be."

The last word may have been left to W. B. Yeats in "A Reason for Keeping Silent":

> I think it better that at times likes these
> We poets keep our mouths shut, for in truth
> We have no gift to set a statesman right;
> He's had enough meddling who can please
> A young girl in the indolence of her youth
> Or an old man upon a winter's night.

Wharton's goal had been publication in October 1915 for the Christmas season, and the contents had to be shipped to America by steamer, avoiding

Henry James photographed in 1913 by Hilaire d'Arois, as a study for a bust of James

German submarines en route. But they had not started until late July, and they missed the October publication date by several months. Still, Wharton plugged the book. "Please boom 'The Book of the Homeless' as hard as you can in New Haven," she wrote Beatrix Farrand, "& get some subscriptions for the edition de luxe."

For the effort involved, however, the book must have been a disappointment. The proceeds for charity, according to R. W. B. Lewis, came to less than $15,000. "If only it could have come out before Christmas we should have made a fortune," Wharton complained afterward.

In November 1915, Edith Wharton began taking breaks from the exhausting war work by visiting the south of France, specifically Hyères, a town on the Mediterranean just east of Toulon that she had first come to know through her visits to the Bourgets' villa at nearby Costebelle. At the end of the month, André Gide was with her, and they went on excursions—lunching one day at Toulon on the quay, another day taking a picnic basket into the mountains. Rosa Fitz-James was expected, as was Robert Norton, for a month's stay.

On December 4 she had a cable from Henry James's secretary, Theodora Bosanquet, reporting that the writer had suffered a stroke and was partially paralyzed. In the beginning of December, James rallied a bit but then suffered a relapse. Wharton was in constant contact about his condition. She wrote to Gaillard Lapsley on December 17 that she had heard from Miss Bosanquet that he was not expected to live: "Yes all my 'blue distances' will be shut out forever when he goes. His friendship has been the pride & honour of my life. Plus ne m'est rien after such a gift as that—except the memory of it." He died on February 28, 1916.

Shortly after James's death, Wharton received the Legion of Honor. In April 1916, she joked with Lizzie Cameron about wearing her new ribbon: "I will conform scrupulously to your instructions as to not hiding my red ribbon under a bushel; but, if the width of the ribbon I wear is to bear any relation to my 'appas' as compared to Miss Marbury's, a 'broad ribbon' on her *wd* mean, on *me*, one that was only visible to the microscope!"

Though Wharton kept in constant correspondence with Elisina Tyler regarding the running of her *ouvroir* and other charities in Paris, at Hyères she was able to recharge by being close to the sea and luxuriating in "the blessed quietness" and the atmosphere of sunshine and flowers. As she wrote to Lizzie Cameron: "It is heavenly here, & I marvel at the thought that I used to be bored on the Riviera! It is delicious just to dawdle about in the sun, & smell the eucalyptus & pines, & arrange bushels of flowers bought for 50 centimes under a yellow awning in a market smelling of tunny fish and olives."

She wrote her best fiction of those war years, *Summer,* over six months during 1916, part of the time while resting in Hyères: "I don't know how on earth the thing got itself written in the scramble and scuffle of my present life: but it did, and I think you'll like it." It came out in *McLure's Magazine* between February and August 1917.

A tale set, like *Ethan Frome,* in western Massachusetts, *Summer* tells the story of Charity Royall, a young girl who longs to escape the small town of North Dormer, but who, after a passionate affair with a young architect, becomes pregnant and marries her foster father, the town lawyer. It takes place in the months of July and August—the hot months Edith Wharton had known well when she lived at the Mount— yet is informed by the brilliance of light of the south of France.

In *Summer,* Wharton celebrated the things that grow, writing that "there had never been such a June in Eagle County." Charity Royall feels "the strong growth of the beeches clothing the ridge, the rounding of pale green cones on countless spruce-branches, the push of myriads of sweet-fern fronds in the cracks of the stony slope below the wood, and the crowding shoots of mead-owsweet and yellow flags in the pasture beyond. All this bubbling of sap and slipping of sheaths and bursting of calyxes was carried to her on mingled cur-rents of fragrance. Every leaf and bud and blade seemed to contribute its exha-lation to the pervading sweetness in which the pungency of pine-sap prevailed over the spice of thyme and the subtle perfume of fern, and all were merged in a moist earth-smell that was like the breath of some huge sun-warmed animal." Charity's love for Lucius Harney is also described in terms of plant images: "The only reality was the wondrous unfolding of her new self, the reaching out to the light of all her contracted tendrils. She had lived all her life among peo-ple whose sensibilities seemed to have withered for lack of use; and more won-derful, at first, than Harney's endearments were the words that were a part of them. She had always thought of love as something confused and furtive, and he made it as bright and open as the summer air."

In 1917 success in her war work brought Wharton a letter of commenda-tion from a busy General Pershing, and she responded like an experienced executive. "A great part of its success," she wrote Pershing, "is to be ascribed to my devoted and indefatigable helpers, to whom a proportionately large share of your praise is due, and who will be as much gratified as I have been by your letter." And then she had Pershing's letter and her reply translated immediately and sent to the French among her helpers.

In April 1917, just before the United States declared war, the French mil-itary called on her again, to inspect the region of German-occupied France, between Montdidier and La Fere, north of Compiègne, just evacuated by the German Army in a move to improve its defenses. Her fiery denunciation of the

Wharton made an official visit to Morocco in 1917, organized by her friend General Lyautey, who was in command there.

destruction the Germans had left in their wake ran on the front page of the April 6 edition of the *New York Sun*. In September 1917 Wharton went off to Morocco with Walter Berry for a VIP tour organized by General Lyautey. The result was another travel book, *In Morocco* (1919).

During the winter of 1917–18, Daisy Chanler remembered how depressed many were in the United States: "The grim deadlock of the trenches seemed to prolong itself indefinitely. We could never forget the horrors of the battlefield, the terrors of the submarine, the many killed in the flower of youth, the hideously wounded and crippled for life, the cruel wanton waste and ruin of it all. This deep throbbing note was with us like an organ point and accompanied every waking moment as day followed day—'How long, O Lord, how long?'" Wharton in Paris remembered "the crushing gloom of the last dark winter."

By July 7, 1918, however, she wrote, "Paris is feeling very confident just now" and described rapturously the Fourth of July parade she watched from the Hotel Crillon. "The great solid 'villas de France' had their stone laps full of American & French soldiers with their arms around each other's necks, & presently down the Champs Elysées trotted the Garde Nationale, & then our wonderful incredible troops, every man the same height, & marching with a long rhythmical musical stride that filled the French with wonder." The American Red Cross nurses scored the biggest success of all. Everything was "beflagged," and "the historic imagination (mine at least) fairly burst in the struggle to deal with all the associations and analogies the scene evoked."

By August 2, 1918, the Allied offensives were at last grinding inexorably forward and victory was only a matter of how long the retreating Germans would endure. General Humbert, commander of the French Third Army throughout the war, took time out to write Wharton a personal note, in which

Survivors of the Great War who participated in the Victory Parade in Paris on July 14, 1919, included many who were permanently disabled, three million of them in France alone. The French called them "les grands mutilés de la guerre."

he told her how magnificently the American soldiers were fighting, as she too had foreseen.

The following July she witnessed the Victory Parade from the balcony of a friend's house in the Champs Elysées. The Allied armies rode under the Arc de Triomphe and down the avenue to the Place de la Concorde. She was dazzled by the sight of the victory parade and in a blur of emotion could just barely distinguish the generals, the massed flags, the names of regiments. She also saw, with pride, a *grand mutilé,* for whom she had secured a wheelchair so that he could take part.

During the war, Edith Wharton had cared for refugees and the homeless. Once the war was over, she turned her energies to taking care of herself. Everything had changed, and old friends had died. The shock of Henry James's death had been followed by news of the deaths of Egerton Winthrop and her faithful helper Anna Bahlmann, plus the many young men who had been killed in the war. She mourned Ronald Simmons, with whom she had worked in her charities, her cousin Newbold Rhinelander, only twenty-three, and many others. She had written in July 1918 about Theodore Roosevelt's sons: "I fear Quentin Roosevelt is dead, though they still hope. Archie is going home, invalided. Their poor father!"

As Wharton watched the parade from a high balcony of a house on the Champs-Elysées, she remembered what Henri Bergson had once said of her inability to memorize great poetry: "You're dazzled by it." Wharton's comment on the Versailles peace treaty that followed: "The criminal mistakes made by the Allies were made in 1919, not in 1914."

She found Paris less and less to her liking—"simply awful—a kind of continuous earthquake of motor busses, trams, lorries, taxis & other howling & swooping & colliding engines, with hundreds of thousands of U.S. citizens rushing about in them & tumbling out of them at one's door—&, through it all, the same people placidly telephoning one to come to tea.—I am 'sensée être' on the move to Jean-Marie—as indeed I shall be in a week, I hope—& have so far seen only Walter, the Tylers, Charlie, & John Hugh. The fact that Rosa is in Austria makes it easy to lie low, as she is almost my only remaining 'Social Welfare Centre.'"

She had exhausted herself physically in the last years, and now she craved the nature and peace of the country. Her doctor Isch Wall told her that if she didn't stop her mad activity, she should break down "permanently this time." Therefore, she decided to leave Paris, giving up the gatherings of intellectuals and French aristocrats that had so excited her since 1907, to find a place where she could be more in control of the atmosphere and the people she saw.

The postwar years brought continuing money worries. During the war, she had been generous with both her time and her money, but now she needed to be practical. "Writing is my business as well as my passion, & again & again I have sacrificed a business opportunity as well as an occasion to write something I longed to express, in order to take up my endless war work." She was glad for what she and her coworkers had accomplished, and proud that that they had been singled out among all American organizations by the Office Publique d'Hygiène and the Ministry of the Interior to continue and develop their tuberculosis sanatoria, "but I have reached the point when I must stop, & rest, & then turn back to my work, & redeem my promises to my publishers." In December 1919, she wrote that she felt "utterly swamped"—then she crossed out 'utterly' and wrote "temporarily swamped"—by her expenses:

1) Having to pay the income tax both in France & America (40,000 fcs. for last year, & the same this, unless our tax is reduced, which is doubtful).

2) Not daring to give up this large & expensive apartment because it's impossible at present to find a foothold anywhere in Paris.

3) Not daring to "put down" the motor temporarily because circulation by taxi & metro is literally impossible except by the young, the acrobatic, & those who can "stand & wait" eternally—& also because, all last summer, I used it to cart coal provisions & furniture the hire of "transport" being beyond the dreams of Rockefeller.

4) Tax on all my literary "output."

5) Doubling of wages, & tripling of all living expenses.

6) &c &c &c &c!

She was confident of her talent and that her work would bring the money to pay her expenses, but, when she picked up her pen to write, she found it difficult. Having seen France and its armies attacked by the Germans and having long struggled in working for the French cause, she had bonded emotionally with France to such an extent that she could not write of it with a sense of proportion. She continued to write propaganda for the French. On February 19, 1919, she told Minnie Jones that she gave her articles "French Ways and Their Meaning" to *Cosmopolitan* because she had discovered it belonged to a group of "desirable magazines. These articles, being good allied propaganda, I was willing to do." Her novels read like propaganda, too: the hyperpatriotic characters in *The Marne* and *Son at the Front* (1923) seem unreal.

Freed from the everyday anxieties of war, she had hoped to be able to resume work immediately on a novel called *Literature*. She wrote to Charles Scribner: "I thought it might be possible to shake off the question which is tormenting all novelists at present: 'Did the adventures related in this book happen before the war or did they happen since?' with the resulting difficulty that, if they happened before the war, I seem to have forgotten how people felt and what their point of view was. Perhaps it will not last much longer & we shall be able to get back some sort of perspective; but at present, between the objection of the public to so called war-stories and the difficulty of the author to send his imagination backward, the situation is a bewildering one."

In the late fall of 1919, she wrote that she hoped "to be rid of this white elephant of an apartment by next autumn, & to wallow in flowers after that all year round." Thus, as the rest of world hurtled on into the twentieth century, Wharton retreated north of Paris to the village of Saint-Brice-sous-Forêt and a milieu that evoked the past. She bought herself an old, eighteenth-century house on seven acres of land, which Elisina Tyler had noticed in 1917 while driving back and forth to the refugee hostel in nearby Groslay. She lived in her new home, which she named Pavillon Colombe, every year from late spring to fall. In the winter she took refuge in Hyères at the Château Sainte-Claire, which she also bought eventually. In both places she was able to indulge her great love, gardening.

She wrote to Berenson in February 1920 about overseeing the work at Jean-Marie, as Pavillon Colombe was then called; clearing out of 53, Rue de Varenne; and supervising the clearing and planting of her gardens at Sainte-Claire: "I talk, I know, as if I were moving into Caprarola, & putting, at the same time, the finishing touches to Chatsworth; & really, I believe those two feats might have been accomplished in 1913 more easily, & at no more expense, than getting settled in my two bicoques of Var & S. & O. today."

In her large new house at Saint-Brice, with its wonderful gardens, Edith Wharton created a refuge from the world where she could write in peace and receive guests. Among the friends who would come out from Paris—ten miles away—for lunch or for dinner were Charles du Bos and his wife, Rosa de Fitz-James, and l'Abbé Mugnier. In addition to her old friends were the many new ones with whom she had worked during the war, including the Tylers; her lawyer and his wife, the André Boccon Gibods; and Louis Gillet, head of the museum near Senlis, and his family.

Wharton loved her new setting. She wrote to Bernard Berenson: "The country—the banlieue even—is divine, and my humble potager gushes with nightingales. The heaps of rubble and various kitchen-midden have been cleared away, & the little place looks really welcoming. May I see you there soon!—"

*Pavillons* were small-scale country residences built by the French nobility out of a desire to get away from the gilded prison Louis XIV had created at his court in Versailles. Pavillon Colombe was built in 1769 by Jean-André Vassal, a rich young man from Montpellier who made it a home for his mistress Marie-Catherine Ruggieri, one of two vivacious sisters of a Venetian family, actresses in Italian comedy, who made their way in the French court through their charms. Marie-Catherine took the stage name "Colombe" (dove). After Vassal married, he gallantly allowed Marie-Catherine to remain in Pavillon Colombe for her lifetime; she lived to be eighty. It was said that she inspired

Pavillon Colombe, on the Rue de Montmorency, Saint-Brice-Sous-Forêt. Walter Berry wrote to Bernard Berenson, July 1, 1920: "Edith is perching rue de Varenne, but moves to St. Brice incessament, in order to avoid the invasion of her compatriots. Every Oshkoshite who contributed $10 to her Fleures de Guerre expects to be 'entertained!' "

Edith Wharton and Robert Norton on the garden side of Pavillon Colombe

artists, and a portrait of her, with doves, by Fragonard hung in her bedroom. Her friend Hubert Robert built the reflecting pool in the garden, which is still there.

A young friend, Vivienne de Watteville, recalled visiting Pavillon Colombe in the 1930s. The visitor's car pulled up before high doors set in a wall on the village street, "and when you stepped into the court-yard beyond, where the geraniums climbed through the dusk to the persiennes, you stepped back two hundred years. You forgot the purring engine of the car which had conveyed you, and heard instead the neat clip-clop of the donkey's hooves upon the cobble-stones as he drew the carriage under the arch-way, and brought home the two lovely demoiselles Colombe." Wharton had perfectly restored the *pavillon* in every detail:

> In the drawing room with the mirrors a l'Italienne (a great novelty of the time), in the tiny boudoir, over the curtained bed, were the little colombes commemorated in plaster, and here and there under the high ceiling were the Maréchal's plumes and bâton. Behind Edith's library was still the closet with the polished wooden bath and its slender brass taps *en tête de cigne.*
>
> The rooms on the ground floor had French windows opening onto the terrace and (as I well remember) communicating doors, so that between the dining room and the library one passed through the whole chain: the long room with the mirrors, the sitting room and the two

little rooms that were Mlle. Colombe's suite, at least five doors which before and after every meal I wanted to open for Edith and she always insisted upon my going through before her. I could not bear doing this, and she, in some ways so ceremonious a hostess, could not give in; but when she saw how much I minded she laughingly took my arm and solved the problem by walking outside along the terrace. About the Pavillon Colombe there was an atmosphere of repose and other-world so strong that one shed one's present day self at the threshold and moved in a continual awareness of the past. . . . Through the window my eyes rested among the green trees whose trunks were shot by the late sun-rays. Stone jars with pink climbing geraniums stood out against the vivid fat grass of a wet summer, and the smell of box rose pungently from the formal clipped hedges. Beyond the garden came the sound of the outer world, voices, autos, the church bell, but so faint that it scarcely touched the consciousness. The  garden itself held such a deep tranquility that one dwelt among its most secret leaves against the quiet sky of evening.

With her two new gardens at Saint-Brice and Hyères, Wharton became known to all her friends as a super-gardener. Madame Saint-René Taillandier,

Walter Berry and a friend on the terrace

Wharton's library at Pavillon Colombe had the same comfortable atmosphere as the one at the Mount. A friend who helped Wharton translate *The Age of Innocence* remembered their meetings at Pavillon Colombe: "Those were delightful afternoons, evenings too, sometimes, in the soft-coloured library, with the low tables covered with new books, the flower-paintings on the walls, the door wide open to the garden and its scents, the bowls of great poppies or blue larkspurs shedding their petals, or a tall white lily, alone in a crystal jar, in noiseless attendance."

Wharton at Pavillon Colombe

The drawing room at Pavillon Colombe, painted by Walter Gay

The drawing room at Pavillon Colombe *(top and middle)* was formal, filled with French furniture and Oriental porcelain vases.

Wharton's friend Madame Saint-René Taillandier remembered: "In nearly every French interior you will notice a clock that betrays the bad taste of the mother-in-law, or a woolwork chair cover, touching relic of 'bonne-maman.' With Mrs. Wharton I was intimidated by the esthetic perfection of everything around her."

The dining room at Pavillon Colombe

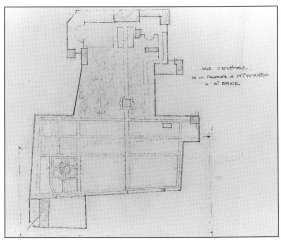

In 1924 Henry Trésol made new plans for Wharton's gardens. The house is at the top. At bottom left are her new rose garden and the blue garden.

"Jean-Marie," as Pavillon Colombe was called before Wharton restored the house and the gardens, in 1918. Ogden Codman wrote to his mother after receiving a postcard "of a *lovely* little house at St. Brice near Paris that [Mrs. Wharton] has just bought. I knew the house well and once I wanted to buy it myself. . . . It has grounds of about four acres and is a gem of 18th century architecture and the grounds contain beautiful trees."

*Below:* Wharton's terrace by the house, where she sat with her friends

The old pool in the *parc,* looking out toward the *potager*

who translated Wharton's fiction in her last years, used the garden as a metaphor for their friendship: "We met, so to put it, in the open, in a garden of the mind, among the choice roses of her growing, the homelier violets of mine; and there we talked at large of other 'garden fancies,' curious and far-fetched, the works of our literary friends. My image is at any rate one that well beseems her. Which of us all who knew her, however slightly, can recall her name without the vision of a garden, perfect in its beauty?"

Wharton delighted in her first French garden, complete with parterres near the house, from which a path led to the *parc,* or wood, and, beyond the wood, a *potager*. The gardens had been abandoned since 1914, however, and had not been well cared for before that.

Upon moving to Pavillon Colombe, Wharton's first task was to restore the gardens to their original splendor. She had found an old picture showing a "jardin à la Française" that the tall windows of the house had once looked out on. It had long since been absorbed into an English-style garden, "but the grove of trees beyond and the oblong basin and fountain beneath their shade were still untouched." She reestablished the original geometric design—first leveling the "humpy modern lawn dotted with coleus and canna beds" that extended from the house to the little grove, then cutting down straggling ornamental

Catharine Gross on the lily path, holding Coony and Linky. L'Abbé Mugnier made a trip each June to Pavillon Colombe "to see the long walk when the Candidum lilies were in bloom; and he really *did* see them, which is more than some visitors do, who make the pilgrimage for the same purpose." Wharton instructed her gardener to plant the monkshood behind the lilies. "In front, we will put some dwarf snapdragons in shades of pink and copper red, like last year."

*Left:* The blue garden, designed with Lawrence Johnston

*Below:* Although the areas near her house were mostly green in the French fashion, the back part of Wharton's property was ablaze with color. As she described it: "My vegetable plots are all bordered with apples 'en cordon,' or with pears and apples trained as pyramids, fans or lyres; and outside these espaliers a box-border edges the alleys. The kitchen garden has three alleys running north and south, and the same number, but much longer, dividing it latitudinally."

She wrote out extensive plant lists (translated here from her French) for herself and her gardener, showing that she planted repeating groups of brightly colored flowers, mostly annuals, creating a picture dazzling in its brilliance.

For the great border in the central allée of the *potager,* to the right of the turnaround, she wished to "repeat as much as possible the effect of last year, but in grouping even more carefully the different colors, that is to say, the oranges, yellows and pale yellows. For example: orange calendula, heliopsis,

yellow calceolaria, white and yellow snapdragons, and behind between the large asters, those yellow very floriferous dahlias which have always been planted in the border of dahlias. Then group the blues, violets and mauves, as for example: anchusas, delphiniums, mauve dwarf asters, heliotrope, violet petunias, violet china asters, *Verbena canadensis*, *Verbena rigida*, ageratum, blue delphiniums."

Farther on, she wanted white and pink colors: white dahlias, pink and white delphiniums, tall scabiosas in various colors, pink and white penstemons, pink and white snapdragons, white browallia; and then large groups of truly blue colors: anchusa, delphinium, lobelia, bachelor's button, blue browallia.

These she "followed again by yellows: at the back, yellow dahlias, then heliopsis and in front of that: some Cape marigolds, Siberian wall flowers, straw and orange nasturtiums, orange California poppies, dwarf yellow calceolaria."

Afterward, she wanted "a large group of violet or blue, and then a group of pink and white and so forth and so on. The essential is that the yellow groups be separated from the pink by the groups of blue and violet. Some strong tufts of perennial plants with silver foliage would be good to separate the groups." She concluded her list with similar instructions for the rest of the border, as well as the border along the east wall, the border of rhododendrons, the penstemons, and the border of lilies.

*Above:* In the *potager,* snapdragons, delphiniums, and other flowers grew in the box-edged beds near a conical topiary, and roses climbed the walls.

In the 1920s, Wharton created a rose garden ("la nouvelle roseraie"). Topiaries punctuated the corners of the central basin, climbing roses were trained on posts, and a line of floribundas ran along the sides backed by hybrid teas, standards, and more climbers.

trees and rooting up laurels and hydrangea borders. "Having retraced the main lines of the old garden, set the fountain playing, and reestablished the lost boundary of a clipped box hedge and a gateway, between the grove and the kitchen garden, I was able to turn my mind to planting."

Eventually, her seven-acre "estate" would consist of several different areas. Near the house was a wide graveled terrace bordered by a row of orange trees in green boxes. Down to the right, looking out from the house, was the "*pelouse*—a lower lawn bordered by a yew hedge." The box-edged squares of lawn in front of the house between the gravel terrace and the wood became her "*parterres à la française*." A path bordered by box hedges led from the house into the wood, where one would discover in the shady cool the handsome old stone pool, which reflected the leafy trees. Here, ivy on the ground was brightened by Solomon's seal and primroses in spring and European cyclamen in the early fall. Wharton also planted expanses of periwinkle and St.-John's-wort, colonies of lily-of-the-valley and autumn crocuses.

The path continued out of the wood and through a grille gateway into the *potager,* or kitchen garden—an elaborate massing of flowers, fruit trees, and vegetables that filled up the rear of the property—dividing it in two under an arcade of pleached limes and abutting ultimately on the southern boundary wall. Along the wall was a wide border of evergreen shrubs, rhododendrons, azaleas, flowering quince, and a few magnolias that, even though they were old and had been neglected, were "in spring a glory of yellow and white and salmon pink."

Her "little world" was a *hortus inclusus,* bounded all around its circumference by old stone walls ten feet high. The walls were covered with ivy in the shady parts and, in the sunny areas, served as a background for roses, clematis, wisteria, and trumpet vine. In the fruit garden, the walls were patterned over with espaliered pears, apples, peaches, and nectarines, and the golden leaves of grapes.

In this part of France just north of Paris, the soil was good but the nights were cold, even in summer. Even so, after two years of gardening in France—"this horticultural heaven"—Wharton rejoiced that "already the New England gardening-wrinkles have been smoothed from my brow and my confidence in the essential reasonableness of Nature has been restored." She explained in the early 1920s:

> At any rate, to one who has fought for years with the ruthless gales of the Rhode Island sea-coast, and the late frosts and burning suns of the Massachusetts mountains, who has watched the mowing-down in a night of painfully nursed "colour-effects," and returned in the spring to the blackened corpses of carefully sheltered hemlock hedges and box-borders, who has learned from cruel experience the uselessness of trying to "protect" ivy, or to persuade even the tough ampelopsis to grow on sunny walls; to a gardener who has battled with such climates for twenty years, for the sake of a few brief weeks of feverish radiance, there is a foretaste of heaven in the long leisurely progression of the French summer.

She was excited to be able to grow box, ivy, jasmine, and climbing hybrid tea roses (which bloom from June until December), all fundamental to the

Edith Wharton and Eunice Maynard in the back garden, 1935. By then, Wharton had planted more lawn and curved beds for her flowers near the back wall.

makeup of any French garden: "Nearly everything is 'remontant' and has plenty of time to flower twice over; this blessed sense of the leisureliness and dependableness of the seasons in France, of the way the picture stays in its frame instead of dissolving like a fidgetty *tableau-vivant,* creates a sense of serenity in the mind inured to transiency and failure."

By the 1930s, Wharton's gardens produced more vegetables and flowers than the household could use. The excess was sold in the village, each sale recorded in the head gardener's account book. In September 1934 alone, for example, they sold:

| | |
|---|---|
| 15K haricots verts (green beans) | 30.00 |
| 20 bottes (bunches) statice | 37.50 |
| 15K pois (peas) | 30.00 |
| 15K tetragonne (like spinach) | 37.50 |
| 50K haricots beurres (butter beans) | 75.00 |
| Dahlias | 26.00 |
| 8K mâche (corn salad) | 10.00 |
| 30K flageolets (kidney beans) | 30.00 |
| 40 choux (cabbage) | 20.00 |
| 55K tomates | 33.00 |
| | TOTAL = 329.00 FF |

Wharton took advantage of the expertise of friends in developing her gardens. Lawrence "Johnnie" Johnston, a fellow American who also chose to live abroad, was famous for his beautiful Cotswolds estate, Hidcote, begun in 1907. Johnston had used hedges to create a number of small isolated gardens without sacrificing the unified effect of the whole. Part of his originality lay in his packing of the plants into the soil until they were overflowing, leaving no space blank or wanting of color. Johnston also skillfully used different shades and textures of green leaves to create breathtaking effects. Wharton sang his praises to Daisy Chanler in 1925: "I had a delightful fortnight in England, though the motor-trip I had projected with Lawrence Johnston to York, Durham, etc. fell through owing to his mother's serious illness. I motored to the Cotswolds to see him, & spent an afternoon in his incomparable garden." At Pavillon Colombe, Johnston helped Wharton create a "blue garden," a formal area devoted solely to blue flowers, including blue hibiscus, enclosed by little box hedges.

She compared garden notes and plans with her niece Beatrix Farrand, as well. Farrand's own Reef Point in Bar Harbor, Maine, was becoming a varied and fascinating nature center for her collections of native and exotic plants. Aunt and niece were in many ways alike—hard-working professional women whose successful careers would save them in this postwar period, when prices had climbed steeply. In July 1923, Edith wrote to Beatrix: "I wish you were lying out under my trees this afternoon—the little place really sparkles with freshness, in spite of the heat, which is creeping up again after a respite. And it's so much tidier, and more nearly finished than last year. . . .Oh, if only you and I could talk across the fence!

"Reynolds's first blue penstemon is in bloom, & the corn is thriving, & the gladioli are lovely. And the chineses are bad but beautiful, & we're all well."

Wharton also shared her own extensive gardening knowledge with her friends. The novelist Louis Bromfield created his wonderful garden having learned from her. According to Russell Page, Bromfield's was the only garden in France "where the hybrid musk roses . . . Penelope and Pax and others . . . were allowed to grow into large loosely trimmed bushes hanging over the river, loveliest with their clusters of cream and white and rose-pink flowers just as the light began to fade."

When she was settled in her new quarters in Saint-Brice, Wharton began to plan her next novel. While many postwar writers used the context of the 1910s and 1920s to experiment with new forms, such as stream of consciousness and interior monologue, Wharton, who still felt unable to address the present without writing about the war, chose to return in her imagination to the past and write a traditional love story about three young people coming of age. Set in 1870s New York, *The Age of Innocence* features all the haunts of Wharton's youth.

The novel concerns the passion of Newland Archer, a staid but intelligent young New Yorker who falls in love with Ellen Olenska, the Europeanized beauty who has returned to her native city to escape a disastrous marriage. Newland, however, is engaged to marry the athletic, unimaginative, and good May Welland, and he cannot break out of the confines of his conventional life to realize his love for Ellen.

Newland Archer is fifty-seven at the conclusion of the novel, the age Edith Wharton was when she began to write it. She told her story from the vantage point of someone who has learned from life, is less angry about the past, and can now appreciate many of the good values of the old New York society. And perhaps she chose to return to this world in which one avoided unpleasant subjects because she wanted to forget so many things—the war and also the personal horrors before the war.

*The Age of Innocence* has an international theme. As Cynthia Wolff points out, the name Newland Archer is a play on the name Isabel Archer, Henry James's heroine in *The Portrait of a Lady*; it is also a play on the name Christopher Newman, from James's *The American*. While Newland and May elect to remain at home to lead the sort of life known to Wharton in her youth—a life filled with pleasant social activities and good manners but little excitement and few intellectual opportunites—Ellen retreats to the lively city of Paris, reflecting Wharton's own feelings about expatriation.

Her portrayal of New York mores here is more affectionate than in previous fictions, particularly *The House of Mirth*. Society seems a less frightening force, and characters can break the rules and get away with it, as long as they understand how social power works. Mrs. Manson Mingott and Julius Beaufort are two such mavericks. Julius Beaufort insists that his wife "slap her new dresses on her back as soon as they arrive from Paris," instead of putting them away for one or two years, as was the rule in New York and the more conservative Boston. Beaufort was modeled on August Belmont, a wealthy German Jew who had emigrated to America and married into the Perry family; he had become assimilated quickly and had acquired all the trappings of wealth—country estates, racehorses, and a gallery of paintings. In the novel, Julius Beaufort is rich enough to get away with being unconventional, but his shady business dealings finally bring him down.

Mrs. Mingott thumbed her nose at convention by building her large house of pale cream-colored stone "(when brown sandstone seemed as much the only wear as a frockcoat in the afternoon) in an inaccessible wilderness near the Central Park. . . . But the cream-colored house (supposed to be modelled on the private hotels of the Parisian aristocracy) was there as a visible proof of her moral courage; and she throned in it, among pre-Revolutionary furniture and souvenirs of the Tuileries of Louis Napoleon (where she had shone in her middle age), as placidly as if there were nothing peculiar in living above Thirty-fourth Street, or in having French windows that opened like doors instead of sashes that pushed up."

Edith Wharton also returned in her imagination to the Newport of her childhood, where Newland and May vacation with May's parents, who are as conventional and predictable as the stodgiest of old New Yorkers who summered there by the sea. Wharton drew on her memories of leaving calling cards at the big summer cottages, driving along Ocean Drive, watching her neighbors the Rutherfurd sisters take part in archery-club contests.

Walter Berry helped with the book, as he had done with *The Valley of Decision, The Decoration of Houses, Ethan Frome,* and *The Reef*. He was with Wharton often, reading, reacting, and advising. In America, she enlisted Minnie Jones to research the back files of the New York *Tribune* and in the Yale University library in order to verify certain facts about the 1870s. Minnie wrote to tell her that Newland "Archer couldn't have received *Middlemarch* because that came out in 1873 and *Daniel Deronda* not until 1876." She also confirmed that Christine Nilsson sang at the old Academy in 1871 and reminded her that

"Ward McAllister started the Patriarchs balls in the winter of 1872/3, and they were going strong in 1875; the Assemblies were not started until several years later, but the F.C.D.C., or Family Circle Dancing Class, was started in 1874; the first meeting of that was at Mr. Butler Duncan's house, 12 Washington Square, but after the first winter those dances, like the Patriarchs, were at Delmonico's (just when Delmonico moved from Fourteenth street to 26th street I haven't found yet). . . .The Beecher case opened in Brooklyn January 11th, 1875, and dragged along all that winter."

Minnie felt she was lowering herself to read Ward McAllister's *Society As I Have Found It*, to clarify details of the social world of her youth: "Little did I think I'd ever consult him and such bosh I never tackled. It was just to be sure about the Patriarchs." She also used souvenirs to trigger her memory, for example, "all the cards of the Assemblies at 21. I was on the Committee of Management from the first to the end, and the changes in the list of subscribers are amusing; I remember we kept Mrs. Vanderbilt, the great Gracie's mother-in-law, waiting for two years at least."

As a result of Minnie Jones's research, Wharton decided to make the date in the opening scene uncertain. She began her novel, "On a January evening of the early 'seventies Christine Nilsson was singing. . . ." This allowed her greater latitude in using the names of famous people from her girlhood. She could "do away with the necessity of substituting Kellogg for Nilsson, and also of putting other obscure names in the places of well-known ones. What I especially want is to give the atmosphere of New York in my youth, keeping the names that have remained familiar and not using those that have long since been forgotten."

She realized that the whole flavor of the book would be lost if "dull names are substituted for vivid ones," and she did not think "accuracy of date in such matters is nearly as important as the rendering of the atmosphere. The unimaginative person who writes a letter to point out that so-and-so did not sing in New York till 1880 is of very little importance." She did not anticipate any chronological difficulties in the latter part of the book as "all the local colour" was in the beginning.

On December 19, 1919, Minnie Jones wrote Wharton: "The Age is very interesting, and your memory quite amazing; you recall things I had entirely forgotten, and you bring back that time as if it were last week. I wonder how many people will recognize old Aunt Mary, and August Belmont—and I do remember your mother's saying that when she was a girl one knew all the carriages in town." Wharton replied, "I am so glad you like it, but I wonder if the public will be interested in so far-off things."

Although the milieu of the novel was historical, the relationships were contemporary. When Ellen Olenska wishes a divorce from her husband—a

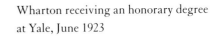

difficult Polish count—her family, fearing the stigma, discourages her. In the character of Ellen, Wharton portrayed a nice woman who struggled with the issue of divorce—one of many in her stories. The idea of divorce had always troubled Wharton. Now she, too, was divorced, as were many of her friends, like Elisina Tyler. Perhaps she was thinking of a composite of all of them when she created Ellen Olenska. In 1919, when she was writing the book, she discussed Elisina's "past" with Minnie Jones:

> With regard to Elisina, there is nothing to do but to laugh at these mysterious allusions! The truth and the whole truth is exactly what everyone knows. She was very unhappily married to Grant Richards, and got a divorce and married Royall.
>
> I don't think anything will shut up a creature like Miss Curtis. But perhaps it would make Mrs. Roger Wolcott (who is a dear) feel better if she knew that Elisina and Royall are life-long friends of the Jack Carters and the Robert Blisses, and that Marie Lee Childe and the

Walter Gays are devoted to them—as well as many other friends of ours. My own idea is that, in such a case, "explaining" is a mistake. Elisina's "past" is what mine is, and yours, and that of any other woman whose marriage has been a calamity—I should have supposed that was no one's affair but her own; but in any case, there is no mystery about it and her friends would laugh if they heard it suggested.

In 1919, Wharton defended her friend Elisina, but in her fiction, she portrayed a "society" from the 1870s that felt otherwise, suggesting her own ambivalence on the subject.

Published in 1920, *The Age of Innocence* brought Wharton the Pulitzer Prize. In June 1923, she was awarded an honorary degree from Yale University, which became the occasion for her last visit to America. She stayed with her friend Mrs. Bayard Cutting at Westbrook, her house on Long Island. Then, with Minnie Jones and Beatrix Farrand, she took the ferry across Long Island Sound and motored to New Haven and dined with the president of the university. On June 20 she walked in a procession to Wolsey Hall as the first woman to receive a doctorate of letters from Yale.

In the next decade, Wharton continued to produce fiction at her steady rate. For story settings, she looked back to the New York of her past, as well as to Europe. In August 1923 she sent a copy of *A Son at the Front* to Daisy Chanler: "I hope you will express your opinion with an equal candor, since most of the help I've had in my writing has come from the plain truths administered by friends." Daisy liked this tale, and Edith wrote her again: "The thing that

Edith Wharton at her writing table in the 1930s

interested me was the love of the ill-assorted quartet for their boy, & the gradual understanding between the two men." Critics had noted that she was losing her ear for the talk of Americans, to which Wharton replied: "No, I'm afraid my young Americans don't talk the language as spoken by the Scott Fitzgerald and Sinclair Lewis jeunesse; but I saw dozens of young Americans from all parts of America during the war, & none of them talked it; any more than your sons-in-law do!" Ronald Simmons, the young man from Providence she became so attached to during the war, was a model for her, and he "never used a word that wasn't real English. So I've really been faithful according to my lights."

She returned to the nineteenth century in four novellas that came out in 1924 under the collective title *Old New York: False Dawn* (set in the 1840s), *The Old Maid* (1850s), *The Spark* (1860s), and *New Year's Day* (1870s). In *The Mother's Recompense*, published in 1925, Wharton envisioned a middle-aged woman, Kate Clephane, who had exiled herself to France after being ostracized in New York for leaving her husband and little girl and running off with another man. Years later, returning to New York for her daughter's wedding, she discovers to her surprise that she is not only forgiven for her old sins—in fact, no one cared—but also that her daughter is in love with a former lover of hers, Chris Fenno. Although she has the chance to marry an old friend, she returns to France to live out her life there. In 1926 a collection of stories, *Here and Beyond,* appeared, and by November of that year she was finishing *Twilight Sleep,* a bizarre novel based on her image of America in which everyone is either obsessed by work or drugged. As she separated herself more and more from the world in her precious retreat, she became increasingly out of touch with modern life as a subject for fiction. Her novels suffered, although from time to time she wrote a short story as good as her best.

During these years, which were marked by the death of Walter Berry in 1927, the solidarity of Edith Wharton's household became increasingly important to her. Her servants, many of whom had been with her for a long time, really were her family. They took good care of her and forgave her her foibles.

Doyley had died long before, and Anna Bahlmann in 1916. Wharton's staff now included two squads of gardeners—one for Saint-Brice and one for Hyères. Catharine Gross ran the household. A native of Alsace who had been with Wharton since a year before her marriage, she turned seventy in 1922. Percy Lubbock wrote of Gross and Edith Wharton, "Their alliance . . . had been long and close, and nothing was pleasanter to see than their meeting again after any separation." In earlier years, Gross had always accompanied Wharton on her travels but now was often replaced by Elise, Wharton's lady's maid. After a trip, "when they met again (after copious correspondence in the inter-

The gardeners at Pavillon Colombe. In 1920 Wharton wrote to Beatrix Farrand that she missed Reynolds, her gardener in Lenox, "for I'm not a working gardener, & never was & never shall be; & when my old gang makes silly answers and objections I never know the counter-answers." By the 1930s, with more experience and much research, Wharton had created gardens of great imagination and flair, particularly at Hyères.

*Above left:* When Wharton traveled, she always took an entourage of servants with her, as in 1914 when she went to Algiers with Percy Lubbock accompanied by Anna Bahlmann, Charles Cook (shown here at left), who took charge of her Mercedes, and Elise, then her new lady's maid.

*Above right:* Smith, the English chauffeur, with Wharton's Peugeot

val), there was Edith greeting and embracing Gross, laughing and chattering to her, excited and delighted as a small girl home for the holidays."

Elise had become Wharton's personal maid beginning around 1914, and she traveled with her from then on. There was a great affection between them. Edith would tell her in a general way where she was going on a trip and for how long, and Elise somehow miraculously packed all the right things. She was very religious; Edith was drawn to her faith and cherished Elise's way of understanding life. One night, in an Algerian town, when Edith asked whether the natives weren't making more noise than usual, Elise replied with authority, "Yes madame. I believe it's the moon."

In April of 1933, Elise collapsed with a nervous breakdown. Edith wrote to Daisy Chanler on April 4: "She herself thinks she is a total & permanent wreck, & it is quite impossible to make her understand that there is no organic trouble, but only a temporary physiological disturbance. The servant class can never grasp anything like that—if they *could* (as dear Egerton used to tell me) they wouldn't be servants, but presidents & prime ministers!" Elise was diagnosed as having pernicious anemia and died in May. Edith found "it is very dull not to have her leaping intelligence always about me—and how she loved dog jokes!" Two weeks after Elise's collapse, Gross had a nervous breakdown and was diagnosed with senile dementia; she died in October 1933. Edith was desolated. She confessed to Mary Berenson: "Since Walter's death I've been incurably lonely *inside,* and these two faithful women kept the heart fire burning."

The Englishman Alfred White was first Wharton's butler; he later became her "agent": He had worked for Edith and Teddy since 1888, in the early years of their marriage, and had taken care of Teddy during his illnesses. Now he managed both of Edith's new places. He served her, according to friends, "with respectful severity; and she very well knew she could rely on him, not only to keep her taste true to the highest mark, but to safe-guard and

help her, to lift trouble off her back, in every way that appertained to his department and I don't know in how many more." After she died in 1937, White wrote, "For 49 years it was my privilege to serve her and protect her from household cares, that she could carry on her work in peace."

Charles Cook, her chauffeur, came from Lee, Massachusetts, the town next to Lenox. Although Wharton did not actually drive her car, she was very involved in getting from place to place. According to Percy Lubbock, it was very difficult for her "to sit submissive and inactive behind her driver"; she was constantly busying herself about the directions, "whether the motor wasn't behaving oddly and what was the meaning of its complaints—who had mislaid the map and whether it was rightly interpreted when found." Cook, however, handled all situations calmly: "Nothing shook his monumental breadth; unknown tongues, strange manners and unhomely customs beat on it in vain." Time and again he saved Wharton from disaster. He repaired the motor on the roads near Lenox. He oversaw the process of letting it down by ropes below the Monastery of La Verna in 1912 when it could not negotiate the narrow road on the side of a cliff. He got the car through to England and back at the beginning of the war, and he drove Wharton and Berry around the war zone in 1915. In the early 1920s, he left Wharton's service after suffering a slight stroke. By this time, according to R. W. B. Lewis, he "had grown corpulent and cosmopolitan" and "was beginning to resemble a somewhat overfed diplomat." He retired to America with a generous pension from his employer.

Wharton had very strong views on the roles of servants and "mistresses," a relationship that was becoming a thing of the past. Just after the war, she wrote to Beatrix about Minnie's personal maid, Murkett, that it was acceptable for Minnie to help her maid make Minnie's bed, "so have I often helped my Gross make mine" in situations "where the lady's maid is supposed to do the work of a housemaid. One can't help such relations between a mistress and

*Above left:* Edith Wharton and Minnie Jones. Wharton wrote to Beatrix Farrand in December 1919 about her sister-in-law Minnie, Beatrix's mother: "The dear darling is as deeply urban as you & I are rustic, & those tendencies are the deepest down & the most unalterable of all."

*Above right:* Linky under the rose pergola

*Below and opposite:* Drawings from Edith Wharton's sketchbook, some labeled by Wharton

"Minnie"

"Tooty pleased"

"Gross"

maid who've been long together." Murkett, Edith felt, was "sincerely devoted to your mother, & gives her the kind of service she most needs. Even if it were not *utterly impossible* to find that kind of decent respectable middle aged maid any longer (so that to part with one who had small failings would be folly) I should still think your mother lucky to have got some one so well suited to her. At your mother's age the feeling of habit and security is all-important."

Wharton knew that finding women who wanted to devote their lives to service was now rare. "Having had four highly recommended maids in succession since Gross became my house keeper, I speak as one who knoweth—and who is now trying to have the Village Idiot as No. 5!!!!—The old type of quiet lady's maid, who is 'in it' for anything but the wardrobe, & high jinks at Palace Hotels, has vanished from the post-war world, and one had best cling to the survivors with hooks of steel."

Servants appear frequently in her fiction. They are often part of the households of the rich—helping the women to dress for dinner and packing the steamer trunks for the next trip abroad. They play prominent parts in the emotional lives of her main characters. Yet it is in Wharton's ghost stories that the reader gets a glimpse of another world, that of the servants' quarters belowstairs and the rivalries and relationships that take place there.

One of her most moving ghost stories is the early "The Lady's Maid's Bell." The central character is Hartley, a young lady's maid who is quiet, well-mannered, and "educated above [her] station." Hartley is recovering from typhoid and seeks a job that will not be too taxing. She is happy, therefore, to serve Mrs. Brympton, who is sickly herself, at Brympton Place, a big and gloomy country house on the Hudson. It is the "right kind of house" where "things were done handsomely."

Soon after her arrival, however, Hartley discovers strange goings-on. There is no bell to call her to her mistress. When Hartley is needed, Agnes, the housemaid, must walk the whole length of the servants' wing to call her. Also, no one is allowed to enter the room of her predecessor, Emma Saxon, now dead, who was very special in her mistress's affections. Hartley sees a woman, whom no one else sees, who may or may not be the ghost of Emma. She learns that there have been four lady's maids in six months.

The cast of characters also includes Mrs. Brympton's coarse, drunk, and demanding husband, who eyes Hartley in a suggestive way, and Mr. Ranford, a kindly neighbor with a warm smile who often visits when the master is away and who loves books. The setting of the story—the long narrow dark halls of the downstairs with the servants' rooms with closed doors—suggests all kinds of happenings of a mysterious, emotional, and sexual nature.

In the 1930s, Wharton wrote two excellent stories depicting the "households" of the rich in interesting detail. In both the mistress of the house is old and her dependence on her servants is a key element of the plot. In "After Holbein," an oft-invited, aging extra man, Anson Warley, dresses in evening clothes—his habit for years—and then attends a dinner party that is a figment of his imagination as well his hostess's. The hostess, Mrs. Jaspar, was modeled after old Mrs. Astor, the queen of New York society when Edith Wharton was young. Even though she has obviously lost her wits, Mrs. Jaspar's loyal household keeps her functioning.

Mrs. Jasper is introduced in the story with her day nurse exclaiming, "She's worse than usual tonight. . . . Absolutely determined to have her jewels out." The longtime members of her household conspire to keep up the charade that Mrs. Jaspar is still the queen of society, still dresses for dinner, and still gives wonderful parties. Her old maid Lavinia—"so old as to make Mrs. Jaspar appear almost young"—knew exactly how to handle her when she rang out, "My sapphire velvet tonight, with the diamond stars. . . . Old Lavinia renewed every morning the roses and carnations in the slim crystal vases between the powder boxes and the nail polishers," probably paying for the flowers herself since the family had shut down the hothouses at the uninhabited country place on the Hudson. The big "high-studded dressing room . . . with its rich dusky carpet and curtains, and its monumental dressing table draped with lace and laden with gold-backed brushes and combs, gold-stoppered toilet bottles and all the charming paraphernalia of beauty," is now the setting of a woman way past her prime dressing and redressing for events that never take place. The role of Munson, the old butler, is to know the combination of the safe where Mrs. Jaspar's jewels are kept.

The day and night nurses and the "stupid footman," George, are not as skilled in the arts of deception; neverthless, the dinner does take place, and the miracle is that someone—the vague Anson Warley—actually comes to dine. The party goes off without a hitch, as the two diners imagine that Apollinaris is "Perrier-Jouet '95," "Château Lafitte '74," and "the old Newbold Madeira"; and that bunched-up newspaper represents "beautiful flowers."

"All Souls'," published just before Wharton's death, is set in one of her many great big country houses, this one called Whitegates, situated five or six miles outside of town. In colonial days, the house had been "foursquare with four spacious rooms on the ground floor, an oak-floored hall dividing them, the usual extension at the back, and a good attic under the roof." In the early 1880s, two wings had been added "at right angles to the south front, so that the old 'circle' before the front door became a grassy court, enclosed on three sides, with a big elm in the middle." It was turned into a roomy dwelling, comfortable and suited to the Clayburns' "large hospitality." The men farmed the considerable land around it for generations and "played a part in state politics."

This detailed description suggests a roomy and pleasant house once

Catharine Gross in the garden where roses climbed on the walls and bloomed below them

thronged by people who enjoyed full, happy lives, yet at the time of the story, the aging Mrs. Clayburn lives there alone, except for her household of servants. On All Souls' Day, the day of remembering the dead, the servants mysteriously desert her, and Mrs. Clayburn, who has been incapacitated with a sprained ankle, finds herself alone in the house, which, like many in Wharton's fiction, changes drastically in personality to become a place of isolation and terror. Wharton, a fiercely energetic person, often had her activities brought to a screeching halt by illness or, in earlier days, by a breakdown; one can imagine what feelings of helplessness she experienced.

Dogs, a key element of Edith Wharton's intimate household, were immortalized in an excellent ghost story, "Kerfol," set at yet another old house—this time in Brittany. This romantic house has an avenue overarched by gray-trunked trees, a chapel belfry, a moat filled with shrubs and brambles,

and proud roofs and gables, all suggesting a "long accumulation of history." When the heroine enters the house, it is deserted except for four dogs: a beautiful Chinese "Sleevedog . . . very small and golden brown, with large eyes and a ruffled throat"; another dog, "a vague rough brindled thing"; a third dog, "a long-haired white mongrel"; and a fourth, "a white pointer with one brown ear." But she discovers that no dogs presently live at Kerfol, and these are ghosts who are said to reappear one day of the year.

This exposition leads into a wonderful story about a woman deserted by her husband who is consoled by another man. In retaliation, her husband murders her beloved dogs. The dogs' ghosts, however, execute her revenge by devouring the husband, a wonderful transference of rage.

As the "châtelaine" of the grandest house in Saint-Brice, Wharton also gained respect as a benefactor for the community, to such an extent that her benefices were formally acknowledged by a resolution of the commune, adopted in 1927. Twice each year she sponsored a village festival and provided tea and refreshments. On July 4, she would fly the American flag and invite all to her open house to celebrate. On August 15, the Feast of the Assumption, the local priest, a standard before him and followed by young girls in bridal veils for their first communion, nuns and villagers *en grand tenu,* would first pause at the statue of the Virgin in a niche in the wall of Pavillon Colombe to sing anthems, then walk in procession through the garden to stop and greet her before the open doors of the house.

Wharton was content in her garden haven during these years. As she wrote, "It used to be said that good Americans went to Paris when they died; but the saying should be qualified by adding that garden-loving Americans go to the suburbs of Paris."

On the Feast of the Assumption, August 15, 1936, the procession sang anthems before the statue of the Virgin in the wall outside, then filed through the garden to the house.

# HYÈRES, "SO WARM, SO GOLDEN, SO FULL OF FLOWERS"

Robert Norton, Walter Berry, Edith Wharton, and Gaillard Lapsley at lunch on the terrace at Château Sainte-Claire, Hyères, in the 1920s

Although she had previously thought Cannes, Nice, and nearby Monte Carlo dull resorts for the moneyed and trivial, Edith Wharton changed her mind about the south of France when she discovered Hyères during the war. Once a popular resort dating back to the sixteenth century—Charles IX and Catherine de Medici wintered there in 1564—Hyères had faded from fashion, though it was still popular with wealthy Russians; its casino and a few large hotels attracted a winter crowd. It was also the center of a farming community that sent two trainloads of vegetables each day to Paris. The mild climate of the western coast of the Riviera near Toulon was perfect for creating a garden completely different from all her others.

In late November 1918, on a motor trip from Paris to Hyères with Robert Norton, a former British diplomat, now a watercolor painter, Wharton talked of her sense of the history of the region. In her reactions, "always so eager when 'on the road,'" there was a new note "that was personal, almost possessive as of one showing for the first time the home he cherishes." She spoke to Norton of "the emotions roused in her by the physical beauty of colour and form and light, and still more by the subtler atmosphere of association and history evoked by every town and hamlet, every mountain chain and river, almost every stone of that favoured land," and of "her own sense of being on holy ground. For her no corner of Mediterranean lands, with such blessings of climate, fertility, and scenery, had played so continuous a role in European history. Phoenicians and Greeks had come to trade, and settled; the Romans had made it the richest province of their Empire—this was the Provincia par excellence, the true Provence, living still as it had lived for two thousand years and more, taking no heed of the artificial life of its coast-line, the cosmopolitan Riviera, the very name of which she hated."

She was fascinated by the vegetation of this region:

> As we neared the Mediterranean and entered tracts of the fragrant maquis that fringes all its coasts, she greeted the green undergrowth of shrubs like old friends and lingered over the musical names—lentisk and cistus and myrtle, rosemary and heath, ilex, juniper and arbutus: they were all pure poetry to her. Through the same evergreen tangle she pictured Miltiades and his handful of men in their heavy armour plunging down on the Persian host at Marathon: Xerxes on his throne watching the battle of Salamis. It was one of those talks, fragmentary,

allusive, half thinking aloud, that linger in the memory. I have dwelt on it as throwing light on her choice of the home where she was to pass . . . the twenty years that remained to her. She was usually reticent about the things she loved, and I doubt if she often spoke of them so freely as at this moment of détente after the four intolerable years of war.

The light of the south, both of sky and sun—the views of mountains and sea, the general atmosphere of peace—charmed and healed her. She raved about it all to Bernard Berenson in 1919: "I read your letter 'stretched on a bank of amaranth & moly,' with the blue sea sending little silver splashes up to my toes, & roses & narcissus & mimosa outdoing Coty's best from the centre all round to the sea. In front of us lay two or three Odyssean isles, & the boat with a Lotean sail which is always in the right place was on duty as usual—& this is the way all my days are spent! Seven hours of blue-&-gold & thyme & rosemary & hyacinth & roses every day that the Lord makes; & in the evenings, dozing over a good book! . . .

"Seriously, you can't think what Provence has been this last month. Never have I seen it so warm, so golden, so windless & full of flowers."

She had found a wonderful house built in the ruins of the château near the top of the hill in the old part of town. The hilltop ruins were owned by Alfred Pechiney, who had made a fortune manufacturing chemicals. He had had work done to restore the fortress towers and walks and the convent buildings, but no one had lived there for many years. Edith Wharton leased the property after the war (she was finally able to buy it in 1927), renovated the existing buildings, and added to them, including a winding access road for motorcars. Here, as at Pavillon Colombe, she established a little world with a rare atmosphere away from the intrusions of reality and the disturbing trends of the twentieth century, and highlighted, of course, by the garden, where she was to "cultive passionément l'art du jardin," as the guidebook now reports.

She quickly became attached to Château Sainte-Claire. By May 1920 she was writing that she "had been torn shrieking from my beloved Hyères," but she was back there again in December, with Robert Norton. She told Bernard Berenson: "It's paralyzing to try to tell you of my life here, so other-dimensional it is to what you are plunged in." They were still at the hotel, but she spent mornings overseeing the making of her garden: "R.N. goes off with his sketching things, we meet at lunch, & in the p.m. usually take one of the tramps in the maquis that you know. The evenings are devoted to tramps in another maquis: 'exploring,' as Mr. Collins would put it, a heap of new books that keep pouring in from Bain & Affolter, with Gilchrist's Blake (we'd neither of us read it) as a background.—Those are the hours when, again & again, we cry: 'Oh, for BB!'

"Meanwhile the heavenly beauty & the heavenly quiet enfold me, & I feel that this really is the Cielo della Quiete to which the soul aspires after its stormy voyage."

Château Sainte-Claire's hilltop dominates the flat farmlands for miles around, from the mountains of the Massif des Maures to the northeast stretching to the Mediterranean coast. The château had been a fortress at the beginning of its history, haunted by ghosts of warriors attacking and defending. The ruined towers and walls around it date from the Middle Ages, but, long before, in Greek and Roman times, a settlement had flourished below the hill under its protection. In 1634 a convent of Clarisses, nuns of the order of Sainte Claire, the companion of Saint Francis of Assisi, was installed in its living quarters, with the approval of the town. The nuns devoted themselves to educating young women there until they were swept away by the French Revolution. The

The towers and ramparts that climbed the steep and rocky hill

The drawing room at Sainte-Claire, like most of the other rooms, was small, with low ceilings, furniture arranged for conversation, and many small tables filled with flowers from her garden.

The same drawing room, where Wharton and her friends read aloud on winter evenings

Library at Sainte-Claire

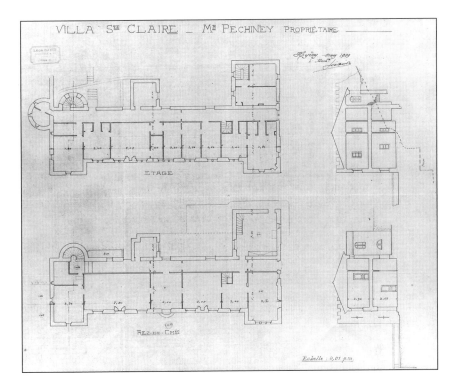

property lay abandoned until 1849, when a soldier of fortune, Olivier Voutier, bought it. Voutier died in 1877; his body is buried on the property.

The existing low, two-story building, untenanted for half a century, was hardly in good repair. Robert Norton described Wharton's enthusiasm about restoring this old place:

> Standing on a rocky ledge cut out of a steep hill-side overlooking Hyères, the oldest houses of which clambered to its gates, its garden a tangled wilderness and no means of access except on foot, it might have daunted many a younger lover of the picturesque than its new tenant. But her imagination was stirred by its romantic associations, by the ruined towers of the castellated peak which rose at its back—a pure Albrecht Dürer background—, and by the old red roofs clustering round a fortress-church at its feet, and she took the difficulties in her stride despite the head-shakings of Paul Bourget and other friends. So the house was gutted, new partitions made, roofs rebuilt, drains installed, and a quarter of a mile of motor-road contrived to wind up-hill through pine trees, with many sharp turns, to reach its door: not to speak of such accessories as garages, housing for chauffeurs and gardeners, all on the same steep hill-side. Chief task of all, perhaps, was providing the denuded rocky surface with soil. Into all this she threw herself intrepidly, and within a year, I think, the old house had come alive.

Norton and Gaillard Lapsley, now a don at Trinity College, Cambridge, were enlisted to help with the move and installation. They were told "to arrange the books, some two or three thousand of which were aligned in neat rows on the drawing-room floor. It would be an over-statement to say that we threw ourselves into the job with zest, but we should have claimed to have embarked on it conscientiously. So that when after two hours of exhausting and sometimes ruffling labour, the hostess coming to review our efforts condemned one shelf after another and ruthlessly ordered all the volumes back upon the floor, we retired, I remember, in some dudgeon. But such incidents are indis-

Frames on which Wharton trained her cypresses at Sainte-Claire

pensable ingredients to the atmosphere of a new house, and no future Christmas passed without reference to our discomfiture. In an incredible short time Edith's personality made itself felt in every room and the house was running on the smoothest of wheels."

The ground floor opened onto a flagged terrace about thirty yards long, which became the gathering place for Edith and her friends. It appeared "almost suspended above the town and was shaded by two pollarded plane trees framing the square tower and rose-coloured roof of the old fortified church. Beyond the town a level plain ran for five or six kilometres to the sea: and along the horizon lay stretched Les Iles d'Or—Porquerolles, Portcros and l'Ile du Levant. To the East rose the Mont des Maures, and westward hills followed the outline of the sea towards Toulon." When Edith had finished making the house her own, it comprised a double library, a dining room, large and small drawing rooms that opened out onto the terrace, seven master bedrooms, and six bathrooms. There were separate houses for the head gardener and chauffeur, as well as accommodations in the house for eight indoor servants and a garage for five cars. Later, Wharton had a separate house for the servants built nearby.

When Wharton and her household moved into the Château Sainte-Claire on December 23, 1920, she was ecstatic:

> The little house is delicious, so friendly & comfortable, & full of sun & air; but what overwhelms us all—though we thought we knew it—is the endless beauty of the view, or rather the views, for we look south, east & west, "miles & miles," & our quiet-coloured end of evening presents us with a full moon standing over the tower of the great Romanesque church just below the house, & a sunset silhouetting the "Iles d'Or" in black on a sea of silver.
>
> It is good to grow old—as well as to die—"in beauty"; & the beauty of this little place is inexhaustible.
>
> Yesterday we had the divinest Riviera weather, & as we sat on the terrace in the sun taking our coffee after luncheon a joint groan of deliverance escaped us at the thought of London, New York & Paris!

Wharton had already begun to redo the garden in 1919, even before she moved in. According to Daisy Chanler, wonderful wild things grew on the twenty-five acres of land: "Ilex, carob trees, and wild olives cluster about the old walls; century plants shoot up their stiff candalabra spikes from a rich undergrowth of *maquis*, the luxuriant tangle, thorny, flowering, always aromatic, which covers the stony hillsides of Provence." She terraced the hillside and connected her terraces by paths, so that about six of her acres became cul-

Arched cypresses and mandarin oranges underplanted with flowers led to a pavilion at the end of a terrace.

tivated gardens in the larger context of the wild growth. She built retaining walls and laid out level patches of lawn. Eventually she trained her cypresses into arches and cultivated all kinds of plants new to her, as well as old favorites. In March 1920 she wrote Beatrix Farrand:

> Ste. Claire, of which I send you some quite inadequate photos, is in the hands of masons & diggers of the earth. It is almost impossible to "take," as it's all up & downhill, but these snaps will give you some idea of its militant air, & the way it leans against the old mur d'enceint, guarded by its 2 towers.

Terrace with lemon trees and
prickly-pear cactus

Mr. Nabormand, the "rosiériste" of Golfe Juan, came to see us (or
rather *it*) the other day, & was in raptures at my series of terraces, & at
the opportunity for growing camellias & gardenias, besides all the roses
that ever *were*. Here, at present, the whole country is gushing with
roses—Banksia, Laevigata & hybrid teas—which, after one outburst in
Dec., & then a gentle steady flowering all winter, have now cast aside all
restraint, & are smothering walls, house fronts & balconies in white &
crimson & golden breakers of bloom.

She felt it was *"agony"* not to talk of all this with Beatrix face to face.

In her introduction to Harriet Martineau's book *Gardening in Sunny
Lands* (1924), Wharton told the reader about the excitement of the northerner
first moving to the south to garden: The first months of planning and planting
are a long honeymoon. Dazzled by the possibilities of growing what previously could be cultivated only under glass or "coaxed through an existence of semi-
invalidism in the uncertainty of the 'sheltered corner,'" he looks around him in
wonder at other people's gardens. "He discovers still newer treasures in the cat-

alogues of the local nurserymen, he summons them in consultation, he wanders through their nurseries; and every visit and every consultation results in a cargo of fascinating novelties." He soon learns, however, that this paradise has its hidden dangers, and is shocked by how vulnerable plants are: "Slight differerences of soil, of exposure, of the degree of shelter available, seem to count far more than in more equable climes. Where the midday sun is so much hotter, proportionately great is the evening chill." A sudden blast of wind off the Alps can do in tender blossoms, and the need for shade and moisture is a new consideration for plants happy in the northern sun and rain.

She had a new palette of plants to work with—different from what she could grow at Newport or Lenox, or even at Saint-Brice. Wharton was not a working gardener—she did not weed or dig and she had a squad of gardeners to tend her place—but she was totally involved, emotionally and intellectually. Her encyclopedic mind filled itself with the names of the many species and types of plants. As one garden writer put it, "Mrs. Wharton is not satisfied with growing the ordinary routine herbs and plants and shrubs, and in most cases her experiments are very successful." An unusual shrub was the *Acacia catheriana,* one of the rarest of late flowering mimosas.

When she described spring in her garden, she pictured a vital and colorful collection of plants all bursting into bloom and complementing each other.

*Above left:* Wharton was known for grouping unusual and different plants not just for their massed effects but because she genuinely appreciated them.

*Above right:* This view of an area bordered by roses and backed by the tower shows Wharton's planting style: a neat terrace of lawn and her packed drifts of many different flowering plants on the slopes that climbed the hill.

Path lined with orange freesias and
African daisies near where olives have
been left to give a natural appearance

The curving path leading up the hill
was planted with a wonderful variety
of shrubs and flowers with contrasting
foliage of various textures and shapes.

She wrote an essay—"Spring in a French Riviera Garden"—in which she used powerful language to describe her garden:

> This transition from winter to spring is perhaps the most exciting moment to garden-lovers in these regions. The roses are over, and have been cut back for April blooming; Narcissus Paper-White and *Iris Tingitana* have shed their last petals, *Bougainvillea Sanderiana* has rolled up its magenta tapestries, and the flowerful *Bignonia Capensis* is only a sheet of brightly varnished foliage. But as one mounts from terrace to terrace what a rush of hurrying flower-feet is in the air! The tireless Laurustinus leads the way, already thrusting its snowy corymbs among last year's blue-black berries; the Photinias are crowning their stately growth with burnished terminal shoots and broad flat flower-clusters; the single-flowered *Kerria Japonica* is breaking into golden bloom, and the single yellow Banksia that climbs through it is already showing a few flowers.
>
> Here clumps of Eremurus are thrusting up between the faded flowers of the Diplopappus; in another corner, tucked away in warm clefts along the path, the species crocuses Tomasinianus and Sieberi are folding up their last blooms; but the purple cups of Imperati and the great vain-glorious chalices of Enchantress still burn in the sunshine, and the vivid golden stars of *Crocus Susianus* nestle low in their striped leaves. Nearby the tulip Kaufmanniana spreads its first water-lily petals,

Like those of the Italian gardens she wrote about in 1903–4, Wharton's terraces at Sainte-Claire were cut out of the hillside. This photograph shows the view looking toward the Villa Saint Bernard, old Hyères and the mountains, and down to a lower terace with a circular garden.

A pergola connected terraces and echium lined the walls.

In the 1930s, Daisy Chanler described how, after her jealously guarded morning with its early breakfast and hours of writing, Wharton came downstairs at 12:15 in time to take a quick walk in the garden and "see what was happening there, before luncheon." According to Chanler, "she loved her flowers as other women love their children, and was tireless in her care of them." The gardener must be interviewed not once but several times a day; every plant was kept in mind. One winter an unusually hard frost did cruel damage, killing fine old trees and plants it had taken many seasons to collect. "Edith was as Rachel weeping for her children, and would not be comforted."

the tiny Humilis has already put up a frail flower of pinkish mauve, Sylvestris is hung with dangling buds, and the plump flowers of *Tulipa Greigii* are forcing apart its thick snake-speckled leaves. Farther on, in another sunny nook, the species Irises are weaving their enchantment; here Sind-pers has already unfurled its ethereally lovely flowers, there the exquisite lilac-blue of *Reticulata Cantab* lies like a fragment of sky on the brown earth. The yellow remontant Pumila, "Souvenir du Lieutenant Siret," which bloomed all through the summer and autumn, is again thick with bursting blossoms, the outspread blue and purple stars of Histroides Major still linger, and Bucharica and Sind-reichii are unfolding their fluted sheaves, and the Hispanicas thrusting up their frail grassy filaments....

But the tale of April in a Riviera garden is too long to tell: as well try to crowd a symphony into a "half-hour of music." When the peaches and cherries are in bloom, and all the late tulips, narcissi, ranonculus, anemones and irises come rushing up, mingling with roses, lilacs and paeonies to swell the mighty chorus, one can only fall back on the closing lines of Schiller's Hymn to Joy, to which Beethoven gave the wings of immortality.

To reach Sainte-Claire, one climbed a steep, winding road, overhung by prickly pear and Judas trees, into a courtyard before the house built into its hillside and surrounded by the old stone towers and walls that were scattered on the hillside. From the broad terrace in front of the house, she and her friends looked out over the town—just below was the old basilica of Saint Paul among the many red-roofed houses—and, in the distance, the sea.

Instead of the level borders in her garden at Saint-Brice, her many drifts of colorful flowers ascended terrace by terrace over the hillside, watered by a system of underground irrigation pipes. A pergola rose out of a bed of tulips and blue violas on one terrace just north of the rock garden. There were two expanses of lawn bordered by roses or santolina, with gardens seats for enjoying the views. She had climbers and crawlers and, behind the wall to the west, cactuses that were protected there from the mistral.

In *Gardening in Sunny Lands,* Harriet Martineau described Wharton's place, which she had visited in late February and early March in 1923 and 1924, as a "series of little gardens, sheltered and sunlit... tucked away on the terraces under the old walls and towers of grey stone. In some of these gardens are freesias and narcissus, in others roses; on one terrace are mandarins, and in a shady corner grow camellias, azaleas, and arums."

Wharton had many species of echium in large masses—blue *Echium fastuosum* near copper-colored cupheas and, on the other steeper side of the path, white and blue biennial *Echium decaisnei* and, behind that among the rocks, many brilliant scarlet aloes. In a sheltered area with a lot of sun grew a collection of rare plants from Morocco and the Canary Islands. Her rock garden was famous for its collection of all the known subtropical plants that flourished in the area, including many cacti and other succulents. "It is said to be more complete than the famous collection at the Prince of Monaco's on the borders of Monte Carlo." Beyond this group among the rocks and gray agaves were drifts of orange and red antholyza, which melted away into bushes of wild mastic. Vivid orange *Lampranthus aureus* carpeted the ground under groups of lilac statice.

Red-flowered grevilleas were grouped with the small shrub *Justica rizzinii* and *Correa bicolor*—both red and yellow. In another part of the grounds, red and partly salmon grevilleas were combined with red and white blooming grevilleas.

The great Judas tree in the center of the courtyard was flanked by a wide border of veronicas in shades ranging from deep purple to pale pink, and, opposite them, was another group of blue echiums. The side of the house was "draped" with purple hardenbergia, while a handsome specimen of silver-leafed *Buddleya madagascariensis* bloomed orange on a wall beyond. Above the buddleya were bushes of *Viburnum suspensum,* which bloomed with "creamy fragrant flower-clusters" through February and March, and, higher still above

Beatrix Farrand at Sainte-Claire

Edith Wharton and friends: Linky is in her left hand, Coony in her right.

Watercolor by Robert Norton. The buttresses below the château were blue with Kennedya in spring.

Looking up from a stone garden path at clumps of variegated agaves to a tower

that, were Wharton's "terraces of freesias and roses, broad walks of white iris and a level stretch of greensward overhanging the view of sea and plain."

Her southern gardening debut received a great blow at Christmastime 1920, as she reported to Minnie Jones:

There was a cold mistral, followed by two nights of severe frost (20 Fahrenheit), & *all* the gardens from Marseilles to Mentone were wiped out. My terraces were just beginning to be full of bursting sprouting things, & it was really sickening to see the black crapy rags which, a few hours before, were heliotropes, "anthémises," tradescantia, plumbago, arums, geraniums—all the stock-in-trade of a Riviera garden—dangling woefully from the denuded terraces. The orange trees were severely frozen, & some of the old ones may be lost; & even my splendid old caroube trees, which had put on their glorious dense shining foliage in October, are all frizzled & brown. Eucalyptus & pepper-trees are shrivelled up, & the huge prickly pears that were the pride of the place are falling apart like paper flowers the day after a procession. Even the native wildflowers, acanthus, fennel and valerian, hung limp from their roots, & are only just picking up.

The poor peasants have lost acres of artichokes & early potatoes—almost all that the floods had spared—& the gardens are a sickening sight.

I had a magnificent climbing buddleya which covered one of my highest terrace walls, & was just preparing to hang out its hundreds of yellow plumes—it is as bare as a ship's rigging in a gale! And so the story goes—& the only consolation people can find is that "it hasn't been known since 1870."

Meanwhile normal weather has come back, & my bulbs are all sprouting, & this prodigal nature will repair things in a year—except that some trees may be lost.

She was further disappointed that a visit from Beatrix Farrand had fallen through, and she wrote her: "I try to extract comfort from the thought that all the 'gardening' we could have done in my stiff & stark frozen garden would have been to mingle our tears over the blackened stumps of the devastated area." The freeze had killed everything that "doesn't resist a Massachusetts winter," although, "in my very sheltered garden almost all the plants are reviving at the root, even heliotrope & Kennedya—but in lower, colder situations, they're stone dead—oh dear—"

After one freeze she wrote: "I thought loving a garden had the immense advantage of sparing me heart-breaks—but that love hasn't yet been invented!"

Her garden always recovered eventually, and she recorded its progress rapturously in her diary. On January 10, 1921: "Daffodils in bloom on tower stairway. Planted roses in upper rose terrace. . . . Garden Glorious." February 7, 1923: "Perfect Day. . . . Pottered about garden all day. House full of violets, narcissus, mimosa, iris, Xmas roses."

During the 1920s and 1930s at Hyères, Wharton continued to see her friends from the past as well as new acquaintances. She visited others who had their own large places and gardens, such as Lawrence Johnston, who gardened farther east at his place, La Serre de la Madone (The Greenhouse of the Madonna), in Menton; or Berthe, the Marquise de Ganay, and her sister, Martine, the Comtesse de Béarn, at La Polynesie. She saw Consuelo Vanderbilt from Newport days, now married to Jacques Balsan. In late February 1923, she went with Harriet Martineau to inspect other big gardens near La Napoule. She had tea with the Hanburys at La Mortola and visited the Villa Eleanne. "Incomparable magnolias," she noted.

A new friend with whom she could share her enthusiasm for gardening was Charles de Noailles. The Vicomte de Noailles owned the property next to Wharton's on the same ridge overlooking Hyères, and, in the mid-1920s, he built the Villa Saint Bernard there. He was married to Marie-Laure Bischoffsheim, daughter of a rich German banker and a friend of Berenson's. In the late 1920s, the young couple gave flamboyant balls at their Paris mansion on the Place des Etats-Unis and entertained artists and members of the avant-garde at the villa in Hyères. It was there that Man Ray filmed *Les Mystères du Château de Dé*. For their costume ball in 1929, the host wore tails made of oilcloth, the hostess a dress of holly. Charles de Noailles eventually decided he was made for a less brilliant and showy existence and his foremost interest became his love of gardens. He would become one of the great horticulturists of France. Wharton would walk along the ridge to see him, and they often dined together.

The Noailles's villa and garden were the first futurist creation of Robert Mallet-Stevens, who before the war had introduced in France the new geometric and graphic architecture of the Austrian Josef Hoffmann. The grounds featured a triangular cubist garden in a checkerboard design by Gabriel Guévrékian and a revolving Lipchitz statue. Indicative of Wharton's attitude toward modernism was that her own villa and garden reflected little of her neighbor's style.

Wharton's winter house parties were made up of Gaillard Lapsley and Robert Norton, who spent every Christmas there, as did John Hugh-Smith; the Berensons and Nicky Mariano visited at some point each winter, and Daisy Chanler came fairly often. Other visitors included the Bourgets, who were close by at Costebelle; new friends such as Aldous Huxley, Kenneth Clark, and

Charles and Marie Laure de Noailles, dressed for their costume ball, 1929

Charles de Noailles and his two daughters in the garden at the Villa Saint Bernard

Philomène de Lévis-Mirepoix, who would become a regular; as well as welcome transients like Sir George and Lady Prothero, who came through in 1920, and Ogden Codman, who would look in occasionally.

Soon after moving into Sainte-Claire, she established a routine for herself and her guests similar to the one she had exercised in Paris. Wharton's afternoons and evenings of leisure were achieved by "the strenuous regulation of the mornings." She would start work at 7:30 and by noon had written for several hours, dictated letters to her secretary, and seen the cook to order the day's meals. Guests told of being sent a note in the morning when she was writing, saying she would see them at lunch.

After lunch on the terrace, if weather permitted, everyone took the obligatory walk—through the garden—and perhaps across the way to see Charles de Noailles. They would then proceed into town or, more ambitiously, drive in the motor to an old château or a nearby village—a picturesque spot where the group could walk. Even now, in her sixties, Wharton was known to walk long distances. She demanded perseverance and action from her guests—Berenson complained that he wasn't allowed to take his afternoon nap.

They sometimes motored to the town of La Lande and walked to the Vieux Porte or to Sainte Eulalie to tramp through the woods, or they might take their lunch and picnic on a ridge overlooking a view. Their picnics, which were the rule on all fine days, also followed a pattern. The hampers contained chicken and ham, chocolate, and oranges, with the portions "efficiently dealt out by the hostess to each in turn." On January 4, 1924, she noted in her diary:

Wharton on the terrace
at Sainte-Claire

Edith Wharton and Catharine Gross on the terrace

"Perfect day. Started 11:30 with R, G. & Phil[omène] for Bormes. Lunched under tower. Walked over hills to Lavandou."

In the evening after dinner, the guests gathered for reading and Edith's great love—conversation. According to Gaillard Lapsley, she would always talk about books but ruled out politics because she didn't like hearing repeated what she or they had just read in the newspapers. She enjoyed discussion but, even more, "one's reaction to the things that matter." Her subjects were, according to Lapsley, music, art and architecture, literature, natural beauty, and civilized human conduct. She was not interested in aesthetic theories. "She was so abundantly and availably well-informed, so documented and experienced by observation, talk and travel that if her interlocutor's resources brought him as far as her point of departure he was lucky. . . . Foolish persons tried to bluff but they did not repeat the experiment if, which was unlikely to happen, the opportunity recurred." With younger people, however, she was patient and responsive.

Some evenings, the group would hear one of Wharton's recently completed chapters. She would be working on two or three things at once—sometimes stories that had begun when someone had given her an episode that sparked her imagination:

Robert Norton

Postcard from Wharton, January 2, 1931: "The party at Ste. Claire (sexes reversed!) . . . The continuation of the heavenly weather has raised our spirits to this pitch, . . ."

It helped her very much, she said, to be able to talk over what she was writing; and she encouraged us to be completely frank in our comments and suggestions. "Of course I'm only the man in the street," someone would begin diffidently, "but I can't see any one in the position of your hero behaving, or speaking like that," etc. etc. Then the psychology of the character and the situation would be argued over, and if the objector made good his point, she would be persuaded and agree. I have known her to re-write a scene four times as the result of one of these discussions; and she listened and replied to suggestions not always helpful, with infinite patience and good temper, which one contrasted mentally with the attitude of other artist friends who would fly into a passion at the least suggestion of disapproval. In this way I watched the Glimpses of the Moon, A Mother's Recompense, the Old New York Stories, The Children, Hudson River Bracketed, and The Gods Arrive, and many of the short stories and articles, take shape. She would never tell one in advance what the dénouement was to be; sometimes she said she was not sure herself. I have known the work on one of her books hung up for weeks when the climax was approaching because she could not find a way that satisfied her for bringing it about. Then she would come down radiant one morning and say, "I've got it!" and the concluding scenes would rush out faster than her pen could write them.

The reading out loud also included poetry, maybe Browning or Shakespeare—a dip, not a whole play—readings from anthologies. One winter the group put together an anthology of "English Love Poetry," inspired by reading the last scene of *Antony and Cleopatra*. Her favorite novels were *War and Peace*, *Anna Karenina*, *The Red and the Black*, *Charterhouse of Parma*, *Vanity Fair*, and *Henry Esmond*. Scenes from these would be read aloud as well as parts of novels from other favorites by Hardy, Conrad, George Eliot, and Jane Austen. She loved the work of Balzac, Flaubert, and Maupassant. The characters of Proust became household words—"That is just what the Duchesse de Guermantes would say"—though she was disappointed with his works after *Swann's Way*.

She read widely, in French, Italian, German, and English. Gaillard Lapsley wrote, "Literature was the centre of her life—indeed her life itself was literature, for the habit of transposing everything into terms of her art, extended to herself. She saw herself, I am convinced, in 'situations' even while she was dealing with them. An experience that in the living of it had been a series of contretemps, she would reset as she would have wished it and was thereafter convinced that it had happened so."

Her humor was not limited by the proprieties. She regretted when the

English press no longer gave details and evidence on divorce cases. She wanted to hear of gossip or scandal—"to know in detail what people did and if possible why they did it"—partly for her writing and partly because "all of human nature was her business." She told Lapsley once that he had a foul mind, and, in reply to his protests, answered, "It is one of your many charms." She loved nonsense and the fantastic or absurd. Upon one encounter with a "fresh vision of the absurd," Lapsley remembered her "speechless with shoulders shaking and the tears running down her cheeks," begging to be spared. Although she openly laughed, she never showed her grief.

She didn't like big gatherings, perhaps because, as she became older, conversation, although her love, was an effort for her. She was naturally shy although not timid, and she became overstimulated with the effort. In her own house, "she had the concentration of intense enjoyment and interest and a responsible consciousness of the whole scene—from what her guests were saying, and how they were reacting, down to the delay of the footman in bringing back the tea kettle she had sent to be refilled. But such talk cost her an effort disproportionate to the occasion, though I don't think it seemed strained or unnatural to those who did not know her well."

She could enjoy her retreat all the more for the honors that were now pouring in. At the end of one letter, she added: "Oh Lord, I was almost forgetting to tell you that, last week, the Académie Française gave me the Prix Montyon (gold medal) for Virtue!!—*Textuel.* Well, it's not a bad thing to have—at 58. It was for oeuvres de guerre—not private ones."

Old-timers in Hyères still remember when she paid to have Château

Successful international lawyer Walter Berry, Wharton's true soul mate, was an intimate friend of Marcel Proust and Henry James.

Edith Wharton and Walter Berry on a picnic

On February 25, 1923, Walter Berry wrote Wharton, thinking back to their early courtship in Bar Harbor in the 1880s, before her marriage: "Dearest— The real dream—mine—was in the canoe and in the night, afterwards,— for I lay awake wondering and wondering,—and then, when morning came, wondering how I could have wondered—*I*, a $less lawyer (not even *that*, yet) with just about enough cash for the canoe and for Rodick's bill—

"And then, later, in the little cottage at Newport I wondered why I *hadn't*— for it would all have been *good*—and the slices of years slid by.

"Well, my dear, I've never 'wondered' about any one else, and there wouldn't be much of me if you were cut out of it. Forty years of it is yours, dear. W."

Sainte-Claire illuminated at night by floodlights, then an astonishing innovation, as part of a town festival. They also talk of a secret charity she maintained: a house in Hyères, which they will point out was a residence for aspiring artists and writers, their rent paid by Edith Wharton.

In the years after the war, Walter Berry had been Wharton's constant companion. In November of 1926, not long after he and Edith had gone to Italy, he was operated on for appendicitis and came down to Hyères at Christmas to recuperate. Back in Paris in January, he had a stroke. Wharton went to Paris to find him very depressed. He returned to Sainte-Claire for a visit, but, the following October, he had another stroke and was paralyzed for a week. At first refusing visitors, he finally asked for "Mme Wharton." She came and was with him off and on for three days. When he died on October 12, 1927, she was devastated.

She wrote to her friend John Hugh-Smith on October 15: "Yes, I am glad indeed that it is over, but I perceive now that I, who thought I loved solitude, was never for one moment alone—& a great dread lies ahead of me.

"The sense of desolation (though of thankfulness too, of course) is unspeakably increased by those last days together, when he wanted me so close, & held me so fast, and all the old flame & glory came back, in the cold shadow of death & parting. Oh, my dear, I sometimes feel I am too old to live through such hours, & take up the daily round again."

Yet she was proud of their friendship and to have felt that "I was there, in the place he put me so many years ago, the place of perfect understanding." She told her cousin Frederick King, "For though I have known intimately two or three great creative intelligences like Henry James's, I have never known a mind as wide in its range as Walter's & at the same time as impartial & as sure in its responses to all that was intellectually of the best."

Walter Berry's funeral, on October 17, 1927, was a major public event, reported on the front page of the Paris edition of the *New York Herald* and attended by "cabinet members, diplomats, and prominent figures in society, literature, and public life." Generals Pershing and Weygand were honorary pall bearers, as was Walter Gay. Edith Wharton "wore a heavy black veil." The funeral cortege started at his home, 53, Rue de Varenne, where Wharton had also lived, led by a carriage heaped with floral tributes and "followed by a delegation of wounded French veterans, for whose welfare Mr. Berry had worked incessantly for many years." Nearly a hundred members of the American Chamber of Commerce walked after them. The procession wound its way along the streets of the Left Bank, then across the Seine and up the Champs Elysées to the American Cathedral on Avenue George V: "A large part of the congregation, it was noticed, was composed of French people," including Paul

**THE NEW YORK HERALD, PARIS, TUESDAY, OCT**

## Hundreds Attend Funeral Services For Walter Van Rensselaer Berry

The funeral procession yesterday from the late Walter Berry's residence in the rue de Varenne to the Cathedral Church of the Holy Trinity.

(Continued from Page ONE.)

Mr. Truxton Beale and Mr. George Washington Lopp.

There were nearly 100 members of the American Chamber of Commerce walking in the cortege, who came to mourn the death of their president from 1916 until 1923.

The only relatives here for the services were: Mr. and Mrs. Harry Crosby, cousins of Mr. Berry. His sister, Mrs. Charles Alden, was unable to come to Paris from Washington because of ill health. Among the mourners, however, was Mrs. Edith Wharton, the novelist, who had been a close friend of the deceased. She wore a heavy black veil.

### Belleau Wood Project Walter Berry's Dream

IT is of interest to all Americans to recall that it was greatly due to Mr. Walter Berry's influence that Belleau Wood was purchased in 1923 by the Belleau Wood Memorial Association, to be conserved, for all time, as an American National Monument in France, commemorating the spot where members of three American divisions—2nd, 3rd and 26th—laid down their lives. Mr. Berry considered Belleau Wood as one of the great bulwarks of American in-

Valéry and Jean Cocteau and many elderly Faubourg aristocrats whom Berry and Wharton had come to know so well.

Often self-contained and guarded, Wharton spoke of her emotions now with unusual directness. As Gaillard Lapsley described it:

> I have only once seen any sign of weakening of the rigid self-control in which she had so long schooled herself. That was when I arrived at Sainte-Claire five or six weeks after Walter Berry's death. Her grief was in complete possession of her, but she spoke of every detail of his illness, death and funeral with the cool detachment of an experienced trained nurse describing a case. One only knew the inner turmoil and the diminished control by a certain disciplined excitement and the fact that she took the earliest opportunity to describe it all to me. Indeed she could not think of or even attend to anything else until that was over. I had arrived as

Walter Berry's grave at the cemetery at Versailles was the site of a ceremony held each year on the anniversary of his death by the Compagnie des Mutilés, of which he had been president. Wharton (shown at center) arranged to be buried nearby.

usual about 9 a.m. and when I came down after all that a night in a sleeping car makes necessary she at once proposed to make the circuit of the *domaine*. I guessed what was needed and used some phrase that opened the gates. But I don't think that any one who did not know her well would have understood that she was under the stress of strong emotion.

The fiction that Wharton wrote in the 1920s and early 1930s is informed by her long residence in Europe. Even though *Summer* was set in New England, it is filled with the light and atmosphere of the south of France. *The Children* (1928), her novel dedicated to "My Patient Listeners at Sainte-Claire," is also informed by images of light and sea. *The Mother's Recompense* (1925) gives a satirical picture of the expatriate colony in the south of France that in real life Wharton knew about and felt superior to.

A plot summary for a novella she called "Beatrice Palmato" was found among her papers at Yale in the 1970s, along with a fragment of text. In this summary, one of the two daughters in the Palmato family commits suicide, the mother has a breakdown and is sent to a sanatorium, and the other daughter, Beatrice, is left to live alone with her father in their English country house near Brighton. When she returns from the sanatorium, Mrs. Palmato grows mad again, tries to kill herself, is sent away again, and soon dies. Mr. Palmato and Beatrice and a governess live together until the father marries the governess and Beatrice marries a "simple-minded country squire with a large property." Although her husband is dull and uninteresting, they have two children, and Beatrice seems happy. "One day the husband has been away for a week. He returns sooner than expected, comes in and finds his little girl in the drawing room. She utters a cry of joy, and he clasps her in his arms and kisses her." Beatrice comes in, is horrified, and screams, "'Don't kiss my child. Put her down! How dare you kiss her?'" Beatrice rushes upstairs and shoots herself.

The text fragment describes Beatrice Palmato making love with her father in an episode that takes place a week after Beatrice's marriage. It is made clear, however, that they have been sexually intimate for some time.

The fragment from "Beatrice Palmato" also has a southern quality to it: in the background of the father, half-Levantine, half-Portuguese, and in the imagery of the incestuous lovemaking, which incorporates the same vocabulary and energy as Wharton's descriptions of the coming of spring to her garden. Her garden verbs—"blooming," "thrusting," "breaking into golden bloom," "unfolding," "blossoming," "bursting," "rushing"—or the adjectives "fiery" and "burnished"—suggest the same blooming and orgasmic bursting as the verbs in the description of lovemaking between Beatrice and her father. The idea is similar, that of arousal, exploding into bloom, all taking place out in the open, in the wonderful light:

"As his hand stole higher she felt the secret bud of her body swelling, yearning, quivering hotly to burst into bloom." The visual element, the eyes caressing the body "with fiery kisses," suggests Wharton's ability to love the world with her eyes—a large element of her old-age life in France, particularly in the south.

In 1928 Wharton was working on *Hudson River Bracketed,* the first of two books, along with *The Gods Arrive*, to deal with her American characters Halo Spear and Vance Weston. Vance is a young writer from the Midwest who comes to the East and finds represented at the Willows, a house on the Hudson, the past—not just his past but that of the Western world—something he had not understood before.

It was in these two novels that Edith Wharton first gave a real analysis of the personality and life of the writer—the moments of inspiration, the moments of block, the nature of the creative process. And in *The Gods Arrive,* she depicted in detail the European haunts she had known for the last twenty years, particularly Paris and the south of France. The unmarried couple are traveling in Europe, where Halo hopes to be Vance's muse and inspire him to finish his novel *Magic.* They live in Spain, Paris, and at Oubli-sur-Mer in the south of France.

Halo masterminds an excursion to Chartres, but Vance is not keen on the trip. The narrator tells us, "It was unlucky that the day before he had been seized by the desire to plan a new book, and was in that state of inward brooding when the visible world becomes a blank." Halo drags him along anyway and, after a full day of sightseeing (she had suggested they spend the night there

Wharton entering the terrace of the château

Picnic near La Roquette, January 8, 1935, with Wharton, an unidentified friend, Robert Norton, and Gaillard Lapsley

so he could see the cathedral "in all its aspects"), they have the following exchange:

> They went to a little tea-shop and had tea (thank God!), and came back and saw twilight fall on towers and buttresses, and dusk deepen to night under the sculpture of the porches. They dined, and came back to see the blueish-grey mass shimmering gigantic under the stars. Then they wandered through the streets and stopped at a cafe for a glass of vermouth. Vance felt that he would soon have to say something, and he would have given the world to slip away before Halo spoke. "Well, dearest—?"
>
> He emptied his glass, and stared sullenly into it. "Well, I just don't see it."
>
> "Don't *see* it?"
>
> "Not a glimmer; not of what you expect me to. . . . It's not my size, I suppose."
>
> "Not your size?" Halo echoed, in the tone of one who has fitted Chartres into her cosmogony without an effort.
>
> Vance felt the inadequacy of words. "I don't *see* it, I tell you. I don't care for it. There's too much of it; yet there isn't anything in it— not for me."
>
> Halo stood up and slipped her arm in his. "You're simply overwhelmed by it—as you were the first evening at Cordova. I was like that when I came here the first time; but tomorrow..."
>
> "Oh, no; I don't want to wait till tomorrow. I want to go home now. Can't we—isn't there a night train? There's sure to be one..."

He would have liked to tell her that his mind was full of his new book, passionately grappling with its subject. If he had, she would have been full of sympathy and understanding; but he did not want sympathy and understanding. He felt sulky and baffled, and wanted to remain so. The masculine longing to be left alone was uppermost; he wanted to hate Chartres without having to give any reason.

"It's not my size," he repeated obstinately.

He saw the immensity of her disappointment. "I know—I'm a Yahoo. But let's go home," he pleaded. They caught a train, and got back to Paris, tired and heavy-eyed, at daylight; and for some time Halo proposed no more weekends.

There is some of Edith Wharton the writer in the character of Vance Weston; there is also much of Morton Fullerton. In the relationship of Vance and Halo, Wharton was writing about her love affair with Fullerton. As a critic has pointed out, Morton Fullerton and Vance Weston have much in common—both pompous and selfish, both three years younger than their lovers (Wharton and Halo), both from families where religion played a big part, and both, of course, writers. The relationships are similar, too, with the female acting as mentor to the male. At the end of the novel, Halo chooses to be alone, and so in a way she emerges victorious, a state that did not characterize the end of Wharton's love affair with Fullerton, in which she was constantly being humiliated. In typical Wharton fashion, Halo plans to return to the Willows, the house she loves, where she will be sheltered and happy.

After reading *Hudson River Bracketed,* Fullerton wrote to Wharton praising the novel but admitting he had read none of her work for some years. She answered him: "Grateful as I am, it is a shock to find that your avoidance of my presence has for so many years extended to my books! I had flattered myself that though you felt only indifference for the old friend, you still followed her through her books. Why have you robbed me of my few remaining illusions? I can only hope that 'Hudson River' may make you feel that you have lost an infinitesimal something by this total rejection of [your Edith]."

In the novel, having endured much of Vance and his moody selfishness, Halo decides not to marry him even though she is pregnant. Critics have made much of this baby—some reading into it Edith Wharton's desire for children, some a symbol for her books, but perhaps it signifies for Halo (and for Wharton, too) the start of a new existence—one in which she doesn't need men to complete her anymore—in which she feels whole by herself.

After the war, Edith Wharton's traveling continued as before. Her diary entries listing the hotels she liked or didn't like give a clue to her itineraries as she traveled in France, Italy, Spain, and England during the 1920s and 1930s: While she loved the Hotel Luxembourg in Moissac, she reminded herself to avoid the "filthy H. de France" in Châteauroux. The Grand Hotel at Le Puy was "impossible." At Bergamo, the Albergo Moderno was "excellent"; at Orta, the Hotel Belvedere only "good." The Miramonti at Cortina was "perfect," as was the Grande Hotel on the Gardone Riviera. She found the Hotel España in Santiago to be "first rate"; the Royal Hotel in Whitby "excellent"; and the Restaurant L'homme at Chartres "very good."

In October 1925, she wrote to Daisy Chanler of her plans for an Aegean and Mediterranean cruise:

> It is a sort of sunset-party that I am hoping to offer to a few chosen friends. I did the same thing in my sunrise days, & never forgot it, or found anything to equal it—& I want the last light to shine again on the same wonders. This sounds much too solemn, & I hope to make many more good trips, & hard over too—but I want to make this one while we're all going fairly full-speed; & though I can't cub-hunt I can still ride a donkey up & down the bed of a mountain torrent with the best of you!—So now's the time. And I've made enough money with "The Mother" to offer myself the supreme treat of inviting you & the Tylers & Robert N. on a two months' cruise. . . . In exchange I ask only a black poodle pup—if you come via Paris! But not the other way, for the journey would be too long & weary for him—& you.

In the spring of 1926, she hired a yacht, the *Osprey*, for the two-month cruise. Daisy Chanler, Logan Pearsall Smith, Robert Norton, and Henry Spencer (who was a late substitute for Walter Berry and Bernard Berenson, both of whom had to turn her down) made up the party. The group boarded in the late afternoon of March 31 at Hyères and set out for Sicily, mainland Greece and several Greek islands, Cyprus and Crete, and Alexandria, to return by way of Syracuse and Naples. The *Osprey* was "very comfortable"; it weighed 361 tons, about the same as "our dear old 'Vanadis,'" the yacht the Whartons and James Van Alen had taken in 1888.

She had always dreamed of returning to the magic of the Hellenic world. As she had noted in her *Vanadis* diary: "Perhaps on a second visit to Athens one

The upper garden, statuary, and pomegranate and lemon trees at the Villa I Tatti, Settignano

might recover one's sense of proportion; I hope some day to find out." Now she could afford to—and did—retrace some of the stops on the 1888 cruise, and she added new wonders, such as Delphi, Mistra, Cyprus, and Crete.

The *Osprey* anchored off the island of Maddalena near Sardinia on April 1 and the next day headed for Palermo. Wharton noted in her diary, "Sat on deck under glorious stars till 10:30. Smooth run to Palermo. Sighted island of Ustica about 2 p.m. Wonderful approach."

At each stop, they went ashore and, riding on donkeys or by motor bus or motorcar, visited temples, monasteries, churches, and museums. From Itea on April 11, everyone (including the maids Elise and Allison) set out for Delphi in a sort of motor bus. On April 16 in Aegina, they rode on donkeys to the temples. They met Minnie Jones in Athens on April 17 and were together with her in Phalerum.

At the end of April, Wharton wrote, "Perfect month, sun every day, blue seas, wonderful scenes, plan carried out successfully. Only 24 hours behind our programme." And at the end of May, "Second month of cruise even more successful and beautiful than the first."

Daisy Chanler described the trip as "like being shown a rainbow bridge to the land of dreams. . . . We were lapped in solid comfort and well taken care of by a pious Scots captain who believed in the strict observance of the Sabbath," as well as a crew of sixteen or eighteen "sailor boys." Although Edith had asked Daisy to bring portable mosquito nets and silk sleeping bags for roughing it in primitive places, they weren't used. They slept on the yacht anchored in the harbors of the various stops they made. As during Wharton's cruise on the *Vanadis*, Butcher and Lang's *Odyssey* was their evening reading.

Wharton wrote later: "Not the least interesting part of the adventure was

The *Osprey* at Delos. Edith wrote after the cruise, "The truth is that I am more and more inconsolable as I get farther away from that perfect beauty & harmony of life, where every demand was satisfied, & every dream surpassed."

*Above left:* The *Osprey* offshore at Delos

*Above right:* The crew of the *Osprey*. Daisy Chanler's "pious Scots captain" is in the center.

the following out, stage by stage, of our old itinerary, and noting the changes produced either by the hand of man (as at Rhodes and the renovated islands of the Dodecanese), or by that other Hand, always written with a capital, which scatters earthquakes and volcanic eruptions throughout those lovely lands as freely as man distributes his administrative changes."

Another stop that brought to mind the 1888 cruise was Amorgos, where both times Wharton made a strenuous climb to the ancient monastery on a ridge at the center of the island. Daisy Chanler described the 1926 climb, made when both she and Wharton were sixty-four years old: "We went ashore after lunch and rode donkeys across the island, then up a very precipitous path. It got so steep and ruinous, a stairway cut in the living rock, that we left our donkeys and reached the astonishing monastery on foot. It perches and clings like a swallow's nest on the face of a perpendicular wall of rock. The rock overhangs it for several hundred feet and below is a sheer precipice to the sea. The

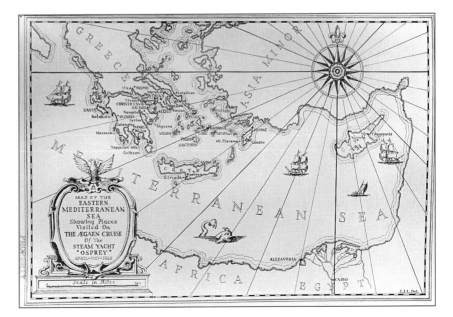

Map of the Aegean cruise from Daisy Chanler's memoir, *Autumn in the Valley*

Daisy Chanler and Edith Wharton on donkeys in Santorini. Daisy, a devout Roman Catholic, wrote in her diary: "Sunday morning we all rode up to the town on donkeys. We heard a jangle of many church bells, among which I thought I distinguished one that sounded Catholic; the Greek Orthodox bells have a different rhythm. Edith was sure I must be mistaken, but when I asked the guide who met us at the top I found I was right and discovered a High Mass going on in a thoroughly Roman looking church, with a Bishop officiating. It is Whitsunday—great luck; I got there for the Gospel."

*Osprey* passengers relaxing on shore

The abbot of the church on Patmos (seen at left), entertained the *Osprey*'s passengers and crew after the Greek Easter service. Daisy described how "he brought out some priceless illuminated mss. and handed them round for us to look at and pass on to one another, as casually as though they were Sunday papers, which our sailor boys would have been better able to appreciate."

Daisy Chanler and Edith Wharton during the *Osprey* cruise

They made the trip to Delphi, Daisy recorded, in "a rattly little bus . . . driven by a light-hearted curly-headed Greek boy who whistled and sang and seemed wholly unconcerned with the dangers of hairpin turns and sheer precipices with no guarding parapets. Our terrors mingled with our ecstasies, but what a drive!"

monastery is built into a cave or grotto, very steep and bare and dead. A few forlorn old monks, dirty and unkempt."

Toward the end of May, the party docked at Alexandria, and Daisy Chanler and Robert Norton went to Cairo to see the Pyramids and the Sphinx, the museums and mosques. Wharton and Logan Pearsall Smith "thought it was a mistake to blur our Aegean-Greek impressions with a short glimpse of Egypt," so they stayed on board. Wharton's 1926 cruise "proved to me again what the first had so fully shown; that *Kein Genuss ist vorübergehend* [no pleasure is transitory], and that no treasure-house of Atreus was ever as rich as a well-stored memory."

Wharton habitually visited Italy by way of Bernard Berenson's Villa I Tatti, near the village of Settignano, a few miles outside Florence. Often she would spend several weeks with the Berensons and then fly off to Rome or Naples in her motor or take excursions to Vallombrosa and the neighboring countryside. Her first visit to the villa had been in the autumn of 1911, two years after she and the Berensons had become friends. By the 1920s, her annual visits had become a ritual, and she could almost consider the place her own. She would arrive either in the spring, after leaving Hyères for the journey back to Paris, or in the fall, on her way south to Sainte-Claire for the winter.

By the 1920s, life at I Tatti also had become a ritual. The house as well as its owner had become a legend. International celebrities, scholars and art collectors, movie stars, and old friends all gathered around the little genius. Houseguests would be met at the train in Florence, taken out to Settignano by motor, up the winding hill covered with olive trees to the ocher-colored villa, which looked over its formal gardens out on the Tuscan countryside. There, at the end of a long hall, whose walls were hung with paintings, in a large room with a stone fireplace, the small figure of Berenson could be seen deep in a chair. Mary Berenson might be working on embroidery, not far away. The genial presence of Nicky Mariano swept through the rooms.

Breakfast arrived on a tray, with a flower in a little vase. The guests took care of themselves in the mornings and met at lunch. Each day included a walk. Wharton and Berenson were legendary walkers and observers. The car would take them to the beginning of the trek somewhere on a hillside or into a field of poppies and then pick them up at the other end. Walking with Berenson in the Tuscan landscape was a great experience, as Iris Origo remembered:

> All affectations cast off, he would leap up the hillside with as much speed and intentness of purpose as if he had still been the young art-student who, in 1888, first gazed upon the Italian scene—his awareness still as fresh as it was then, but enriched and sharpened by every day

that had since passed. Whether he took us to see a fading fresco in some remote little country church, or merely stood in the aromatic woods of cypress and pine, looking at the serene outline of a distant hill, or, nearer by, at a happily-placed farm with its dovecot and clump of trees ("Look, a Corot," he would say, or "a Perugino"); to be with him, was to realise, once for all, what was meant by the art of looking. One day, after taking us to see some frescoes, he told the Indian tale of how the God of Bow and Arrow taught his little boy to hit a mark. "He took him into a wood and asked him what he saw. The boy said, 'I see a tree.' 'Look again'—'I see a bird'—'Look again'—'I see its head'—'Again'—'I see its eye'—'Then shoot!'" It was the same, BB said, in looking. "One moment is enough, if the concentration is absolute."

After the walk, there would be more guests for tea and others at dinner, always in evening dress.

For Wharton, the visits to I Tatti were visits with old friends, and as such she was privy to all of their many intrigues—Mary's sickness, BB's self-absorption—as well as their charms. There were always amorous intrigues, as Wharton reported to Daisy Chanler on June 22, 1926: "You can see that Pellegrina [Pellegrina del Turco, a young woman whom Berenson fancied] is enjoying a love-drama. I don't believe they're ever really happy at I Tatti without one."

Berenson, who as a young man was "elegant and exotic in appearance and manner . . . serious and sensitive, with dark hair, slav features, and wide-set gray eyes," had many love affairs, starting with Mary—they had married in

View from Mary Berenson's bedroom at I Tatti, overlooking the Arno valley

Bernard Berenson and Geoffrey Scott in the garden at I Tatti, 1915

*Above left and right:* I Tatti had its own Italian gardens surrounding the house—the old part flanked the house, and new terraces, designed by Cecil Pinset starting in 1910, descended the hill. Off to the side was an old cypress allée with statues at the end.

1900, after living together for ten years—and followed by Belle da Costa Greene, Sybil Cutting, Hortense Serristori, Gladys Deacon, Aline Sassoon, Gabrielle La Caze, Natalie Barney, Nicky Mariano, and Clothilde Marghieri. As for brief encounters, BB philandered with gusto: he was not above enjoying sex with any of the staff or with a guest there. Mary once caught him kissing I Tatti's Swedish masseuse, and an Italian countess on first meeting got at least a kiss in the back of his car.

Like BB, Mary also tended to throw herself into love affairs, most notoriously with Geoffrey Scott, "my penguin Geoffrey," who left her in 1918 to marry Sybil Cutting, who concurrently left BB. The newlyweds took up residence at the Villa Medici, within walking distance from I Tatti, with everyone trying to pretend that nothing unusual had just occurred. In 1944, the year

The Villa Medici was the home of Sybil Cutting. Her daughter, Iris Origo, remembered, "At the end of the terrace stood a square house with a deep loggia, looking due west towards the sunset over the whole valley of the Arno."

"The Ritz," as everyone called Wharton's suite at I Tatti, consisted of two rooms filled with eighteenth-century Italian furniture—one room was for sleeping, the other for writing (*above and below left*).

Wharton's writing room at I Tatti featured walls covered with yellow silk, a Longhi painting, *The Card Game,* a portrait of the duchess of Orléans by Jean Marc Nattier, and a view out to the upper terrace of the garden. The bookcases were filled with her books, and there was a wonderful carved secretary and small tables and a colored marble fireplace. The total impression was of exquisite details that suggested the fine craftsmanship and taste of the past.

Sybil Cutting at the Villa Medici

*Below left:* Logan Pearsall Smith, Mary Berenson, and Desmond MacCarthy in Italy, 1932

*Below right:* Geoffrey Scott and Bessy Berenson, Bernard's sister

before she died, an invalid in pain since an operation in 1932, Mary wrote BB: "I cannot seem to get beyond the different so-called love affairs that took up a good deal of time and thought when I was younger; I can explain a good many of them and one or two I deeply regret, but they are falling off like dying leaves from a tree, and only what refers to you has any vitality left. The one I chiefly regret is Geoffrey, because it gave you so much annoyance and inconvenience, and was so full of absurdity in itself."

When Wharton came to I Tatti, she would encounter all the Berensons' guests and hangers-on. One who was put off by her was Clothilde Marghieri. When the Neapolitan writer met Edith Wharton at I Tatti in the late 1920s, Wharton was famous, the author of many novels, winner of the Pulitzer Prize and many other honors. Marghieri found Wharton intimidating.

Berenson had spoken to Marghieri of Wharton's success as a writer and her beautiful villa at Hyères where he spent a month each year and returned refreshed and full of enthusiasm. During the afternoon tea in the library, however, Marghieri noticed that Wharton seemed preoccupied. She did not exchange greetings with the younger women but would fondle her Pekinese, letting it drink tea from her cup. Marghieri complained to Berenson: "But she is an old woman." Berenson's reaction was violent: "What you have said is vulgar. I hope you are not so foolish to think that youth is a merit. Even Cretans are young, but to be an old woman like Wharton takes decades of education of the spirit. It takes a whole life dedicated to work of intelligence and when time is short it takes courage."

Nicky Mariano (here with Berenson) had known Edith Wharton since 1923, about four years after she had gone to live at I Tatti with the Berensons. Wharton had never made her feel like "anything more than an outsider to whom one had to be polite," until 1926, when Nicky and BB were in Naples and the *Osprey* arrived in the harbor. They went out to the boat and there was Edith, surrounded by a party of friends, glowing after her cruise. Nicky asked about Edith's maid Elise, who had often stayed at I Tatti. After Nicky went below deck to talk to Elise on Edith's urging, she became aware of a change: "There was a warmth, a tone of intimacy that I had never known before. A gesture that was natural to me had let down a drawbridge leading into the small fortress of her small intimate circle."

Nothing bored Berenson more than the *femmes des lettres,* whom he thought the most detestable of human types. "And what of La Wharton?" Marghieri asked him. "La Wharton," he replied, "I see her as the perfect friend who absolves the job of living by paying the right dues to joy and suffering, and then also writes some very beautiful books. They, her books, are like leaves detached from a tree and it is her tree that I like."

In the autumn of 1931, Edith Wharton decided to go to Rome for the first time in seventeen years. She had last been there in 1913, just before the war. Now, almost seventy, she was returning to the city where she had lived as a child before the Risorgimento. She arrived at I Tatti at the end of October, exhausted, but her "beautific fortnight" there cured her of her accumulated fatigue and gave her the energy to enjoy a Roman holiday. She and Nicky Mariano took the train and talked of gardens along the way. At the hotel in the Via Veneto, her room looked out on the Via Liguria, which was "roaring with noise," and the heat gushed out of the radiators. The weather was tropical and she was upset that she had brought only winter clothes, yet she was excited to be there and felt that "Rome has changed much more than I have."

BB and Mary in 1931

Edith Wharton and Carlo Placci

On their first day, November 13, she and Nicky went to "the divine golden chapel at S. Prassede, and the restored Santa Maria and Cosmedia; not to speak of S. Giovanni in Porta Latina," with its glorious cedar which was quite unknown to her. On November 14 it poured rain, but after seeing the Villa di Papa Giulio, one of Wharton's favorite places, its vaulted arcade decorated with the frescoes of "putti peeping through vine-wreathed trellises" and the lovely caryatids in the grotto-like bath, they drove out to the Villa Livia, which she had never seen.

That night the writers Umberto Morra and Alberto Moravia, friends of Berenson's, came to dine. Wharton found Morra more interesting than the younger writer, "who seems to me too self-engrossed to develop much. . . . But," Wharton wrote to Mary Berenson, "who knows?"

Three days later, she wrote to Berenson, "Here we continue to 'savour' every drop of this rich vintage, to eat our early Christian monuments leaf by leaf, & in between times revel in sights by the way." She did not find Rome "nearly as disastrously ruined" as she had been told. "No second calamity has befallen her equal to the Victor Emmanuel monument" and new buildings have "increased the beauty of the old familiar quarters."

Although their paths had crossed on previous trips, Edith and Nicky had never traveled together before 1931, and the idea of a prolonged tête-à-tête in Rome filled the younger woman with apprehension. Wharton still gave her, Mariano wrote, "the sense of being weighed in the balance and found wanting," as if she were not "coming up to her expectation, and did not entertain her and amuse her enough."

On the third day, Edith asked Nicky whether they had any chance of hearing some good church music, or at least of watching one of the more important religious functions. As Mariano later described it:

> As it happened, the feast of St. Peter and St. Paul was quite near, and I learned that a pontifical mass would be sung by the Benedictine fathers at S. Paolo fuori le Mura in celebration of it. I expected a refusal from Edith on account of the rather early hour; but no she accepted with alacrity, and both she and her maid (a very pious Catholic by the way) were ready before nine; so we got there in good time. In the dim light of a muggy November morning the Basilica looked even vaster and emptier than usual; a small group of poorly clad parishioners from the quarter S. Paolo was waiting before the central apse and watching the candles being lit by the sacristans. Never have I been present at a more magnificent and sumptuous and yet dignified and, I would almost say, severely classical ceremony, enhanced by the smallness and quietness of the congregation, which helped one to concentrate on what was going

on in the apse. I felt deeply moved and at the same time acutely aware of Edith's presence—the presence not, as I feared of an impatient rather spoiled woman, easily bored and anxious to move on, but of someone quite close to me, carried away with me and like me into another sphere, with no stiffness and impatience left in her, no thought of the passing hour or of other plans. We stayed to the very end and followed the procession carrying the Blessed Sacrament all round the Basilica until it had disappeared into the sacristy and the bell had stopped ringing and the candles had been put out.

That same day, at vesper hour, we went to St. Peter's and watched the relics being shown there; and during the following days we assisted at other functions and loved it all and felt in great sympathy; but the particular "Stimmung" of that dim November morning at S. Paolo never came back. It left me in the belief that Edith may perhaps have been much nearer to actual conversion to the church than any of her friends ever thought.

Although Edith's enthusiasm for church ceremonies in Rome convinced Nicky that Edith was about to convert, Berenson was skeptical. Certainly she was very sensitive to the beauty of ritual, but he could not imagine that there could be more to it than that. "Anyway," he said, "if Edith should be converted to Catholicism, my heart would go out to her confessor."

As Berenson could sense, Wharton probably never shared Nicky's sphere of religious faith. Wharton's "seeming spirituality as revealed in her Roman church tours with Nicky" had been evoked by impressions she had come to associate with Italy, impressions of beauty derived from the Italian landscape, art, and history, which the Christian faith had contributed to but never overpowered. Visits to Italy had always been escapes into a world of history, art, spirit, and imagination, out of her own obsessive life as a disciplined writer, businesswoman, and head of a complicated household (not of family but of servants). Wharton had always been moved by church services, and simply sitting in a church could bring on overwhelming associations of history and religious feelings for her. She coupled going to church with going to the theater, two events of "great emotion" in which she had taken "an active part" as a child. "I venture to group them together because, looking back across the blurred expanse of a long life, I see them standing up side by side, like summits catching the light when all else is in shadow." The ceremonies of the Roman Catholic Church were one of the last available demonstrations of the ritual and pageantry Wharton always loved. The distinction could have escaped Nicky, a younger woman perhaps disconcerted by discovering this aspect of the forbidding author.

At Christmastime, Mary Berenson was sick again, but BB came for his annual visit to Château Sainte-Claire. Other friends were there: Gaillard Lapsley, Robert Norton, and John Hugh-Smith. They went on their usual walks and read out loud after dinner. Berenson told a friend, "There is no such company as three men with one woman whom they all love without having been or wanting to be her lovers."

Six months later, in May of 1932, Wharton was again in Rome. At a time when many were anxious about the future, she was able to escape again into her glorious world of light, landscape, and memory. "In Italy," she wrote to a friend, "it was all sunshine and fiestas, at any rate, in my happy attic on the Via Sistina." She had gone there with Nicky Mariano again and with BB and had stayed at the Hotel de la Ville. From her terrace on the seventh floor, she could look out over the Trinita dei Monti and all of southwestern Rome on the one side; on the other she could see the Villa Medici and the Villa Malta. Rome in the late spring was a "volupté of roses, orange blossoms and nightingales and really all die Romanticker seem to come to life and walk its streets between the sun gold and the indigo shadows."

The good roads made it possible for daily afternoon *giri* in her large, comfortable car that could sweep them out to the campagna, "making all the Alban, Volscian and Sabine wonders so easily accessible." The whole character of the place and her experience of it was changed by motoring: "To be able to float or fly, every afternoon to some remote loveliness on the sea or among the hills, without hurry or fatigue, is simply enchanting." An afternooon at Ostia "was particularly dreamy and Browningesque." Every now and then, she and Nicky would escape to hear some church music, and "let BB wallow alone in the museums." Berenson wrote to Mary at I Tatti on May 28, "Nicky, who had been grumbling over Edith's tyranny and caprice, returned from an afternoon's visit to the churches in ecstasy over her tenderness and her childlike pleasure in little things and her fun."

There were many invitations to luncheons and dinners, and Berenson and Mariano reflected on her temperamental reactions to other people: "Edith got on well with Steinman," but, "when an elderly American galleon sailed in, a Miss Drake of Philadelphia, Edith bristled and froze," until Berenson signaled to Steinman to take her away and show her the library.

Mrs. Parry, Wharton's maid, had arrived almost two weeks before to replace Elise, who had been ill. Now, Elise was back, and often they both helped Wharton dress. She laughed at the picture of herself standing in her hotel room: "Mrs. Parry does the pulling and hauling (I don't mean on my person but on my belongings) while Elise stands by to direct and occasionally I stand between them in the attitude of the 'Orante' while one buttons one sleeve and one the other." Since she was so well taken care of, she was able to abandon herself to "the Roman rapture which at this season amounts to intoxication; one heavenly day follows another and each, thanks to the wise prevoyance of BB and Nicky are packed to the brim, for me, with enchanting sights and sounds—the latter including yesterday a beautiful high mass at S. Anselmo with the Benedictines, candle in hands, walking in procession around the cloister singing the Corpus Christi anthems and treading on box leaves and rose petals."

After the sojourn in Rome came a motor trip north to Assisi with Elisina Tyler, and then to Milan, which in 1932 was as full of pleasure as any trip taken in all the years of Italian travel: "The run today was indescribably beautiful, with the changing skies and such endless play of mountain forms."

Wharton was not above boasting of her foresight as a traveler: "It's lucky, by the way, that I phoned for rooms, for 2 big 'tours' arrived before me, & unhappy motorists who neglected the same precaution are wandering mournfully from hotel to hotel as I write." Before reaching Assisi during a "glorious run" from Spoleto, they had stopped at Spello, where "the old lady couldn't turn the key in the padlock of the Pinturicchio chapel, & I filled her with mingled dismay and admiration by vaulting lightly (from a chair) over the barrier, and turning on the electric lights myself!!" Halfway to Assisi, Edith remembered: "'Oh, dear, I forgot to turn off the electric lights, & she can't get at them, and she'll be sacked by the Bishop!' *What* a donnée!" She asked Berenson, "Would *you* have gone back?"

They arrived at Assisi in the pouring rain. She rushed to the lower church of the great pink and white stone basilica. It was "dark as a pit; but the monks were singing vespers or some hymn or 'hour' in the dark depths of the apse, with a faint glimmer on the altar, so I listened instead of looking."

The next morning she was so keen to witness another high mass that she imagined one in the upper church when she heard a "deep, distant murmur," but "it was only the guides megaphoning [to the tourists] & the responses were the tramp of their hurrying feet."

Elise, who was full of admiration for the beautiful church of Saint Francis, confessed as they were leaving that she really wanted to visit the tomb of Santa Chiara (Sainte Claire)—who, along with Saint Francis, is a patron saint of Assisi—"because Madame lives at Sainte-Claire," making the connection between the saint and the name of Edith Wharton's house in Hyères.

They left Assisi at about eleven in the morning and drove to Recanati, "a splendidly perched & proud little town," the birthplace of the poet Leopardi. The facade of the great brick palace of the poet's family impressed Wharton, but she was not able to see his room because Leopardi's grandnephews who still lived there were away on holiday. They reached Loreto on the last day of a religious festival, and "the high altar of the Basilica flamed with lights, & canons

Edith Wharton, 1925

in glorious reds & purples intoned without ceasing, while in the Casa Santa two nuns remained in adoration, & a young Franciscan knelt on the door steps in pallid ecstasy."

Wharton motored on to Rimini, Ravenna, and Ferrara, and then, feeling a sudden yearning to have "two nights at the old stand," she stopped at her familiar haunt, the Grand Hotel des Thermes at Salsomaggiore, where she had often taken the cure. The whole establishment rushed out to welcome her. The hotel was nearly empty, and "round faces grew long & dimples were replaced by lines of care when I said I was leaving in two days." The manager was wan with anxiety over the lack of business: "What do you think? Will it be better? Nobody knows!" She had no comfort for him, "though I persist in thinking that the universal cataclysm is largely hysterical (chez nous at any rate) that one day human nature will get tired of wailing & being frightened & begin to shake off the nightmare."

Yet the world was intruding painfully on Wharton's last ten years. For Wharton the world's ominous descent into barbarism was cause for despair. Mussolini had been in power since 1922, and the consequences were increasingly horrifying. In 1933 Hitler had triumphed in Germany, and she feared that the forces of "Bolshevism," backed by Stalin in Russia, were rising to power in France and Spain: "All the shattering, crashing, smashing, that has gone on" foreshadowed a "roaring chaos."

She worried continually about money. The crash in 1929, followed by the Great Depression, hurt in the pocketbook. The publishers offered much less for her work and her trust income from New York real estate dropped. Her friends were hit hard as well—at one point Berenson considered selling I Tatti—but somehow they managed to adjust their life-styles and continue much as before.

Her constant literary output continued, and she was determined that it should bring her the returns she needed. Five years before, the *Ladies Home Journal* had offered her $25,000 for her reminiscences, but now, in the Depression year of 1933, they did not want to pay that much: "Any offer that might have been made for such a work during the past two years would have been at a considerably reduced sale of price, in recognition of the changed conditions and the fact that our issues are so much smaller than formerly with a consequent reduction in the length of stories and serial installments." Her editor at Appleton, Rutger Jewett, wrote Wharton about the conditions of the bookselling world: "Today the booksellers would not purchase even a copy of a book unless it is on some timely popular subject and promises a quick turn over. You cannot blame them. They are bankrupt, banks will not extend credit, they have more clerks on the payroll than customers in the store."

By early summer 1933, Wharton had almost completed her memoirs,
which she titled *A Backward Glance*. She knew she was a writer of considerable
standing and she refused to capitulate on her fee. She did, however, propose
one plan of compromise. She would omit the chapter on Henry James and take
a reduced fee of $21,000. She would then place the chapter on Henry James in
another journal, *Life and Letters*, which was already anxious to have it. Wharton cabled her editor: "I authorize editor make proposed cuts but absolutely
decline reducing price: will sue unless agreement kept."

By the end of May, she heard that the *Ladies Home Journal* did not want
to relinquish the sections dealing with Henry James. They finally agreed to pay
the full $25,000.

In October 1933, Wharton wrote Jewett that "I am in as much need of
money as everybody else at the moment and if I could turn out a series of pot
boilers for magazine consumption I should be only too glad to do so." She was
afraid, however, she could not write down to the present standard of the American picture magazines.

The review of *A Backward Glance* in *The Times* said, "She has written one
of her most delightful books . . . evoking a vanished world and investing it with
body and warmth and a peculiar leisured and gracious charm." Other reviewers used the words "wise and gracious," "golden twist of wit," "restful charm,"
and a "gracious charming narrative."

As she had in her fiction, in her memoirs Wharton created marvelous
scenes, drawing characters in carefully depicted settings, all against a larger
architectural background suggesting time and place. For example, on a
sparkling afternoon at the Blanches' house at Offranville, in June 1914:
"Brightly dressed groups were gathered at tea-tables beneath the overhanging
boughs. . . . An exceptionally gay season drawing to its close, the air was full of

Robert Norton, Bernard Berenson, Edith Wharton, and Gaillard Lapsley at Château Sainte-Claire

new literary and artistic emotions, and that dust of ideas with which the atmosphere of Paris is always laden sparkled like motes in the sun. . . . 'Haven't you heard? The Archduke Ferdinand assassinated . . . at Sarajevo . . . where *is* Sarajevo? His wife was with him. What was her name? Both shot dead.'"

Beneath the descriptions of happy throngs at one party or another and accounts of the many occasions that she witnessed runs the real story of her life, the story of escape from the conventional world of her New York childhood into a self-created world in which she could be herself and could write. Although her memories recap the main events of her life, there is much they avoid. She tells of her escape from the world of Fifth Avenue to later settings—Paris and then Saint-Brice and Hyères—but she does not tell her reader about the feelings with which the escape was made. Nor are the most important people nor the complicated relationships honestly depicted in the book. To find the rage and the true nature of the relationships, one must look at her more confessional memoir, *Life and I*, which has only recently been published, and, of course, to her fiction.

In the spring of 1934, Edith wrote to Mary Berenson that she hoped to go, not just to Rome, but also "down to St. Angelo in Formis and Capua Vetera, and also to see Paestum again, and the new Pompeii—all that is new to me, for I haven't excursioned in those parts for over twenty years; so for me at least, there will be plenty of novelty." She did get to Rome in May but on her arrival came down with flu and spent her two weeks languishing in a hotel overlooking the Pincio and Saint Peter's. She was unable to take her motor flights, unable to visit the dark, cool churches, unable to move. She wrote to Gaillard Lapsley about the experience: "And my whole visit has become a feverish witches' dance ever since—ten days in bed, the last four just within range of the teabasket afternoons on the Campagna!"

Lady Wemyss, Wharton, and H. G. Wells (right) in England

With all its frustrations, however, this stay in Rome did bring forth a wonderful story, "Roman Fever," which evokes the experience of American travelers to Italy while portraying one of Wharton's passionate triangular relationships. Two middle-aged women, Grace Ansley and Alida Slade, from Wharton's old New York world, lifelong friends, sit and talk during a spring afternoon on the verandah of a restaurant ovelooking the ruins of the forum. Mrs. Slade mentions how her great-aunt Harriet had lured her sister there and the poor girl caught the fever and died. Like Alida Slade and Grace Ansley, the two had loved the same man. As the shadows lengthen and they recall what took place nearby, their conversation gradually exposes the rivalry and hatred that has lain beneath the surface of their friendship.

They have known each other all their lives, having grown up together in fashionable New York, married at the same time, and settled down in houses across the street from each other. Now, as they sit fascinated by the evocative view, each reflects on what she thought of the other. Mrs. Slade sees Mrs. Ansley as dull and cannot abide her knitting in the face of all this glory. Mrs. Ansley feels that Mrs. Slade is brilliant, "but not as brilliant as she thinks."

The relationship changes from one of detached and guarded friendship to that of rivalrous fury. Mrs. Slade confesses to having lured the young Grace Ansley out to the Colosseum years ago, when they were both in Rome, by forging a note from her fiancé, Delphin. All these years Mrs. Slade had enjoyed her triumph thinking Grace had wandered around in the dark of night trying to get into the Colosseum and then caught a chill, and now she discovers the young couple had indeed met. Mrs. Slade feels beaten, but, "'I oughtn't to begrudge you, I suppose. . . . After all I had everything; I had him for twenty-five years and you had nothing but that one letter he didn't write.'

"Mrs. Ansley was again silent. At length she turned toward the door of the terrace. She took a step, and turned back, facing her companion," and delivered the brief sentence that creates the wonderful surprise ending.

Wharton had often used a double heroine in her novels—including *The Valley of Decision*, *Ethan Frome*, *The Reef,* and *The Age of Innocence*—but in this, the last of her fictions about two women, there is an unusual confrontation, as one almost admits to wishing to kill the other. The charm of the story lies in the subtle way its situation is revealed in the powerfully suggestive descriptions of the landscape.

Like *A Backward Glance*, "Roman Fever" speaks about the passing of eras and the values that went with them. While writing her memoirs, Wharton had remembered four generations of Americans in Rome, drawing on the travel diary of her father's 1848 trip to Europe, and writing of her own Italian travels as a child in the 1870s, as a young married woman in the 1890s, and again just before World War I. In "Roman Fever," she again chose Rome, not New York, as the place that provides continuity for two women to reflect on their own experiences and those of others in their families, locating their pivotal final encounter in Italy rather than America.

Edith Wharton, the writer who had always seen the world as "a series of pictures" and who had delighted in observing beautiful settings as well as creating them in her writing, used this setting masterfully. These women look out over the ruins of Rome, where their own drama had been played out a generation before. As the golden light of day fades, the reader and the women witness the hour when it becomes "deathly cold," as it had for Great-aunt Harriet's younger sister, but not for Mrs. Ansley and Delphin Slade. The different eras of Roman experience are suggested by the mention of the generations of Roman visitors and, as the conversation moves from silence to the exchange of pleasantries, to more pointed remarks and finally to the vengeful attack and counterattack, we observe this new kind of Roman fever—rage.

When the mothers of Alida Slade and Grace Ansley had been girls in Rome, people could catch malaria, the "Roman fever" of that day, and die, as James's Daisy Miller had after she insisted that her Italian suitor take her to see the Colosseum in the moonlight. When Alida and Grace were girls, their Roman fever had been passion. Now, their daughters, Barbara and Jenny, rush off unchaperoned to Tarquinia with two young Italian aviators (reminding the reader that this is Mussolini's Italy), and the older women lament that the familiarity and casualness in relations between the sexes deprive this younger generation of the romance and magic of passion. At the story's end, the reader learns that one of the women had allowed herself a moment of passion that changed her life.

"Roman Fever" was Wharton's last writing about Italy and her best short story with an Italian setting. Italy had always held for her the promise of fulfillment, the satisfaction of all her sensuous, intellectual, and aesthetic impulses. In contrast to her late novels, "Roman Fever" shows the author at the height of her powers, three years before her death. With the Italian subject, she regained her touch and revealed Italy as the place she could best associate with the honest feelings of rage she had harbored for so long.

Memory figures strongly in several works written toward the end of Wharton's life. A number of her later characters are happier with their memories of the past and unwilling to replace them with a reality in the present that may not be as precious. When visiting Paris as an older man, Newland Archer of *The Age of Innocence* will not call on the Countess Olenska; he prefers his memory of her. Kate Clephane of *The Mother's Recompense* is happier with her memories of passion than the reality of an uninteresting but secure marriage to an old friend. Memories also figure strongly in "Roman Fever." They have nurtured Grace Ansley: "All these years the woman had been living on that letter. How she must have loved him, to treasure the mere memory of its ashes."

It is tempting to suppose that Edith Wharton is Grace Ansley. Here is the private self, happy in her memories. Perhaps she represents the author, finally satisfied with her life and her accomplishments, survived by her writing instead of children. Yet there are also elements of Alida Slade in Edith Wharton. She is the assertive woman, the public self, who dresses well, entertains beautifully, and is impressive to those with conventional values. Alida Slade was married to an international lawyer (like Wharton's friend Walter Berry), the interesting husband whom Wharton never had. Easily irritated, she feels that she has somehow missed out and harbors a deep anger that can surface when provoked. She has no immortality, for her child is not heir to her nature. The two women can be seen as representing the two sides of Edith Wharton's personality: one is competitive, feels cheated, and is often angry and exasperated (as Wharton was when she fell sick in Rome); the other enjoys her memories, muses on her victories, and says, "I have lived."

In December 1936, Edith Wharton visited I Tatti for the last time and wrote Mary Berenson on her way home: "It deluged nearly all the way to Spezia; but as soon as we began to descend on the Southern side of the Velvas pass there was that old humbug the Mediterranean, all peacock & gold, doing her postcard stunt; and after that it was roses, roses all the way."

That Christmas, Berenson broke his usual routine and did not visit Wharton at Château Sainte-Claire, explaining that he was at last beginning to write something important, "out of the depths," and "must stick to it now until I come to a stop."

In April of 1937, Edith Wharton wrote what turned out to be her last letter to Berenson: "Dearest BB, Alas, what shall we do? My vista of recovered health in the spring has been clouded over by *three* successive attacks of flu . . . I have lost a week, nearly, of heavenly capricious spring weather, with a garden tuning up here & there like a symphony orchestra, & suddenly bursting into a glorious 'tutti.' But I'm used to invalidism now, & find it full of oases & hidden springs; & I should bear it all with equanimity except missing I Tatti, which I find intolerable." She wished to go to him, but "instead I've had to be content with lingering here, fighting one tidal wave of fatigue after another," and occasionally doing some writing.

She planned "to meet Elisina [Tyler] in Venice next month, take a look at the Tintorets, and go on [to] see that little corner still unfamiliar to me, Aquileia, Grado, Cividale, etc." Berenson was to go to Cyprus and Crete, and she advised him on what to see: "Don't fail . . . to stop & picnic beside a stream smothered in blossoming oleander, with snow-covered Ida soaring in the blue above.

One of the last known photographs of Edith Wharton, standing in the door at Pavillon Colombe. After Edith Wharton died her friends remembered her at Pavillon Colombe, standing "on the good soil of her garden, with her broadleafed hat and her basket on her arm, calling and waving to the window where Gross looked out . . ." or "when she whisked round and made off to her business among the flowers, with her pair of toy dogs sputtering and scuffling at her heels."

Edith Wharton with three friends—
Berenson is hidden just behind her.

"Oh me, how thankful I am to remember that, whether as to people or as to places & occasions, I've *always* known the gods the moment I met them. Oh, how clearly I remember saying to myself that day by the stream, as I looked up at the snow through the pink oleanders: 'Old girl, this is one of the pinnacles—'

"I expect to leave for Italy at the end of this month if I'm well enough, to get to Pav. Colombe about June 8th or 10th."

Her last letter to Berenson expresses all the enthusiasm for the things they loved. It contains memories of places they knew and the sense of their "inalienable ownership of beauty." Berenson was moved by her letter, and he answered it at once:

Dearest Edith
Thanks for one of the most delightful letters ever addressed to me by yourself or anyone else. On the whole you give me a good account of yourself. Of course *à notre âge* one must walk in fear of the Lord, and we often enough find ouselves clinging to a bush which rats are gnawing away while dragons [glower] beneath us and wild beasts prowl above. We find honey on a perpendicular wall within reach of our tongues and lick it.

I feel a real *Wehmut* over yr. spending May in Italy without my seeing you. Friuli is too lovely in that month, and I used to know it well, having been almost in every village before motors came into the world. What idyllic landskip—the background of Palma's Jacob and Rachel. Be very careful about fatigue. That you surely know is our worst enemy.

Wharton was growing increasingly feeble. She had had an attack of heart palpitations in 1929 and experienced total exhaustion, an episode that greatly slowed her down and caused her friends to notice the change in her. She continued to write, however, and, after finishing *A Backward Glance*, she began *The Buccaneers*, a novel she never completed, about a rich American girl who marries into the English nobility. In April of 1935 Wharton suffered a mild stroke at Sainte-Claire; on June 1, 1937, she had another stroke while staying at Ogden Codman's Château de Grégy south of Paris. Codman described it to a friend: "Poor Mrs. Wharton had a very sad visit here, she arrived on Saturday, and seemed very unwell, and could only just crawl about, but on Tuesday she collapsed, and for days we were very much alarmed indeed. Her doctors decided to move her to her own house at Saint-Brice yesterday, and she was taken over in an ambulance with a doctor, a trained nurse, and an *infirmier* in the ambulance, followed by her own car containing her secretary and two maids. Her secretary telephoned over that she reached there at 4:30 p.m. apparently no worse for her journey."

Two months later, in August 1937, she died, before she could make that last trip to Italy, the place where she had met the gods so often. Alfred White, Edith's agent, wrote to Berenson: "She had a simple funeral full of dignity surrounded with loyal friends and flowers. They all knew her love for flowers. And here in this little village, where she had won the respect and affection of all through her endless charity for all, les Pompieux, Ancien Combattants, Mutilés de guerre, formed a guard of honneur, in the Court, and as the body was carried out they dipped their flags & sounded the last Post." At Versailles, where she was buried, "the body was met by a deputation of Ancien Combattants who led the Cortege to the grave, it was very satisfying such respect shown by men who are supposed to be Red.

"Now it's all over. I can't believe she's gone forever—it seems she's on one of her little motor trips and will come back again."

Berenson wrote to Louis Gillet: "For me she can never be dead. She will remain while consciousness lasts in me, a projected emotion & ideal, a cultural term of reference. How can it be otherwise, after thirty years of such spiritual intimacy and of such fraternal affection. She is only out of reach whence answers may not be expected. That is bad enough but it is not death."

Wharton wrote: "W. always said that success in life depended more on luck than was generally admitted. In the main I agree; but there are people who knock bad luck into good by just butting at it.

——

"My ruling passions:
Justice—Order—
Dogs—
Books—
Flowers
Architecture—
Travel—
a good joke—&
perhaps that should
have come first—"

# NOTES

*Numbers preceding entries refer to page numbers.*

**6:** Edith Wharton letter to Charles Scribner in R. W. B. Lewis and Nancy Lewis, eds., *The Letters of Edith Wharton.*

**7:** Winthrop Chanler letter to Margaret Chanler, October 29, 1905, in *Winthrop Chanler's Letters.*

**7–8:** Edith Wharton's letters concerning *The House of Mirth* are in the Norton Critical edition of *The House of Mirth*, edited by Elizabeth Ammons.

**9:** For more about the Vanderbilt weddings, see Louis Auchincloss, *Maverick in Mauve* and *The Vanderbilt Era.*

**10:** Many critics, including Cynthia Wolff in *A Feast of Words: The Triumph of Edith Wharton* and Judith Fryer in *Felicitous Space,* have written about Lily Bart's being an object of art, not an artist.

**11:** The letter from the *New York Times Saturday Review of Books* is among Wharton's papers at the Beinecke Rare Book and Manuscript Library at Yale University. Mary Berenson's remarks on Edith Wharton are in *Mary Berenson: A Self-Portrait from Her Diaries and Letters.*

**12:** History of New York City described in Charles Lockwood, *Manhattan Moves Uptown* and Henry Collins Brown, *Fifth Avenue Old and New.*

**12:** Edith Wharton's references to her childhood in Europe and New York are found in *A Backward Glance,* "Life and I," and "A Little Girl's New York."

**12:** Family history is in R. W. B. Lewis, *Edith Wharton,* and in Edith Wharton's memoirs. Also, the Jones family genealogy is in the Louis Auchincloss collection of the Wharton Archives at the Beinecke Library.

**12:** Wharton's family was well off and she inherited a great deal of money; she also earned—and spent—a large income from her writing during her lifetime. According to R. W. B. Lewis, in 1883 she received $20,000 outright under her father's will (as did her brothers) plus an equal share of his remaining estate in trust, which provided her with about $9,000 a year. In 1888 her grandfather's childless cousin, Joshua Jones, died and left an unexpected $120,000 each to her and her brothers. In 1901, she began to receive the income from a trust of about $90,000 as her share of her mother's estate. Her total income then was about $22,000 a year from trusts and investments, mainly in New York City real property.

Her writing income started modestly in 1898 with the first royalty check for $39.60 from *The Decoration of Houses,* which would pay her royalties indefinitely. Next year, *The Greater Inclination,* a collection of short stories, provided $441 as a first royalty payment. The following year *The Touchstone,* a novella, brought an advance of $500, $750 for serialization rights, and royalty payments of $514. The breakthrough came with *The Valley of Decision,* published in 1903, which commanded a $2,000 advance and earned more than $10,000 in royalties on more than 35,000 copies sold, followed by her first best-seller, *The House of Mirth* (1905): she received $5,000 for serial rights, with royalties of $30,000 earned by the end of the year. Her writing income in 1905, more than $20,000, was for the first time equivalent to her income from trusts and investments. For the three years 1905–7 she earned more than $65,000. In 1907, she received a $10,000 advance for her next novel, *The Fruit of the Tree.* It was well reviewed but did not sell as well; her writing income for 1908 was about $15,000, mainly from its royalties.

By this time she was publishing at the rate of about one volume per year, a pace she maintained until her death. Even during the Great War, she managed *Fighting France* (1915), *Summer* (1917), *The Marne* (1918), and *French Ways and Their Meaning* (1919), a collection of articles first published in several magazines. *Ethan Frome* (1911) was not a commercial success and *The Reef* (1912) did not earn back its $15,000 advance, her largest to that time. *The Custom of the Country* (1913) was a commercial success, likewise *Fighting France* (1915). *Summer,* published in 1917, produced an advance of $7,000 plus $7,000 more for serial rights. In 1919, *The Age of Innocence* brought an advance of $15,000 and $13,000 for serial rights. It was a best-seller, earning her nearly $70,000 during 1920 and 1921, including $15,000 for film rights. *The Glimpses of the Moon* (1922) was another best-seller; she received $17,000 for serial rights, $28,000 in royalties, and $13,500 for film rights. The *Ladies Home Journal* paid her $5,500 in 1922 to publish the short story *False Dawn.* In 1923 she was paid $15,000 for serial rights to *A Son at the Front,* not a commercial success. In 1924 she earned $15,000 in royalties from sales of a four-volume boxed set of *Old New York,* a collection of four novellas. For her next novel, *The Mother's Recompense* (1925), she received $32,000 for serial rights.

R. W. B. Lewis estimates her literary income at about $50,000 a year for the years 1920 through 1924, in addition to her $30,000 a year from trusts and investments. In 1925, *The Mother's Recompense* earned her $55,000 in royalties before the summer; she asked her publisher to defer further payments until the next year. *Twilight Sleep* (1928), another best-seller, brought $30,000 for serial rights plus $21,000 in royalties. In 1928–29, the Broadway production of *The Age of Innocence* earned her $23,500. *Hudson River Bracketed* in 1929 brought $60,000. *The Gods Arrive* (1932) brought $50,000 for serial rights, but only $8,500 in royalties. In 1933, she haggled for and won $25,000 for her memoirs, *A Backward Glance.* In 1934, her literary earnings had fallen to about $20,000, but for the three years remaining of her life, she enjoyed an income of about $130,000 from two successful Broadway productions of *The Old Maid* and *Ethan Frome.*

**12:** Wharton was not close to either of her brothers, although she saw Harry more than Freddy. She wrote to Elizabeth Cameron after Freddy's death in June of 1918: "Minnie & Trix make up to me for my own wretched family, & all my thoughts & interests are with them."

**14:** Her father's travel descriptions are from George Frederic Jones's Travel Diary, 1847–48, which is at the Lilly Library, University of Indiana, Bloomington.

**15–16:** Descriptions of the American colony in Rome during the 1860s are from Margaret Terry Chanler, *Roman Spring,* and Maud Howe Elliot, *My Cousin Marion Crawford.*

**16:** R. W. B. Lewis writes that Wharton's mother called her "Puss" or "Pussy," as did Ogden Codman, Beatrix Farrand, Daisy Chanler, and many close friends in America.

**18:** Notes for *A Backward Glance,* entitled "Memories," are at the Lilly Library. Her story about writing her childhood novel (see p. 25) also comes from here.

**19:** In *A Feast of Words,* Cynthia Wolff discusses Edith Wharton's projection of her anger onto the mother of the dance teacher.

**19–20:** The letter from Alice James to William James is quoted in Jean Strouse's *Alice James.*

**20–21:** Edith Wharton letter to Mary Berenson, June 4, 1932.

**22:** Descriptions of the Joneses' house are from Scott Marshall's *The Mount: A Historic Structure Report,* and from Edith Wharton's "A Little Girl's New York." Scott Marshall kindly helped me with the details of the Joneses' neighborhood.

**26:** Viola Winner comments on *Fast and Loose* in her introduction to the 1977 University of Virginia Press edition of that novel.

**27:** In her confessional memoir, *Life and I,* Wharton recalls enjoying herself immensely at her debut; in *A Backward Glance,* she pictures herself as shy and fearful.

**28:** *Portrait of a Knight of Saint John* by Franciabigio, the Florentine painter Francesco di Cristofano (1482/3–1535).

**31:** Louis Auchincloss and R. W. B. Lewis tell the story of the broken engagement.

**31:** Edith's friend Ethel King described the breaking off of the engagement to Harry Stevens in a letter to her sister Alice, July 15, 1883, at the Redwood Library and Athenaeum in Newport.

**32:** See Gloria Ehrlich on Wharton's lack of knowledge of sex; for other emotional unreadiness for marriage, see R. W. B. Lewis, Cynthia Wolff, and Wharton's descriptions in "Life and I."

**32:** Renata Propper, a graphologist, analyzed the handwriting of Edith Wharton and Teddy Wharton and confirmed what I had learned through my study: Teddy's writing was one of a childish and dependent, insecure person, while Edith's hand showed the personality of an intensely intelligent, strong, confident, dominating, energetic, and accomplished woman, who was creative within a conventional framework.

**32:** Gaillard Lapsley's comment on Teddy Wharton is in his notes for Percy Lubbock, *A Portrait of Edith Wharton,* at the Beinecke Library.

**33:** Newport's history is described in Cleveland Amory's *The Last Resorts,* Mrs. Van Rensselaer's *Newport, Our Social Capital,* Maud Howe Elliott's *This Was My Newport,* Edith Wharton's *A Backward Glance,* and Margaret Terry Chanler's *Roman Spring.*

**33:** I have drawn heavily on Ogden Codman's letters to his mother and Edith Wharton's letters to Ogden Codman, found at the Society for the Preservation of New England Antiquities (SPNEA), Boston. I also quote from Edith Wharton's letters to Sara Norton, which are at the Beinecke Library at Yale and the Houghton Library at Harvard, letters from Edith Wharton to Margaret Chanler, and letters to her editor Edward Burlingame at the Firestone Library at Princeton University and in the Lewises' *Letters of Edith Wharton.*

**38:** Although R. W. B. Lewis calls Mr. White *Arthur* White, in his letter to Bernard Berenson after Edith Wharton's death White signs himself, "Yours very respectfully, *Alfred* White."

**39:** Mrs. William Backhouse Astor, born Caroline Schermerhorn, was the daughter-in-law of William Backhouse Astor, Sr., who died in 1875. She became "the" Mrs. Astor of New York and Newport society.

**40:** Daniel Berkeley Updike's memories of the Whartons at Newport and later in Lenox are in *A Portrait of Edith Wharton.*

**40:** William L. Van Alen, "Wakehurst," published by the Numismatic and Antiquarian Society of Philadelphia, 1974.

**41:** Edith Wharton's travel journal was not actually published as *The Cruise of the Vanadis* until 1991, after the manuscript was discovered by the French scholar Claudine Lesage in the municipal library of Hyères. See Eleanor Dwight, "The Cruise of the Vanadis" [book review], in the *Edith Wharton Review* (Spring 1993).

**41:** Wharton's travel accounts show she was a fearless explorer. When the travelers reached Mount Athos, she had to stay on board the yacht, as "the early established rule that no female, human or animal is to set foot on the promontory, is maintained as strictly as ever; and as hens fall under this ban, the eggs for the monastic tables have to be brought all the way from Lemnos." Not to be left out, however, she "ordered up steam in the launch, and started out on a voyage of discovery, going so close to the forbidden shore first to photograph and then to look" that the lay brothers on the shore "clambered hurriedly down the hill to prevent my landing and with their shocks of black hair and long woolen robes flying behind them, they were a wild enough looking set to frighten any intruder away."

**42:** Paul Bourget's impressions of America and Newport can be found in *Outre-Mer*, published in 1895. Details of his visit are also in Edith Wharton's obituary essay on Bourget, translated from the French by Adeline Tintner. The *Edith Wharton Review*, "Souvenirs de Bourget Outre-mer," Spring 1991. Tintner writes in another article, "Portrait of Edith Wharton in Bourget's 'L'Indicatrice,'" that the American woman in this tale (1905) is a portrait of the Edith Wharton whom Bourget has gotten to know and respect after ten years of friendship so that her "humanity, kindness, and generosity," come out in this tale, which may be a kind of "making up" for the earlier picture in *Outre-Mer.*

**42:** Bourget's fiction pictured the freer social and sexual mores in France and influenced Henry James to be more open in writing about love affairs. See Adeline Tintner, *The Cosmopolitan World of Henry James.* Having read Bourget's fiction, Wharton too may have seen France as a place where liaisons were possible.

**46:** Albert Léon Guérard discusses Bourget in *Five Masters of French Romance.*

**47:** Clare Colquitt discusses the passage in Wharton's *The Writing of Fiction,* pp. 20–21, about the creative artist needing an ideal other in her excellent essay, "Unpacking Her Treasures: Edith Wharton's 'Mysterious Correspondence' with Morton Fullerton."

**48:** For background on Ogden Codman, his friendship with Edith Wharton, and the writing of their book, see *Ogden Codman and the Decoration of Houses,* edited by Pauline C. Metcalf.

**52:** The late Nicholas King describes the Codman attitude toward the Vanderbilts in his excellent essay, "Living with Codman," in *Ogden Codman and the Decoration of Houses.*

**63:** Although previous autobiographical studies have claimed that Wharton had a long, drawn-out breakdown in the mid- and late-1890s, her letters to Codman suggest that her depressions and physical collapses were short-lived and that she was on her feet before too long, rushing off on another trip or beginning another project. Her letters to Sally Norton after finishing *The Valley of Decision* in January 1902 suggest that she, like many authors, suffered depression after completing a book. (She also collapsed in August 1913, after finishing *The Custom of the County*—see pp. 173–77.) All her life she experienced wide mood swings and physical ailments requiring her to withdraw from life (which she often did by traveling somewhere to "change the scene"), but generally she was fiercely energetic.

**63:** Susan Goodman discusses Wharton's friendship with Sally Norton in *Edith Wharton's Women: Friends & Rivals.*

**64:** Although there are several apocryphal stories (including this one) about Edith Wharton and Isabella Stewart Gardner putting each other down, there is little to document this poor relationship. They saw each other from time to time and seem to have maintained a cordial, if distant, friendship. This letter to Codman suggests that Edith Wharton saw Mrs. Jack's "new pictures" at the Gardner house on Beacon Street as they were apparently installed at Fenway Court in 1901 or in 1902, after Mrs. Gardner moved there. The grand opening of "the Palace" was held on January 1, 1903, at which time Edith Wharton was supposed to have said (in French) that she had had better food in a French railway station and her hostess to have replied, "Never darken my door again."

**65:** Reading her writing about interiors in the 1890s, in *The Decoration of Houses* and the short stories, one senses that Wharton was often projecting sexual feelings onto rooms and houses. The fear of entrapment, the obsession with entrances keeping out and letting in, and the fascination with privacy can be seen as expressing sexual desire.

**67:** For an analysis of Edith Wharton's early short stories, see Cynthia Wolff's *A Feast of Words.*

**67:** In her introduction to *The Muse's Tragedy and Other Stories,* Candace Waid writes about Wharton's ambivalence about art.

**69:** Wharton's reflections on Italian travel are recorded in *A Backward Glance,* her obituary essay on Paul Bourget, her travel essays collected in *Italian Backgrounds,* and her letters to Margaret Chanler, Ogden Codman, Sally Norton, and her editors.

**69:** In her introduction to the 1991 Northern Illinois Press edition of *A Motor-Flight Through France,* Mary Suzanne Schriber writes that in the nineteenth century more than fifteen hundred American books on travel were published in the United States: "They were written by such authors as Mark Twain, Henry James, Henry Adams and William Dean Howells, but they were also written by female journalists and occasional writers, some among them otherwise unpublished."

**69–70:** Cynthia Wolff has pointed out that the soul mate in Wharton's story who offers just what the woman wants is a replica of herself, "like a parody of Little Sir Echo." But it is also a parody of the art critics Edith Wharton had read—the aesthetes John Ruskin and Walter Pater. See Ruskin, *Mornings in Florence,* in *Complete Works,* 23: 308, and Pater, *Renaissance,* 101–2.

**73:** After Wharton's essay appeared in 1895, scholars gradually came to agree that these figures popularly attributed to Giovanni Gonelli had been made earlier. In Emmanuelle Repetti's *Dizionario Geographico, Fisico, Storico* (1843), they are listed as Gonelli's work, as they are in the *Allgemeines Lexikon* as late as 1921. In 1920, however, Alan Marquand, an American authority on the Della Robbias, wrote that two of the groups might be attributed to Giovanni della Robbia, and the scholarship done by Antonio Paolucci in 1976 concludes that the groups were done between 1500 and 1515 by artists of the Florentine School. The convent was built with the financial support of the Florentine friars, linking it with Florence. There are similarities between the works at San Vivaldo and authenticated works by Benedetto Buglioni and Giovanni della Robbia, two gifted artists in this sort of sculpture. Modern scholars feel that many different artists participated in creating the figures, but that three groups, *Lo Spasimo, L'Ascensione,* and *La Maddalena ai Piedi,* three of the five Wharton had singled out, are similar to the known style of Giovanni della Robbia. See Repetti, *Dizionario Geographico, Fisico, Storico Della Toscana* 5: 175; Thieme and Becker, *Allgemeines Lexikon der Bildenden Kunstler* 14: 371; Marquand, *Giovanni della Robbia,* 219; *Guida d'Italia Toscano,* 502; and Paolucci, *Guida de S. Vivaldo,* 22–23.

**73–74:** The Berensons' comments about Wharton and the terra-cottas are in R. W. B. Lewis's *Edith Wharton* and in *The Letters of Bernard Berenson to Isabella Stewart Gardner, 1887–1924,* edited by Rollin Hadley.

**74:** Mary Berenson recorded her impressions on meeting Wharton in her diary, found in *Mary Berenson: A Self-Portrait from Her Diaries and Letters.*

**74–75:** Information on Vernon Lee can be found in the Colby College Library, whose quarterly journal has published numerous articles about her. Wharton drew heavily on her *Studies of the Eighteenth Century in Italy* for *The Valley.* Lee's *Euphorion,* subtitled *Studies of the Antique and the Mediaeval in the Renaissance,* had interested Wharton greatly with its chapters on the Italy of the Elizabethan dramatists and Medieval Love. In a fragment called "Italy Again," written at the end of her life, Wharton praises the "impressionistic sketches of travel" of her youth by Bourget, Vernon Lee, and John Addington Symonds and admits to having written one or two "pretty books" herself, noting the value of the "experienced amateur."

**75:** Information on John Singer Sargent and Ralph Curtis is from Hugh Honour and John Fleming, *The Venetian Hours of Henry James, Whistler and Sargent.*

**78–79:** Sybil Cutting's memories of Teddy are in Percy Lubbock's *A Portrait of Edith Wharton.*

**79:** See Blake Nevius's *Edith Wharton: A Study of Her Fiction* on "Soul's Belated" for an analysis of Lydia's dilemma.

**79–80:** While the Whartons and Bourgets were traveling together in 1899 in Italy, the Dreyfus affair became a test for their friendship. Dreyfus, a captain in the French Army and a Jew, had been falsely convicted of treason in a case that eventually involved most French intellectuals as partisans for or against Dreyfus. Bourget was outspokenly anti-Dreyfus: "He always told me that personally he had no closed opinion on the guilt of Dreyfus. For him, that which counted first was the political obligation to defend the army, by no matter what means." Wharton remembers they spoke of it together from morning to night, but out of Minnie's hearing and presumably Teddy's also: "Whenever we were alone we resumed our arguments." Edith was firmly pro–Dreyfus, "but he never got angry while listening to my arguments." She concludes: "I can say that nothing gave me as high an idea of his intellectual independence as did this sojourn near him at a moment when many Frenchmen, and the most intelligent, submitted to the pressures of an atmosphere overheated by political hatreds." A credit also to Wharton's intellectual independence and her affection for Bourget as well: she disagreed with him and must have become bored with their discussions—she called them "interminable"—and rancorous political issues were not usually her favorite subject for conversation.

**80–83:** Illustrations are from Wharton's essays "A Midsummer Week's Dream" and "Sub Umbra Liliorum," published in *Scribner's Magazine.*

**80:** If Wharton was trying to emulate George Eliot, one of her favorite authors, when she wrote *The Valley,* in one way she considered that she had surpassed her mentor, as indicated by this untitled fragment in the Beinecke Library: "Our conception of the men and women who lived three or four hundred years ago is made up not from personal experience, but from literature and art—from the books they wrote, the pictures thay painted, and the houses they lived in. From the books we obtain, with more or less efforts of mental adjustment, a notion of what they thought and how they expressed their ideas; but much more vivid is the notion formed of them from their appearance and environment. And it is for this reason that the visualizing gift is of the first importance to the novelist. George Eliot did not possess it. Her letters from Italy show her curious insensibility to qualities of atmosphere, to values of form and colour. And for this reason her Florence, for all its carefully studied detail, remains a pasteboard performance."

**80:** Sources for *The Valley of Decision* can be found in the Ph.D. dissertation of Eleanor Dwight, New York University, 1984, "The Influence of Italy on Edith Wharton." Although she claimed later that the writing of the book was not prepared for by months of hard study, Wharton's research was impressive: the most important sources were Stendhal's *Charterhouse of Parma* and Goethe's *Italian Journey,* but she also read many accounts of travelers to Italy in the settecento such as those of Mrs. Piozzi, John Moore, Arthur Young, Giuseppe Baretti, Henry Swinburne; the writings of Gozzi, Goldoni, and Casanova as well as Copping's biography of Alfieri and Goldoni; studies of the period by Vernon Lee, Antonio Galenga, John Addington Symonds; and fiction set there such as Shorthouse's *John Inglesant* and Madame de Staël's *Corinne, or Italy.*

**80:** Letters to William Brownell about *The Valley of Decision* and travel essays are at the Firestone Library at Princeton.

**82–83:** At the heart of the book is the conflict which Wharton was then struggling with: whether to live as a conventional member of the privileged elite or to use her talents to improve the world. Also featured is the longing for escape from this conflict in pleasurable activities such as travel.

**84:** Wharton discussed with her publisher the idea of having Maxfield Parrish illustrate *The Valley of Decision;* these illustrations, found among her papers at Beinecke, may be Parrish's.

**85:** Her hero, Guido Villalba, was reputedly the son of a bastard, whose parents were the Marquis Trescorre and, it was rumored, the Duchess Maria Clementina, by whom he was created Count Villalba "and treated with peculiar distinction."

**85:** The "New York novel" eventually became *The House of Mirth.*

**85:** Review of Edwin H. and Evangeline W. Blashfield's book *Italian Cities,* in *Bookman* 13 (August 1901): 563–64.

**86:** Wharton knew the Italian background, or the well-known travel haunts, as Brigitte Bailey discussed in her paper given at the conference "Edith Wharton in Paris," June 1991.

**86:** Perhaps most important, it was Wharton's habit of taking "imaginative possession of the settecento world" (as R. W. B. Lewis writes), of being able to fantasize about Italy and its history, which led to her first serious creative accomplishments.

**87:** For history of Lenox, see *The Berkshire Hills,* by the Writers Project of the WPA; *Lenox and the Berkshire Highlands,* by Raymond Dewitt Mallary; and *The Berkshire Cottages,* by Carole Owen.

**90:** For information on the design of the Mount and Edith's relationship with Ogden Codman, see *Ogden Codman and the Decoration of Houses.* I drew heavily on Part One of *The Mount, A Historic Structure Report,* by Scott Marshall, and *The Landscape Architectural Analysis and Master Plan for the Mount,* prepared by David Bennett, Wendy Baker, and Diane Dierkes. I also used Edith Wharton's letters to Ogden Codman and Codman's letters to his mother, at SPNEA, as well as Wharton's letters to Sara Norton, Margaret Chanler, and George B. Dorr at Beinecke; and letters to her editors at Scribner's, which are at the Firestone Library; and to Richard Watson Gilder at the Beinecke and New York Public libraries.

**90–91:** When there were bills outstanding after the decoration of the Mount, Codman started a legal proceeding, and the Whartons hired Walter Berry to represent them. After some years of discord, the Whartons finally paid Codman what he had asked. The rift was not repaired, however, for when Codman became engaged to marry Leila Morgan in the early 1900s, he wrote to Edith Wharton and she never answered the letter. It was not until the early 1920s, some time after his wife's death, that they began to see each other again. During the war, "Coddy" contributed money to her charities and in the 1920s and 30s they met often and swapped gardening advice. In 1937 her final sickness struck her while staying at his château.

**91:** I am grateful to Scott Marshall for the articles in *Lenox Life* and *Berkshire Resort Topics,* which I used in the Lenox and Motor-Car chapters.

**94:** Richard Guy Wilson writes that the approach is "reminiscent of French country estates near Compèigne or Versailles. The opening onto a broad green lawn, upon which the house sits, is American suburban. The form of the house is usually called Georgian, though the English label 'Wrenaissance' would be more accurate." He sees the Italian villa as the ultimate source for the English model, "as Charles McKim had noted in his memorandum to Edith and as she and Ogden had argued in *The Decoration of Houses.* The plan, however, was French, while the interior was American in convenience and mechanics though the decor recalled French, English, and Italian sources." He finds the terrace and gardens also Italian "in inspiration," and "beyond an English-style meadow lay the American landscape." His excellent essay in *Ogden Codman and The Decoration of Houses* discusses all the influences on the house.

**94:** Farrand would eventually become one of America's greatest landscape designers, doing both city and country gardens for clients such as the Rockefellers, Mrs. Woodrow Wilson at the White House, Otto Kahn, as well as several universities, including Princeton and Yale, and Oberlin College. In 1905, during the time when Wharton's *The House of Mirth* was being serialized in *Scribner's Magazine,* Beatrix also published an article there, on the gardens of Le Nôtre, the great French landscape designer.

In Italy in 1895, she toured many villas and gardens. On Friday, March 22, she wrote, "Joined

P. W. & went to the Casino Raspiglicias to see Guido's Aurora." This was most likely Pussy Wharton she joined, as Wharton was in Italy that spring looking at gardens herself. This is the only documented instance I have found of their being together in Italy.

**94:** Beatrix Farrand's plans for gardens of Lenox clients are in the College of Environmental Design Documents Collection at the University of California at Berkeley.

**96:** The list of visitors draws on Scott Marshall's *Historic Structures Report*. In 1906 Clyde Fitch dramatized *The House of Mirth*.

**97:** Updike's description of Ethel Cram is from *A Portrait of Edith Wharton*.

**100:** Louis Auchincloss described to me the Sloanes' marital troubles, which became the source for Edith Wharton's story "The Line of Least Resistance."

**100:** In "The Line of Least Resistance," even the walls appear to speak back to the often humiliated Mr. Mindon: "'And who are you?' the walls seemed to say.' 'Who am I?' Mr. Mindon heard himself retorting. 'I'll tell you, by God! I'm the man that paid for you—paid for every scrap of you: silk hangings, china rubbish, glasses, chandeliers—every Frenchified rag of you.'" Wharton is using the details of house furnishing, which so fascinated her especially in the 1890s, to suggest the excesses of the rich.

**103:** The descriptions of Italian villas and gardens are quoted from Wharton's *Italian Villas and Their Gardens* and *A Backward Glance*.

**106:** William Buckler's memories are in the memoirs collected by Percy Lubbock for *A Portrait of Edith Wharton*.

**109 ff:** Scott Marshall, David Bennett, and Nicolas Ekstrom kindly helped me with the captions for the photos of the Mount's gardens.

**113–14:** The description of the Whartons' gardens at the Mount is taken from "Gardens of Well Known People," in Hildegarde Hawthorne, *The Lure of the Garden*.

**114:** Wharton's prize-winning flowers are detailed in *Lenox Life*.

**114:** *Memoirs of a Sculptor's Wife*, by Mrs. Daniel French.

**115:** Mark Alan Hewitt, *The Architect and the American Country House*.

**116–17:** Letter to W. Morton Fullerton in *The Letters of Edith Wharton*.

**117:** When writing his mother on September 20, 1910, about Teddy, Ogden Codman mentioned Teddy's father's suicide: "She no sooner gets him settled in one place than he wants to go somewhere else, and is constantly in tears complaining either that he is spoiling her life or that he is being shamefully neglected—Really if he cannot die, it would seem as if he might as well follow his father's example and kill himself!! The more I think of it all the more sorry I feel for them both."

**118:** Gaillard Lapsley's memory is in the material for *A Portrait of Edith Wharton*.

**119:** I am indebted to Lyall Powers for his description of the motor-flighting of James and Wharton and other friends in his "Les Liaisons Non Dangereux." I used his superbly edited book, *The Letters of Henry James and Edith Wharton*, and benefited from his many insights on their friendship. Additional details of motoring are from Wharton's letters to Sara Norton and Margaret Chanler. I have also quoted from James's letters in Leon Edel, ed., *The Letters of Henry James*, vol. 4, *1895–1916*, and *The Selected Letters of Henry James*.

**121:** The fact that Wharton mentions sleeping well after motoring suggests that she may not always have slept so well, and her familiarity with chloral, which Lily Bart takes in *The House of Mirth*, suggests she took it herself.

**122:** The Backs are the system of canals at Cambridge, England.

**124–25:** The story of the accident is told in an unpublished reminiscence of Katharine Sargent Osborn, a niece of Ethel Cram, about her childhood summers in the Berkshires, and Nini Gilder kindly gave it to me. I also used Wharton's letters to Sally Norton and excerpts from the *Pittsfield Sun*, which Scott Marshall gave to me. Scott Marshall discusses the accident in his article "Edith Wharton, Kate Spencer, and *Ethan Frome*," *The Edith Wharton Review* (Spring 1993).

**125 ff:** Wharton's memories of first knowing Henry James and entertaining at the Mount are from *A Backward Glance*.

**126:** Note that in describing her meeting Henry James, Wharton uses the metaphor of John the Baptist and Christ.

**133:** Charles Eliot Norton letter to Ruskin, 1873, is in the *Letters of Charles Eliot Norton* 2: 14–15.

**134:** Wharton's approval of the Christmas celebration at Biltmore in which everyone was thought of reflects her social interests at the time she was working on *The Fruit of the Tree*.

**139:** According to R. W. B. Lewis, Edith Wharton toured a mill in North Adams, Massachusetts, to gain information for *The Fruit of the Tree*.

**141:** Edith Wharton's two diaries for 1908 are at the Lilly Library; some of her letters to W. Morton Fullerton are published in *The Letters of Edith Wharton*. Other sources for the chapter are Edith Wharton's letters to Sara Norton, Charles Eliot Norton, Elizabeth Cameron, John Hugh Smith, Bernard Berenson, and Mary Berenson, as well as *A Backward Glance*, *A Portrait of Edith Wharton*, *Edith Wharton: A Biography*, and "Unpacking Her Treasures: Edith Wharton's 'Mysterious Correspondence' with Morton Fullerton."

**143:** Henry James letter to W. E. Norris. Although Wharton often urged that he come to France, James preferred staying in Rye: "I have lived into my little old home and gardens so thoroughly that they have become a kind of domiciliary skin; that can't be pulled off without pain."

**147:** The passage from Dante's *Inferno* is quoted in *Edith Wharton: A Biography*.

**148:** R. W. B. Lewis connects Wharton's reflecting on the times she wore her gowns with Lily Bart's similar reflections at the end of *The House of Mirth*.

**149:** Edith Wharton composed a poem as she sailed for America, parting from Fullerton temporarily.

Written in her diary, it is quoted by R. W. B. Lewis.

**151:** Gloria Ehrlich analyzes the affair between Wharton and Fullerton in *The Sexual Education of Edith Wharton*. Cynthia Wolff also provides an excellent discussion of the liaison in *A Feast of Words*.

**151:** Edith Wharton wanted desperately to keep her affair secret. Perhaps James and her servants were the only ones who knew of it.

**152:** Margaret Terry Chanler, *Autumn in the Valley* and *Memory Makes Music,* and *A Portrait of Edith Wharton* were sources for information about many of the friends Wharton saw in Paris.

**153–55:** See *The Complete Letters of Henry Adams*, vol. 6. At the turn of the century, Adams had turned to writing his great work, *The Education of Henry Adams*, in which he described growing up as the grandson and great-grandson of presidents and trying to use his talents in a confusing world. In the process he recorded brilliantly America in the last half of the nineteenth century, and gave his analysis of the "multiplicity" of modern times. In love with the medieval architecture of France, he had just written *Mont-Saint-Michel and Chartres*. He was surrounded by adoring women of all ages—his "nieces," Lizzie Cameron and others—whom he would lunch and dine with and take on excursions: "My idea of paradise is a perfect automobile going thirty miles an hour on a smooth road to a twelfth century cathedral."

**161:** The journal of L'Abbé Mugnier was my source for understanding him and other friends.

**163:** Teddy Roosevelt's visit is detailed in *The Letters of Edith Wharton*.

**165:** From her window Wharton could see la cité de Varenne, a complex of *hôtels particuliers* and lovely gardens.

**165:** The background on the flood is from the biography of Marcel Proust by George D. Painter.

**165–66:** Edith Wharton's comments on the flood in Paris are in a letter to Elizabeth Cameron, February 9, 1910, at the Library of Congress.

**167:** Sexual passion as a theme in Edith Wharton's writing is discussed by Judith Fryer in *Felicitous Space*.

**167:** See Cynthia Wolff's comments on the similarities between Undine Spragg's personality and that of her creator in *A Feast of Words*.

**170:** See Louis Auchincloss's introduction to Scribner's edition of *The Reef*.

**170:** When Wharton was studying the language, her tutor was too polite to correct her spoken mistakes and asked her to prepare a written exercise before each visit: "The easiest thing for me was to write a story; and thus the French version of 'Ethan Frome' was begun." This first version, written in 1907, had no first-person narrator, so important in the final *Ethan Frome*, and there is no sledding accident.

**171:** For the background on the sledding accident that occured in Lenox, see Scott Marshall's article in the *Edith Wharton Review* (Spring 1993).

**171:** James Tuttleton discusses how Wharton's affair influenced her writing of *The Reef* in "Mocking Fate: Romantic Idealism in Edith Wharton's *Reef,*" in *Studies in the Novel*, 1987, 19: 459–74.

**173:** Information on Mary and Bernard Berenson is found in the two-volume biography by Ernest Samuels; in Meryle Secrest's *Being Bernard Berenson*; and in *Mary Berenson: A Self-Portrait from Her Diaries and Letters*, edited by Barbara Strachey and Jayne Samuels. I also refer to letters read at the Villa I Tatti, including letters Bernard Berenson wrote to Mary Berenson, in 1913 and in the early 1930s, describing Edith Wharton.

**174:** Wharton was thinking of being "so happy" in the Valtelline with the Bourgets in the late 1890s.

**177:** Cynthia Ozick discusses Wharton's habit of writing in bed in "Justice Again to Edith Wharton," *Commentary* (1976).

**178:** While Wharton and Berenson were in Berlin he reported to Mary on their different way of seeing things: "Edith was impressed as indeed she is by the spacious avenues leading out of the town, the freshness of the grass and flowers everywhere, the look of order and tidiness. The 'handsomeness' of the place."

**178:** See Meryle Secrest's *Being Bernard Berenson*.

**179:** The information on Edith Wharton's wartime activities between August 1914 and 1916 comes from *Fighting France* and letters to friends—especially Henry James, Sara Norton, and Bernard Berenson—as well as *A Backward Glance*, *The Book of the Homeless*, and her article "My Work Among the Women of Paris," in the *New York Times Magazine*.

**182:** "Mme Laonnois," the German gun, was thought to be located in a forest near the town of Laon.

**182:** The quotes on the war are from André Gide in his *Journals*, Henry James, and a letter dated August 29, 1914, from Ralph Curtis to Bernard Berenson at I Tatti.

**183:** Blanche's description is from his memoir for *A Portrait of Edith Wharton*.

**184:** Information on the Comtesse d'Haussonville was kindly given to me by her great-grandson, the Comte d'Haussonville.

**186:** The story of Elsie de Wolfe and her friends is told in the biography *Elsie de Wolfe: A Life in High Style*.

**187:** Ralph Curtis's letter to Berenson, dated September 23, 1915. Letters from Curtis to Berenson at the beginning of the Great War are in the Berenson Archives at I Tatti.

**187–88:** Wharton's letter to Elisina Tyler is formal. It begins, "Dear Mrs. Tyler," and is signed, "yrs ever sincerely, E. Wharton."

**188:** In December 1914, Wharton wrote Beatrix Farrand about raising money in America: "I don't care how much people have given over there. They ought to give more, & give most of all to the Belgians. When a great nation like ours has dishonored herself forever by not protesting at the violation of a treaty which she signed to protect a weaker country, the individual members of that nation ought to make every sacrifice to atone for the cowardice of their government." Then she added: "The whole thing makes me so sick with shame that if I had time—& it mattered—I'd run round to the Préfecture de Police & get myself naturalized, almost anything rather than continue to be an American. . . . But it's much more important to try to make oneself useful."

**188:** For the story of Edith Wharton and the Red Cross, see Alan Price's article "Edith Wharton at War with the American Red Cross," in *Women's Studies*, and his forthcoming book, *The Tremolo Note: Edith Wharton and the First World War*.

**193:** When Wharton and Berry visited Verdun in February 1915, it was a quiet sector. A year later the Germans attacked and quickly overran the field hospital she had inspected "not far from the enemy's lines near Cosenvoye." The one-lane back road to Bar-le-Duc they took when they motored from Verdun to Paris was destined to become the Voie Sacré, the French lifeline for supplies and reenforcements for the Verdun battlefield.

**195:** Wharton's description of the *Rire* cartoon is found in her letter to Alice Garrett at Johns Hopkins University.

**201:** "The Hymn of the Lusitania" continues: "A war ship, and one of the foe's best workers, / Not penned with her rusting harbor shirkers. / Now the Flanders guns lack their daily bread, / And shipper and buyer are sick with dread; / For neutral as Uncle Sam may be, / Your surest neutral's the deep, green sea. / Just one ship sunk with lives and shell, / And thousands of German graycoats—well! / And for each of the graycoats German hate / Would have sunk ten ships with all their freight. / Yea, ten such ships are a paltry fine / For one good life in our fighting line. / Let England ponder the crimson text—/ 'Torpedo, strike! And Hurrah for the next!'"

**202:** Alan Price told me that movies as well as photographs were used to publicize Wharton's charities and appeal to donors.

**205:** Edith Wharton letter to Lizzie Cameron.

**206:** Edith Wharton letter to General John J. Pershing dated July 22, 1917, from *The Letters of Edith Wharton*.

**209:** Edith Wharton explained her fears about finances to Beatrix Farrand.

**211:** Edith Wharton often described her house and garden in letters to Beatrix Farrand, Minnie Jones, and Bernard Berenson.

**211:** Background on Pavillon Colombe is from Cyril Connoly and Jerome Zerbe, *Les Pavillons: French Pavillons of the Eighteenth Century*.

**211:** Some sources say there were two Ruggieri sisters, others say there were three.

**212:** Vivian de Watteville's description of Pavillon Colombe is from her memories written for *A Portrait of Edith Wharton*.

**215:** Madame Saint-René Taillandier's thoughts are from *A Portrait of Edith Wharton*.

**217 ff:** Edith Wharton's description of her garden is from her "Gardening in France," at the Beinecke Library.

**219:** Wharton wrote out detailed lists of flowers for the different borders of the potager. She sent her gardener questionnaires to get his ideas and he filled them out and returned them.

**221–22:** Account of the sale of produce from Pavillon Colombe was found in the head gardener's notebook, which Jacques Fosse kindly showed me at Saint-Brice.

**223:** Russell Page discusses Louis Bromfield in *The Education of a Gardener*.

**223:** Another famous gardener whom Edith Wharton met was Gertrude Jekyll, but Wharton's shyness prevented a satisfactory exchange between the two when they met at Miss Jekyll's famous garden, Great Warley. "On that long-desired day I had a hundred questions to ask, a thousand things to learn. . . . I put one timid question to Miss Jekyll, who answered curtly, and turned her back on me to point out a hybrid iris to an eminent statesman who knew neither what a hybrid nor an iris was: and for the rest of the visit she gave me no chance of exchanging a word with her."

**223:** At this time, Beatrix Farrand was working on the Rockefeller garden in Seal Harbor, Maine, and others.

**223:** The memories of Teddy's adultery and her brother Harry's (according to Codman's letters to his mother), of her own affair and the horrors of her divorce (see R. W. B. Lewis), and the horrors of the war were lingering just below the surface when Wharton returned in her imagination to the world of the 1870s and wrote of the conflict between social duty and personal and sexual realization.

**225:** The correspondence with Minnie Jones is at the Beinecke Library.

**227:** Wharton recorded brief details of her visit to America in her diary for 1923. She stayed at Westbrook before the trip to New Haven and with her friends the Maynards on Long Island afterward.

**228 ff:** Wharton's servants are described in *Edith Wharton: A Biography,* and in *A Portrait of Edith Wharton*, and are mentioned many times in her letters. Letters from Catharine Gross to Edith Wharton are at Beinecke.

**229:** Letter from Alfred White to Bernard Berenson is at the Villa I Tatti.

**231:** One reading of the ghost stories is to see the "downstairs" as corresponding to the subconscious, another world behind the scenes where unmentionable strange things happen according to another standard.

**232:** See Annette Zilversmit's essay "All Souls': Wharton's Last Haunted House and Future Directions for Criticism," in *Edith Wharton New Critical Essays*, ed. Bendixen and Zilversmit.

**234:** Jacques Fosse gave me the resolution of Saint-Brice, which reads: "Le conseil, sur la proposition du maire et à l'unanimité des membres présents, adresse ses remerciements à Madame Wharton pour le joli don de volumes offerts aux bibliothèques des écoles. Egalement de toutes les générosités adressées à la Caisse des écoles, au bureau de bien-faisance et à la commune par cette généreuse donatrice."

**235:** Much of the information about Château Sainte-Claire and Hyères I found at an exhibit in the house itself during a 1992 visit. I was given generous help by Jean-Claude Barrois in the office of the national park of Port Cros, the botanical conservatory of the Porquerolles Islands, whose offices are in the house. Pierre Quillier, the gardener at the

Villa Saint Bernard next door, took me through the gardens (which are very changed since Wharton's time) and explained the planting. I have drawn also on memoirs written by Gaillard Lapsley and Robert Norton for *A Portrait of Edith Wharton*.

**242:** Margaret Terry Chanler, *Autumn in the Valley*.

**243:** Harriet Martineau visited Sainte-Claire in 1923 and 1924 and described Wharton's garden in her book *Gardening in Sunny Lands*, for which Wharton wrote the introduction.

**243–47:** Garden descriptions are based on *Gardening in Sunny Lands;* Edith Wharton's "December in a French Riviera Garden," "Spring in a French Riviera Garden," as well as E. C., "A Riviera Garden: Sainte-Claire le Château, Hyères," in *Country Life* (November 3, 1928).

**244:** The *Country Life* article mentions the rare *Acacia catheriana*, which was probably a nursery owner's designation, as it is not a valid scientific name.

**245–46:** Some of the plant names Edith Wharton mentioned are no longer used. The following names and their contemporary equivalents have been kindly compiled by Nicolas H. Ekstrom: Bougainvillea Sanderiana = *Bougainvillea glabra* 'Sanderiana'; Bignonia capensis = *Tecomaria capensis;* Laurustinus = *Viburnum tinus*; Banksia = *Rosa banksiae*; Diplopappus = *Aster* sp.; Tomasinianus = *Crocus tommasinianus*; Enchantress = *Crocus vernus* 'Enchantress'; Crocus Susianus = *Crocus angustifolius;* Sind-pers = *Iris* 'Sindpur'; Reticulata Cantab = *Iris reticulata* 'Cantab'; Histriodes Major = *Iris histriodes* 'Major'; Hispanicas = *Iris xiphium*.

**249:** Wharton's reactions to her garden are recorded between 1919 and 1935 in her diaries now at the Lilly Library.

**255:** Information on Walter Berry's death came from the Paris edition of the *New York Herald*, October 1927.

**255:** Letter from Edith Wharton to Frederick King is at Redwood Library and Athenaeum.

**257–58:** Beatrix Palmato fragment is in Appendix C of *Edith Wharton: A Biography*.

**260:** See "Edith Wharton's Subtle Revenge?: Morton Fullerton and the Female Artist in *Hudson River Bracketed* and *The Gods Arrive*," by Abby H. Werlock.

**260:** Although Fullerton did not read Wharton's works, he saved her letters, which were discovered in Paris in the 1980s and sold to the Harry Ransom Humanities Research Center at the University of Texas in Austin.

**261:** Margaret Chanler describes the cruise of the *Osprey* in *Autumn in the Valley*.

**261:** Notes on hotels are on the end papers in Edith Wharton's diaries at the Lilly Library.

**265:** For the atmosphere at I Tatti, see Carter Brown's introduction to *Looking at Paintings with Bernard Berenson*. For more information on the relationship between Bernard Berenson and Nicky Mariano, see Mariano's book, *Forty Years with Berenson*.

**265:** I draw on Edith Wharton's letters to Mary and Bernard Berenson and Berenson's letters to Mary when he was with Edith Wharton.

**265:** Iris Origo, *Images and Shadows*.

**266:** See description of Berenson in *Mary Berenson, A Self Portrait from Her Diaries and Letters*.

**269–70:** The reactions of Clothilde Marghieri toward Edith Wharton are recorded in her *Trilogia*. This passage was translated for me by Franca Lally.

**271:** Nicky Mariano, in *A Portrait of Edith Wharton*.

**275:** Edith Wharton, letters to Rutger Jewett.

**278–79:** In 1903 Wharton had cautioned writers to be careful in writing about Italy: "He who has anything to say about Rome, Florence and Siena must justify himself by saying it extraordinarily well." "Roman Fever" is filled with literary echoes of others who wrote so well about Rome: Lord Byron, Madame de Staël, and Wharton's compatriates James and Hawthorne. At the beginning of *The Marble Faun*, Hawthorne has us glance "at this bright sky, and those blue distant mountains, and at the ruins, Etruscan, Roman, Christian, venerable with threefold antiquity, and at the company of

world-famous statues in the saloon—in the hope of putting the reader into that state of feeling which is experienced oftenest at Rome."

**282:** During Wharton's illness, Elisina Tyler cared for her at Pavillon Colombe.

**282:** Ogden Codman wrote his brother, Thomas, on June 5, after Wharton's visit: "I feel as if a great responsibility has been removed from my shoulders. It has been no joke putting up all her people. She had her own maid, then added her secretary, then a housemaid, then a nurse, and her chauffeur was here all the time, although as she arrived from the South in Paris, I had to send in for her with my car. Daisy got some one to assist the cook by washing dishes, etc., but every one was on the jump all the time. It was all very complicated and upsetting. Her almost last words as she left in the ambulance were, 'This will teach you not to ask decrepit old ladies to stay.' *I think it will.*"

**282:** Alfred White letter to Bernard Berenson.

**282:** Edith Wharton's will left the bulk of her estate, including her mother's trust, to Elisina Tyler and made Gaillard Lapsley her literary executor. Wharton believed she had been given the right to dispose of this trust to whomever she pleased as a result of an agreement she forced her two brothers to make with her, in effect rewriting her mother's will after her mother's death. Wharton's lawyers at that time made what turned out to be an egregious blunder, however: they did not insist that Beatrix Jones Farrand, Freddy's daughter and then in her mid-twenties, join with her father in the agreement, thus leaving it open for her to challenge its interpretation after Wharton's death. An embarrassing feud developed between Tyler and Farrand, who called Tyler a gold-digger to her friends. After appearing to turn the other cheek for a while, Tyler unloaded a bitter letter on Farrand that ended all civilities between them, however insincere. Their respective law firms battled on to an eventual compromise, whereby Farrand received a substantial part of Wharton's mother's trust.

**283:** Bernard Berenson to Louis Gillet.

# CHRONOLOGY

1844 Lucretia Stevens Rhinelander marries George Frederic Jones.

1847–48 With their son Freddy, the Joneses tour Europe. They are in Paris during the revolution that deposes King Louis Phillipe.

1862 Edith Newbold Jones is born January 24 at 14 West 23rd Street.

1866–72 Edith's family, with Edith, tours Europe for six years, living in Paris, Florence, Rome, and Germany.

1872 The Jones family returns to the United States to live in New York City and summer in Newport.

1879 Edith makes her debut in New York City.

1880 The Jones family returns to Europe.

1882 George Frederic Jones dies in Cannes. Edith and her mother return to New York City afterward.

1885 Edith Jones marries Edward Wharton on April 29 in New York City. The newlyweds set up housekeeping in Pencraig Cottage, Newport.

1888 Edith and Teddy Wharton cruise the Aegean with James Van Alen, from February 18 through May 7, on the steam yacht *Vanadis*, which they had chartered jointly.

1889 Four of Wharton's poems are accepted for magazine publication.

1890 A short story, "Mrs. Manstey's View," is accepted for publication in *Scribner's Magazine*.

1892 The Whartons move to Land's End in Newport, a spacious cottage with an ocean view.

1893 Paul and Minnie Bourget visit Newport with a letter of introduction to the Whartons and become Edith's friends for life.

1895 Wharton's first travel essay, "A Tuscan Shrine," is published in *Scribner's Magazine*.

1897 *The Decoration of Houses*, written with

interior designer Ogden Codman, is published. It becomes a classic, and Wharton and Codman become close friends.

1899   *The Greater Inclination*, a first collection of short stories, is published by Scribner's. The Whartons travel in Italy with the Bourgets.

1900   *The Touchstone*, a novella, is published by Scribner's.

1901   *Crucial Instances*, a second collection of short stories, is published by Scribner's. Lucretia Jones dies in Paris. Edith inherits $90,000 in trust.

1902   Scribner's publishes *The Valley of Decision*, Wharton's first novel. The Whartons move into the Mount at Lenox, Massachusetts.

1903   The Whartons spend the winter and early spring in Italy, Edith writing *Italian Villas and Their Gardens*.

1904   *Italian Villas and Their Gardens* is published in *Century* magazine. Edith Wharton begins friendship with Henry James.

1905   *The House of Mirth*, Edith's first novel set within old New York society, and *Italian Backgrounds*, a collection of travel essays, are published by Scribner's. *The House of Mirth* becomes a bestseller, after successful serialization in *Scribner's Magazine*.

1906   The Whartons spend several months in Paris and in England with Henry James.

1907   The Whartons live in Paris and travel with Henry James through France. Edith meets W. Morton Fullerton in Paris and entertains him at the Mount in October. The Whartons return to Paris in late December. Wharton sees Fullerton again in Paris. *The Fruit of the Tree* is published after serialization in *Scribner's Magazine*.

1908   While in Paris, Edith and W. Morton Fullerton begin their affair. There she also develops a friendship with Henry Adams. After spending the summer at the Mount, Edith returns to Europe in October. Scribner's publishes *A Motor-Flight Through France*, a collection of travel essays. During a social tour of England toward the end of the year, Edith meets John Hugh Smith and Robert Norton, who become lifelong friends.

1909   Edith Wharton meets Bernard Berenson in Paris. They become instant friends and remain close for the rest of her life. For the first time since she bought it, Edith Wharton does not spend the summer at the Mount.

1911   Wharton's love affair with W. Morton Fullerton ends. With Walter Berry, she visits Berenson and his wife Mary at the Villa I Tatti near Florence for the first time. *Ethan Frome* is published by Scribner's.

1912   *The Reef* is published by D. Appleton & Company. The Mount is sold.

1913   *The Custom of the Country* is published by Scribner's, after serialization in *Scribner's Magazine*. In April the Whartons are divorced by decree of a French court. Edith travels to Sicily with Walter Berry. In December she makes a brief trip back to New York City for the wedding of her niece Beatrix to Max Farrand.

1914   Before outbreak of the Great War, Wharton tours Algeria and Tunisia with Percy Lubbock and Spain with Berry; they drive back to Paris as the war begins. She immediately plunges into charitable war work there.

1915   With the permission of the French High Command, Wharton and Berry tour the military zone, making five or six motor trips from February through August. Her reports are published in *Scribner's Magazine* and then collected in *Fighting France*. Wharton and Elisina Tyler work together organizing assistance for Belgian and French refugees, with Wharton as the fund-raiser in France and, increasingly, the United States. As a fund-raiser, Wharton organizes *The Book of the Homeless*, published in early 1916.

1916   Wharton mourns the deaths of Henry James, Egerton Winthrop, and Anna Bahlman, her longtime secretary. The French government makes her a Chevalier of the Legion of Honor for her services to France.

1917   *Summer*, a novella set, like *Ethan Frome*, in a village of western Massachusetts, is published by Appleton after magazine serialization. Wharton wrote it during breaks from war work in 1916. In September Wharton makes an official tour of Morocco with Walter Berry as the guest of General Lyautey.

1918   *The Marne*, a war novel, is published by Appleton. Wharton rejoices for the U.S. soldiers marching in the Bastille Day parade in Paris, July 14.

1919   Wharton moves to two country residences: Pavillon Colombe in Saint-Brice-sous-Forêt, north of Paris, and Saint-Claire in Hyères, near Toulon. Each has an elaborate garden in which Wharton immerses herself. She gives up her Paris apartment in the early 1920s.

1920   *The Age of Innocence* is published after magazine serialization and is a best-seller.

1921   Wharton is awarded the Pulitzer Prize for *The Age of Innocence*, a first for a woman.

1922   Wharton mourns the death of Sara Norton, her longtime friend and steady correspondent. *The Glimpses of the Moon* is published after magazine serialization.

1923   Wharton makes her last trip to the United States to receive an honorary degree from Yale University, the first time it honors a woman this way. *A Son at the Front*, a war novel, is published.

1924   *Old New York*, a collection of four novellas, is published.

1925   *The Mother's Recompense* is published after magazine serialization.

1926   Wharton makes her long-dreamed-of return to the Aegean. She charters the steam yacht *Osprey* for a ten-week cruise with Daisy Chanler, Robert Norton, Logan Pearsall Smith, and Henry Spencer.

1927   Wharton mourns the death of Walter Berry, her oldest and dearest friend. *Twilight Sleep* is published after magazine serialization.

1928   *The Children* is published, after magazine serialization. A dramatization of *The Age of Innocence* begins a successful Broadway run.

1929   Wharton has a severe attack of pneumonia and is unable to work for four months. *Hudson River Bracketed* is published, after magazine serialization.

1932   *The Gods Arrive* is published, after magazine serialization.

1933   Wharton mourns the deaths of her two longtime servants, Catharine Gross and Elise Duvlenck.

1934   *A Backward Glance*, Wharton's autobiography, is published, after magazine serialization.

1935   A dramatization of *The Old Maid* begins a successful Broadway run. Wharton mourns the death of Minnie Jones in London. She travels to England to make funeral arrangements. She suffers a mild stroke and loses sight in one eye temporarily but is able to return to work.

1936   A dramatization of *Ethan Frome* is successfully produced on Broadway.

1937   Edith Wharton dies on August 11 at Pavillon Colombe after having been crippled by another stroke earlier in the year.

# SELECTED BIBLIOGRAPHY

## EDITH WHARTON'S WRITINGS

### BOOKS

*The Decoration of Houses* (with Ogden Codman, Jr.). New York: Scribner's, 1897.

*The Greater Inclination.* New York: Scribner's, 1899.

*The Touchstone.* New York: Scribner's, 1900.

*Crucial Instances.* New York: Scribner's, 1901.

*The Valley of Decision.* 2 vols. New York: Scribner's, 1902.

*Italian Villas and Their Gardens.* New York: Century, 1904.

*The House of Mirth.* New York: Scribner's, 1905.

*Italian Backgrounds.* New York: Scribner's, 1905.

*The Fruit of the Tree.* New York: Scribner's, 1907.

*Madame de Treymes.* New York: Scribner's, 1907.

*A Motor-Flight through France.* New York: Scribner's, 1908.

*Artemis to Actaeon and Other Verse.* New York: Scribner's, 1909.

*Ethan Frome.* New York: Appleton, 1912.

*The Reef.* New York: Appleton, 1912.

*The Custom of the Country.* New York: Scribner's, 1913.

*Fighting France, from Dunkerque to Belfort.* New York: Scribner's, 1915.

*The Book of the Homeless.* New York: Scribner's, 1916.

*Xingu and Other Stories.* New York: Scribner's, 1916.

*Summer.* New York: Appleton, 1917.

*The Marne.* New York: Appleton, 1918.

*French Ways and Their Meaning.* New York: Appleton, 1919.

*The Age of Innocence.* New York: Appleton, 1920.

*In Morocco.* New York: Scribner's, 1920.

*The Glimpses of the Moon.* New York: Appleton, 1922.

*A Son at the Front.* New York: Scribner's, 1923.

*Old New York.* New York: Appleton, 1924.

*The Mother's Recompense.* New York: Appleton, 1925.

*The Writing of Fiction.* New York: Scribner's, 1925.

*Here and Beyond.* New York: Appleton, 1926.

*Twelve Poems.* London: The Medici Society, 1926.

*Twilight Sleep.* New York: Appleton, 1927.

*The Children.* New York: Appleton, 1928.

*Hudson River Bracketed.* New York: Appleton, 1929.

*The Gods Arrive.* New York: Appleton, 1932.

*A Backward Glance.* New York: Appleton-Century, 1934.

*The Buccaneers.* New York: Appleton-Century, 1938.

"Life and I," in *Edith Wharton Novellas and Other Writings,* ed. Cynthia Griffin Wolff. The Library of America.

*The Collected Short Stories of Edith Wharton.* Ed. R. W. B. Lewis. New York: Scribner's, 1968.

*Fast and Loose.* Charlottesville: University Press of Virginia, 1977.

*The Letters of Edith Wharton.* Ed. R. W. B. Lewis and Nancy Lewis. New York: Macmillan, 1988.

*The Cruise of the Vanadis.* Amiens: Sterne Presses de L'Ufr Clerc Université Picardie, 1991.

### ARTICLES

"The Three Francescas." *North American Review* 175 (July 1902): 17–30.

"The Great American Novel." *Yale Review* 16 (July 1927): 646–56.

"A Little Girl's New York." *Harper's Magazine* 176 (March 1938): 356–64.

"Memories of Bourget from Across the Sea." *The Edith Wharton Review* 8, no. 1 (Spring 1991): 23–31.

### REVIEWS

Blashfield, Edwin H. and Evangeline W. "Italian Cities." *Bookman* 13 (August 1901): 563–64.

Stephen, Leslie. "George Eliot." *Bookman* 15 (May 1902): 247–51.

## GENERAL SOURCES

### BOOKS

Adams, Henry. *Mont-Saint-Michel and Chartres.* Boston: Houghton Mifflin, 1905.

———. *The Education of Henry Adams.* Boston: Houghton Mifflin, 1918, rpt. 1961.

Amory, Cleveland. *The Last Resorts.* New York: Harper and Brothers, 1948.

Andrews, Wayne. *Architecture, Ambition, and Americans.* New York: Macmillan, 1978.

Auchincloss, Louis. *Edith Wharton.* University of Minnesota pamphlets on American writers. Minneapolis, 1961.

———. *Edith Wharton: A Woman in Her Time.* New York: Viking, 1971.

———. *The Vanderbilt Era.* New York: Macmillan, 1989.

Bell, Millicent. *Edith Wharton and Henry James.* New York: Braziller, 1965.

Bell, Quentin. *Ruskin.* New York: Braziller, 1978.

Bendixen, Alfred, and Annette Zilversmit, eds. *Edith Wharton: New Critical Essays.* New York: Garland, 1992.

Bennett, David, Wendy Baker, and Diane Dierkes. *Landscape Architectural Analysis and Master Plan for The Mount.* Cambridge: Harvard University Press.

Benstock, Shari. *Women of the Left Bank: Paris, 1900–1940.* Austin: University of Texas Press, 1986.

Berenson, Bernard. *The Italian Painters of the Renaissance.* London: Oxford University Press, 1932.

———. *Sunset and Twilight.* New York: Harcourt, Brace and World, 1963.

*Berkshire Hills,* by Members of the Federal Writers Project of the WPA. New York: Funk & Wagnells, 1939.

Biocca, Dario, ed. *A Matter of Passion: Letters of Bernard Berenson and Clothilde Marghieri.* Berkeley: University of California Press, 1989.

Blanche, Jacques-Emile. *Cahier d'un Artiste.* 6 vols. Paris: Élie-Paul Frères, 1916.

Bourget, Paul. *Sensations d'Italie.* Paris: Alphonse Lemerre, 1892.

———. *Outre-Mer.* New York: Scribner's, 1895.

Bourne, J. M. *Britain and the Great War: 1914–1918.* London: Hodder & Stoughton, 1989.

Brooks, Van Wyck. *Dream of Arcadia: American Writers and Artists in Italy 1760–1915.* New York: Dutton, 1958.

Brown, David Alan. *Berenson and the Connoisseurship of Italian Painting.* Washington, D.C.: National Gallery of Art, 1979.

Brown, Henry Collins. *Fifth Avenue Old and New.* New York: The Fifth Avenue Association, 1924.

Chanler, Mrs. Winthrop. *Autumn in the Valley.* Boston: Little, Brown, 1936.

———. *Roman Spring.* Boston: Little, Brown, 1936.

Chanler, Margaret. *Memory Makes Music.* New York: Stephen-Paul, 1948.

———, ed. *Winthrop Chanler's Letters.* New York: printed privately, 1951.

Connolly, Cyril, and Jerome Zerbe. *Les Pavillons: French Pavillons of the Eighteenth Century.* New York: Macmillan, 1962.

Edel, Leon. *Henry James.* 5 vols. Philadelphia: Lippincott, 1953–72.

———, ed. *The Letters of Henry James.* Vol. 4, *1895–1916.* Cambridge: Belknap, 1984.

———, ed. *Henry James, Selected Letters.* Cambridge: Belknap, 1987.

Elliott, Maud Howe. *My Cousin, F. Marion Crawford.* New York: Macmillan, 1934.

———. *This Was My Newport.* Cambridge: The Mythology Company, 1944.

Erlich, Gloria. *The Sexual Education of Edith Wharton.* Berkeley: Univeristy of California Press, 1992.

Flink, James E. *America Adopts the Automobile 1895–1910.* Cambridge: MIT Press, 1970.

French, Mrs. Daniel Chester. *Memoirs of a Sculptor's Wife.* Boston and New York: Houghton Mifflin, 1928.

Fryer, Judith. *Felicitous Space.* Chapel Hill: University of North Carolina Press, 1986.

Gallatin, Eugene, ed. *Walter Gay Paintings of French Interiors.* New York: Dutton, 1920.

Gilbert, Sandra M., and Susan Gubar. *No Man's Land: The Place of the Woman Writer in the Twentieth Century.* Vol. 1, *The War of the Worlds.* Vol. 2, *Sexchanges.* New

Haven: Yale University Press, 1989.

Gimbel, Wendy. *Orphanage and Survival*. Landmark Dissertations in Women's Studies series. New York: Praeger, 1984.

Goethe, Johann Wolfgang von. *Italian Journey 1786–1788*. Trans. W. H. Auden and Eliz. Mayer. New York: Pantheon, 1962.

Goodman, Susan. *Edith Wharton's Women: Friends and Rivals*. Hanover and London: University Press of New England, 1990.

Griswold, Mac, and Eleanor Weller. *The Golden Age of American Gardens*. New York: Abrams, 1992.

Guérard, Léon Albert. *Five Masters of French Romance*. New York: Scribner's, 1916.

*Guida d'Italia del Touring Club Italiano, Toscano*. Milan, 1959.

Gwilt, Joseph. *Encyclopedia of Architecture, Historical, Theoretical and Practical*. London: Longman, Brown Green and Longmans, 1842.

Hadley, Rollin, ed. *The Letters of Bernard Berenson and Isabella Stewart Gardner, 1887–1924*. Boston: Northeastern University Press, 1987.

Hawthorne, Hildegarde. *The Lure of the Garden*. New York: Century, 1911.

Hayman, Ronald. *Proust: A Biography*. New York: Carroll & Graff, 1990.

Hewitt, Mark Alan. *The Architect and the American Country House 1890–1940*. New Haven: Yale University Press, 1940.

Honour, Hugh, and John Fleming. *The Venetian Hours of Henry James, Whistler and Sargent*. Boston: Little, Brown, 1991.

Horn, Alistair. *Verdun*. New York: St. Martin's Press.

Howe, Irving, ed. *Edith Wharton. A Collection of Critical Essays*. Englewood Cliffs: Prentice Hall, 1962.

James, Henry. *William Wetmore Story and His Friends*. Boston: Houghton Mifflin, 1906.

————. *The American Scene*. Bloomington: Indiana University Press, 1987.

Jameson, Anna Brownell Murphy. *Legend of the Madonna As Represented in the Fine Arts*. London: Longmans Green, 1896.

————. *Sacred and Legendary Art*. London: Longmans Green, 1896.

Joslin, Katherine. *Edith Wharton*. New York: St. Martin's Press, 1991.

Kugler, Franz Theodor. *History of Italian Painting*. London: Murray, 1842–46.

Levenson, J. C., Ernest Samuels, Charles Vandersee, Viola Hopkins Winner, eds. *The Letters of Henry Adams*. Vol. 6, *1906–1918*. Cambridge: Harvard University Press, 1988.

Lewis, R. W. B. *Edith Wharton. A Biography*. New York: Harper and Row, 1975.

Lockwood, Charles. *Manhattan Moves Uptown*. Boston: Houghton Mifflin, 1976.

Lowell, Guy. *American Gardens*. Boston: Bates & Guild, 1902.

Lubbock, Percy. *Portrait of Edith Wharton*. New York: Appleton Century Crofts, 1947.

Mallary, Raymond DeWitt. *Lenox and the Berkshire Highlands*. New York: Putnam, 1902.

Marghieri, Clothilde. *Trilogia*. Milan: Rusconi, 1982.

Mariano, Nicky. *Forty Years with Berenson*. New York: Knopf, 1966.

Marquard, Alan. *Giovanni della Robbia*. Princeton: Princeton University Press, 1920.

Marshall, Scott. *The Mount, Home of Edith Wharton: A Historic Structures Report*. Lenox, Mass.: Edith Wharton Restoration, 1997.

Martineau, Mrs. Philip. *Gardening in Sunny Lands*. New York: Appleton, 1924.

Masson, Georgina. *Italian Villas and Palaces*. New York: Abrams, 1959.

————. *Italian Gardens*. New York: Abrams, 1961.

Metcalf, Pauline, ed. *Ogden Codman and The Decoration of Houses*. Boston: Boston Athenaenum, 1988.

Moers, Ellen. *Literary Women, The Great Writers*. Garden City, N.Y.: Doubleday, 1976.

Mugnier, L'Abbé. *Journal de L'Abbé Mugnier*. Paris: Mercure de France, 1985.

Nevius, Blake. *Edith Wharton. A Study of Her Fiction*. Berkeley: University of California Press, 1953.

Norton, Charles Eliot. *Notes of Travel and Study in Italy*. Boston: Houghton Mifflin, 1881.

————. *The Letters of Charles Eliot Norton*. Ed. Sara Norton and M. A. De Wolfe Howe. Boston: Houghton Mifflin, 1913.

Novak, Barbara. *Nature and Culture*. New York: Oxford University Press, 1980.

O'Brien, Justin, ed. *The Journals of André Gide*. New York: Knopf, 1949.

Origo, Iris. *Images and Shadows*. New York: Harcourt, Brace, Jovanovich, 1970.

Owen, Carole. *The Berkshire Cottages*. New Jersey: Cottage Press Inc., 1984.

Page, Russell. *The Education of a Garden*. New York: Random House, 1983.

Paget, Violet. *Euphorion*. Boston: Roberts, 1884.

————. *Studies of the Eighteenth Century in Italy*. London: Unwin, 1887.

Painter, George. *Marcel Proust. A Biography*. New York: Random House, 1959.

Paolucci, Antonio. *Guida de San Vivaldo*. Firenze, 1976.

Pater, Walter. *The Renaissance*. New York: Macmillan, 1894.

Powers, Lyall, ed. *Henry James and Edith Wharton Letters: 1900–1915*. New York: Scribner's, 1990.

Quest-Ritson, Charles. *The English Garden Abroad*. London: Viking, 1992.

Repetti, Emmanuelle. *Dizionario Geographico, Fisico, Storico Della Toscana*. Vol. 5. Firenze, 1843.

Ruskin, John. *Modern Painters*, in *Complete Works*, vols. 2–6. London: G. Allen, New York: Longmans Green, 1903–12.

————. *The Stones of Venice*, in *Complete Works*, vols. 7–10. London: G. Allen, New York: Longmans Green, 1903– 12.

————. *Mornings in Florence*, in *Complete Works*, vol. 23. London: G. Allen, New York: Longmans Green, 1903–12.

Samuels, Ernest. *Bernard Berenson: The Making of a Connoisseur*. Cambridge: Belknap, 1979.

————, and Jayne Newcomer Samuels. *Bernard Berenson: The Making of a Legend*. Cambridge: Belknap, 1987.

Secrest, Meryle. *Being Bernard Berenson*. New York: Holt, Rinehart and Winston, 1979.

Sloane, Florence Adele. *Maverick in Mauve*. New York: Doubleday, 1983. With a commentary by Louis Auchincloss.

Smith, Jane S. *Elsie de Wolfe: A Life in High Style*. New York: Atheneum, 1982.

Spacks, Patricia Meyer. *The Female Imagination*. New York: Knopf, 1975.

Steegmuller, Francis. *The Two Lives of James Jackson Jarves*. New Haven: Yale University Press, 1951.

Strachey, Barbara, and Jayne Samuels, eds. *Mary Berenson: A Self-Portrait from Her Diaries and Letters*. New York: W. W. Norton, 1983.

Strouse, Jean. *Alice James: A Biography*. Boston: Houghton Mifflin, 1980.

Thieme, Ulrich, and Felix Becker. *Allgemeines Lexicon der Bildenden Kunstler*. Leipzig: Seeman, 1921.

Tintner, Adeline. *The Cosmopolitan World of Henry James*. Baton Rouge: Louisiana State University Press, 1991.

Tuchman, Barbara. *The Guns of August*. New York: Macmillan, 1962.

Tuttleton, James. *The Novel of Manners in America*. Chapel Hill: University of North Carolina Press, 1972.

Tuttleton, James, Kristin O. Lauer, and Margaret P. Murray, eds. *Edith Wharton: The Contemporary Reviews*. New York: Cambridge University Press, 1992.

Van Rensselaer, May King. *Newport, Our Social Capital*. Philadelphia and London: Lippincott, 1905.

Viollet-le-Duc, Eugène. *Dictionnaire Raisonné de l'Architecture Française*. 1858.

Waid, Candace. *Edith Wharton's Letters from the Underworld*. Chapel Hill: University of North Carolina Press, 1991.

Winner, Viola Hopkins. *Henry James and the Visual Arts*. Charlottesville: University of Virginia Press, 1970.

Wolff, Cynthia Griffin. *A Feast of Words: The Triumph of Edith Wharton*. New York: Oxford University Press, 1977.

Wright, Nathalia. *American Novelists in Italy. The Discoverers: Allston to James*. Philadelphia: University of Pennsylvania Press, 1965.

ARTICLES AND ESSAYS

Colquitt, Clare. "Unpacking Her Treasures:

'Edith Wharton's Mysterious Correspondence' with Morton Fullerton." *The Library Chronicle of the University of Texas at Austin* 31 (1985).

Hughes, Robert. "Only in America." *The New York Review of Books,* December 20, 1979.

Marshall, Scott. "Edith Wharton, Kate Spencer, and *Ethan Frome.*" *Edith Wharton Review* (Spring 1993).

Ozick, Cynthia. "Justice Again to Edith Wharton." *Commentary,* no. 62 (October 1976): 48–57.

Powers, Lyall. "Les Liaisons Non Dangereux". Papers given at La Journée d'Edith Wharton, les Amis de Vieux Saint-Brice (September 1987).

Price, Alan. "Writing Home from the Front: Edith Wharton and Dorothy Canfield Fisher Present Wartime France to the United States: 1917–1919." *Edith Wharton Review* (Fall 1988).

———. "Edith Wharton at War with the American Red Cross," in *Women's Studies.*

Schriber, Mary Suzanne. Introduction to *A Motor-Flight Through France.* New York: Scribner's, 1908.

Tinter, Adeline R. "Portrait of Edith Wharton in Bourget's 'L'Indicatrice'." *Edith Wharton Review* (Spring 1990).

———. "Edith Wharton and Paul Bourget." *Edith Wharton Review* (Spring 1991).

Tuttleton, James. "Edith Wharton: The Archeological Motive." *The Yale Review* 61 (Summer 1972).

———. "Mocking Fate: Romantic Idealism in Edith Wharton's *Reef.*" *Studies in the Novel* 19 (1987).

Van Alen, William L. "Wakehurst." The Numismatic and Antiquarian Society of Philadelphia, 1974.

## UNPUBLISHED LETTERS, MEMOIRS, DIARIES, AND MANUSCRIPTS

The Wharton Archives, Beinecke Rare Book and Manuscript Library, Yale University, New Haven, Conn.: Edith Wharton letters to Sara Norton, Mary Cadwalader Jones, Beatrix Jones Farrand, Richard Watson Gilder, Rutgers Jewett, Gaillard Lapsley, Henry James, Margaret Terry Chanler, John Hugh Smith, George B. Dorr; Edward Wharton letter to Sara Norton; Mary Cadwalader Jones letters to Edith Wharton; Beatrix Jones Farrand letters to Edith Wharton; Walter Van Rensselaer Berry letters to Edith Wharton; Edith Wharton writings on gardens: "Spring in a French Riviera Garden," "Gardening in France," "December in a French Riviera Garden"; Wharton's garden lists and plans.

The Berenson Archives, The Villa I Tatti, Settignano, Florence, Italy: Edith Wharton letters to Bernard Berenson and Mary Berenson; Bernard Berenson letters to Mary Berenson; Ralph Curtis letters to Bernard Berenson; Marie Laure de Noailles letters to Bernard Berenson; Louis Gillet letters to Bernard Berenson; Alfred White letter to Bernard Berenson.

The Boston Athenaeum, Boston, Mass.: Ogden Codman letters to Julian Sampson.

Colby College, Waterville, Me.: Edith Wharton letters to Vernon Lee.

Dwight, Eleanor. "The Influence of Italy on Edith Wharton." Ph.D. diss., New York University, 1984.

The John Work Garrett Library, Johns Hopkins University, Baltimore, Md.: Edith Wharton letters to John and Alice Garrett and Walter Berry.

The Houghton Library, Harvard University, Cambridge, Mass.: Edith Wharton letters to Sara Norton and Charles Eliot Norton.

The Nelson Miles Papers at the Library of Congress: Edith Wharton letters to Elizabeth Cameron.

Wharton Papers, Lilly Library, University of Indiana, Bloomington, Ind.: Edith Wharton diaries, including "The Life Apart" and untitled ones; Edith Wharton letters to Elisina Tyler; Edith Wharton notes for *A Backward Glance* and "Memories."

The New York Public Library: Edith Wharton letters to Richard Watson Gilder.

The Redwood Library and Athenaeum, Newport, R.I.: Edith Wharton letters to Ethel King and LeRoy King.

The Scribner's Archives at the Firestone Library, Princeton University, Princeton, N.J.: Edith Wharton letters to Edward Burlingame and Charles Scribner.

The Society for the Preservation of New England Antiquities, Boston, Mass.: Edith Wharton letters to Ogden Codman; Ogden Codman letters to Sarah Codman and Thomas Codman.

# INDEX

# PHOTOGRAPH CREDITS

The author and publisher wish to thank all the collectors and institutions, many of them listed in the captions, who made photographs available for reproduction. Additional photograph credits appear below. Numbers refer to page numbers.

Stephane-Jacques Addade, 157R; Alinari, 16T, 72, 73T, *106*; AP / Wide World Photos, 214BL, 226; Ashmolean Museum, Oxford, 75B; Louis Auchincloss, 10, 12, 163B, Bar Harbor Historical Society, Maine, 24; Mme. Bialek, 157L; Bibliothèque historique de la Ville de Paris, 195R: photo by Jean-Loup Charmet; Photo. Bibliothèque Nationale, Paris, 142T, 142B, 143, 160, 164, 165, 179, 180, 181T, 181B, 194B, 208; Beinecke Rare Book and Manuscript Library, Yale University, New Haven, CT, 18, 22, 27, 29, 32, 33TL, 35B, 37B, 38B, 38TR, 39L, 39R, 40, 41, 50T, 51B, 56B, 57, 62, 84T, 84B, 90, 92B, 93T, 93B, 94, 95B, 96B, 97, 98M, 100T, 101, 102, 109, 110T, 110B, 113T, 114, 115, 116, 121T, 121B, 127, 128, 129, 141, 144, 145, 166, 172T, 172B, 173B, 173T, 174, 185, 190, 191M, 191T, 191B, 192L, 192R, 193, 194T, 195L, 196, 197, 200, 206, 211, 212, 213, 214T, 215T, 215M, 215B, 216TL, 216TR, 218M, 218B, 220, 221, 227, 229L, 232, 234, 235, 241, 248B, 248T, 249, 252B, 254T, 255, 276, 277B, 280, 281, back cover; College of Environmental Design Documents Collection, University of California, Berkeley, 95TR, 95TL, 96T, 98L; Museum Archives, Chesterwood, a Property of the National Trust for Historic Preservation, Stockbridge, MA, 131T, 131B; Special Collections, Colby College Library, Waterville, ME 77B; *Country Life* Picture Library, 242, 243, 244R, 245T, 246T; Culver Pictures, Inc., 126, 150, 163T; from *Portrait of Edith Wharton* by Percy Lubbock. Copyright 1947 by D. Appleton-Century, Inc. Used by permission of Dutton Signet, a division of Penguin Books USA Inc., 168L, 168R; Edith Wharton Restoration at the Mount, Lenox, MA, 14T, 14B, 15T: photographs by Robert D. Lohbauer Lee, 112; Florence, Berenson Collection, reproduced by permission of the President and fellows of Harvard College, 73B, 74B, 78, 175, 176T, 176B, 177L, 177R, 244L, 261, 266T, 267, 268T, 268B, 269; Courtesy of the Fogg Art Museum, Harvard University Art Museums, Gift of Mrs. Francis Ormond, 75T; The private collection of Jacques Fosse, 228, 229R, 230TL, 233; Four Brooks Farms Collection, 130T, 130B; Isabella Stewart Gardner Museum Archives, Boston, 43, 74T, 76T, 77; HOH Associates, © 1992, 113B; by permission of Houghton Library, Harvard University, 132, 133T, 133B, 134, 138, 139, 154; Comte d'Haussonville, 184; Knickerbocker Club, New York, 47; Courtesy of Lenox Library, 87, 88T, 89T, 89B, 92T, 107; Francis Benjamin Johnston Collection, Prints and Photographs Division, Library of Congress, 216B, 219; Wharton mss, Lilly Library, Indiana University, Bloomington, 2, 6, 15B, 26, 38TL, 42B, 44, 45, 100B, 119, 123, 125, 146, 182, 183, 188, 201, 217, 218T, 230B, 230TR, 231T, 231M, 231B, 236, 237, 238M, 238T, 238B, 239, 240T, 240B, 245B, 246B, 247, 249BL, 251B, 252T, 253, 254B, 257, 258, 259, 262, 263TL, 263TR, 264T, 264B, 264M, 265B, 265T, 271B, 275, 277T, 282; by permission of Little, Brown and Company, 16B, 17, 35T, 68, 186, 263B; The Metropolitan Museum of Art, Gift of the Estate of Ogden Codman, Jr., 1951 [#51.644.73 (13), #51.644.75 (1)], 49, 59B; Museum of the City of New York, 21, 23, 28; National Portrait Gallery, London, 205; The New York Herald, 256; New York Historical Society, 20, 30T, 64, 99BR, 99TL, 99TM, 99TR, 99BL; New York Society Library, 30B, 46L, 46R, 71, 80, 81, 82, 83, 98R; Edmond de la Haye Jousselin, 250, 251T; From the Collection of the Newport Historical Society, 33B, 34, 36T, 36B, 37T, 42T, 67; Roger Viollet, Paris, 156, 161, 207; Charles Scribner's Sons, 9L, 9R, 13B, 52, 53, 54L, 54R, 55, 69: illustrations by E. C. Peixotto, 103, 104B, 104T, 105TL, 105TR, 105BR, 136, 199, 202, 203T, 203B; Codman Family Manuscripts Collection, Society for the Preservation of New England Antiquities, 25, 48, 50B, 51T, 56T, 59T, 61, 63, 88B; Courtesy Smith College Archives, Smith College, 271T; U.S. Capitol Art Collection, 13T; Barbara Strachey Halpern, 266B, 270; Walter Gay Papers, Archives of American Art, Smithsonian Institution, 153.

# ACKNOWLEDGMENTS

On November 15, 1900, Edith Wharton wrote her editor William Brownell, "I don't care for illustrated books." (She was discussing the possibility of Maxfield Parrish doing drawings for *The Valley of Decision*.) I found writing and doing the research for this illustrated book exhilarating because it took me to many places Edith Wharton had known well—to Paris, to Pavillon Colombe and to Hyères, and all over Italy. I learned many things, and I met many kind people.

I would like to thank those in France who welcomed me into their homes and helped me with my research or lent me photographs: Princesse Isabelle von Liechtenstein, Comte Charles de Cossé-Brissac, the Comte d'Haussonville, M. and Mme. André de Bocon-Gibbod, M. and Mme. Jerome Gillet, Jacques and Paulette Fosse, Mme. Bialek, Stephane-Jacques Addade, and Pierre Quillier.

Special thanks to my friends, family, and colleagues who read my chapters in different stages and gave me all kinds of good suggestions: Frank MacShane, Daphne Trotter, Andrew Trotter, Sargent Gardiner, Pauline Metcalf, Gigi Wilmers, David Bennett, Scott Marshall, Pascale Mallaby, Mary Crowley, James Tuttleton, Carole Hill, Alan Price, Viola Winner, Lisa Semple, Hope Cooke, and Tom Maren.

And thanks to others who helped me find and identify photographs and illustrations: Louis Auchincloss, R. W. B. Lewis and Nancy Lewis, Willard Gardiner, Susannah D. Prout, Barbara Strachey Halpern, Fiorella Superbi, Linn Sage, Carole Palermo Schulz, James Clark, Nini Gilder, and Gilder Palmer.

I owe thanks to those who helped in other ways, such as translating, finding sources, helping with captions, or suggesting contacts: Sargent Collier, Tom Hayes, Edward Luke Stone and Cassandra Stone, Mary Mallet, Frank Cabot, Gerd Grace, Patrick Chassé, Melanie Wisner, Franca Lally, Isabelle Storey, William L. Van Alen, Julia Smith, Cynthia Jay, Caroline Milbank, and Deborah Dyer.

Thanks also to the Edith Wharton Society, at whose conferences I gave several papers. Thanks to those who gave me moral support: Bambi Schwartz, Ed Schwartz, Lissa Hodder, Andy Austin, Elaine Gould, and many others.

Thanks to everyone at Abrams including my superb designer, Carol Robson; Margaret Kaplan, who believed in the project from the beginning; Gilda Hannah, who masterfully integrated the illustrations and text; Nanice Lund; and to my graceful and skillful editor, Harriet Whelchel, who was a pleasure to work with.

Thanks to those at libraries and museums who helped: Lorna Condon at the Society for the Preservation of New England Antiquities, Fiorella Superbi at the Villa I Tatti, Melanie Wisner at the Houghton Library, Rebecca Cape and Saundra Taylor at the Lilly Library, Patricia Willis and Lori Misura at the Beinecke, Susan Sinclair at the Gardner Museum, Wanda Styka at Chesterwood, and P. A. Lenk at the Miller Library at Colby College. And many, many thanks to everyone at the New York Society Library, especially the librarian Mark Piel, Rita Atterton, Doris Glick, Sharon Brown, and Bill Watson.

Special thanks to the Edith Wharton Estate and William Tyler, to my agent, William Reiss, to Vicki Dwight, who helped me with the printing of many photographs, to my hard-working and wonderful editorial assistants, Erica Santos, Tiffany Smythe, and Jennifer Kelley, to Nicolas H. Ekstrom, and my two resourceful photo researchers in France, Jean Martin and Leslie Fayard.

And very special thanks to my mother, Eleanor Collier, who showed her wonderful enthusiasm, to Candida Dixon for her continual good advice, and, of course, to my husband, George Dwight.